School-Based Family Counseling

D1602839

Written by experts in the field, *School-Based Family Counseling: An Interdisciplinary Practitioner's Guide* focuses on how to make integrated School-Based Family Counseling (SBFC) interventions, with a focus on integrating schools and family interventions, in an explicit step-by-step manner. Departing from the general language used in most texts to discuss a technique, this guide's concrete yet user-friendly chapters are structured using the SBFC metamodel as an organizing framework, covering background information, procedure, evidence-based support, multicultural counseling considerations, challenges and solutions, and resources.

Written in discipline-neutral language, this text benefits a wide variety of mental health professionals looking to implement SBFC in their work with children; professionals such as school counselors and social workers, school psychologists, family therapists, and psychiatrists. The book is accompanied by online video resources with lectures and simulations illustrating how to implement specific SBFC interventions. A decision tree is included to guide intervention.

Brian A. Gerrard, PhD is chair of the Institute for School-Based Family Counseling and director for the Oxford Symposium in School-Based Family Counseling which has members in 22 countries.

Michael J. Carter, PhD teaches the School-Based Family Counseling graduate students and directs the Counseling & Assessment Clinic at California State University, Los Angeles. He believes that multiculturally focused family therapy is critical to our future.

Deborah Ribera, PhD is an assistant professor of Counseling at California State University, Los Angeles, a marriage and family therapist, a school counselor, and founder of the nonprofit organization Beyond the Block.

School-Based Family Counseling

An Interdisciplinary
Practitioner's Guide

**Edited by Brian A. Gerrard,
Michael J. Carter, and Deborah
Ribera**

Routledge
Taylor & Francis Group

NEW YORK AND LONDON

First published 2020
by Routledge
52 Vanderbilt Avenue, New York, NY 10017

and by Routledge
2 Park Square, Milton Park, Abingdon, Oxon, OX14 4RN

Routledge is an imprint of the Taylor & Francis Group, an informa business

© 2020 Taylor & Francis

Library of Congress Cataloging-in-Publication Data
Names: Gerrard, Brian A., editor. | Carter, Michael J.
(Michael Joseph), editor. | Ribera, Deborah, editor.
Title: School-based family counseling : an interdisciplinary practitioner's guide / edited by Brian A. Gerrard, Michael J. Carter, and Deborah Ribera.
Description: New York, NY : Routledge, 2019. |
Includes bibliographical references and index.
Identifiers: LCCN 2019011074 (print) | LCCN 2019012919 (ebook)
| ISBN 9781351029988 (E-book) | ISBN 9781138492660 (hbk) |
ISBN 9781138492677 (pbk) | ISBN 9781351029988 (ebk)
Subjects: | MESH: Family Therapy–methods | School Health
Services | Counseling–methods | Family Relations | Schools
Classification: LCC RC489.F33 (ebook) | LCC RC489.F33 (print) |
NLM WM 430.5.F2 | DDC 616.89/156–dc23
LC record available at https://lccn.loc.gov/2019011074

ISBN: 978-1-138-49266-0 (hbk)
ISBN: 978-1-138-49267-7 (pbk)
ISBN: 978-1-351-02998-8 (ebk)

Typeset in Baskerville
by Swales & Willis, Exeter, Devon, UK

Visit the eResources: www.routledge.com/9781138492677

Contents

Acknowledgements

First, we owe a great debt of thanks to School-Based Family Counseling pioneer Dr. John Friesen who in 1974 placed family counselors in the *University of British Columbia-New Westminster School District Community Counseling Center*. This was the inspiration for the development of a) the University of San Francisco Center for Child & Family Development: the largest, longest lasting (37 years) university-school partnership in SBFC in the USA; and b) the development of the School-Based Family Counseling MSc program at California State University, Los Angeles: the first academic program in SBFC in the USA. These are SBFC programs we were influential in developing, in which we continue to participate, and which have had a significant impact in helping children and families over more than three decades.

Second, we would like to thank all our School-Based Family Counseling colleagues at the University of San Francisco; California State University, Los Angeles; the Institute for School-Based Family Counseling; and the Oxford Symposium in School-Based Family Counseling for their support over many years in pioneering SBFC to empower students, families, and schools. Because SBFC is interdisciplinary in nature, not all mental health professionals are able to easily embrace it because of the narrowness of training in many disciplines. Our colleagues, however, were able to support and help extend our vision and we are deeply grateful.

Third, we want to thank our family members who supported our late-night vigils writing and editing.

Brian: Many thanks to my wife Olive Powell who patiently reviewed my chapters.

Michael: To my mom and dad, Pat and Tom; my siblings, Catherine, Tom, Tricia, Ellen, and Vince; my wife, Laurie; and our children, Kenya, Kristina, and Tomas. They have all given me the greatest privilege of all, a loving family. I hope that this book helps to extend this privilege to many more children and families.

Debbie: *Mil gracias* to my partners in life and encouragers of balance: my husband, Nate, and best doggie buddy, Russ. Our life of adventure continues! I'm also extremely grateful to my friends and family who provide me with smiles, laughs, and support. Thank you to Michael and Brian for including me in this endeavor. Thank you to all of the students and former students who participated in creating our video materials and made the process so fun and enjoyable! Kimberly Cheng, Keila Mejia, Nancy Rendon, Celia Fang, Sally Chung, Melody Villar, Christopher Yanez, Natalie Reynoso, and Takashi Matsumoto—you are hilarious people and awesome counselors. Lastly, thank you to all the clients, students, kids, and adults who have trusted me with their stories over the years in counseling, therapy, and Beyond the Block. I treasure the marks you've left on my soul!

Foreword

Our age has been called the Age of Anxiety. Never before have as many people sought advanced training in psychology and never before have as many clients sought the services of counsellor/therapists, psychiatrists and social workers. Counselling/therapy is a burgeoning field of research, study, theory building and professional practice.

An index expressing the status of this profession is the number of registrants in the American Psychological Association. In 1918 there were only 318 members while today there are considerably over 60,000 registrants with many thousands attending the annual conventions. Many other professional associations have been formed including the American Counseling Association, the Oxford Symposium in School-Based Family Counseling and many others. Similarly, there are currently over 300 identifiable kinds of therapy in America. Each therapy has its own journals, research activities, adherents and supporting books and services.

This growth and need for counselling/psychotherapy arises during a time of immense social and cultural change. It is a time when society fails to provide its members with the myths, values and understandings to adequately address anxiety, stress, relationship disruptions and painful emotions. It is also a time with mounting problems of divorce, parenting, poverty, homelessness and finding meaningful employment.

This is also a time in history in which many people have experienced intense violence, verbal and physical abuse, and carry with them deeply troubling narratives of trauma, post-traumatic stress disorder (PTSD) and related symptoms. Current studies in epigenetics provide evidence that narratives of trauma are transmitted from generation to generation. I am well aware of such phenomena. In 1919, during the early phase of the communist revolution in Russia, unbelievable and gruesome atrocities occurred. While my family was living peacefully on an estate, roving bandits murdered my father's wife, mother, infants, several relatives, and brutally killed workers and estate management personnel. Many other estate owners in Russia experienced similar atrocities.

Father remarried and moved to Canada. He carried with him deeply troubling narratives of trauma which were transmitted from generation to generation. My profound interest in psychology and psychological healing can undoubtedly be traced back to the often unconscious narratives associated with father's profound experience of trauma and abuse.

The book *School-Based Family Counseling: An Interdisciplinary Practitioner's Guide*, edited by Gerrard, Carter and Ribera, is a penetrating and sensitive work which speaks to the needs of a changing society. It makes important contributions to the literature on mental health in families and schools.

I am particularly proud of Brian Gerrard, a senior editor of this book who was my graduate student and research assistant in the early 1970s. Brian has made numerous contributions to the development of school-based family counselling in many parts of the world. He has provided outstanding leadership and unwavering support to this very important and innovative approach to mental health in families and schools. A vast literature, annual conferences, a journal and other publications are now available addressing the topic of school-based family counselling.

Perhaps the most unique feature of this book on school-based family counselling is the underlying theoretical framework of this work. Based on systemic formulations and hypotheses, the book addresses the key features of systemic thought including a focus on relationships, connections, interactions and healthy mental health functioning in families, schools, communities and the world. The book includes a vast array of worksheets, theoretical explanations, research findings, references, clinical case studies and audiovisual materials and practical advice on how to structure and practice school-based family counselling.

This book is important not only for students engaged in training for the profession of counselling/psychotherapy but also for all those interested in understanding the theory and research associated with school-based family counselling. The book is strongly oriented for use by practitioners of counselling/therapy and those interested in developing the skills and practices associated with this profession. The book could also be used by administrators in schools and other institutions focusing on the development of healthy mental health practices.

Whether we agree with the authors of this book in every detail is not important. The book provides a comprehensive understanding of the work of school-based family counselling. As a well-experienced professional counsellor/therapist, researcher, professor and former administrator who has worked with hundreds of troubled families and school systems, I am profoundly impressed with this book. It has the potential to make a significant contribution to the future well-being of individuals and families. It offers a rich learning experience to the reader and to those interested in the development of research hypotheses and theory building.

John Friesen, PhD
Emeritus Professor
Educational and Counselling Psychology, and Special Education
University of British Columbia
Vancouver, British Columbia, Canada

Contributors

Michael J. Carter, PhD, Associate Professor and Co-Coordinator: School-Based Family Counseling Program, Department of Special Education & Counseling, Charter College of Education, California State University, Los Angeles

Caroline Doyle, MSW, Top Priority Care Services, Greensboro, North Carolina, USA

Margaret Garcia, PhD, Associate Dean: Undergraduate Studies, Division of Academic Affairs, California State University, Los Angeles

Brian A. Gerrard, PhD, Institute for School-Based Family Counseling, Stuart, Florida

Emily J. Hernandez, PhD, Assistant Professor and Co-Coordinator: School-Based Family Counseling Program, Department of Special Education & Counseling, Charter College of Education, California State University, Los Angeles

Michael Kelly, PhD, Professor and Director: Family & School Partnership Program, School of Social Work, Loyola University, Chicago, Illinois

Gema Macias, Principal: Richard Garvey Intermediate School, Rosemead, California

Allan Morotti, PhD, Dean Emeritus: School of Education, University of Alaska, Fairbanks; Senior Editor: *International Journal for School-Based Family Counseling*

Joelle D. Powers, PhD, Associate Dean and Professor: College of Health Sciences, Boise State University, Boise, Idaho

Deborah Ribera, PhD, Assistant Professor: School-Based Family Counseling Program, Department of Special Education & Counseling, Charter College of Education, California State University, Los Angeles

Nancy Rosenbledt, EdD, Family Therapist, San Francisco, California

Phillip Slee, PhD, Professor, Human Development, and Director of the Student Wellbeing & Prevention of Violence (SWAPv) Research Centre, School of Education Flinders University, Adelaide, South Australia

Marcel Soriano, Emeritus Professor, Department of Special Education & Counseling, Charter College of Education, California State University, Los Angeles

Danielle D. Swick, PhD, Associate Professor: Department of Social Work, University of North Carolina at Greensboro, North Carolina

Michele D. Wallace, PhD, Professor and Program Coordinator: Applied Behavior Analysis, Department of Special Education & Counseling, Charter College of Education, California State University, Los Angeles

Gertina J. Van Schalkwyk, PhD, Emeritus Faculty, Department of Psychology, University of Macau, Macao (SAR), China

1 School-Based Family Counseling

The Revolutionary Paradigm

Brian A. Gerrard and Marcel Soriano

Overview: This chapter defines School-Based Family Counseling (SBFC), and explains its origins, scope of practice, and unique strengths. The SBFC metamodel is introduced with guidelines on how to use this book to make effective SBFC interventions.

Background

School-Based Family Counseling (SBFC) is an integrative, systems approach to helping children succeed academically and personally through mental health approaches that link family and school. The earliest large-scale application of SBFC was made by the psychiatrist Alfred Adler who developed 30 guidance clinics attached to schools in Vienna in the 1920s. Adler believed that schools were a logical and constructive place to bring mental health services for children and families because schools and families are the two most important institutions affecting the lives of children. Adler frequently held demonstrations of interviews with children and their parents and teachers, before an audience of teachers and parents, as a way to demonstrate his approach to helping children and in order to educate parents and teachers in effective approaches to helping children with behavior problems. In recent years continued research into the importance of both school connectedness and family involvement for the promotion of children's academic success and mental health have underscored the value of mental health practitioners working with both schools and families (see Boxes 1.1 and 1.2). Although the idea of SBFC has been around since the time of Adler, the tendency of the mental health professions to focus on either school intervention or family intervention, makes SBFC still a revolutionary approach.

Box 1.1 Evidence-Based Support for the Benefits of School Involvement for Children

Aldridge, J. M., Fraser, B. J., Fozdar, F., Ala'l, K., Earnest, J., & Afari, E. (2016). Students' perceptions of school climate as determinants of well-being, resilience and identity. *Improving Schools*, 19(1), 5–26.

Chapman, R. L., Buckley, L., Sheehan, M., & Shochet, I. (2013). School-based programs for increasing connectedness and reducing risk behaviour: A systematic review. *Educational Psychology Review*, 25(1), 95–114.

Denman S. (1999). Health promoting schools in England – a way forward in development. *Journal of Public Health Medicine*, 21(2), 215–20.

Frydenberg, E., Care, E., Freeman, E., & Chan, E. (2009). Interrelationships between coping, school connectedness and wellbeing. *Australian Journal of Education*, 53(3), 261–276.

García-Moya, I., Brooks, F., Morgan, A., & Moreno, C. (2015). Subjective well-being in adolescence and teacher connectedness. A health asset analysis. *Health Education Journal*, 74(6), 641–654.

Huang K, Cheng S, & Theise R. (2013). School contexts as social determinants of child health: current practices and implications for future public health practice. *Public Health Reports*, 128(S3), 21–28.

Jose, P. E., & Pryor, J. (2010). New Zealand youth benefit from being connected to their family, school, peer group and community. *Youth Studies Australia*, 29(4), 30–37.

Jose, P. E., Ryan, N., & Pryor, J. (2012) Does social connectedness promote a greater sense of well-being in adolescence over time? *Journal of Research on Adolescence*, 22(2), 235–251.

Konishi, C., Hymel, S., Zumbo, B. D., & Li, Z. (2010). Do school bullying and student teacher relationships matter for academic achievement? A multilevel analysis. *Canadian Journal of School Psychology*, 25(1), 19–39.

Lau, M., & Li, W. (2011). The extent of family and school social capital promoting positive subjective well-being among primary school children in Shenzhen, China. *Children and Youth Services Review*, 33(9), 1573–1582.

Maddox, S. J., & Prinz, R. J. (2003). School bonding in children and adolescents: Conceptualization, assessment, and associated variables. *Clinical Child and Family Psychology Review*, 6(1), 31–49.

McGraw, K., Moore, S., Fuller, A., & Bates, G. (2008). Family, peer and school connectedness in final year secondary school students. *Australian Psychologist*, 43(1), 27–37.

McNeely, C., & Falci, C. (2004). School connectedness and the transition into and out of health-risk behavior among adolescents: A comparison of social belonging and teacher support. *Journal of School Health*, 74(7), 284–292.

Niehaus, K., Rudasill, K. M., & Rakes, C. R. (2012). A longitudinal study of school connectedness and academic outcomes across sixth grade. *Journal of School Psychology*, 50(4), 443–460.

Oberle, E., Schonert-Reichl, K. A., & Zumbo, B. D. (2011). Life satisfaction in early adolescence:Personal, neighborhood, school, family, and peer influences. *Journal of Youth and Adolescence*, 40(7), 899–901.

Prelow, H. M., Bowman, M. A., & Weaver, S. R. (2007). Predictors of psychosocial 1 wellbeing in Urban African American and European American youth: The role of ecological factors. *Journal of Youth and Adolescence*, 36(4), 543–553.

Resnick, M. D., Bearman, P. S., Blum, R. W., Bauman, K. E., Harris, K. M., Jones, J., & Udry, J. R. (1997). Protecting adolescents from harm: Findings from the National Longitudinal Study on Adolescent Health. *JAMA*, 278 (10), 823–832.

Svavarsdottir, E. K., & Orlygsdottir, B. (2006) Health-related quality of life in Icelandic school children. *Scandinavian Journal of Caring Sciences*, 20(2), 209–215.

Thomson, K. C., Schonert-Reichl, K. A., & Oberle, (2015). Optimism in early adolescence: Relations to individual characteristics and ecological assets in families, schools, and neighborhoods. *Journal of Happiness Studies*, 16(4), 889–913.

Wang, M-T. & Degol, J. L. (2016). School climate: A review of the construct, measurement, and impact on student outcomes. *Educational Psychology Review*, 28(2), 315–352.

Box 1.2 Evidence-Based Support for the Effect of Parent Involvement on School Achievement

Anguiano, R. P. (2004). Families and schools: The effect of parental involvement on high school completion. *Journal of Family Issues*, 25, 61–85.

Chen, W., & Gregory, A. (2009). Parental involvement as a protective factor during the transition to high school. *Journal of Educational Research*, 103, 53–62.

Cheung, C. S., & Pomerantz, E. M. (2011). Parents' involvement in children's learning in the United States and China: Implications for children's academic and emotional adjustment. *Child Development*, 82, 932–950.

Deslandes, R., & Cloutier, R. (2002). Adolescents' perception of parental involvement in schooling. *School Psychology International*, 23, 220–232.

Eccles, J. S., & Harold, R. D. (1996). Family involvement in children's and adolescents' schooling. In A. Booth & J. F. Dunn (Eds.), *Family-school links: How do they affect educational outcomes?* (pp. 3–34). Mahwah, NJ: Erlbaum.

Fan, X., & Chen, M. (2001). Parental involvement and students' academic achievement: A meta-analysis. *Educational Psychology Review*, 13,1–22.

Fan, W., & Williams, C. (2010). The effects of parental involvement on students' academic self-efficacy, engagement and intrinsic motivation. *Educational Psychology*, 30, 53–74.

Flouri, E., & Buchanan, A. (2003). The role of father involvement and mother involvement in adolescents' psychological well-being. *British Journal of Social Work*, 33, 399–406.

Grolnick, W. S., Kurowski, C. O., Dunlap, K. G., & Hevey, C. (2000). Parental resources and the transition to junior high. *Journal of Research on Adolescence*, 10, 465–488.

Grolnick, W. S., & Slowiaczek, M. L. (1994). Parents' involvement in children's schooling: A multidimensional conceptualization and motivational model. *Child Development*, 65, 237–252.

Hill, N. E., Castellino, D. R., Lansford, J. E., Nowlin, P., Dodge, K. A., Bates, J. E., et al. (2004). Parent academic involvement as related to school behavior, achievement, and aspirations: Demographic variations across adolescence. *Child Development*, 75, 1491–1509.

Hill, N. E., & Tyson, D. F. (2009). Parental involvement in middle school: A meta-analytic assessment of the strategies that promote achievement. *Developmental Psychology*, 45, 740–763.

Jeynes, W. H. (2009). The relationship between parental involvement and urban secondary school student academic achievement: A meta-analysis. *Urban Education*, 42, 82–92.

Johnson, M. K., Crosnoe, R., & Elder, G. H., Jr. (2001). Students' attachment and academic engagement: The role of race and ethnicity. *Sociology of Education*, 74, 318–340.

Newman, B., Newman, P., Griffen, S., O'Connor, K. & Spas, J. (2007). The relationship of social support to depressive symptoms during the transition to high school. *Adolescence*, 42, 441–459.

Patall, E. A., Cooper, H., & Robinson, J. C. (2008). Parent involvement in homework: A research synthesis. *Review of Educational Research*, 78, 1039–1101.

Shumow, L., & Lomax, R. (2002). Parental efficacy: Predictor of parenting behavior and adolescent outcomes. *Parenting: Science and Practice*, 2, 127–150.

Simons-Morton, B. G., & Crump, A. D. (2003). Association of parental involvement and social competence with school adjustment and engagement among sixth graders. *Journal of School Health*, 73, 121–126.

Spera, C. (2005). A review of the relationship among parenting practices, parenting styles, and adolescent school achievement. *Educational Psychology Review*, 17,125–146.

Wang, M. T., Brinkworth, M. B., & Eccles, J. S. (2013). The moderation effect of teacher-student relationship on the association between adolescents' self-regulation ability, family conflict, and developmental problems. *Developmental Psychology*, 49, 690–705

Wang, M. T., & Eccles, J. S. (2012a). Social support matters: Longitudinal effects of social support on three dimensions of school engagement from middle to high school. *Child Development*, 83, 877–895.

Wang, M. T., & Eccles, J. S. (2012b). Adolescent behavioral, emotional, and cognitive engagement trajectories in school and their differential relations to educational success. *Journal of Research on Adolescence*, 22, 31–39.

Wang, M. T., & Eccles, J. S. (2013). School context, achievement motivation, and academic engagement: A longitudinal study of school engagement using a multi-dimensional perspective. *Learning and Instruction*, 28, 12–23.

The Strengths of School-Based Family Counseling

SBFC has eight strengths:

- School and Family Focus
- Systems Orientation

- Educational Focus
- Parent Partnership
- Multicultural Sensitivity
- Child Advocacy
- Promotion of School Transformation
- Interdisciplinary Focus

School and Family Focus

In the lives of children, especially young children, family and school are the two most important social institutions affecting their development. In an SBFC approach an assessment is always made of the positive, as well as negative, influences school and family environments have on a particular child. Where negative family behaviors (e.g. family stress, child abuse, etc.) or negative school behaviors (e.g. bullying, poor teaching, etc.) affect a child, the SBFC practitioner will implement preventive and intervention techniques to remediate the situation and build positive connections. Where positive family behaviors (e.g. family members who are supportive of a child, or who maintain positive discipline, etc.) or positive school behaviors (e.g. a supportive teacher or students, the presence of engaging after-school programs, etc.) exist, the SBFC practitioner will mobilize these resources in the service of a child needing additional support. In SBFC building family and school strengths is as important as remedying deficits. The hallmark of the SBFC approach is that the SBFC practitioner will work with both the family and the school to help the student.

Systems Orientation

SBFC is a systems approach, drawing from ecological theories like Bronfenbrenner (1979) and from family systems theory.

> The problems in schools are but a reflection of the problems in society. The solution to those problems lies in understanding the systemic nature and interdependence of school, families and communities.
>
> (Dear, 1995)

A core assumption in systems theory is that the "identified patient" or client is embedded in a matrix of relationships and that the problem to be dealt with does not solely reside in the individual client. The SBFC practitioner strives to facilitate change in the client's various relationship systems (family, school, peer, community) in order to reduce dysfunctional behavior affecting the client and bring about improved support and more positive communication in the client's contacts with others. When a mental health practitioner lacking a systems focus deals with a client who is being bullied at school, he or she may only work with the child. An SBFC practitioner will involve the child, the child's family, the bully and the bully's family, and the teacher, classroom, and possibly the entire school. This is because the SBFC practitioner conceptualizes "individual" problems as being maintained by relationships in the child's family and school system.

Educational Focus

In SBFC there is an explicit focus on promoting children's school success. This educational focus has the effect of de-stigmatizing the SBFC practitioner's use of mental health intervention. Consider how a parent might feel receiving these two phone calls from a principal, teacher, or school mental health professional:

> "Hello Mrs. Jones, I am the school mental health professional at Meadow Middle School and I am calling about your daughter Alicia. Alicia has been crying in class and seems very depressed. My impression is that she is disturbed about stress in the family. I think that Alicia and your family would benefit from seeing a therapist at a community counseling center. Would you be willing to meet with me about getting psychological help for your daughter?"
>
> "Hello Mrs. Jones, I am the school mental health professional at Meadow Middle School and I am calling about your daughter Alicia. I had the pleasure of meeting Alicia the other day. I learned from Alicia's teacher, Miss Smith, that Alicia is experiencing some challenges with her schoolwork. It is my role at the school to work with teachers and parents to help children do well at school. Because you as her parents know much more about Alicia, would you be willing to meet with me to discuss ways we can help Alicia be more comfortable at school? I would really appreciate having your advice on how we can help Alicia."

As you can see, these are very different ways of approaching a parent about her child. The first approach communicates to the mother that the family is deficient and needs remediation. The suggestion that the family needs mental health counseling will be experienced by most families as an insult and a negative comment on their parenting. The second approach – which is typical of an SBFC approach – engages the parent as an equal who has wisdom and who would be an active collaborator in promoting her child's school success. What parent would not want her child to succeed at school? The SBFC approach engages the parent and family around an educational focus that does not make them feel deficient.

Parent Partnership

SBFC practitioners use a collaborative approach with parents and engage with them as sources of wisdom and important resources for their children. This represents a significant shift away from the "therapist-client" relationship which emphasizes hierarchy. While some families may be very dysfunctional and some parents deficient in parenting skills, these families and parents can potentially engage with their children in more effective ways and this is something the SBFC practitioner never loses sight of. Indeed, by engaging with parents as partners with the SBFC practitioner, the parents feel respected and therefore more likely to engage with the SBFC practitioner. What SBFC holds in common with Narrative, Solution-focused and other strength-based approaches to mental health is an understanding of the importance of honoring the strengths that parents and families bring to the "table."

Multicultural Sensitivity

SBFC is a multiculturally sensitive approach because of its family and educational focus. Most mental health approaches are derived from a western individualistic model which considerable research has shown is inappropriate with many collectivist cultures, including Asian, Latino, African and Middle Eastern (Dana, 2000; Pope-Davis & Coleman, 2015, Sue & Sue, 2008).

> For example, a majority of Mexican immigrants do not share the Western assumptive set that when one has a family problem, one goes to a therapist. Instead, the assumptive set of most traditional Mexicans is to seek guidance from a family elder, from a priest or even a "curandero" (an indigenous healer). Thus counselors offering "therapy" or "counseling" meet with great resistance, even when the problems are significantly stressful. However, an SBFC counselor understands that while a Mexican client may resist "counseling" he/she would eagerly seek "educational help" for his/her child or adolescent. Thus the reframing of "counseling" into a psycho-educational model of service reaches both parents and their children.
>
> (Soriano & Gerrard, p. 10)

For many minority families, a visit to the community mental health clinic for therapy or counseling would be a sign the family is crazy or "loco." However, a visit by parents to the school to discuss with the school mental health professional educational matters relating to their child, is quite a different matter and one that most minority families are open to. The educational focus de-stigmatizes the mental health context.

Child Advocacy

SBFC is a child advocacy approach. The central focus of SBFC is the child and advocating for the child in all the child's relevant social systems: family, school, peer, community. SBFC recognizes that children are embedded in and deeply affected by their multiple social networks. By working with the child's family, school, peer group and community, the SBFC practitioner's goal is always empowerment of the child. The child, the family, and the school are all clients of the SBFC practitioner. However, because the child is more vulnerable than the family or the school, the SBFC practitioner gives primary advocacy emphasis to the child.

Promotion of School Transformation

Schools, like families, can be very dysfunctional. Like families they can be classified using the Circumplex Model (see Chapter 2). There are Rigid classrooms in which the teacher is authoritarian and strict to a point that interferes with children's learning. There are also Chaotic classrooms in which the teacher exercises so little control that children are unfocused and undisciplined, and this too interferes with their learning. Principals who have an authoritarian or laissez-faire leadership style may instigate Rigid or Chaotic environments in their schools. When bullying of a student occurs in a school it is often not an isolated event, but reflective of classroom dynamics involving bystanders (Padgett & Notar, 2013). Similarly, there is research connecting school shootings with broader dynamics in school systems: for example, large schools that have low connectedness (Wike & Fraser, 2009). These are examples of some of the problems that emanate from the classroom and school social climates and affect individual students. They represent major detriments to students' learning and academic success and would need to be addressed by the SBFC practitioner.

Interdisciplinary Focus

SBFC is an approach that can be used by any of the mental health disciplines: social work, counseling, psychology, marital and family therapy, psychiatry, and by professions such as special education and teaching. The mental health approaches used include: consultation, advice-giving, therapy, psychotherapy, counseling, psycho-education, and prevention. The integrating discipline in SBFC is family therapy. Family therapy, as a discipline, developed alongside the other mental health disciplines, and as its efficacy became clearer to the other mental health disciplines family therapy became integrated with many of them (hence: family counseling, family social work, family psychology, and family psychiatry). The word "counseling" is used in the term "school-based family counseling," however, because it is more acceptable than the word "therapy" to school personnel, and does not detract from SBFC's educational focus. However, we regard counseling, therapy, and psychotherapy as synonyms. SBFC also draws on techniques from diverse theoretical orientations. For example, an SBFC practitioner might use a classroom meeting based on Reality therapy, a family council meeting based on Adlerian therapy, assessment using a genogram based on Bowen Family Systems therapy, positive reinforcement drawn from Behavior therapy, cognitive restructuring based on Cognitive therapy, the empty chair technique based on Gestalt therapy, and community intervention based on the strategies from Social work or Community Psychology. To intervene in a school the SBFC practitioner needs to understand school and classroom organizational dynamics and how school cultures and school climates differ. To intervene in a family the SBFC practitioner needs to understand families from both systems and multicultural perspectives. The SBFC practitioner must also have skills in working with children of various ages, adolescents, and adults: teachers, principals, parents, and guardians, as well as with the elderly. This all requires that the SBFC practitioner have a broad rather than a narrow training – which is the essence of an interdisciplinary orientation.

How to Use This Book

This book is a "how to" manual on how to do SBFC. It is intended for practicing SBFC practitioners who wish to sharpen their skills, and for mental health practitioners, and mental health profession students, who wish to learn the skills of SBFC.

The SBFC Metamodel

This book is organized around the SBFC Metamodel. The SBFC Metamodel is a trans-disciplinary model for conceptualizing the skills needed for SBFC (see Figure 1.1).

The metamodel is organized around two axes: Family Focus vs. School Focus and Intervention Focus vs. Prevention Focus. The resulting matrix consists of four quadrants: School Intervention, School Prevention, Family Intervention, and Family prevention. Community is represented by a dotted line encompassing the family and school quadrants. School Intervention refers to remedial interventions that focus on modifying school environments: parent consultation, teacher consultation, group counseling, crisis intervention, student support groups. School Prevention refers to strategies used to prevent problems from occurring: guidance groups, classroom management, classroom meetings, stress management, anti-bullying programs. Family Intervention refers to remedial interventions that address serious family problems affecting children: parent consultation, conjoint family counseling, family counseling with individuals, couples counseling. Family Prevention refers to psycho-educational strategies to prevent problems from developing in families: parent education workshops, parent support groups. Community Intervention refers to interventions aimed at advocating for children, families, and schools through the mobilization of community resources.

The specific techniques chapters relating to the SBFC Metamodel (Chapters 3–10) are shown in Figure 1.2.

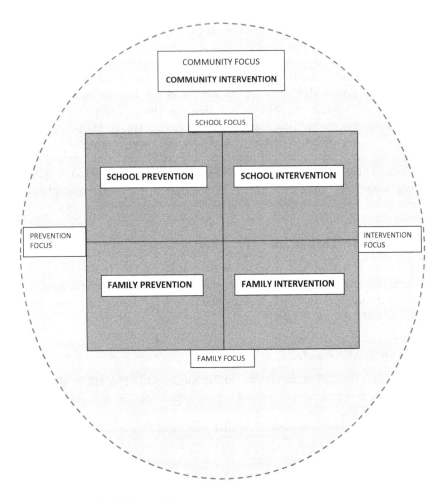

Figure 1.1 The SBFC Metamodel

This book does not cover all the skills that an SBFC practitioner might use, but it does describe in detail the basic techniques essential for SBFC practice. A description of the full range of SBFC competencies may be found in Gerrard & Soriano (2013) p. 7. To make the most effective use of this book, we recommend you begin with Chapter 2: How to Develop an SBFC Case Conceptualization. The importance of the SBFC practitioner developing a comprehensive SBFC case conceptualization is illustrated by the following story. A homeowner discovers during the winter that the furnace is not working. A furnace repair shop is quickly called. The repair person arrives with a bag of tools, removes a panel, and studies the furnace mechanism carefully for several minutes. Then the repair person takes out

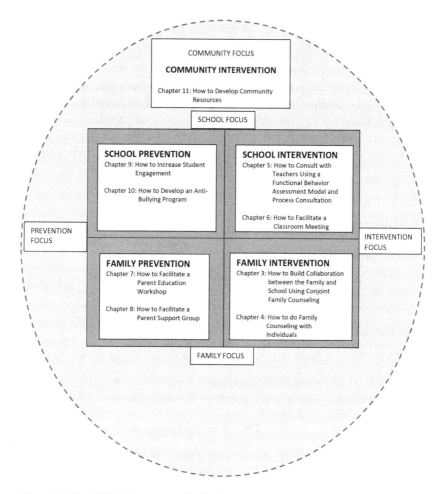

Figure 1.2 The SBFC Metamodel with Techniques Chapters

a small hammer and taps something. In a few minutes the furnace starts and runs fine. A week later the homeowner receives a bill for $100. The bill is itemized:

Tapping with hammer $1.
Knowing where to tap $99.

To be an effective SBFC practitioner you have to know where to "tap." This means having a solid grasp of the interpersonal and intrapersonal dynamics affecting a child and her social systems. Chapter 2 provides a starting point for thinking more systematically about interventions that link school and family. Chapters 3–11 deal with specific strategies in intervention or prevention in school and family systems. Each of these chapters contains specific instructions an SBFC practitioner could use to implement SBFC techniques. The techniques chapters are also organized around the headings: Overview, Background, Evidence-Based Support, Procedure, Multicultural Counseling Considerations, Challenges and Solutions, Resources, and Bibliography. Chapter 11 describes strategies for mobilizing important community resources to aid children, families, and schools. Chapter 12 identifies common obstacles SBFC practitioners experience and suggests strategies for overcoming them. Chapters 13–15 describe examples of SBFC case studies. In addition, this book contains links to videos of role-played demonstrations of important techniques described in the chapters.

Resources

Literature Review on SBFC

Gerrard, B. (2008). School-based family counseling: Overview, trends, and recommendations for future research. *International Journal for School-Based Family Counseling*, 1, 1–30.

Books on SBFC

Boyd-Franklin, L. & Hafer Bry, B. (2000). *Reaching out in family therapy*. New York: The Guilford Press.

Dreikurs, R. Cassel, P. (1965). *Discipline without tears*. New York: Harper and Row.

Fine, Marvin J. & Carlson C. (Eds.) (1992). *Family-school intervention: A systems perspective*. New York: Allyn and Bacon.

Gerrard, B. & Soriano, M. (Eds.) (2013). *School-based family counseling: Transforming family-school relationships*. Phoenix, AZ: Createspace.

Hinckle, J. & Wells, M. (1995). *Family counseling in the schools*. Greensboro, NC: ERIC/CASS Publications.

Laundy, K. C. (2015). *Building school-based collaborative mental health teams: A systems approach to student achievement*. Camp Hill, PA: TPI Press.

Miller, L. D. (Ed.) (2002). *Integrating school and family counseling: Practical solutions*. Alexandria, VA: American Counseling Association.

Palmatier Larry L. (1998). *Crisis counseling for a quality school community: A family perspective*. New York: Taylor & Francis.

Peacock, G. & Collett, B. (2010). *Collaborative home/school interventions: Evidence-based solutions for emotional, behavioral, and academic problems*. New York: Guilford.

Sherman, R., Shumsky, A. & Roundtree, Y. (1994). *Enlarging the therapeutic circle*. New York: Brunner/Mazel.

Sheridan, S. & Kratochwill, T. (2008). *Conjoint behavioral consultation: Promoting family-based connections and interventions*. New York: Springer.

Steele W. & Raider M. (1991). *Working with families in crisis: School-based intervention*. New York: Guilford.

Walsh, W. & Giblen, N. (Eds.) (1988). *Family counseling in school settings*. Springfield, IL: Charles C. Thomas.

Walsh, W. & Williams, G. (1997). *Schools and family therapy: Using systems theory and family therapy in the resolution of school problems*. New York: Charles C. Thomas.

Examples of SBFC Academic and Educational Programs

California State University, Los Angeles SBFC Master's Degree Program
This was the first master's degree program in SBFC in the USA. This Master of Science in Counseling School-Based Family Counseling Program is accredited by the Council for Accreditation of Counseling and Related Educational Programs (CACREP).

Central Connecticut State University Certificate Program in School-Based Marriage and Family Therapy
"For post-graduate students of master's or doctoral programs in Marriage and Family Therapy who wish to complete requirements for a Provisional Educator Certificate in Marriage and Family Therapy through the State of CT Department of Education."

The Loyola University, Chicago Family-School Partnership Program
"The Family and School Partnership Program (FSPP) was launched in 1996 to provide postmaster's training and consultation to school social workers and other school mental health professionals. To date, the FSPP has trained over 800 SBMHPs [school-based mental health professionals] via our Annual Summer Institutes and bi-monthly Consultation Groups."

The Loyola University Advanced School Mental Health Practice Certificate
"This post-master's certificate program equips mental health professionals to better affect positive psychosocial development of their student clients. Primary takeaways from the program will include: fostering collaboration between schools and families, implementing strength-based interventions in schools, advocating for whole-school interventions, and becoming more data driven and evidence informed as School-Based Mental Health Practitioners (SBMHP)."

Oxford Symposium in School-Based Family Counseling
Sponsored by the Institute for School-Based Family Counseling and co-sponsored by the University of San Francisco Center for Child and Family Development, the Oxford Symposium in SBFC is a small, invited, residential, international conference limited to around 25 members and their guests. The objective of the Oxford Symposium in SBFC is to make visible the "invisible college" of international experts in School-Based Family Counseling and to provide opportunity for information exchange, co-operation and collegial networking.

For links to these programs see SBFC EResources.

Examples of SBFC Service Delivery Programs

Families and Schools Together, Inc. (FAST)
"FAST® is a prevention and early intervention program that helps children succeed by empowering parents, connecting families, improving the school climate and strengthening

community engagement." The FAST program has been in existence for 25 years and has strong evidence-based support in the form of randomized control group studies with diverse populations. Educators who wish to implement the FAST program in their schools are provided with grant-seeking assistance by the FAST program.

The Place2Be Program
Place2Be is an SBFC program in over 257 schools in the UK. "Place2Be is the leading national children's mental health charity. Our Patron is The Duchess of Cambridge. We provide in-school counselling support & expert training to improve the emotional wellbeing of pupils, families, teachers & school staff." Funding comes from the schools, grants, and donations.

University of San Francisco Center for Child and Family Development SBFC Program
The Center for Child and Family Development has managed an SBFC service delivery program for 34 years. Marital and Family Therapy trainees and interns practice SBFC in 20–30 San Francisco-Bay area public and private schools. Funding is provided by the schools and foundation grants.

For links to these programs see SBFC EResources.

Journals That Publish Articles on SBFC

Child & Family Behavior Therapy
Child & Family Social Work
International Journal for School-Based Family Counseling
International Journal of Child, Youth and Family Studies
International Journal of School and Educational Psychology
International Journal of School Social Work
Journal of Child and Family Studies
Journal of School-based Counseling Policy and Evaluation

Brief Videos on SBFC

Krause, R. (2016, May 4). *School-based family counseling: An overview*
Krause, R. (2017, July 23). *School-based family counseling: Strengths*
For links to these videos see SBFC EResources.

Internet Resources on SBFC

Child and Adolescent Psychological and Educational Resources
"This site has been active since 2001 and, over time, has built up a large information base, accessed internationally by students, teachers, researchers and other professionals interested in research and practical resources relating to children, adolescents and families. Particular focus is given to issues relating to peer relationships, including bullying, as well as stress and wellbeing."

Institute for School-Based Family Counseling
The Institute for School-Based Family Counseling exists to promote the development of SBFC as a discipline through multiculturally sensitive programs that educate mental health professionals, educators, and the general public on the nature and value of SBFC. The Institute's website contains SBFC resources for mental health professionals, teachers, and parents.

UCLA School Mental Health Project
"Stated simply, our mission is to improve outcomes for students by helping districts and their schools enhance how they address barriers to learning and teaching and re-engage disconnected students. One way we do this is by providing information and links for leaders and practitioners to access a range of no-cost resources developed by us and others that can be used for: school improvement, professional development, direct student/learning support."

Schoolsocialwork.net
"SchoolSocialWork.net is a free online resource and community dedicated to supporting the professional practice of school social workers and other school mental health professionals."

For links to these programs see SBFC EResources.

Bibliography

Bronfenbrenner, U. (1979). *The ecology of human development.* Cambridge, MA: Harvard University Press.

Dana, R. (Ed.). (2000). *Handbook of cross-cultural and multicultural personality assessment.* Mahwah, NJ: Erlbaum.

Dear, J. (1995). *Creating caring relationships to foster academic excellence: Recommendations for reducing violence in California schools.* Sacramento, CA: CCTC.

Gerrard, B. & Soriano, M. (2013). *School-based family counseling: Transforming family-school relationships.* Phoenix, AZ: Createspace.

Padgett, S. & Notar, C. (2013). Bystanders are the key to stopping bullying. *Universal Journal of Educational Research,* 1(2): 33–41.

Pope-Davis, D. B. & Coleman, H. L. K. (2015). *Multicultural counseling competencies: Assessment, education and training, and supervision.* Thousand Oaks, CA: Sage.

Sue, D.W. & Sue, D. (2008). *Counseling the culturally diverse: Theory and practice* (5th Edition). New York, NY: John Wiley & Sons.

Wike, T. & Fraser, M. (2009). School shootings: Making sense of the senseless. *Aggression and Violent Behavior,* 14, 162–169.

2 How to Develop an SBFC Case Conceptualization

Brian A. Gerrard

Overview: *This chapter shows how to develop a comprehensive SBFC case conceptualization based on the SBFC metamodel. The central relationship of case conceptualization to assessment, diagnosis, and the treatment plan is described.*

Background

Case conceptualization refers to the process by which an SBFC practitioner takes assessment information and makes sense of a client's situation in a way that facilitates the development of an effective treatment plan to resolve the client's presenting symptoms. A comprehensive SBFC case conceptualization involves a diagnosis of the individual client's functioning and a diagnosis of the family, peer, school, and community systems affecting the client. The individual client's view of the problem is typically very different from the SBFC practitioner's view of the client's problem. For example, a Hispanic student Kylie Gonzalez, age 14, has been cutting herself and seems depressed, according to her teacher and parents. When Kylie is asked about what is going on with her, the SBFC practitioner Ramona is told: "No one at school likes me. Nothing really interests me." After interviewing Kylie, Kylie's parents and teacher, and observing Kylie in the classroom and at recess, Ramona develops an initial case conceptualization, shown in Table 2.1.

What is missing from Kylie's conceptualization of her problems is the theoretical and systems thinking that Ramona brings. Ramona's analysis is that Kylie's cutting, low self-esteem, and weak friendship skills are related to problems in her family and in her classroom. Furthermore, the marital tension between Kylie's parents is compounded by institutional racism that is affecting Kylie's father at work. A comprehensive SBFC treatment plan to help Kylie will involve interventions at all four SBFC levels (see the SBFC metamodel in Figure 1.1). What is critical, however, is the ability of the SBFC practitioner to identify the challenges at each level. To intervene only at the individual level – with no understanding of how the family, school, and community levels are maintaining Kylie's problems – would be a mistake and represent only partial treatment.

Table 2.1 Case Conceptualization for Kylie

SBFC Focus	Challenges
Individual level	Kylie's unrealistic thinking about her self-worth
	Lack of friends
Family level	Marital discord between parents
	Tense home atmosphere
	Conflict between Kylie's mother and Kylie
School level	Kylie being cyber-bullied by a girls' clique
	Kylie's school having a disengaged, impersonal "climate"
Community level	Kylie's father experiencing discrimination at work

Procedure

To conduct a comprehensive SBFC case conceptualization there are six main steps:

Step 1: Collecting Assessment Information
Step 2: Developing the Case Conceptualization
Step 3: Developing a Treatment Plan Informed by the Case Conceptualization
Step 4: Using an Intervention with the Client
Step 5: Monitoring the Client's Response to the Intervention
Step 6: Modifying the Case Conceptualization, Treatment Plan, and Intervention depending on additional Information

As can be seen in Figure 2.1, case conceptualization occurs within a dynamic relationship with assessment, treatment planning, intervention, and client response to intervention. It is important to note that developing an accurate case conceptualization is a *process that undergoes modification* depending on the client's response to intervention and additional information that the SBFC practitioner may learn about the client.

The intervention may not work and may therefore require modification. Or the SBFC practitioner may learn some new information about the client, the family, or the school that requires a significant change in the case conceptualization or the treatment plan and intervention. That is, the final case conceptualization used by the SBFC practitioner could be quite different from the original case conceptualization, depending on important new information about the client's family, the school, or the intervention. If the SBFC practitioner is skilled, she/he will be open to modifying the case conceptualization, treatment plan, and intervention as necessary. This is because when you work with a client it is impossible to have every significant piece of information available at the first session. Because trust builds over time, clients – as they experience greater trust – feel more comfortable revealing information they withheld at the earlier sessions.

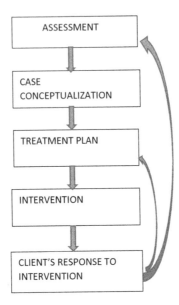

Figure 2.1 The Case Conceptualization – Intervention Cycle

It is very rare that an SBFC practitioner will meet with a student, their teacher, and parents for several sessions and only then formulate a case conceptualization. The more skilled an SBFC practitioner is the more likely that they will very quickly form a hypothesis (a guess) about what the psychological and systems nature of the client's problem is, and then ask questions and look for behavior that indicates whether the SBFC practitioner is on the right track. In Kylie's case, Ramona might think initially that Kylie's problem only has to do with bullies in her classroom. However, based on comments Kylie made during the end of their first meeting, Ramona realizes that a more critical piece has to do with martial stress between Kylie's parents that is causing Kylie to feel depressed and is making her more vulnerable to being bullied. Three sessions into working with Kylie and her family, Ramona next discovers from comments by students during recess that bullying is a problem throughout the school and that this systemic problem is underpinning Kylie's problems. It also becomes clear to Ramona that the counseling goal Kylie wants most to work on is improving her relationship with her mother.

Step 1: Collecting Assessment Information

Step 1A: Establishing a Reputation for Being Trustworthy with Students, Parents, and Families

In order to collect useful information about a client's situation, it is essential the SBFC practitioner have a relationship of trust with everyone the SBFC practitioner interviews. Before any student, parent, or teacher meets with you, they will likely have some information about who you are and what sort of person you are. That is, you will have a "reputation" for acting a certain way with others. When you enter a school as the SBFC practitioner for the first time, you can establish a reputation for being a helpful (and therefore trustworthy) professional by following the strategies shown in Box 2.1 Tips for Joining with the School Community and Box 2.2 Tips for Joining with Families. These strategies establish you as an SBFC professional who is available, concerned, and friendly.

Box 2.1 Tips for Joining with the School Community

Set up a regular time to consult with the Principal, e.g. a weekly 15 minute meeting.

Familiarize yourself with the school's rules and procedures.

Make friends with the school secretary.

Be punctual in attending meetings.

Think of yourself as being part of the school staff.

Send a letter to the teachers and parents/guardians introducing yourself.

Emphasize that as a SBFC professional one of your primary goals is to help children succeed academically.

Participate actively in the school community. Show up at the school play, basketball game, etc.

Make yourself available before school starts and after it ends (e.g. for 30 minutes) to increase your accessibility to staff.

Have lunch with other school staff (rather than in your office).

Be visible to teachers, students and parents/guardians.

Introduce yourself and explain your role to teachers, students, and parents/guardians. If you are an introvert, consider this an important part of your personal growth.

If there are other mental health professionals working in the school who do not have an SBFC background, make friends with them. Let them know that you are there to collaborate with them.

Consult with the person referring a student.

Meet with student clients at a time that fits into their school schedule.

Remember that parents/guardians may not be able to meet with you during school hours because they are working.

Box 2.2 Tips for Joining with Families

Send a letter introducing yourself as a school mental health professional to all the parents/guardians in the school community.

Emphasize the importance of collaborating with parents/guardians in order to help their children succeed in school.

Be flexible in scheduling meetings with parents/guardians who are working.

During a first meeting, explain your role in collaborating with families to help children succeed academically.

Be sure to discuss confidentiality with the family.

Use empathy to show you understand each family member's point of view.

During the meeting be sure to hear from everyone, especially the adult who has the most influence in the family.

Remember that there is a power structure in every family and that if you alienate the person with the most authority, the family will be unlikely to return for counseling.

Use a strength-based approach to encourage the family members and give them hope.

As you speak with each family member, look for positives as well as things you may have in common with the family member. Briefly sharing a connection you may have (e.g. with sports, TV shows watched, etc.) with a family member facilitates the building of trust.

At the end of a first session, summarize what you understand to be the different family members' concerns and hopes.

Point out a strength you see in the family and indicate what you think you and the family working together could do to help their child.

After the first meeting, develop a beginning case conceptualization for the family that moves from a description of the "identified patient" to a broader systems conceptualization of how family and school strengths and challenges affect the behavior of the referred student.

When you ask to meet with a student, parent, or teacher, they will have heard good things about you. Your reputation "goes before" you and makes it easier for you to get an interview and build trust during the interview. By actively involving yourself in the life of the school and by actively engaging with parents (e.g. by introducing yourself at a PTA meeting) you will be more likely to have access to information about: the social climate in the school, teachers who have challenges with their students, the principal's relationship with staff, how families feel about the school, and the presence of different student cliques and groupings within the school. The importance of this step cannot be emphasized enough.

Step 1B: Interview the Person who Made the Referral

This could be a teacher, principal, parent/guardian, or a self-referred student. Find out what their view of the problem is and their thoughts about what is causing the problem and what needs to be done to improve things. If the referring person is an adult, your interview might be brief as teachers and principals are busy persons, and a parent/guardian might initially only be available by phone.

Step 1C: Interview the Student

Irrespective of the approach you use to interview the student (e.g. client-centered, CBT, multimodal, narrative, strength-based, etc.) your goal should be to make friends with the student and earn enough trust so that you will be told the student's most important concerns. This early phase of intervention, called Stage 1: Preparing for Change, has two essential components: building rapport with the client and getting the client to tell her/his "story." The use of empathic listening ("It sounds like you felt really upset when your classmate made fun of you.") and open-ended questions ("What did it mean to you when she said that?") are useful responses for building trust. In a first interview, discussion of your role and confidentiality, as well as any need for parent permission, will be important to cover.

Step 1D: Interview the Parents/Guardians

There are two reasons for interviewing the parents/guardians: a) they may be contributing to the student's problems and you will need to figure out how; and b) they may be able to provide positive resources to help support and empower the student. You should not be quick to assume that the family is a "problem." The problem affecting the student may be at the school level. Keep in mind that schools, like families, can be dysfunctional. Box 2.3 The First Interview with the Parents/Guardians contains sample model dialogue you can use in a first interview.

Box 2.3 The First SBFC Interview with the Parents/Guardians

Note: Step 4 of this interview guide is worded for a mental health trainee (e.g. school counselor, school social worker, school psychologist, marriage and family therapist, etc.).

Goal of the First Meeting:	– To make friends with the parents/guardians – To identify a counseling goal – To form a partnership with the parents/guardians
STEP	**DESCRIPTION**
1. Welcome (1 min.)	Hello My name is … I am the school mental health professional for (name agency/school) Thank you for coming …
2. Small Talk (1 min.)	Did you have any trouble parking?
3. Overview (0.5 min.)	I'd like to tell you a little bit about who I am and my role as the school mental health professional. Then I'd like to talk with you about how we can work together to help (Name of Child).
4. Explain Role (5 min.)	I am a mental health professional trainee. A trainee is … – not a licensed professional yet – a student in the Master's degree program at … – under the licensed supervision of … – my professors have determined that I am now qualified … – my traineeship placement is in this school until … – my role is to work in partnership with parents – to help students succeed at school – Everything we discuss is confidential with three exceptions: I have to discuss how I am doing with my supervisor and supervision group; I have to report any danger to self or others; with a court order I would have to share some of my counseling notes. – Do you have any questions?
5. Explain Reason for Meeting	As I indicated on the phone, the reason I wanted to meet with you is because_____. As the parents/

(1 min.)	guardians of (Name) you are experts on your child. It is therefore very important that I consult with you.
6. Introduce a Strength-Based Focus (5 min.)	What do you see as your child's greatest strengths? What are your wishes for your child's future? *Use Active Listening / Validation*
7. Get the Parent's/ Guardian's View of the Situation (10 min.)	How do you feel (Name) is doing in school? How do you feel about (Name)'s teacher? How do you feel about the school? *Use Active Listening / Validation*
8. Introduce a Counseling Goal (5 min.)	Are there any areas in which you would like (Name) to improve at school or at home? Would you like to see (Name): • get along better with_____? • do better at_____? • get better grades? If we work together there are some things we can do that would help (Name) to_____. *Use Active Listening / Validation*
9. Secure a Commitment (2 min.)	Would you be willing to work with me to help (Name) do better at_____? This would mean our meeting to discuss how things are going. I recommend we meet three times and then review how things are going. (If resistance: phone check-in once a week)
10. Set Next Meeting/ Contact (1 min.)	Would this time work for you next week?
11. Thank Them for Coming (1 min.)	I just want to tell you how much I appreciate that you met with me today. (Name) is very lucky to have such caring parents/ guardians as you. I am very optimistic that together we can help (Name) do better at_____.

Step 2: Develop the Case Conceptualization

A comprehensive SBFC case conceptualization has seven components:

a) A *counseling readiness* assessment.
b) An assessment of the client's *individual and interpersonal functioning*.
c) An assessment of the client's *family system* as it affects the client.
d) An assessment of the client's *school system* as it affects the client.

e) An assessment of how *multicultural variables* (e.g. ethnicity, discrimination, etc.) affect the client

f) An assessment of how *other socio-demographic variables* (e.g. age, religion, sexual orientation, gender orientation, social class, etc.) affect the client.

g) An assessment of *family strengths*.

Step 2A: Make a Counseling Readiness Assessment

One of the signs of an inexperienced or incompetent mental health professional is the inability to recognize when a client is ready to participate in counseling. Between 20% and 57% of therapy clients do not return after their initial session and 37% to 45% attend therapy a total of only two times (Schwartz & Flowers, 2010). The Client Readiness for Change Model (see Table 2.2) developed by Prochasa, DiClemente, and Norcross (1992) is a useful guide to help you identify the stages many clients go through.

Strategic therapists sometimes describe the Precontemplation stage as one in which the potential client is deciding whether to become a "customer." During the Precontemplation and Contemplation stages, critical counseling skills to use are the client-centered therapy triad of empathy, warmth, and respect.

It is important to keep in mind the many reasons why some persons may not want to see you for counseling:

• They have an alternate source of support (friends, family, spiritual advisor).
• They fear being labelled as "crazy" for seeking mental health services.
• They may not be "psychological minded" and not understand how counseling can be helpful.
• They may be open to counseling but feel you are not the right person to help them (because you are a beginning SBFC practitioner, of a different ethnicity, gender, etc.).
• They may be affected by negative stereotypes of mental health professionals as portrayed on TV(often as "crazy").
• They may have had a prior experience with a mental health professional that did not go well.

If your "client" is in the Precontemplation or Contemplation stage, avoid assigning homework or implementing behavior change activities as this is

Table 2.2 The Client Readiness for Change Model

Readiness for Change Stage	*Description*
Precontemplation	Individual does not see the need for counseling
Contemplation	Client is open to seeing the need for counseling
Preparation	Client is open to planning for change
Action	Client implements change
Maintenance	Client takes steps to maintain change

likely to result in the "client" not returning. Keep your emphasis on making friends, making it easy for the "client" to tell you their story, and communicating that you have ways to assist them in dealing with their challenges when they are ready to do so.

Step 2B: Make an Assessment of the Client's Individual and Interpersonal Functioning

If you are successful in building trust with your client and they move into the Contemplation and Preparation stages, it is important to assess your client's emotional, cognitive, and interpersonal functioning. Assessing this involves taking a history that taps into the different ways the client deals with stress. A useful approach to obtaining this information is to conduct a **Multimodal assessment** of the client. This CBT approach, which was developed by Lazarus (2006), involves asking the client about their functioning across the seven basic personality modalities: Behavior, Affect, Sensation, Imagery, Cognition, Interpersonal, and Drug/Physiological – what Lazarus refers to as the BASIC ID. Box 2.4 contains useful questions you can ask a client to obtain their BASIC ID.

Box 2.4 Questions for Multimodal Assessment

Multimodal Assessment Questions for a Specific Issue

Behavior: "What do you typically say or do with_____ (problematic situation or person)?"
SBFC example: "What do you typically do when other kids bully you?"

Affect: "What sort of emotions or feeling do you typically have with_____?"
SBFC example: "When the teacher ignores you how do you feel?"

Sensation: "What sensations or tensions do you experience when_____?"
SBFC example: "When the other girls send you a nasty text, do you feel tense anywhere in your body?"

Imagery: "What images or fantasies do you have when dealing with_____?"
SBFC example: "What images or fantasies do you have when the teacher asks the class to form work pairs and nobody chooses you?"

Cognition: "What does it mean to you when_____?"
"What kinds of thoughts do you have about_____?"
SBFC example: "What does it mean to you when you get these text messages?"

Interpersonal: "What does (name person) typically do when_____?"
"How does (name person) treat you when_____?"

SBFC example: "What does the teacher do when she sees you don't have a work partner?"

Drug/
Physiological:
"When you are dealing with_____", how is your body affected?"
(e.g. "Feel ill, sleep affected, need medication, etc").
SBFC example: "When you get a nasty text message, how is your body affected?"

General Multimodal Assessment Questions for Family

Behavior:
"What sort of things do you do during a typical weekend at home?"
"What do you do in the morning? Afternoon? Evening?"

Affect:
"What feelings or emotions do you typically have when you are with your family?
With your mother? With your father? With _____ (other family members)?"

Sensation:
"What sensations (for example: feeling tense or relaxed) do you experience when you are with your family?"

Imagery:
"What images or fantasies do you have when you are with your family? With your mother? With your father? With other family members?"

Cognition:
"When you are with your family, what sort of thoughts do you have about them? About yourself?"
"What would be something your family does that you really like? When they do that what does it mean to you?"
"What would be something you family does that you don't like? When they do that what does it mean to you?"

Interpersonal:
"How does your family generally treat you?" "Can you give me an example of that?"
"What sort of things do they say to you?"
"How does your mother generally treat you?" (repeat for father, other family members)

Drug/
Physiological:
"Sometimes families upset us and we can't sleep or even feel ill. Does that ever happen to you?" "Can you please tell me about a time that happened?"

General Multimodal Assessment Questions for School

Behavior:
"What sort of things do you do during a typical day at school?"
"What do you do in the morning? At lunch? At recess? In the afternoon?"

Affect:
"What feelings or emotions do you typically have when you are at school?"
"Can you please tell me about the last time you had those feelings at school?"

Sensation:
"What sensations (for example: feeling tense or relaxed) do you experience when you are at school?"

Imagery:
"What images or fantasies do you have when you are at school?"

Cognition:	"When you are at school, what sort of thoughts do you have? What sort of thoughts do you have about your teacher? About yourself?" "What would be something your teachers do that you really like? When they do that what does it mean to you?" "What would be something your teachers do that you don't like? When they do that what does it mean to you?" "What would be something students at school do that you really like? When they do that what does it mean to you?" "What would be something students at school do that you don't like? When they do that what does it mean to you?"
Interpersonal:	"How do students at school treat you?" "What sort of things do they say to you?" "How do teachers treat you?" "What sort of things do they say to you?"
Drug/ Physiological:	"Sometimes things at school upset us and we can't sleep or even feel ill later. Does that ever happen to you?" "Can you please tell me about a time that happened?"

General Multimodal Assessment Questions for Friends

Ask:	"Do you have any friends?" If client answers no, skip this section.
Behavior:	"What sort of things do you like to do with your friend(s)?" "Can you please give me an example of that?"
Affect:	"What feelings or emotions do you have when you are with your friend(s)?"
Sensation:	"What sensations (for example: feeling tense or relaxed) do you experience when you are with your friend(s)?"
Imagery:	"What images or fantasies do you have when you are with your friend(s)?"
Cognition:	"When you are with your friend(s), what sort of thoughts do you have? What sort of thoughts do you have about your friend(s)? About yourself?" "What would be something your friend(s) do that you really like? When they do that what does it mean to you?" "What would be something your friend(s) do that you don't like? When they do that what does it mean to you?"
Interpersonal:	"How do your friends treat you?" "What sort of things do they say to you?"
Drug/ Physiological:	"Sometimes things friends do upset us and we can't sleep or even feel ill later. Does that ever happen to you?" "Can you please tell me about a time that happened?"

****

Tips for using Multimodal Assessment:

1. Begin by saying: "I'd like to ask you some questions to help me get a better understanding of how you experience_____ (e.g. school, your family, or specific incident)."

2. Use empathy/active listening statements between questions (e.g. "When your friend yelled at you that must have been upsetting.").
3. When asking questions about a specific incident, start with the Interpersonal modality.
4. Use bridging to link modalities, e.g. "When you felt angry [*Affect*] at what your friend said, what did you do [*Behavior*]?"; "When your father criticized you [*Interpersonal*], how did you feel [*Affect*]?"

With respect to Kylie described above, the BASIC ID assessment may be of Kylie's a) life situation in general, b) her relationship with a specific person or group, or c) a specific incident involving another person or group. As illustrated below for Behavior, the wording for specific levels of BASIC ID assessment will differ:

BASIC ID Assessment of Kylie's Life Situation:
"What do you generally do during a typical day at school?"
"What are some things you do at school that you would like to do more of?"
"What sort of behaviors would you like to do less of?"

BASIC ID of Relationship with a Specific Person or Group:
"What do you say and do when you are with_____(e.g your mother)?"

BASIC ID of Specific Incident Involving Another Person or Group:
"When_____occurred (e.g. your parents were arguing), what did you say or do?"

When doing a BASIC ID assessment, it is useful to use the multimodal assessment questions to map out all three levels: life situation, specific relationship, and specific incident. The value of conducting a multimodal assessment is that by identifying challenges the client is experiencing in specific BASIC ID areas, you can formulate a treatment plan that addresses each area.

This is illustrated in Table 2.3.

An alternative way to assess the client's individual and interpersonal functioning is to use a **Narrative Therapy** interview approach. This approach developed by White and Epston (1990) emphasizes asking the client questions that "externalize the problem." The client is invited to re-story their relationship with their problem from a story about deficiency and failure to a story about resilience and competence. The client is asked to give a name to their problem and then the SBFC practitioner conducts a client history asking the client about the renamed problem as though it were an entity separate from the client. In their book, Epston and White

Table 2.3 A Multimodal Assessment and Treatment Plan for Kylie

Modality	Problem	Proposed Intervention
Behavior	When Kylie is bullied she keeps silent. She cuts herself after being bullied.	Assertion Training
Affect	Kylie frequently feels depressed because she feels her parents will divorce.	Desensitization to parents' arguments, couple counseling for parents
Sensation	Kylie feels very tense all the time.	Systematic muscle relaxation
Imagery	Kylie has fantasies about being abandoned by her parents if they divorce.	Thought-stopping with Positive Imagery
Cognition	Kylie has thoughts like: "I am worthless." "No one likes me." "Something terrible is going to happen to me."	Cognitive restructuring
Interpersonal	A girls' clique with a ringleader Jessica is cyberbullying Kylie.	Classroom meeting to address the classroom bullying
Drug/ Physiological	Kylie has trouble sleeping at night.	Guided meditation tape to relax

describe a child who had severe encopresis. They invited the family to give this problem a name: "Sneaky Poo" then proceeded to ask questions about how "Sneaky Poo" had been affecting the family. By treating the family problem as though it were an unwanted visitor, the therapists helped the family to externalize the problem rather than view it as a sign of family psychopathology. This avoidance of deficiency labelling reduces client resistance and facilitates history taking. Externalizing the problem is a first step in doing Narrative Therapy. A second step is to develop with the client "unique outcomes": instances in which the client does not experience the problem. These two steps are illustrated by the questions in Box 2.5. The advantage of using a Narrative Therapy approach to exploring the client's history with a problem is that it generates valuable information about the client's problem without making the client feel deficient; it produces information about client resources (i.e. instances when the client doesn't have the problem); and it empowers the client by avoiding deficiency language and suggesting ways the client could defeat the problem.

Box 2.5 Interview Guide for Narrative Therapy

STEP 1: INVITATION TO TALK

"What are you most interested in talking about today?"
"As you talk I'm going to just take some brief notes in order to ..."

STEPS 2–5 EXTERNALIZING THE PROBLEM

STEP 2: GIVE THE PROBLEM A NAME (Dominant Plot Name)

"If you were to give this problem a name, what would it be?"

STEP 3: EXPLORE THE EFFECTS OF THE PROBLEM ON
           THEIR LIVES

"How has _____(Insert 'the Name' e.g. CONFLICT) been
affecting you?"

"When does CONFLICT seem to show up?"

"What has _____ (e.g. CONFLICT) got you into believing
about yourself?"

"What has _____ (e.g. CONFLICT) got you doing that gets
you into trouble?"

"How has _____ (e.g. CONFLICT) got you into acting in
ways you don't want?"

If client gives example: "Give me an example of what you would
rather have happened.")

STEP 4: ASK CLIENT TO EVALUATE AND JUSTIFY THE
           EFFECTS OF THE PROBLEM

"What about _____ (e.g. CONFLICT) is most upsetting
to you?"

"Why is this upsetting? Does it have any positive effects?"
(Have client justify their position.)

STEP 5: ASK RECRUITMENT QUESTIONS
(Establishing the Context of the Problem)

"How did _____(CONFLICT) trick you into a relationship?"

"Have you witnessed_____(CONFLICT) in your family or other
families?"

If so: "Tell me about how observing_____ (CONFLICT)
affected you."

STEPS 6–9 IDENTIFYING NEW PATTERNS (UNIQUE OUTCOMES)

STEP 6: IDENTIFY AN INSTANCE OF POSITIVE
           INTERACTION

"Have there been any times that _____ (e.g. CONFLICT)
didn't get the better of you?"

"Was that positive or negative?"

If positive: "Why do you regard that as positive?"

STEP 7: GIVE THE POSITIVE BEHAVIOR A NAME (Alternative Plot Name)

"What Name might you give this Positive Behavior?"(e.g. COURAGE)

STEP 8: EXPLORE THE EFFECTS OF THE POSITIVE BEHAVIOR_____
(e.g. COURAGE)

"What did you do that facilitated the presence of _____ (e.g. COURAGE)?"

"How has _____ (e.g. COURAGE) helped you?"

"What do you like best about_____(e.g. COURAGE)?"

STEP 9: EXPLORE THE CLIENT'S POSSIBLE FUTURE WITH _____ (e.g. COURAGE)

"If _____ (e.g. COURAGE) were to become stronger in your life, how would that affect you?"

"If you wanted to do one thing to increase to presence of _____ (e.g. COURAGE) in your life, what might you try?"

"Who do you know who would not be surprised at all to learn that you took this step?"

Step 2C: Assessing the Client's Family System

Two useful models for assessing families are the Bowen Family Systems Model and the Circumplex Model. Some key aspects of each model are described below.

BOWEN FAMILY SYSTEMS MODEL

This assessment model was developed by Murray Bowen who is considered one of the founders of the family therapy approach (Bowen, 1978). The advantages of conducting a Bowen family assessment are:

• The genogram is a useful visual tool that helps the SBFC practitioner to quickly identify all the members of the family system and take a basic family history in a way that engages families.
• Identifying triangles in a family represents a sophisticated level of systems thinking that goes beyond the analysis of dyads.
• The concept of Family Projection Process helps the SBFC practitioner to identify not only how a family member gets a negative identity, but also how the family currently reinforces that identity.

- The identification of each family member's level of differentiation of self helps the SBFC practitioner to conceptualize a communication training plan for the different family members.

A minimal Bowen assessment consists of an assessment based on: a) Genogram, b) Triangles and Scapegoating, c) Family Projection Process, and d) Differentiation of Self.

The Genogram. The Genogram is a sophisticated type of family tree that visually presents important information about the family members across two

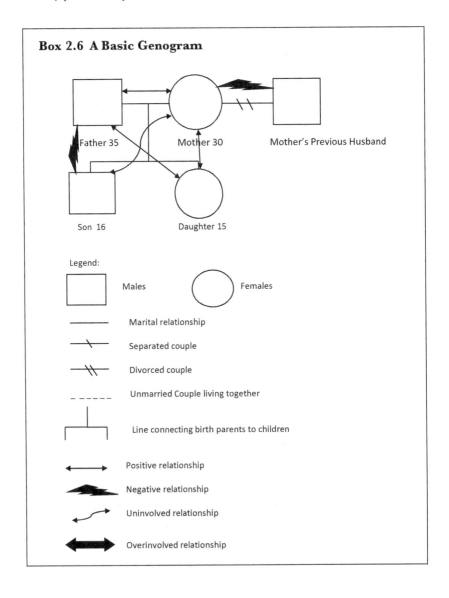

Box 2.6 A Basic Genogram

Father 35   Mother 30   Mother's Previous Husband

Son 16   Daughter 15

Legend:

☐ Males   ◯ Females

——— Marital relationship

—✕— Separated couple

—✕✕— Divorced couple

- - - - - Unmarried Couple living together

Line connecting birth parents to children

←——→ Positive relationship

Negative relationship

Uninvolved relationship

◀——▶ Overinvolved relationship

to three generations (Bowen, 1978). This information includes using circles for females, squares for males, ages, birth order (indicated by oldest sibling placed to the left), symbols that indicate death, marital and common law relationships, positive and negative relationships, medical and other information. A sample genogram is shown in Box 2.6.

As can be seen from the genogram for Kylie's family in Box 2.7 Kylie has an uninvolved relationship with her parents, who have a negative relationship with each other. Kylie has a positive relationship with her maternal grandmother and her younger brother. However, there is a lot of tension in this family with negative relationships between Kylie's father and both sons, and between Kylie's mother and her father. We see also a history of marital difficulty across two generations.

The genogram has two strengths: families tend to enjoy completing it and it provides the SBFC practitioner with a lot of useful information in a visual format.

Assessing Triangles and Scapegoating. A fundamental assumption in Bowen theory is that when family members become anxious about each other a common way to reduce the anxiety is to form triangles which are typically coalitions of two against one. Some common triangles are shown in Figure 2.2.

The upper triangle showing a coalition of parents against a child is a common form of a scapegoating triangle. The dynamic here is that of two parents with significant marital difficulties who are not openly dealing with each other about their frustrations and anger. Instead their tension with each other is displaced onto a child who is misbehaving and acting out. This child is typically brought to counseling by a parent and is considered by

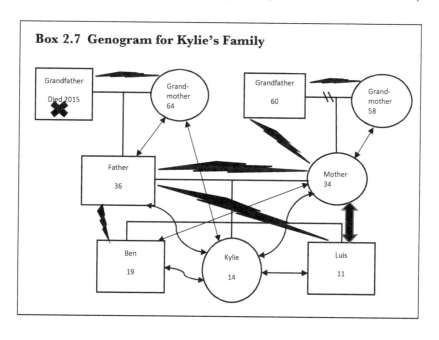

Box 2.7 Genogram for Kylie's Family

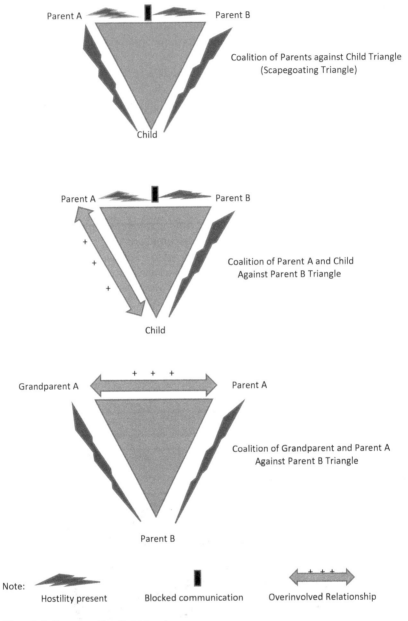

Figure 2.2 Common Family Triangles

family therapists to be the "identified patient." The tense relationship between the parents and the child brings the parents together in a way that lessens their marital tension. The second triangle is that of a parent–child coalition against the other parent. Parent A has a tense relationship with Parent B, but rather than dealing directly with Parent B, Parent A encourages the child to act out against Parent B. This type of triangle is present in the Gonzalez family in two triangles – each involving a coalition of mother and child against father (see Figure 2.3). The third type of triangle is a grandparent coalition with a parent against the other parent. In the Gonzalez family there is this third triangle present (shown in Figure 2.3) – a coalition of Grandmother and Mother against Grandfather.

Although this triangle involves two grandparents, its structure is basically that of a parental coalition with a child against another parent. The value in doing an assessment of triangles in a family is that it helps to identify dyads characterized by hostility and poor communication and which attempt to reduce their stress by drawing in a third family member.

Family Projection Process.   This is the process by which a family member is given a negative identity. Its presence is most obvious in families where there is a scapegoating triangle, often where a child is labelled uncooperative or "bad" by other family members. This process is one where family members "project" their own hostile and negative characteristics onto another family member, the "identified patient." The identified patient may have his or her identity shaped by being told (often by a parent): "This is who you are." For example, "You have a mean streak, just like uncle Eddie who is in prison." In addition, significant family members may pay attention to the identified patient only when the identified patient is misbehaving or showing symptoms. This serves to reinforce the identified patient's negative behavior and identity. In the Gonzalez family the father Raoul has a tense relationship with his wife and with his sons, Ben and Luis. However, Mrs. Gonzalez (Margarita) has encouraged the boys to rebel against the father on the grounds that "Father is unfair and rigid." The times when Raoul acts fairly and flexibly with his sons are ignored. This negative perception of the father is an example of Family Projection Process.

Differentiation of Self.   This Bowen concept refers to the ability of a family member to develop a separate identity from the family. Bowen used the term "undifferentiated family ego mass" to describe families where independence and separateness are not tolerated and are viewed as acts of disloyalty. The differentiated family member, however, is able to act independently of the family and hold opinions that the family might not approve of. A sign of a very highly differentiated family member is someone who is interdependent and can maintain contact with the family without losing a sense of emotional balance and independence. Family members who score low on Differentiation of Self tend to have enmeshed, dependent relationships or counter-dependent, hostile relationships with other family members. Bowen used a Differentiation of Self Scale using ratings from 0 (no differentiation of self at all) to 100 (complete differentiation of self) to measure degree of differentiation. With the caveat that this is not a reliable, standardized measure, the

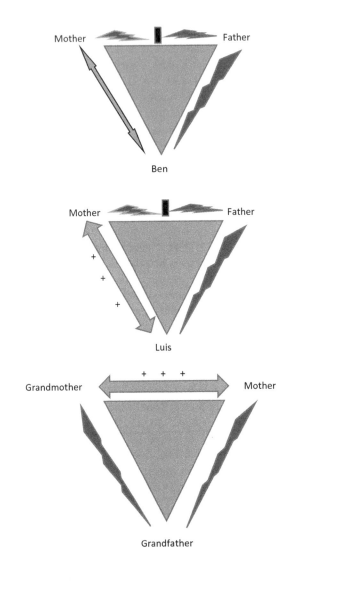

Mother

Father

Ben

Mother

Father

+
+
+

Luis

Grandmother

+ + +

Mother

Grandfather

Note:

Hostility present

Blocked communication

Overinvolved Relationship

Figure 2.3 Gonzalez Family Triangles

probable ratings for Kylie's family would be: Raoul (50), Margarita (55), Kylie (25), Ben (20), Luis (15).

Table 2.4 summarizes challenges identified in the Gonzalez family by a Bowen family assessment and some possible interventions to address those challenges.

THE CIRCUMPLEX MODEL

The Circumplex Model has several advantages for family assessment:

- It is a metamodel that can be easily used with any intervention approach.
- Its core concepts are easily understood by beginning SBFC practitioners.
- It is a true systems assessment model focusing on relationships.
- It can be used to describe the entire family as well as specific pairs of relationships.
- It is a trans-systems model useful for assessing both families and schools.
- It can be used with observational and standardized assessment tools.
- It has very good reliability and validity established in over 500 studies.
- It offers a visual (diagram) display of information.

The Circumplex Model is a family systems map of the relationship between family members on two dimensions: Flexibility and Cohesion (Olson, Russell, & Sprenkle, 1989). Flexibility refers to the ability of a family to adapt to change. Cohesion refers to the family's degree of closeness between family members. Each dimension has five subcategories (see Table 2.5).

Each Circumplex dimension is a continuum. For example, Cohesion ranges from Enmeshed (where Cohesion is too high) to Disengaged (where Cohesion is too low). The cohesion sub-categories in the middle – Very

Table 2.4 Treatment Plan for Kylie's Family Based on Bowen Assessment

Bowen Assessment	Presence in Gonzalez Family	Proposed Intervention
Triangles	Mother and Luis against Father Mother and Ben against Father Grandmother and Margarita against Grandfather	Marital counseling & Parent consultation Encourage Margarita to disengage from her parents' conflict
Family Projection Process	Labeling of father as cold, rigid	Use of reframing to highlight Father's caring and flexible side
Differentiation of Self	Moderate differentiation scores for parents; Low differentiation scores for children	Communication training to promote use of "I" messages

Table 2.5 Description of the Circumplex Model

Dimension	Sub-category	Description
Flexibility	Rigid	Authoritarian parenting: children have no input
	Somewhat Flexible	Slightly democratic parenting: children have some input
	Flexible	Democratic parenting: children have moderate input
	Very Flexible	Very democratic parenting: children have a lot of input
	Chaotic	Absence of parental control: children have too much input
Cohesion	Enmeshed	Dependent, overinvolved relationships
	Very Connected	Very caring, close relationships
	Connected	Caring, close relationships
	Somewhat Connected	Somewhat caring, close relationships
	Disengaged	Lack of close relationships

Connected, Connected, and Somewhat Connected – represent more balanced, moderate, and healthy forms of Cohesion. Flexibility ranges from Rigid (where Flexibility is absent) to Chaotic (where there is too much Flexibility). The Flexibility sub-categories in the middle – Very Flexible, Flexible, and Somewhat Flexible – represent more balanced, moderate, and healthy forms of Flexibility. These two sets of five sub-categories form a matrix of 25 sub-categories as shown in Figure 2.4.

While the extreme sub-categories are more frequently associated with dysfunctional families, there are cultural exceptions. For example, in some cultures, a more enmeshed relationship that would be viewed as pathological in an Anglo cultural context could be normal in a culture that places a higher value on cohesion and a lower value on independence. It is important that the SBFC practitioner take cultural context into consideration when using the Circumplex Model.

The Circumplex Model is considered a family systems approach to assessment because it does not assess individual behavior. It assesses relationships *between* persons. The Circumplex Model can be used to assess an entire family or it can be used to assess dyads – two-person groups within a family. A Circumplex Model for Kylie's family is shown in Figure 2.5.

Although not all members of the extended family have been included in this figure, it can be seen that when dyads are diagrammed, very different clusters of relationships emerge within the family. There is a Chaotically Disengaged cluster involving Kylie and her parents. There is a Rigidly Disengaged cluster involving the marital dyad, and the father-Ben relationship. There is a Connected – Very Connected cluster for relationships between Kylie and Luis and between Kylie and her maternal grandmother. Connected to this cluster are a Flexibly Enmeshed relationship between mother and Luis and a Somewhat Flexibly Connected relationship between father and Luis. An

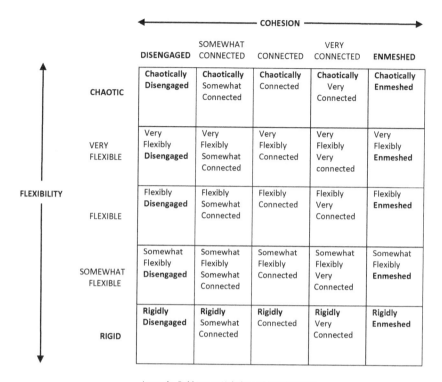

Legend: Bold type = Unbalanced Family Types
No bold type = Balanced Family Types
Bold and No bold together = Midrange Family Types

Figure 2.4 Circumplex Model

"X" marks the spot where a Circumplex diagnosis for the entire family would occur and mask the three very different clusters of relationships. It is sometimes the case that an entire family has relationships that clearly fit into one of the Circumplex Model's cells. However, because there are generally variations in relations within a family, it is recommended that you always do a dyadic analysis like that in Figure 2.5.

There are four basic ways to develop your Circumplex Model of a family: by observing actual interaction between family members, by using the Clinical Rating Scale (CRS) that identifies the different components of Cohesion and Flexibility in the family (see Resources below), by giving family members an inventory called the Family Adaptability and Cohesion Scale (FACES-IV) which has very good reliability and validity and is available for a fee (Olson, 2011), or by asking family members questions about their family cohesion and flexibility (see Box 2.8).

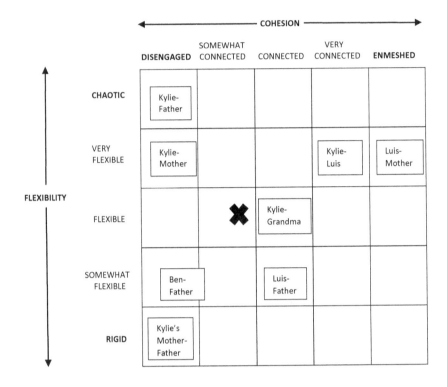

Figure 2.5 Circumplex Model for Kylie's Family

Box 2.8 Circumplex Model Assessment Questions

1. Cohesion Assessment Questions

Whole Family:

"How well do your family members get along with each other?"

"What percentage of the time would you say your family members get along with each other: 100% 75%, 50%, 25% ?"

"What sort of things does your family like to do as a family?"

"What does your family do to have fun together?"

"If someone in your family is upset, how much support do they get from the rest of the family?"

"What happens when someone doesn't want to join in a family activity?"

"Are there any family members who you think spend too much time together?"

Specific Relationships between Family Members:

"Which family members get along best with each other?"

"Which family members sometimes don't get along so well?"

"Who in your family do you feel closest to?"
    "What sort of things do the two of you do that are enjoyable?"

"Who in your family do you feel least close to?"

"How well do your parents (or guardians) get along with each other?"

"How close a relationship do you have with your father?"

"How close a relationship do you have with your mother?"

    (repeat for sister, brother, other family members)

2. Flexibility Assessment Questions

Whole Family:

"What sort of rules do family members have to follow?"

"Are these good rules or bad rules?" "Why are they good (or bad)?"

"Who makes these rules?"

"What happens when someone breaks a family rule?"

"Who makes the important decisions in your family?"

"Who has the most say about important decisions in your family?"
    "Who has the next most say?"
    "And after that person, who has the next most say?"

"Do the children in your family ever get to participate in family decisions?"

Specific Relationships between Family Members:

a) Student:

"How strict is your father with you?"
"How strict is your mother with you?"

b) Parents:

"How are decisions made in your family about things involving the
   children?"
"How are decisions made about big things like finances, budget,
   buying a car, where to live?"
"Are there any decisions that the children are allowed to make?"

The setting of treatment goals when using the Circumplex Model generally involves helping family members to move out of unbalanced relationships and engage in more balanced interactions. Persons in a Rigid
relationship are encouraged to be more Flexible. Persons in a Chaotic
relationship are encouraged to be more Flexible (that is more structured).
Family members in Enmeshed or Disengaged relationships are encouraged
to become more Connected. Figure 2.6 illustrates the Circumplex Model
goals Ramona might have for Kylie's family.

Table 2.6 lists sample family counseling techniques that might be used to
achieve these Circumplex goals.

The general strategy Olson recommends is to work at changing one
dimension – Cohesion or Flexibility – at a time. For example, in Kylie's
relationship with her mother, it is the Disengaged aspect of the relationship
that is having the most negative effect on Kylie. Because Margarita, Kylie's
mother, is so stressed by conflict with her husband, Margarita may be
unaware of how her lack of attention to Kylie is affecting Kylie. To help
increase cohesion in the relationship between Kylie and her mother,
Ramona could encourage Kylie to speak directly to her mother about her
wish to have a closer relationship and she could teach Margarita how to use
active listening with Kylie. These would represent basic steps to increase
cohesion between Margarita and Kylie. To help improve the relationship
between Kylie and her father Raoul, Ramona might initially work on the
Flexibility dimension, if she felt that changing Cohesion would be more
challenging for Oscar. That is, Ramona might encourage Raoul to relate to
Kylie in a more structured way, for example by checking her homework
each day. This slight increase in parental control from Raoul would likely be
viewed as appropriate parental interest by Kylie and an antidote to the lack
of contact that characterized the relationship previously. As a later step
Ramona might discuss with Raoul the importance of a father expressing his
caring towards his daughter in a more tangible way, for example by telling
her he is proud of how she is doing in school. In addition, Ramona might
encourage Kylie's maternal grandmother to develop a more connected
relationship with Kylie by having her to lunch on Saturdays. This would
decrease Kylie's sense of isolation while Ramona is working to strengthen

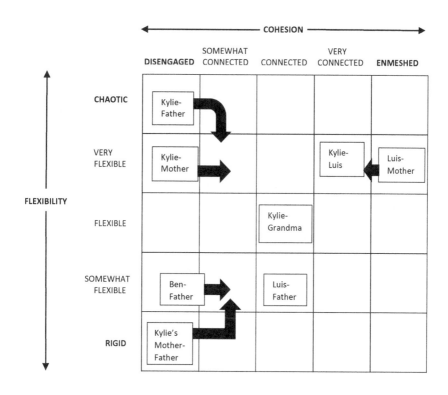

Figure 2.6 Circumplex Model Treatment Goals for Kylie's Family

Table 2.6 Treatment Plan to Achieve Circumplex Goals for Kylie's Family

Relationship	Circumplex Diagnosis	Circumplex Goal	Family Counseling Technique
Kylie-Mother	Very Flexibly-Disengaged	Very Flexibly-Somewhat Connected	Parent Consultation Parenting Skills Training
Kylie-Father	Chaotically Disengaged	Very Flexibly-Somewhat Connected	Parent Consultation Parenting Skills Training
Mother-Father	Rigidly-Disengaged	Somewhat Flexibly-Somewhat Connected	Marital Counseling
Mother-Luis	Very Flexibly-Enmeshed	Very Flexibly-Very Connected	Parent Consultation Parenting Skills Training

Kylie's relationship with her parents. The goal in all these interventions is to shift relationships in the family from unbalanced to balanced.

As Lusterman (1988) has shown, the Circumplex Model is a systems assessment approach that can be used to diagnose relationships in families and at school. It is well known in teacher education that many beginning teachers lack classroom management skills and have classrooms that are Chaotic (often so noisy with students out of their seats and ignoring the befuddled teacher that the principal has to intervene). And there are few students who have not at some stage in their education had the misfortune to attend a Rigidly-Disengaged classroom where the teacher is authoritarian, cold and punitive. Some of the relationships the Circumplex Model can be used to diagnose in a school are:

Groups:

The entire school
A specific classroom
A clique within a classroom

Dyads:

Principal – Teacher
Principal – Parent
Principal – Student
Teacher – Parent
Teacher – Student
Student – Student

A strength of the Circumplex Model is that it is a form of trans-system assessment. That is, it can be used to provide a similar type of assessment across different systems such as families and organizations, such as schools. This facilitates a comparison of a student's relationships within their social networks. Table 2.7 illustrates how the Circumplex Model does this for family and school.

A Circumplex Model diagram for Kylie's classroom is shown in Figure 2.7.

The central problem Kylie is experiencing at school is her Rigidly-Disengaged relationship with a girls' clique made up of other 14-year-old girls led by Roxie. Roxie herself has an unbalanced family characterized by a Chaotically-Disengaged relationship between Roxie and her parents. While the girls' clique has close relationships, Roxie is the dominant and authoritarian leader. Kylie's parents and Kylie's teacher have a Disengaged relationship. There is minimal contact between these parties. Once, the

Table 2.7 Examples of Circumplex Model Categories Comparing Family and School

Circumplex Category	Brief Example for Family and School
Cohesion: Enmeshed	*Family*: Parent may be overprotective of child Partner A is very dependent on Partner B Family member interrupts and speaks for another family member Family time is compulsory *School*: Teacher may be overprotective of student ("teacher's pet")
Very Connected	*Family*: Family members have a very warm, respectful relationship Family members prefer to spend their time together *School*: Teacher and student have a very warm, respectful relationship Teacher and parents may be on a first-name basis
Connected	*Family*: Family members have a warm, respectful relationship Family member A listens to and appreciates feelings of Family member B Family time is valued *School*: Teacher and student have a warm, respectful relationship Teacher and parent have a warm, respectful relationship
Somewhat Connected	*Family*: Family members are caring but engage in a lot of independent activity Family time is valued but occurs less often *School* Teacher is polite, but reserved with student and parent
Disengaged	*Family*: Family members lack emotional closeness with each other Family time is avoided Relationships characterized by coldness or hostility *School*: Teacher is coldly matter-of-fact or demonstrates lack of caring towards student and/or parent
Flexibility: Chaotic	*Family*: Parents/guardians are not in charge: no clear family hierarchy Conversations are a "free-for-all" Family rules are unclear; Family rules not enforced *School*: Teacher lacks classroom discipline skills Teacher has difficulty getting students to remain in seats or focus Teacher unable to implement lesson plan
Very Flexible	*Family*: Parents/guardians use a very egalitarian leadership style Children may have an "equal vote" on family matters

(*Continued*)

Circumplex Category	Brief Example for Family and School
Flexible	*School*: Teacher frequently modifies lesson plan to accommodate student interests *Family*: Parents/guardians use a moderate egalitarian leadership style Children included in decision-making often by consensus
Somewhat Flexible	*School*: Teacher is willing to occasionally modify lesson plan to accommodate student interests *Family*: Parents/guardians make the rules, but occasionally consider children's views *School*: Teacher is clearly in charge, but occasionally modifies lesson plan to accommodate student interests
Rigid	*Family*: Parents/guardians make the rules in an arbitrary fashion A family rule is almost never changed despite the circumstances Punishment swiftly follows the breaking of a family rule *School*: Teacher is inflexible about the rules or lesson plan Student failure to conform is swiftly punished

teacher sent Kylie's parents a note home requesting a meeting to discuss why Kylie seemed inattentive in the classroom. The parents didn't respond. A month later Kylie's mother Margarita called the school asking to speak with Kylie's teacher, but Margarita did not get a call back. This type of Disengaged relationship, where teacher and parents do not have an ongoing even Slightly Connected relationship, prevents adult problem-solving that can help a student like Kylie. As can be seen in Figure 2.7 Kylie has a balanced relationship with her teacher and with another student in her classroom, Maggie.

The Circumplex Model goals for Kylie's classroom situation are shown in Figure 2.8.

The most important intervention involves blocking the cyberbullying of Kylie by the girls' clique and getting these girls to relate to Kylie in a Somewhat Flexible/Somewhat Connected way. Ramona will also need to meet with Roxie and her parents to discuss Roxie's leadership role in bullying. It is possible that Roxie is being bullied herself at home. The Disengaged relationship between Kylie's parents and teacher needs to move in a more Connected direction so that these adults can collaborate to help Kylie. Increasing connectedness between Kylie and her teacher and Maggie will help reduce Kylie's sense of alienation at school. Some specific treatment strategies that could help attain these Circumplex Model goals are shown in Table 2.8.

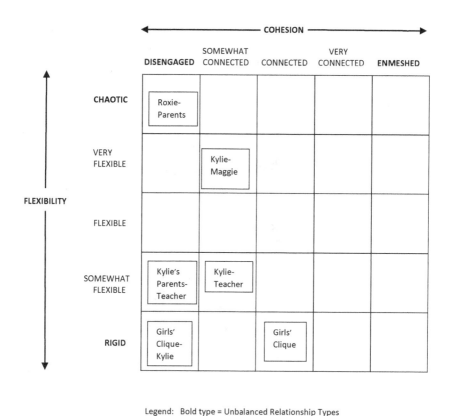

Figure 2.7 Circumplex Model for Kylie's Classroom

In the course of working with Kylie's teacher and spending time in Kylie's school, Ramona soon discovered that bullying and cyberbullying were occurring in many other classrooms at the school. Ramona's conclusion was that Rigidly Disengaged relationships were occurring between numerous students in the school. It should be noted that Kylie's school was a large one with over 1000 students. As is common in some large schools, student engagement can be low for students who experience the school as imperso-nal, especially if class sizes are large (Kylie's class has 35 students). When class sizes are large, teachers have difficulties maintaining connected rela-tionships with students. In addition, while many teachers in Kylie's school are aware there is some bullying going on, there has been little to no school intervention to stop the bullying. From a Circumplex Model point of view the school staff have a Chaotically Disengaged relationship with the bullies and their victims. That is, the school is not exercising leadership to prevent

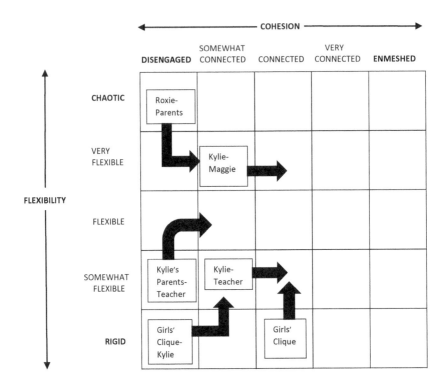

Figure 2.8 Circumplex Model Goals for Kylie's Classroom

the bullying. A Circumplex Model diagnosis and goals for this school-wide problem is shown in Figure 2.9.

This Circumplex Model does not diagram all the relationships in the school. What are diagrammed are the bullying encounters that Ramona has heard about – most of which occur in classrooms that are Disengaged. The school staff (principal, vice-principal, and teachers) have a Chaotically Disengaged relationship with the students doing the bullying (most often cyberbullyiing). The staff attitude seems to be: "It happens after school hours mostly so it's not our problem." The Circumplex Model goal here is to put in place and strictly enforce rules that block bullying and have consequences for bullies: to have a structured response – as opposed to no response. The school staff and the victims also have a Chaotically Disengaged relationship because nothing is being done to help the victims. The Circumplex Model goal here is to put in place a Flexible structure that provides Connected support for the victims. After

Table 2.8 Treatment Plan to Achieve Circumplex Goals for Kylie's Classroom

Relationship	Circumplex Diagnosis	Circumplex Goal	Counseling Technique
Kylie-Girls' Clique	Rigidly Disengaged	Somewhat Flexible-Somewhat Connected	Classroom Meeting to address bullying in the classroom Principal, teacher, SBFC practitioner meeting with the parents of the bullying girls
Kylie's Parents-Teacher	Somewhat Flexible-Disengaged	Flexibly Connected	SBFC practitioner hosts meeting with parents and teacher
Roxie-Parents	Rigidly Disengaged	Very Flexible-Somewhat Connected	Conjoint family counseling Parent consultation Parent support group
Kylie-Teacher	Somewhat Flexible-Somewhat Connected	Somewhat Flexible-Somewhat Connected	Teacher consultation to have teacher give more attention to Kylie
Kylie-Maggie	Very Flexible-Somewhat Connected	Very Flexible-Connected	Teacher moves Kylie to sit next to her friend; Margarita lets Kylie invite Maggie to visit Kylie on Saturdays

discussing the problem with the principal, Ramona receives approval to develop an evidence-based anti-bullying program for the school.

There is no Circumplex Model rating scale or inventory for use in schools. However, SBFC practitioners who become familiar with the Circumplex Model can easily apply it to a student's classroom by observing the classroom (with teacher permission). As the SBFC practitioner spends more time in the school, she/he should get a better sense of how students and teachers feel about the school.

If you wish to use an inventory to measure Cohesion in a school, there are several available that assess social climate, which refers to the overall atmosphere in the school that facilitates a sense of belongingness and connectedness in students. The four inventories referred to in Table 2.9 are all free and available on the internet.

All have good reliability and validity and most are available in student (elementary and secondary) versions, as well as teacher and parent versions. This represents an alternative, and a standardized, way of assessing a school's degree of cohesion. It is important for SBFC practitioners to be aware of this because of the research that shows a connection between low school cohesion, low school achievement, and bullying (Wang et al., 2014). If you decide to administer a school climate instrument in your school, it is important that you have principal, parent, and likely school district approval. It is important to understand that if the school turns out to have very low

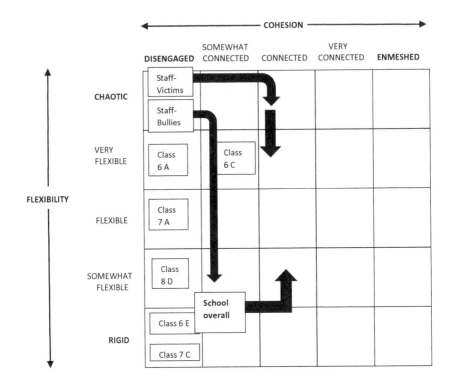

Figure 2.9 Circumplex Model for Kylie's School

Table 2.9 Comparison of Free School Social Climate Instruments

Instrument	No. of Items	Versions				Empirical Support
		Elementary	Secondary	Parent	Teacher	
1. Delaware School Climate Survey*	75	Yes	Yes	Yes	Yes	Yes
2. School Climate Assessment Instrument*	57	Yes	Yes	Yes	Yes	Yes
3. The Hemingway Measure of Adolescent Connectedness*	57	No	Yes	No	No	Yes
4. Georgia Brief School Climate Inventory	11	Yes	Yes	No	No	Yes

*Also available in Spanish

cohesion and this is tangibly demonstrated in the scores on the instrument you selected, the principal may feel this reflects badly on her or his administration (and indeed it may). The principal is to the school as a parent is to a family. When a family has low cohesion, it generally has to do with the parenting. You can increase the chances of being successful at formally assessing a school's social climate by your building a relationship of trust with the principal.

Step 2E: Assessment of Multicultural Variables

> But all our phrasing – race relations, racial chasm, racial justice, racial profiling, white privilege, even white supremacy – serves to obscure that racism is a visceral experience, that it dislodges brains, blocks airways, rips muscle, extracts organs, cracks bones, breaks teeth. You must never look away from this. You must always remember that the sociology, the history, the economics, the graphs, the charts, the regressions all land, with great violence, upon the body.
>
> (Coates, 2015)

> Individual clients are influenced by race, ethnicity, national origin, life stage, educational level, social class, and sex roles (Ibrahim, 1985). Counselors must view the identity and development of culturally diverse people in terms of multiple, interactive factors, rather than a strictly cultural framework (Romero, 1985). A pluralistic counselor considers all facets of the client's personal history, family history, and social and cultural orientation.
>
> (Arcinega & Newlou, 1981, p. 90)

MULTICULTURAL VARIABLES AFFECTING THE FAMILY: DISCRIMINATION ASSESSMENT

When working with students and families of color, it is important to remember that racism and discrimination may be commonplace occurrences for your clients. If your own background is one of white privilege, this may not be obvious to you. Your client (whether student or family) may experience discrimination in a direct personal form (e.g. a student of a different ethnicity shouting an insult at your client or the less obvious micro-aggression of a white teacher never calling on the student in class) or the discrimination may consist of institutional racism as in the family having difficulty getting a housing loan, or having to live in a poorer neighborhood where the school offers a lower quality of teaching.

> When white terrorists bomb a black church and kill five black children, that is an act of individual racism, widely deplored by most segments of the society. But when in that same city – Birmingham, Alabama – five hundred black babies die each year because of the lack of power, food,

shelter and medical facilities, and thousands more are destroyed and maimed physically, emotionally and intellectually because of conditions of poverty and discrimination in the black community, that is a function of institutional racism. When a black family moves into a home in a white neighborhood and is stoned, burned or routed out, they are victims of an overt act of individual racism which most people will condemn. But it is institutional racism that keeps black people locked in dilapidated slum tenements, subject to the daily prey of exploitative slumlords, merchants, loan sharks and discriminatory real estate agents. The society either pretends it does not know of this latter situation, or is in fact incapable of doing anything meaningful about it.

(Ture & Hamilton, 1967, p. 4)

In working with a student of color or her/his family it is important you assess the impact of discrimination on the student and the family by asking direct questions about it. In order to build trust for the discussion of this topic, a starting point – if you are of a different ethnicity than that of your clients – would be to ask: "How do you feel about working with me as a school staff member who is (mention your ethnicity)?" Follow-up questions could include: "Students of color often are treated differently by some teachers. Has this ever happened to you?" During her first session with the Gonzalez family Ramona discovered that Mr. Gonzalez (Raoul) was a taxi driver and that frequently white passengers would say derogatory things about Mexico. Raoul's supervisor was white and would often yell at Raoul, but speak politely to the white taxi drivers. This was a significant source of tension for Raoul. Mrs. Gonzalez (Margarita) experienced discrimination in a variety of ways. For example, she noticed that when she was in a waiting room at her bank to see about sending money to her parents in Mexico, customers who came to the waiting room after her were often served first by bank staff. At the grocery store, when she was at the meat counter to obtain sliced turkey, the white server behind the counter would frequently serve the white customers before Margarita, even though they arrived at the counter after Margarita. Box 2.9 contains additional questions for exploring cultural factors.

Box 2.9 Questions for Exploring Cultural Factors

1. Possible Cultural Issues with the SBFC Practitioner

"How do you feel about working with me as someone with a different ethnicity (or different cultural background)?"

2. Cultural Identity Questions

"How have the experiences you had in your native country influenced your life?"

"Please tell me about these experiences and how they affected you."

"What about your native country are you most proud of?"

"How have the experiences you have had in the host country influenced your life?"

"Please tell me about these experiences and how they affected you."

"What about your host country are you most proud of?"

"Do you think of yourself as a (member of the host country) or as a (member of your native country) or as both?" (Example: "Do you think of yourself as an American or as a Mexican or as a Mexican-American?")

"Do you think of your values as being more like those of the host country or more like those of your native country?"

"Please tell me about those values and why they are important to you."

2. Degree of Acculturation Questions

"How many friends do you have who speak (the dominant host-country language) (e.g. English)?"

"What language to you speak at home?"

"What language do you speak with your friends?"

"What language do you read in at home?"

"What language do you think in?"

3. Migration Experience

"What was it like migrating here? For some families migrating can be very challenging."

"What was the hardest thing for your family about leaving your native country?"

"When you (or your family) first came to this country, how did people treat you?"

4. Experience of Discrimination

"Persons who belong to a minority culture sometimes are treated poorly by some members of the dominant culture. Have you had any experiences like that?"

"Please tell me about them."

5. Client's Cultural Explanation for Problems

"Why do you think you are having these problems?"

"What do you think you need to do to overcome these problems?"

(Issue: does client think of the causes and solutions for interpersonal and emotional problems in terms of mental health, counseling, scientific reasoning, rationality, or in other cultural terms?)

MULTICULTURAL VARIABLES AFFECTING THE FAMILY: FAMILY VALUES ASSESSMENT

Based on a family's ethnicity and cultural background, families may differ significantly on values. For example, some families may value conforming to the social order, being spiritual, and having very close family relationships. Other families may value challenging the social order, being pleasure-seeking, and valuing independence. A family that values expressing anger will relate very differently in counseling from a family that values withholding anger.

If you are multiculturally competent you will be sensitive to cultural differences between families. You will also not automatically assume that because a family is of a particular ethnicity that family will necessarily hold values traditionally associated with that ethnic group. The multiculturally competent SBFC practitioner will withhold assumptions, but be sensitive to the cultural differences that families bring.

A useful way to look at families is in terms of their values which are culturally influenced. The super-grouping of values diagram based on Schwartz (1992) is shown in Figure 2.10.

Families and individuals can be viewed in terms of their positioning on two sets of opposing values: Conservation vs. Openness to Change; and

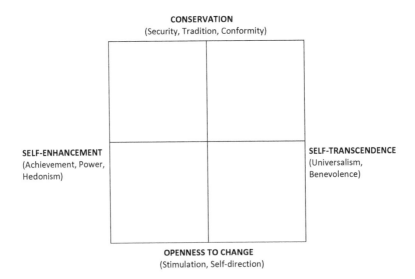

Figure 2.10 Super-Grouping of Cultural Values

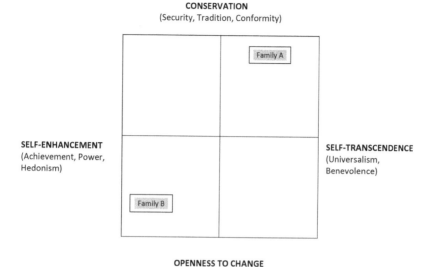

Figure 2.11 Comparison of Families on Super-Grouping of Cultural Values

Self-enhancement vs. Self-transcendence. Conservation refers to a cluster of values that include conformity to the social order, valuing tradition, and security. Openness to Change refers to valuing independence, risk-taking, and challenging the social order. Self-enhancement refers to valuing achievement, power, and competition. Self-transcendence refers to valuing spirituality, benevolence, and cooperation. Figure 2.11 shows how two families with different cultural backgrounds might be positioned on this values map.

Box 2.10 shows a Basic Family Values Scale that contains sixteen pairs of opposing values and was adapted from Collin (n.d.) and can be used to identify how a student may have the same – or different – values as her/his family.

Box 2.10 Basic Family Values Scale

Instructions: On the sheet below please read each pair of values and indicate which one is the most important to your family by placing an "F" on the line joining the values. If you strongly agree that one value is important to your family, you would place the "F" closest to that value. If you feel that neither value is more important, then you would check the line in the middle. After rating your family values, rate where you are on each value using an "S" for Self.

	Very Important	Moderately Important	Slightly Important	In-between	Slightly Important	Moderately Important	Very Important	
1. Punctuality								Being flexible with time
2. Controlling the environment								Not controlling the environment
3. Sticking with tradition								Developing new traditions
4. Task-centered								Relationship-centered
5. Thoughts								Feelings
6. Expressing anger								Withholding anger
7. Family								Friends
8. Following the "letter" of the law								Following the "spirit" of the law
9. Being assertive								Being kind
10. Sitting very close while talking								Not sitting too close while talking
11. Being Independent								Fitting in with the group
12. Being competitive								Being cooperative
13. Predictability								Flexibility
14. Justice								Mercy
15. Spirituality								Rationality
16. Supporting the Social order								Challenging the social order

Initially Ramona had assumed that Kylie's mother Margarita was pathologically enmeshed with her son Luis, with whom Margarita had a Very Flexible-Enmeshed relationship. After a conjoint family session in which Ramona had an opportunity to observe Margarita and Luis interacting, Ramona concluded that the mother-son relationship was culturally normal given the context that the family had recently immigrated to the USA from Mexico and lived in a neighborhood where there was gang activity.

The fourfold model of acculturation examines the extent to which an individual accepts or rejects one's native (minority) culture and one's host (dominant) culture. There are 4 types of acculturation: assimilation, separation, integration, and marginalization (Berry, 1997). Assimilation occurs when individuals completely adopt the cultural norms of the dominant culture. Separation occurs when individuals reject the dominant culture in order to preserve their culture of origin. Integration (sometimes referred to as bi-culturalism) refers to an individual valuing both the dominant culture and their native culture. Marginalization refers to a rejection of both the native and dominant cultures. In examining the values of Kylie and her parents, Ramona asked Kylie to complete the Basic Family Values Scale. Kylie's completed scale (Box 2.11) shows both her value ratings for herself and for her family.

Box 2.11 Basic Family Values Scale for Kylie

Instructions: On the sheet below please read each pair of values and indicate which one is the most important to your family by placing an "F" on the line joining the values. If you strongly agree that one value is important to your family, you would place the "F" closest to that value. If you feel that neither value is more important, then you would check the line in the middle. After rating your family values, rate where you are on each value using an "S" for Self.

	Very Important	Moderately Important	Slightly Important	In-between	Slightly Important	Moderately Important	Very Important	
1. Punctuality		Kylie		Family				Being flexible with time
2. Controlling the environment		Kylie				Family		Not controlling the environment
3. Sticking with tradition	Family			Kylie				Developing new traditions
4. Task-centered		Kylie			Family			Relationship-centered
5. Thoughts			Kylie		Family			Feelings
6. Expressing anger					Kylie Family			Withholding anger
7. Family	Family		Kylie					Friends
8. Following the "letter" of the law	Family		Kylie					Following the "spirit" of the law
9. Being assertive					Kylie	Family		Being kind
10. Sitting very close while talking	Family	Kylie						Not sitting too close while talking
11. Being Independent		Kylie				Family		Fitting in with the group
12. Being competitive			Kylie		Family			Being cooperative
13. Predictability	Family	Kylie						Flexibility
14. Justice				Family Kylie				Mercy
15. Spirituality	Family			Kylie				Rationality
16. Supporting the Social order	Family		Kylie					Challenging the social order

---

Table 2.10 summarizes the value similarities and differences for Kylie and her family. The ratings suggest that while Kylie's parents are at an

Table 2.10 Summary of Basic Values for Kylie and her Family

	Value Direction for Family	*Value Direction for Kylie*
Values not Shared	Being flexible with time	Punctuality
	Not controlling the environment	Controlling the environment
	Sticking with tradition	Developing new traditions
	Relationship-centered	Task-centered
	Feelings	Thoughts
	Family	Friends
	Following the "letter" of the law	Following the "spirit" of the law
	Fitting in with the group	Being independent
	Being cooperative	Being competitive
	Spirituality	Rationality
	Supporting the social order	Challenging the social order
Shared Values	Withholding anger	
	Being kind	
	Sitting very close while talking	
	Predictability	
	Mercy	

Integration stage of acculturation, Kylie is moving towards an Assimilation stage. Degree of acculturation can be assessed by asking:

"What language do you speak at home?"
"What language do you read in at home?"
"What language to you speak with your friends?"
"What language do you think in?"

The more the client uses the dominant language, the more acculturated they are considered to be.

MULTICULTURAL VARIABLES AFFECTING THE SCHOOL: DISCRIMINATION ANALYSIS

When discrimination occurs in a school, it is usually student-student or teacher-student. The discrimination may be based on ethnicity or other differences such as gender orientation. In the case of Kylie, the girls' clique cyberbullying her had seen Kylie holding hands with her friend Maggie. Their internet tweets referred to Kylie as a "lesbo." After speaking to other students at the school Ramona discovered a pattern of bullying at the school that targeted LGBTQ students in particular. To remedy this problem across the school, Ramona secured the principal's support for staff training on how to support LGBTQ students, arranged for guidance classes on gender identity for all the grades, and implemented an anti-bullying program called the P.E.A.C.E. Pack in the school.

Step 2F: Assessment of Other Socio-Demographic Variables

These other socio-demographic variables include: age, religion, sexual orientation, gender orientation, social class, and educational level. During Ramona's first interview with Kylie's parents, Raoul and Margarita, she learned that Raoul was driving a taxi for a living. She assumed, based on his occupation, that this was a lower-class family and likely one that was unused to thinking about psychological issues. But she was wrong. During the second interview with Raoul and Margarita, Ramona learned that Raoul had been a physician in Mexico. The only reason he was driving a taxi was because that was the only job he could get while preparing to take the physician licensing exam in his new country. It became clear to Ramona that Raoul was as educated, and likely more educated, than she was. Furthermore, she discovered that Margarita had a master's degree in political science from the Universidad México Internacional. Both parents were very religious and were concerned about how Kylie seemed to be drifting away from the church. They attributed this to Kylie's friend Maggie whose family was not religious. Ramona found this additional socio-demographic information very important in shaping the way Ramona would approach Margarita and Raoul about Kylie's wish for more independence.

Step 2G: Assessment of Family Strengths

It is important to assess family strengths for three reasons. First, it de-pathologizes the family's experience of participating in mental health services. Many families are worried about being labelled as "crazy" or otherwise deficient. By asking a family about their strengths, the members leave the interview feeling a sense of pride in their family and also a feeling of being respected and admired by the SBFC practitioner. Second, it provides the SBFC practitioner with valuable information for reframing negative family identities ("Mr. Gonzalez, you say that you feel a failure as a parent yet you have a daughter who gets As in Art and shares your appreciation of photography and painting."). Third, mental health approaches have a long history of being deficit-focused (e.g. DSM labels generally, Bowen's multigenerational transmission of neurosis, CBT's irrational beliefs, etc.). A focus on family strengths is congruent with asset-based approaches to mental health such as Narrative Therapy and Solution-Focused Therapy. This emphasis on a strength-based orientation gives hope not only to the family, but to the SBFC practitioner as well. Box 2.12 provides a checklist of positive family characteristics based on the work of Peterson (2006) and adapted from a list developed by Wright (2012). This checklist could be given to a family as an in-session assignment (e.g. where the family is asked to have each member fill out the checklist during a 20-minute period which is followed by a sharing with the SBFC practitioner). Alternatively, it could be given as a homework assignment for the family to bring back at the next session.

Box 2.12 List of Positive Family Characteristics

Instructions: Place an "X" next to any of the positive characteristics that you think your family has. In a few words identify one example of each characteristic you selected.

<u>Family Example</u>

Strengths of Wisdom and Knowledge
___ Creativity _____
___ Curiosity _____
___ Open-mindedness _____
___ Love of learning _____
___ Perspective [wisdom] _____

Strengths of Courage
___ Bravery _____
___ Persistence _____
___ Integrity [authenticity, honesty] _____
___ Vitality [zest, enthusiasm] _____

Strengths of Humanity
___ Love _____
___ Kindness _____
___ Social intelligence _____
    (understanding relationships)

Strengths of Justice
___ Citizenship [social responsibility, teamwork]_____
___ Fairness _____
___ Leadership _____

Strengths of Temperance
___ Forgiveness and mercy _____
___ Humility/Modesty _____
___ Prudence (being careful) _____
___ Self-regulation [self-control] _____

Strengths of Transcendence
___ Appreciation of beauty and excellence _____
___ Gratitude _____
___ Hope _____
___ Humor _____
___ Spirituality _____

Step 3: Development of a Comprehensive Treatment Plan Based on the SBFC Metamodel

A treatment plan based on the SBFC Metamodel addresses presenting problems affecting the client (e.g. being bullied and cutting) as well as systemic problems affecting the client and other students and families (e.g. a lack of cohesion in the school or families lacking knowledge in how to help a child who is being bullied). A comprehensive SBFC treatment plan will consider the need to possibly intervene in all four of the SBFC Metamodel quadrants: School Intervention, School Prevention, Family Intervention, and Family Prevention. To illustrate this *some* elements of Ramona's SBFC treatment plan for Kylie are summarized in Table 2.11.

What makes this a comprehensive SBFC treatment plan is that it systematically addresses all the core systems that Kylie is part of and addresses the challenges she experiences in each. The assessment strategies illustrated here – Multimodal Assessment, Genogram, Circumplex Model, Questions for Cultural Assessment, Basic Values assessment, and List of Family Strengths – are only one way of creating a comprehensive SBFC case conceptualization. Alternative assessment models can be used. For example, the McMaster model, the Beavers System model, or a classic Bowen Systems model could be used instead of the Circumplex Model to assess the family. What is important is that whatever assessment models you use (until research clearly establishes that a particular model has better client outcomes), you should be systematic, and your assessment should cover individual, family, school, cultural, socio-demographic, and family strengths aspects, and your SBFC treatment plan should consider intervention and prevention at both school and family levels. As a further aid to selecting SBFC strategies, SBFC Decision Trees are shown as Box 2.13. These can be used to quickly identify the specific quadrants of the SBFC Metamodel relevant for intervention.

Steps 4, 5 and 6 (Using an Intervention with the Client; Monitoring the Client's Response to the Intervention; and Modifying the Case Conceptualization, Treatment Plan, and Intervention Depending on Additional Information) basically involve monitoring the client's response to your interventions and making "course corrections" as necessary. This is important because as the SBFC practitioner interacts more with the client and the client's social systems, new information typically comes to light, and this often requires making modifications to the case conceptualization (see Figure 2.1).

Table 2.11 A Comprehensive SBFC Treatment Plan for Kylie

SBFC Metamodel Quadrant	Diagnosis / Problem	Goal	Proposed Intervention
School Intervention	Rigidly Disengaged relationship between Kylie and girls' clique (bullying)	Eliminate bullying	Meet with clique's parents and principal, Classroom meeting to change Classroom norms re bullying, Individual counseling for Roxie, the clique's leader
	Kylie non-assertive and feeling depressed (cutting self)	Strengthen Kylie's coping skills	CBT (cognitive restructuring, desensitization, assertion training, relaxation training)
	Kylie Disengaged from school	Increase Cohesion between Kylie and teacher, other students	Consultation with teacher to encourage teacher to: spend more time with Kylie and facilitate Kylie working on in-class assignments with other sympathetic students; seat Kylie next to Maggie
School Prevention	Disengaged social climate in the school	Increase school Cohesion	Implementation of the P.E.A.C.E. Pack anti-bullying program which builds general school support
	Teachers and students lacking LGBTQ knowledge and sensitivity	Increase LBGTQ knowledge and sensitivity	Guidance modules in senior grades on LGBTQ needs and issues
Family Intervention	Kylie Disengaged from parents	Increase Cohesion in family	Parent consultation to promote better collaboration between the parents, Parenting skills training, Marital counseling, Family meetings.
	Raoul dealing with discrimination at work	Develop assertion skills	Supportive counseling, Assertion training
	Roxie and her parents in Chaotically Disengaged relationship	Increase Cohesion and Flexibility	Conjoint family counseling with Roxie's family
Family Prevention	Many school parents unsure how to help their children deal with cyberbullyiing	Increase parents' knowledge on how to deal with cyberbullying	Lecture to Parent-Teacher Association (PTA) on cyberbullying; follow-up workshop for parents

Box 2.13 Decision Trees for SBFC Model

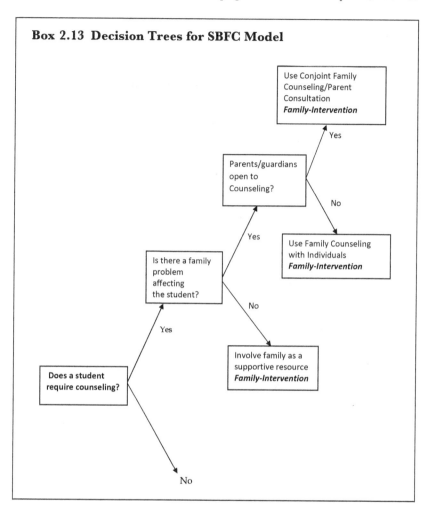

Box 2.13

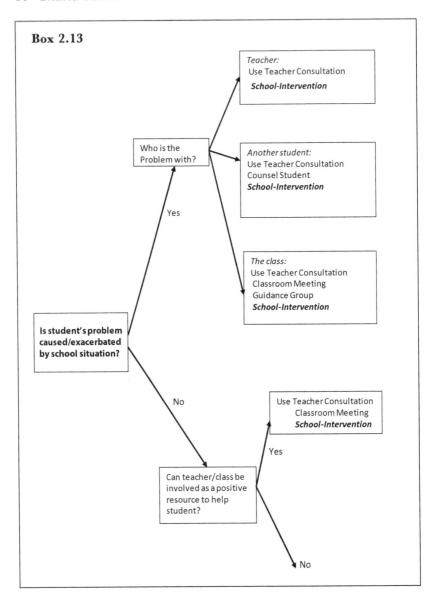

Box 2.13

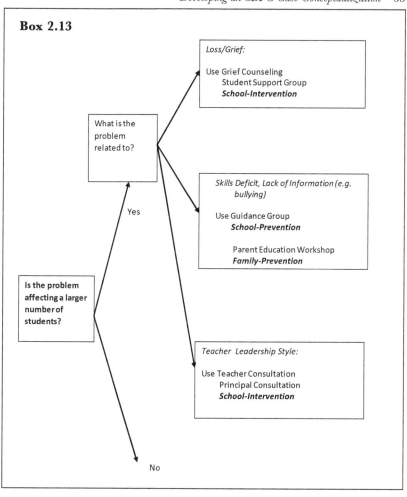

Box 2.13

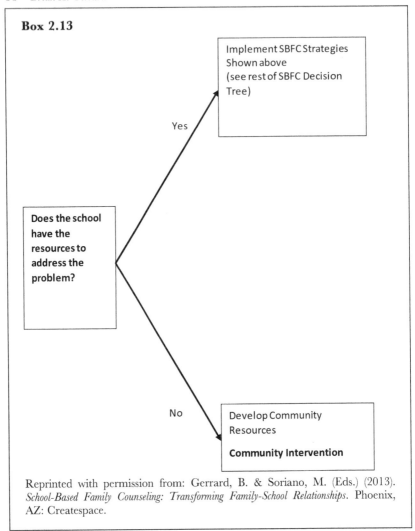

Reprinted with permission from: Gerrard, B. & Soriano, M. (Eds.) (2013). *School-Based Family Counseling: Transforming Family-School Relationships.* Phoenix, AZ: Createspace.

Resources

To order FACES IV contact:

www.facesiv.com/

To view the Clinical Rating Scale for the Circumplex Model:

Olson, D.H. (1999). Empirical approaches to family assessment. *Journal of Family Therapy, Special Edition.*

See SBFC EResources for link.

Bibliography

Arcinega, M. & B. J. Newlou (1981). A theoretical rationale for cross-cultural family counseling. *The School Counselor*, 28, 89–96.

Berry, J. (1997). Immigration, acculturation, and adaptation. *Applied Psychology*, 46 (1), 10. 10.1111/j.1464-0597.

Bolton-Brownlee, A. (1987). Issues in multicultural counseling. Highlights: An ERIC/ CAPS digest. ERIC Identifier: ED279995, ERIC Clearinghouse on Counseling and Personnel Services Ann Arbor MI.

Bowen, M. (1978). *Family Therapy in Clinical Practice*. New York, NY: Aronson.

Coates, T. (2015). Retrieved November 7, 2018 from www.goodreads.com/quotes/ 7184083-but-all-our-phrasing-race-relations-racial-chasm-racial-justice-racial

Ibrahim, F. (1985). Effective cross-cultural counseling and psychotherapy. *The Counseling Psychologist*, 13, 625–638.

Lazarus, A. (2006). *Brief But Comprehensive Psychotherapy: The Multimodal Way*. New York, NY: Guilford Press.

Lusterman, D. (1988). School-family intervention and the circumplex model. *Journal of Psychotherapy and the Family*, 4 (12), 267–283.

McGoldrick, M., Gerson, R., & Shellenberger, S. (1999). *Genograms: Assessment and Intervention*. New York, NY: Norton. RESOURCE.

Olson, D. H. (1999). Empirical approaches to family assessment. *Journal of Family Therapy, Special Edition*, RESOURCES Appendix 1 and Appendix 2 http://citeseerx. ist.psu.edu/viewdoc/download?doi=10.1.1.554.7050&rep=rep1&type=pdf.

Olson, D. H. (2011). FACES IV and the circumplex model: Validation study. *Journal of Marital and Family Therapy*, 3 (1), 64–80.

Olson, D. H., Russell, C. S., & Sprenkle, D. H. (Eds.). (1989). *Circumplex Model: Systemic Assessment and Treatment of Families*. Binghampton, NY: Haworth Press.

Peterson, C. (2006). *A Primer on Positive Psychology*. Oxford, UK: Oxford University Press.

Prochasa, J., DiClemente, C., & Norcross, J. (1992). In search of how people change: Applications to addictive behaviors. *American Psychologist*, 47, 1102–1114.

Romero, D. (1985). Cross-cultural counseling: Brief reactions for the practitioner. *The Counseling Psychologist*, 13, 665–671.

Schwartz, B. & Flowers, J. (2010). *How to Fail as a Therapist: 50+ Ways to Lose or Damage Your Patients*. Santa Clarita, CA: Impact Publishing.

Schwartz, S. H. (1992). Universals in the content and structure of values: Theoretical advances and empirical tests in 20 countries. *Advances in Experimental Social Psychology*. San Diego, CA: Academic Press.

Ture, K. & Hamilton, C. (1967). *Black Power: The Politics of Liberation*. New York, NY: Random House.

Wang, W., Vaillancourt, T., Brittain, H. L., McDougall, P., Krygsman, A., Smith, D., & Hymel, S. (2014). School climate, peer victimization, and academic achievement: Results from a multi-informant study. *School Psychology Quarterly*, 29 (3), 360–377.

White, M. & Epston, D. (1990). *Narrative Means to Therapeutic Ends*. New York, NY: Norton. RESOURCE.

Wright, S. (2012, May 5). List of personal strengths. Retrieved November 7, 2017 from http://meaningandhappiness.com/psychology-research/list-of-personal-strengths.html

3 Family Intervention

How to Build Collaboration between the Family and School Using Conjoint Family Counseling

Emily J. Hernandez, Deborah Ribera and Michael J. Carter

Overview: *This chapter describes a seven-step procedure that can be used by School-Based Family Counseling (SBFC) practitioners who are interested in integrating conjoint family counseling processes within a school context. Understanding the importance of conjoint family counseling and being able to incorporate it into one's counseling practice is an essential part of being an SBFC practitioner. Though the reader will need experience in family therapy before implementing the process described in this chapter, the procedure described will assist trained mental health practitioners with the challenging task of applying conjoint family counseling to a school setting.*

Background

The skills of conjoint family counseling are a critical component of School-Based Family Counseling (SBFC). SBFC is a specific conceptualization of how conjoint family counseling processes can be applied directly to dealing with student problems in a school environment. SBFC can be implemented by mental health professionals in a school setting; professionals such as school counselors, school social workers, and school psychologists, so long as those professionals are trained in its core processes. These professionals should have education and training in addressing the complex problems that can arise in a family system (Carter & Evans, 2008). School personnel may be in the best position to implement SBFC because the focus in a school setting is on improving student functioning for success as opposed to addressing mental health issues. In our experience, most parents are more willing to attend counseling sessions or parent education meetings at a school versus attending family therapy at a community mental health clinic. This is likely because parental support of student achievement is highly regarded and rewarded in society and school, whereas mental illness still carries a stigma that affects whether or not one chooses to attend therapy (Glied & Cuellar, 2003).

Conjoint family therapy applied in SBFC can also be useful for schools because of its collaborative and open processes. For example, the SBFC practitioner can be a key asset in helping schools handle sensitive family issues like child abuse reporting. The SBFC practitioner can avoid the frequent alienation caused by reporting parents for child abuse by staying focused on the goal of improved family functioning and by being transparent throughout the process. The SBFC practitioner is trained to treat the whole family while also ensuring the safety of the children. This ensures that the needs of the parents, siblings, and other relatives can be met as well.

Karpel & Strauss's (1983) multidimensional model of family evaluation is recommended for anyone interested in conjoint family therapy and will be referred to throughout this chapter. Their description of family evaluation and the assessment of the Factual, Individual, Systemic, and Ethical dimensions enables SBFC practitioners to obtain information that creates a more comprehensive view of family functioning while determining the most important issues for the whole family. These issues then become the focus of developing more effective treatment plans with prioritization of specific goals and delineation of the concrete, and specific steps necessary to accomplish them.

Family counseling is very different from individual or group counseling because it typically involves dealing with a high degree of interpersonal conflict and requires a more active and directive approach. At its core, effective family counseling often requires mental health practitioners to help a family to address the unresolved conflicts that create so much anxiety for family members, especially children. Skill in family therapy requires knowledge of individual cognitive and emotional development and understanding of what these look like in natural settings from infant to grandparent. It also requires familiarity with the stages of the family life cycle, and normal and abnormal responses to stage transitions for a family from the birth of a child to the aging and death of parents. Family therapy involves the willingness to bring out conflict and the skills to resolve it in ways that help members develop greater awareness and compassion for each other. These skills enable a mental health practitioner to feel prepared to handle a lot of what happens in assisting parents to help their children develop, especially in the emotional and behavior areas.

Evidence-based support

The articles shown in Box 3.1 demonstrate the effectiveness of the technique of family therapy.

Box 3.1 Evidence-Based Support for Family Therapy

Asen, E. (2002). Outcome research in family therapy. *Advances in Psychiatric Treatment, 8*, 230–238.

Carr, A. (2009). The effectiveness of family therapy and systemic interventions for child-focused problems. *Journal of Family Therapy, 31*, 3–45.

Cookerly, J. R. (1973). The outcome of the six major forms of marriage counseling compared: a pilot study. *Journal of Marriage and Family, 35*, 4, 608–611.

Cottrell, D. & Boston, P. (2002). Practitioner review: the effectiveness of systemic family therapy for children and adolescents. *Journal of Child Psychology and Psychiatry, 43*, 5, 573–586.

DeWitt, K. N. (1978). The effectiveness of family therapy: a review of outcome research. *Archives of General Psychiatry, 35*, 5, 549–561.

Diamond, G. & Josephson, A. (2005). Family-Based Treatment Research: a 10-year update. *Journal of the American Academy of Child and Adolescent Psychiatry, 44*, 9, 872–887.

Rowe, C. L. (2010). Multidimensional Family Therapy: addressing co-occurring substance abuse and other problems among adolescents with comprehensive family-based treatment. *Child and Adolescent Psychiatric Clinics of North America, 19*, 3, 563–576.

Stratton, P. (2005). *The Evidence Base of Systemic Family Therapy* (pp. 1–12). Warrington, UK: Association for Family Therapy.

Williams, R. & Chang, S. (2000). A comprehensive and comparative review of adolescent substance abuse treatment outcome. *Clinical Psychology: Science and Practice, 7*, 138–166.

Procedure

Definition

The following seven-step procedure can be used by SBFC practitioners who are interested in integrating conjoint family therapy processes within a school context. The procedure involves working with the family to develop a behavior management process consistent with the school around the three rules of kindergarten so that parents can teach and manage the skills necessary for the three outcomes of young adulthood and to increase the primary protective factors against the three high-risk factors of adolescence. The procedure assists families to co-construct rules and consequences between parents and children, with the mental health practitioner facilitating in the process. The procedure consists of seven steps, with six of the steps being in direct contact with the family. The first step, while not in direct contact with the family, is included because the initial referral and information-gathering process is crucial to establishing the foundation for the work with the family. The seven-step SBFC procedure is outlined in Box 3.2.

Box 3.2 Seven-Step SBFC Procedure for Integrating Conjoint Family Counseling Processes in a School Setting

Step   Description
1   Initial Referral/Information gathering
2   Phone Call: How to get the family in

---

3   The First Family Meeting: Learning more about strengths and challenges
4   The Second Family Meeting: Psycho-education
5   The Third Family Meeting: Co-Constructing rules, expectations, and consequences
6   The Fourth Family Meeting: Family fun
7   Termination: Generalization and transfer

Procedural steps

Step 1: Initial referral/information gathering

The first step in the process begins with the need for an initial referral. The initial referral usually comes from the school or community agency by a service provider, educator, or administrator. Referrals are normally initiated by the referring party after a multitude of initial interventions have already been completed in and out of the classroom. These interventions may include individual meetings with the student, classroom observations, conferences with the counselor and teacher, parent conferences, multi-disciplinary meetings at the school with the student and family, and/or other school-related interventions as needed. Within these initial interventions, either additional information is obtained that warrants more intensive services to be provided for the student and family, or the student and/or family makes a request for additional services. The initial referral for services includes basic information about the student, family, and the presenting problem. Once the initial referral is received, additional information is gathered by the SBFC professional.

Information gathering is an important part of the process in step one. Having a good understanding of the presenting problem is crucial to the next steps. Box 3.3 provides additional information that is helpful to fully understand the presenting problem.

Box 3.3 Additional Information that is Helpful to Fully Understand the Presenting Problem

1a. Obtain a thorough understanding of the presenting problem. The presenting problem should be clear, and provide an operationalized description of what it is, and its duration, frequency, and intensity.

1b. Complete a review of student information available (school history [cumulative file], grade retentions, discipline/behavioral history, attendance history, individualized academic plans [IEP] or assessments, retention history, any changes in grades, attendance, and/or behavior).

1c. Complete a review of academic progress (grade history, current and past grades) and take note of any changes (increases or decreases).

1d. Complete a review of previous and current interventions/services and outcomes.

1e. Make a brief observation of the student (in and out of the classroom). For elementary age students, observing the student in the classroom and during outside play is helpful (recess, lunch, physical education class, after-school program, etc.). For secondary students, observing the student in multiple class periods to get a better understanding of any fluctuations in behavior, and during out-of-class time (transitions, recess, lunch, physical education, etc.).

1f. Develop different perspectives of the presenting problem. Understanding the teacher's view of the presenting problem, the school counselor's view, and student's view. This may require the SBFC practitioner to schedule a time to meet with the student's teacher(s) and school counselor, to discuss the student in more depth.

1g. Hold an individual meeting with student. In order to get an understanding of the student view of the presenting problem, an individual meeting with the student is needed. The primary focus of this meeting is to introduce self to the student, develop rapport, establish a positive connection with the student, and gain an understanding of the student's perspective and level of awareness and insight of the presenting problem. A family perspective of the presenting problem is crucial, but this information is gathered later in step three.

The important aspect of this information-gathering process is to get a comprehensive view of the student's academic history and a better understanding of the presenting problem. Reviewing previous academic records (as far back as available, preferably kindergarten) allows a holistic view of the student and may shed light on the current presenting problem and provide a guide to be able to pinpoint when difficulties may have started. Frequently, problems in school reflect problems either at home, or in another important part of the student's life. Having an understanding of the academic history will help the SBFC professional have a more in-depth understanding of the root of the presenting problem, and provide for a more accurate plan and intervention for working with the student and family. Additional information is available about this process with the SBFC Interview Procedure and format provided (see Appendix A).

Step 2: Phone call – how to get the family in

The collaborative process between families and schools begins with the first telephone contact with the student's parent(s) or guardian(s). As with most collaborative strategies, the establishment of rapport is the first, most critical process. This begins by clearly communicating to the parent(s) the need for the family to be involved in order to assist the student, who may be the primary reason why the family is seeking help. It is important to remember that many parents do not truly understand what mental health intervention is about and may feel very defensive about a request for their child or themselves to be involved in therapy. They may have learned from their own culture or family that therapy is only for "crazy people" or that personal information should never be shared outside the family. In these cases, it is critical for the SBFC practitioner to explain to the parents that this type of intervention is part of the educational process that helps children learn.

For example:

> "Hi Mrs. _____, I am _____, the _____ (school counselor, school social worker, etc.) at _____ school. I am calling because _____. One of the most important parts of a child's learning process is the ability to pay close attention to verbal or written instructions. Whenever a person is feeling strong emotions such as anxiety or frustration, it is difficult to maintain attention on academic information. This often results in classroom behavior problems, such as: inattention to the teacher, not following directions, "daydreaming," or fidgeting. Counseling with the child and the family can help to address these emotions so that they do not interfere with the child's availability for learning and developing social relationships."

In many cases involving referral for school-related problems, parents may feel that only the child needs to be involved in counseling. Helping parents to understand why their involvement is required is an important first step in establishing rapport. Some parents may ask: "If my child is having the problem why do I need to be involved?" Great care should be taken in answering this question because parents may become defensive if it is implied that they need to be involved because they are the *source* of the problem. This is a natural phenomenon that has been labeled the "source-solution attribution" (Compas, Adelman, Freundl, Nelson, & Taylor, 1982). In a few words, a "source-solution attribution" occurs when parents assume that if the *solution* to a problem is their involvement, then the *source* of the problem must be themselves. It is important to interrupt this attribution by explaining to the parents that:

> "While there may be many things that cause children difficulty, parents have a unique relationship with a child that puts them in the best position to be a part of helping to address the child's problems."

Most parents readily accept these explanations, which may increase their willingness to be directly involved in conjoint family counseling. If not, it is important for the SBFC practitioner to continue to push for full involvement by the family. As Carl Whitaker would say, this "battle for structure" must the won by the therapist (Whitaker & Keith, 1981). This is a critical aspect of effective conjoint family counseling. Once a commitment has been gained for the parents to attend counseling, along with any other family members who may be helpful, the first session is then scheduled.

Step 3: The first family meeting – learning more about strengths and challenges

The first session with the family is the most important because it sets the stage for all the sessions that follow. The most important thing to accomplish in this session is to *make a strong connection with the parents and family* so that they will return for subsequent sessions. This rapport is more important than anything that is discussed and should always be the *utmost priority*. Some of the following suggestions will help to establish this connection, but mindfulness about what is happening during the session and sensitivity to how each person feels (especially those who have power in the family) will be most important.

3A THINGS TO REMEMBER ABOUT THE COUNSELOR'S ROLE IN FAMILY COUNSELING PROCESSES

As a counselor, you are *always* modeling effective communication for the family in: how you **LISTEN;** how you **ADDRESS** each person **NON-VERBALLY**; and in how you **SPEAK** to each person, especially children who need accommodations to their developmental level in order to understand what is being said. Adults often fail to remember that children do not process information in the same way that adults do.

3B INTRODUCTIONS

After introducing yourself, ask each person in the family: what their name is, where they work or go to school, and what they like to do for fun. (Remember, you're establishing connections with **e**ach person – be warm and speak with each member in a manner appropriate to their developmental level). Also find out the names of any immediate family members not present. Thank them for coming.

3C DISCUSSION OF WHAT FAMILY COUNSELING IS ABOUT AND HOW IT MIGHT HELP THE CHILD TO EARN MORE MONEY AND EXPERIENCE LESS ANXIETY (I.E., DUE TO UNEMPLOYMENT) WHEN THEY BECOME ADULTS

For many parents, there may be a lack of understanding of what family counseling is and how it can be helpful to their child. In many cultures, there is more concern for economic survival than there is an appreciation of issues related to mental health, although most place great value on happiness and less anxiety. Accordingly, it is often good to frame counseling as a means of helping children to become more financially successful and less anxious as they grow up. In order to facilitate this, it is often useful to show parents the connection between the level of education that a person attains and the corresponding earning potential and level of unemployment expected across their lifespan. The family is presented with a chart produced by the US Department of the Interior that indicates the weekly salary and percentage of unemployment associated with an individual's educational achievement (see Figure 3.1). Once this chart is presented to the parents and student, we often keep the chart in full view for continued reference throughout the session.

An example of how this might be presented to the family is:

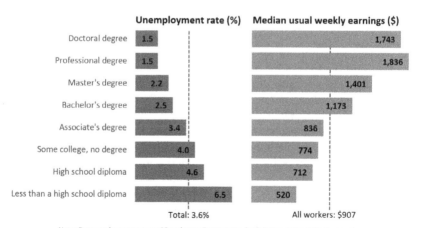

Unemployment rates and earnings by educational attainment, 2017

	Unemployment rate (%)	Median usual weekly earnings ($)
Doctoral degree	1.5	1,743
Professional degree	1.5	1,836
Master's degree	2.2	1,401
Bachelor's degree	2.5	1,173
Associate's degree	3.4	836
Some college, no degree	4.0	774
High school diploma	4.6	712
Less than a high school diploma	6.5	520
	Total: 3.6%	All workers: $907

Note: Data are for persons age 25 and over. Earnings are for full-time wage and salary workers.
Source: U.S. Bureau of Labor Statistics, Current Population Survey.

Figure 3.1 USA Unemployment Rates and Earnings by Educational Attainment, 2016

"Before we begin, I'd like to talk a little bit about what family counseling is about and how it can help your child. Most parents have two general hopes for their children when they grow older and become adults: one is to make enough money to live comfortably and the other is to avoid excessive worry. This chart indicates the connection between a person's level of education and their average amount of income earned and percentage of unemployment across their lifespan. As you can see, if a person completes just two years of college, they almost double their average earnings and reduce their chances of unemployment by half compared with someone who does not finish high school. Some of the biggest obstacles to educational achievement are distractions caused by emotional and social factors that reduce a child's availability for learning. Family counseling can help your children to improve their emotional and social functioning so that they can focus better on learning. This counseling can also help you and your child to communicate better and improve your relationships, which is a protective factor in helping your child to avoid the high-risk behaviors of adolescence, which are: drug and alcohol abuse, issues related to romantic relationships, and the negative influence of peers."

3D DISCUSSION OF FAMILY COUNSELING AND THE FOCUS ON COMMUNICATION AND LEARNING ABOUT OUR STRENGTHS AND CHALLENGES

This is a continued discussion on the introduction to family counseling and the focus on communication within the family, and learning more about strengths and challenges.

An example of how this might be presented to the family is:

"As we begin, I wanted to tell you a little bit about what I hope this experience will be like. First, I know that every family has strengths and challenges. I want to learn more about the strengths in your family and how you can use these to work on the challenges that are facing your family right now and in the future. So, I see this as a learning process that improves communication between family members so that you all know where you stand with each other and how best to help each other. I also want to focus on how your family can help each person to be as successful as possible in school, work, and with friends. We'll also work to develop a partnership with the teachers and school to help your child be more successful. Then, as we learn more about what's going on, we'll work together to come up with some strategies to help make things better. Some ideas will help and some may not, but we'll keep working together to find out what works the best."

Ask the family what they think of this:
"*How does this sound to you?*"

3E EXPECTATIONS AND GROUND RULES

The expectations and ground rules are discussed together with the family. This involves revising the commitment to each other by attending all session appointments and having a review of communication and confidentiality. Communication and confidentiality focuses on the importance of the family's openness about what is going on in their lives and what they think and feel about it, freedom for every member to feel open to share without fear of punishment, and a review of the safety and protection of each member of the family. An example of how this might be presented to the family is provided in Box 3.4.

Box 3.4 Example of Reviewing Expectations and Ground Rules with Family

Commitment to Each Other

We're all going to work together as a group to make this happen and we want to make the most of the time that we have available. We'll meet for from three to five sessions over the course of the coming weeks and we hope that you'll be able to attend as *consistently* as possible so that we can all get the most out of this experience. We know that emergencies come up, but be sure to *call* as soon as possible if you can't be here so that we'll know that you're okay. Before you leave today, we'll give you our card with the phone number and appointment times.

Communication and Confidentiality

a) **The importance of the family's openness about what's going on in their lives and what they think and feel about this:**

One of the most important things that we'll work on is communication. A lot of problems are caused by misunderstandings between people about what's going on. In order to improve your ability to communicate with each other, we hope that you can all be as open as possible with us about what's going on in your lives and how you feel about things, and what *you* **think** of what *we* **say**. We will have ideas and suggestions about what's going on and what might make things better, but we need to be sure that these fit with *your* ideas of what is best for your family. If you ever disagree, please let us know as soon as possible so that we can resolve any misunderstandings or differences.

---

b) **Freedom for everyone to be open during sessions without fear of punishment:**
Another thing that will help make this experience more valuable is if everyone can speak freely without worrying about getting in trouble for what they say during the sessions here. We'd like to ask the parents' permission that no one will get in trouble for what is said here. There are a lot of thoughts and feelings that we all have and we can't help straighten things out unless everyone feels free to talk about things without worrying about getting in trouble. Is this okay with both parents?

REMEMBER to remind everyone of this promise at the end of this session and any future session involving conflict.

c) **Safety and protection of everyone:**
We're also responsible for dealing with issues of safety. What we talk about in here is confidential and won't be shared with anyone else unless there is a need to protect you or others. If we feel that someone might hurt themselves or someone else, we need to do whatever is necessary to make sure that that doesn't happen. If something like this comes up, we'll talk about it and work out a way to make sure that everyone is safe. Any questions?

3F ASSESSMENT PLAN REGARDING IDENTIFYING STRENGTHS AND CHALLENGES INCLUDING THE PRESENTING PROBLEM

The assessment will begin by interviewing the parents with the SBFC Interview Procedure (Carter & Evans, 2008) (Appendix A). This procedure involves interviewing the parents, children and teacher, with a focus on learning more about strengths, challenges, and what has been tried to address these challenges (see Box 3.5). The teacher and child portion of this interview should already be completed (see Box 3.3, 1g).

Box. 3.5 SBFC Interview Procedure Basic Information. See Appendix A for complete procedure.

Interview Content

Exploration of Student Strengths. The respondent is first asked to comment on the student's *strengths*. This question is a critical initial step because it frames subsequent discussions within a balanced perspective of positive and challenging traits and behaviors. Helping participants to acknowledge positive aspects of the student is an important part of the process of addressing challenging behaviors. As described later, this balanced perspective is also important in reducing defensiveness on the part of parents and students. At times, it may be difficult for parents and teachers to come up with strengths, and the SBFC may need to help them define and explore these aspects. In addition, it is often necessary to reframe negative comments into positive ones. For example, a mother responded to a question about her child's strengths by saying, "Well, he's not a total slob." The SBFC then reframed this in terms of the student's ability to sometimes clean up after himself.

Exploration of Student Challenges. The respondent is then asked to describe the student's challenges. These challenges are separated into challenges to the student, to those around him or her, and to the teacher or parent. Part of this discussion is to ascertain the respondent's view of how well the student is able to satisfy the "Three Rules of Kindergarten" discussed earlier. While these may seem to be more applicable to the school setting, they are in fact important parts of the student's functioning in home and social environments as well.

Exploration of Previously Attempted Interventions. In order to prevent redundancy and to communicate respect, the respondent is then asked to describe what attempts, if any, they have made to address the above challenges. These responses are separated into what has seemed to work and what has not seemed to work. The respondent is also asked if they know of any specific obstacles that may have hindered these interventions.

Exploration of Underlying Causes. The respondent is then asked to comment on what they think might be underlying factors of the problem behavior. This information typically involves discussion of feelings, situational variables, current stressors and other aspects that may be critical to developing strategies that address the most important issues involved in the behavior.

Interview Process. One of the most important aspects of the SBFC Interview format is the *process* of how the interview is conducted. While the information obtained through the questions is vital, the process of developing a collaborative relationship between parents and teachers may be more important to the overall success of the intervention. In order to begin this process, the interviewer actively searches for any similarities in the views of the current respondent (e.g., the parent) and previous respondents (e.g., teachers), particularly in the area of student strengths. If any exist and confidentiality is not violated, the interviewer then shares this information with the respondent about the specific similarities between their responses and those of others.

When interviewing the parents it would also be important to include the following:

a) The parents' viewpoint of the history of the problem
b) Anything they would like you to know in order to help the family
c) Their viewpoint of how well they operate together as a team
d) The general level of marital satisfaction and any unresolved conflicts
e) Family genogram

3G EXPLORATION OF FAMILY CHALLENGES AND THE PRESENTING PROBLEM

The family challenges and presenting problems will be explored with the family. While some of this information may be known from the initial referral, it is still important to explore this with the family.

An example of how this might be presented to the family is:

> "Now, let's talk about the challenges of the family and for the student. We want to find out what each of you thinks about this."

Explain that it is normal for each family member to have different views of what the family needs to work on. In general, start by asking the *student* what they think the family needs to work on and then move up, finishing with the father or mother. This allows the children to have some input before the parents give more detailed descriptions. As the family talks, be sure to explore *each* person's perspective and **summarize** what they say and how they feel. (As soon as you start to feel "overloaded" by the amount of information, it's time to summarize – e.g., "Let me make sure that I understand what you're saying. You feel that ....". Then, check with that person to make sure that your perceptions are accurate. As you listen, think about how the problem may be related to normal stresses that occur during each of the Family Life Cycles, shown in Box 3.6, that the family may be in at this time.

Box 3.6 Family Life Cycle Stages (Karpel & Strauss, 1983)

The study of family life cycles is based on the notion that there are predictable stages of family life. While there is variation in when and how families move through these stages, all families do go through each stage. Each stage is precipitated by a particular life event, and each stage presents the family with a "crisis." Given this crisis, there are major tasks for the family to achieve at each stage to overcome the "crisis."

Marriage/Relationship
Major Task: Related to both partners' shifts (physically and emotionally) away from their families of origin and toward one another.

Birth of the Children
Major Task: Involves both parents' attempts to integrate their new relationships to the child with the relationship that already exists between the two of them.

Individuation of the Children
Major Task: Trying to balance the growing autonomy of the child with their sense of belonging and loyalty to the family, and trying to maintain a reasonable and fair balance of accountability between parent and child without overburdening the child with expectations and missions or expecting too little, or nothing, from the child.

Individuation of the Adolescent
Major Task: To redefine the terms of the parent-child relationship primarily regarding issues of autonomy, responsibility and control, without fundamentally violating their basic trustworthiness.

Departure of the Children
Major Task: Associated with moves toward independent living; the basic task is to separate without breaking ties.

Aging and Death of the Parents
Major Task: For all family members involved to face and accept a variety of losses (relational, physical, vocational and possibly financial) without damaging the basic level of trustworthiness which as been built up in these relationships.

3H ADDITIONAL FAMILY COUNSELING TECHNIQUES TO FACILITATE THE FIRST SESSION

Exploring the family challenges and presenting problem is likely to bring about some intensity or conflict in the session. There are several family counseling techniques that may need to be used throughout the session(s) as needed to facilitate exploration. The SBFC practitioner may need to use reframing, interrupting and interventions to address the family conflict as needed.

Reframing. A major component of the counselor's work during this family discussion is the *reframing* of what family members say about a problem *into more positive words*. It is often helpful to summarize what the family says in a way that frames the problem in terms of:

GOALS – what they *want* to have happen
OBSTACLES – what *gets in the way* of reaching this goal

For example, when someone says, "Jimmy's teacher's a jerk, she doesn't care about anyone but herself!" a possible reframe might be: "So you want Jimmy to do better in school, but you feel that the teacher doesn't care about him." Or, when a parent says: "My husband wants me to be all lovey-dovey, but when it's time for the kids to do homework, he just sits around on his butt," a possible reframe might be: "So you think that your husband wants to be closer to you, but it's hard for you because you get angry when he won't help you with the kids."

Interrupting.   You may have to interrupt some family members if they jump in to answer. If this is necessary, explain that you don't want to seem rude in interrupting, but that you need to hear *each* member's viewpoint so that you can help the *whole* family. It's also important for the family to help each family member to learn to express their own views.

Family or Parental Disagreements About Issues.   If family members interrupt and disagree with each other, reiterate that it's natural for every person to have their own viewpoint and that each person will get a chance to give their view. If the parents start to discuss marital issues or other issues that violate healthy subsystem boundaries, then immediately interrupt them with a brief explanation of the types of issues that are best discussed together as a family (e.g., expectations of parents and children, family rules and consequences, etc.) and the types of issues that are best talked about in private (issues that the parents have with each other, or issues that the parents have with a child that might embarrass the child if discussed with siblings, etc.). Then ask the parents to save that discussion for later when you will talk with them separately from the kids.

3I SUMMARIZING THE FIRST SESSION

It is unlikely that you will be able to complete the Assessment in the first session, but it is very important to save time to summarize what has happened in the first session. After each person has given their view, tell the family that the plan is to address *each* of the problems that they have talked about, but that the family will have to work on one at a time in order to make progress so that everyone will feel better. As you summarize what the family has done to deal with the problem remember to:

Acknowledge the family and individual strengths and specifically *praise* the family *for their effort* in trying to make things better, even if it didn't seem to solve the problem. Remind them that if they *continue to try*, things will get better. Assure the family that, while it will take time for things to get better, today is a great start because everyone knows more about the situation and we can now start to help the family to work together to improve the situation a little each day.

Introduce "Shut-down, Write-down" procedure. Explain to the family the importance of trying to save their arguments for when they meet with the family counselor. Watching them argue will enable the counselor to learn about how they communicate their disagreements and resolve their differences.

This will then help the counselor to work with the family to develop better ways of communicating and solving problems.

An example of this could be as follows:

> "So, if you start to get into any arguments while discussing anything that happened today and anyone starts to feel bad, then stop the discussion and help each person to write down what the argument was about. At the next family session, these arguments will be explored to see if they can be used to help the family learn how to communicate better and to resolve conflicts with fewer hurt feelings."

Get a Consent for Counseling form signed and, if necessary, get a Consent to Release Information form signed in order to talk with other important parties (e.g., outside service provider, other professionals, other family or community members). Use the forms provided and approved by the school/district. Remind the family of the next session date and time, give them an appointment card with this information and your phone number and then say good-bye.

Step 4: The second parent meeting – psycho-education

The second parent meeting consists of psycho-education, a process of providing information, education, and support to assist the family to understand their situation and cope. Psycho-education topics may vary depending on the specific case, but in general psycho-education should always consist of the following for the purposes of the SBFC professional in a school setting:

4A THE MOST IMPORTANT ISSUES AND CURRENT CRISES

The SBFC practitioner provides a summary of the first session to remind the family of what was done, and the reason for working together. Following this narrative discussion, the parents are then presented with the SBFC practitioner's view of the family's most important issues and current crises, the latter being the initial focus of treatment. The SBFC practitioner considers all of the information obtained from the family and then prioritizes "The Most Important Issues," including any crises that the family is currently involved with. The Most Important Issues usually are related to the Presenting Problem, although the SBFC practitioner's view of the Presenting Problem is typically different from the family's because the counselor is objectively considering many more aspects of the family from the dimensional analysis. After speaking with the parents, the counselor then gives feedback to the whole family with an emphasis on strengths and family life cycle stressors that normally challenge all families, while safeguarding any information that would increase anxiety.

An example of this could be as follows:

> "After talking with each of you, it is clear that there are many strengths in this family. One of them is the family's willingness to seek help from outside sources in order to address problems. Another is your ability to be open and honest about what's going on in your lives and how you feel. There are also individual strengths such as _____.

> There are also some challenges for the family, some of which are experienced by many families going through the family life cycle stages that you are going through. For example, your family is involved in the Individuation of Adolescents stage where families are trying to help their adolescent children to learn more about their own individual viewpoints and desires. Consequently, many families experiencing this stage have more arguments and conflict than they had when the children were younger."

Throughout the evaluation process, the SBFC practitioner is looking for any crises that need immediate attention before continuing with further treatment. These are typically any situation where someone may get hurt, either physically or emotionally, or basic needs (from the Factual Dimension) such health, food, rent, or other time-sensitive issues. These require the SBFC practitioner to engage in Crisis Counseling, which typically involves:

a) Identifying the possible harm that may occur and helping the family to understand that immediate action must be taken to *prevent harm to anyone*.
b) Developing a specific behavioral plan to assist the family in helping each other to cope constructively with the crisis.
c) Assisting the family to recognize what the crisis reveals about their family dynamics and what they can do to prevent further occurrence of the crisis.

If crisis counseling is involved, this becomes the priority. An additional session may be required in this procedure after the crisis is stabilized to review psycho-educational information with the family.

4B GENERAL PSYCHO-EDUCATIONAL TOPICS TO INTRODUCE

A general introduction to these topics is provided in this session. Since this procedure is an abbreviated form of a longer-term conjoint family therapy intervention, these psycho-educational topics may be applied as needed, or as appropriate. These topics will be reviewed again during additional sessions and integrated into the treatment plan.

The psycho-educational topics include the following:

*   The three rules of kindergarten
*   The three high-risk behaviors associated with middle and high school
*   The three main protective factors to prevent these "high-risk behaviors"

- The three outcomes of young adulthood
- Introduction and review of basic academic school counseling information
- The 10 positive methods of discipline and redirection techniques

Developmentally, this teaching process should begin when the child is about 2 years old, but some parents begin much earlier. It is important to note that many parents may not be consciously aware of their role in teaching their children how to behave. Most rely upon their own cultural and familial experiences to make decisions regarding how best to deal with their children. Consequently, the discussion of the three rules of kindergarten (Box 3.7) may cover unfamiliar ground for some parents. Many parents may feel uncomfortable discussing their own discipline techniques that include yelling or spanking.

Box 3.7 The Three Rules of Kindergarten

1) Keep your hands and feet to self
2) Follow adult directions
3) Respect others and their property

In these cases, it is often helpful to use the following words:

> "Research shows that most parents use conscious and unconscious information and personal experience in deciding how to discipline their children. Research also indicates that children learn best when discipline methods are consistent across all environments, especially in school. That's why it's important for us to explore the specific techniques that you have used in the past so that any necessary modifications can be made in the present in order to maximize your child's academic and personal development."

Another aspect to explore in the parental subsystem with preadolescent or adolescent children concerns the "three high-risk behaviors of adolescence" (see Box 3.8) and the main protective factors to prevent these (Box 3.9) (Fraser, 2004). Parents often become anxious as their children approach adolescence and most parents will share their concern about these high-risk behaviors, which often have great ramifications for the future happiness of their children. Many parents, however, are not aware of the protective factors that can help to prevent significant problems regarding these high-risk behaviors.

Box 3.8 The Three High-Risk Behaviors Associated with Middle and High School

1. Issues regarding substance and alcohol abuse
2. Issues regarding romantic relationships, sexual behavior, and pregnancy

---

3. Issues related to negative influence of peers, including involvement in gangs

There are three main protective factors that can prevent negative experiences with these issues of high-risk behaviors (see Box 3.9). For many children, the latter two protective factors are very difficult to achieve, especially during adolescence. Therefore, the main protective factor to focus upon for most parents is the nature of their relationship with their adolescent. This protective factor is maximized when children and their parents have a good relationship with clear and effective communication and a willingness to discuss mistakes constructively.

Box 3.9 The Three Main Protective Factors to Prevent these "High Risk Behaviors"

1. Strong relationship with a parent or significant adult where the adolescent is able to talk about mistakes with sensitive topics without fear of anger or punishment
2. When the adolescent has a unique strength in a meaningful skill such as a sport, artistic skill, or academics
3. When the adolescent has very close friends who are a positive influence and are willing to confront the adolescent about negative behaviors (Fraser, 2004)

For older children, the focus is typically centered on the "three outcomes of young adulthood" (see Box 3.10). These three outcomes are achieved when the adult child (usually in their early 20s) is able to 1) be self-maintaining, 2) have one good friend, and 3) stay out of jail. These three outcomes may seem minimal, but if a child is able to accomplish these, they'll have a good chance of being happy and successful. Realizing each of these outcomes requires the child to develop of variety of skills related to these areas during adolescence.

Box 3.10 The Three Outcomes of Young Adulthood

1. Be self-maintaining
2. Have one good friend
3. Stay out of jail

Being self-maintaining requires a person to be able to take care of all of their physical, financial, and psychological needs. These include taking care of one's health; cooking and cleaning; developing work skills to earn enough money to survive; living within one's means with a minimum of debt; and numerous other skills required to live independently. Having one good friend requires the ability to identify and control one's own emotions; express thoughts and feelings adequately and listen carefully to others; be flexible enough to accommodate the needs of others while also advocating for one's own needs; as well as having a number of other relationship skills. Staying out of jail requires the ability to understand and follow rules; respect authority; and understand the social consequences of human behavior. These "three outcomes of young adulthood" often become the basis for the development of family rules within the household as children grow older. It's also necessary to acknowledge the increased ability of the adolescent to participate in and give input into family discussions regarding decisions that affect them and to also take more responsibility for their part in implementing these.

4C INTRODUCTION AND REVIEW OF BASIC ACADEMIC SCHOOL COUNSELING INFORMATION WITH THE STUDENT AND FAMILY (MIDDLE AND HIGH SCHOOL STUDENTS)

This part of this session includes an individual review of the student's academic information, or transcript, with the family, including grades, test scores, credits, college course requirements, and progress towards graduation (or culmination for middle school students) (see Box 3.11). Review with them where the student has been academically, where they are at now, and what is needed to move forward.

Box 3.11 Review of Basic Academic Information

1. Grades
2. Grade point average (GPA)
3. High School Diploma

    a) Credits needed to graduate
    b) A–G course requirements

4. Review of high school graduation, college and career options and pathways
5. Student review of transcript, grades, GPA, course credits, and A–G

(courses required for college acceptance) course completion progress

---

While this information may appear to be general knowledge, it is very common for students to move through high school and not have an understanding of what is needed to graduate and what options are available to them. Many times this information is provided in large-group settings such as assemblies, classroom presentations, or workshops, and students may not be fully attending due to distractions, and/or feeling that the information does not yet apply to them. "Teaching" the basics of academic counseling to students in an important aspect for SBFC practitioners. Providing this information with the student and the family within a family counseling context allows for improved grasp and understanding of the concepts and a good opportunity to assess the level of knowledge they already have, and provide individualized assistance and support as needed. The SBFC practitioner can also assess for nonverbal reactions on the part of the student and/or family, and use that information in the counseling process.

Reviewing academic information with the family provides a basic common knowledge of academic information and helps the family be on the same page to establish family expectations, rules, and goals. In general, the SBFC practitioner should conduct a basic review of grades, and how grades are converted into points which becomes a GPA. In addition, there should be a review of high school credits, how they are earned, and how many credits are needed to graduate (this information varies by school, district, and state). It is important that students understand that a grade of an F equals 0 credits, and will most likely require that class to be repeated. Also, depending on the state, many high school graduation requirements have changed requiring students to complete an A–G course curriculum (courses required for college acceptance) in order to be competitive to apply to a 4-year university. Understanding what A–G means is an important part of the school counseling process, especially if a student is interested in attending a 4-year college. For these reasons, exploring graduation and post-graduation options are important. For students interested in applying to a 4-year college, they will need to understand that while earning a D in a class may allow them to graduate high school, it will disqualify them from applying to a 4-year college, unless they retake the class. This is a good opportunity to link back to the "Education Pays" connection between education and employment to help personalize the information for them.

4D POSITIVE METHODS OF DISCIPLINE AND REDIRECTION TECHNIQUES

The positive methods of discipline and redirection techniques are reviewed with the parents only. The student can be excused to return to class or work on an independent assignment if it is after school hours. This information is adopted from Kay Manning: Positive Methods of Discipline and Redirection (2018) (Box 3.12).

Box 3.12 List of the 10 Positive Methods of Discipline and Redirection (K. Manning, 2018)

1. Identify feelings
2. Positive redirection

3. Giving choices
4. Positive reinforcement
5. Give "I" messages
6. Avoid labeling children
7. Use the positive
8. Model your feelings in a positive way
9. Explain
10. Trust

This is often the beginning of helping parents to see the connection between early childhood experiences of parental discipline and the quality of the parent-child relationship during adolescence. This is a good time to reiterate that this relationship constitutes the primary protective factor against the three high-risk behaviors of adolescence. This discussion typically leads to explanation and training of positive discipline techniques that acknowledge the child's feelings and give two structured choices of how to deal with their feelings and also include a specific, detailed procedure that uses "breaks", which are modified "time-outs" that allow the child a chance to think about their behavior and more constructive ways of getting what they want (see Box 3.13). Let family know that this use of time-outs or breaks will come next session because kids need to have consistent attention to positive behaviors before time-outs or breaks will work.

Box 3.13 Positive Methods of Discipline and Redirection (K. Manning, 2018)

As family therapists, we are responsible for maintaining a safe, calm, therapeutic environment where families can learn and work together. We also need to model appropriate discipline techniques so that parents learn to discipline their children without yelling, belittling, or becoming physically aggressive. We also want to "give" parents tools to replace discipline what has been labeled inappropriate and taken away (physical punishment, yelling, belittling, etc.). Many times we tell parents what "not-to-do", but we also need to tell parents what they "can-do" to effectively discipline their children in a loving way. These techniques are called positive methods of discipline and redirection. These positive methods will serve:

(1) To preserve and enhance the self-esteem of the child,
(2) To create a positive relationship between the parent(s) and child,
(3) To provide opportunities for children to accept responsibility for their own actions,
(4) To challenge children to develop problem solving techniques,

(5) And to maintain an atmosphere where all children in the family feel safe and relaxed.

POSITIVE DISCIPLINE

I believe that there is no such thing as a bad child; however, I do know that there are children with inappropriate behaviors. These inappropriate behaviors may include (but are not limited to), hitting, biting, scratching, screaming, temper tantrums, foul or hurtful language, abuse of materials or property, and an unwillingness to show respect or follow directions. The child's motivation for inappropriate behaviors varies, and may include:

(1) Ignorance (lack of experience) – not knowing the rules or what is expected; they are still learning.
(2) Fear – children have fears of abandonment, not having their basic needs met, not knowing what to do, embarrassment, not feeling safe.
(3) Hunger – most of us are a little restive when we are hungry.
(4) Tiredness – lack of sleep can make us irritable.
(5) Lack of positive attention – no one likes to be ignored.
(6) Lack of self-worth – an attitude of, "No matter what I do, it will be wrong anyway."
(7) Growth – gaining competency by trial and error.
(8) Lack of stimuli – try hot sauce on bland food; bored children make things more interesting For themselves.
(9) Communication – children do not have complex verbal or thinking skills.
(10) Inconsistency – in their past experiences with one adult this behavior was okay, why not now?
(11) They may have special needs such as a disability.
(12) Not understanding, such as semantics, sarcasm, humor.
(13) Family pressures – the squeaky wheel gets the oil. (A cry for help.)
(14) They may be a victim of abuse.

When children's behavior is inappropriate, we need to empower parents to remain the "adult." We can respond calmly and positively. As the adult, we "model" appropriate responses when we are angry or upset, which need not include physical or verbal abuse or punishment.

Below are some methods to positively discipline children:

I. Identify Feelings:

Children's inappropriate behavior is communication. Try to help them express their feeling.
"Can you tell me about that?"

"Tell me what you are feeling."
"You must have had a good reason for doing that; tell me about it."
"Something has made you really angry. Let's discuss it."

Help them label and clarify their feelings. Give them *appropriate* words and an "ear" to help them verbally express feelings. Avoid asking "Why?"

II. Positive Redirection:
"I can let you hit the pillow, but I can't let you hit your sister."
"I can let you say that in the bathroom; we don't use that word in the kitchen."
"If you feel angry, you can use your words and say, 'It makes me angry when you …'"

Second Chance: "Can you say that again so I can understand?"
(Tell them what they may do as an alternative to their inappropriate behavior.)

III. Giving Choices:
"I know you don't want to leave the park. I was having fun, too, but it's time to go. Do you want to walk to the car or skip to the car?"
"I know you don't want to wear a jacket. But today it is cold. Do you want to wear the blue one or the yellow one?" or "Do you want to zip it or do you want me to zip it?"

Be matter-of-fact, and then give them two choices that they can accept. Only give them reasonable choices that you are also willing to accept.

With older kids, let them state the options or choices. "What are your options?"

IV. Positive Reinforcement:
Give them positive attention, validation, reinforcement.
"I saw that you were taking turns."
"I saw you getting angry and you remembered to use your words."
"You were patiently helping your sister."
"You did it!"

Catch them when they are engaged in what is appropriate behavior – being "good," and notice them honestly and often. You do not have to evaluate, "good job," "well done," etc.

Use encouragement and attention, rather than praise. We don't have to label the behavior.

V. Give "I" Messages:
"I like the colors in your painting."

"I like the way you remember to walk around the puddle."

People have different viewpoints.

VI. Avoid Labeling Children:
Try not to say:
"Oh, you are such a shy girl!" "You are such a good boy." "He is so hyper."

Children are not good or bad, but their behaviors may be pleasing or inappropriate. Children often live up to their labels; however, a "good" child will not learn how to handle mistakes.

VII. Use the positive. Avoid saying "No":
Child: "I want to eat a cookie!"
Adult: "I know you would like a cookie, but an apple is healthier for you. Would you like a red apple or a yellow apple?" or "Do you want it cut or whole?"

Saying, "No!" turns people off. Children hear it too often. They may not hear the rest of what you are trying to communicate.

VIII. Model your feelings in a positive way:
Calmly say, "I feel angry when you bump into my leg with the tricycle. If you want to ride the tricycle, you need to drive carefully."

If parents or teachers yell and scream, it teaches children that these behaviors are appropriate; however, do express your feelings. Adults feel angry, sad, etc., too.

IX. Explain:
"I can let you throw the ball, but when we throw sand, it hurts other people's eyes."
"I can let you run on the grass, but I care about you; it is not safe to run up the slide."

Sometimes there is not a clear "good" reason (e.g., "You don't wear your bathing suit to church").

Give them reasons – in one short sentence, not a lecture. This helps them develop logical thinking, and cause-and-effect relationships.

X. Trust:
"I'm going to ask you to carry this bowl of water to the table, because I know you will try your best." "Yesterday I saw you sit so quietly during the story that I know you can sit quietly today."

Trust the child. Assume the best. Your confidence will give them self-confidence to develop competency.

Using positive methods of discipline and redirection takes some getting used to. We weren't all raised this way. You may find that this positive attitude will change your whole day. You will start to see the "good" in everybody.

Step 5: The third family meeting: co-constructing rules, expectations, and consequences

The third family session is an important one because it helps the family to co-construct a positively oriented system of behavior management based on what is consistent with societal and school system requirements in order to be successful. Again, it is emphasized that this work at home can help the child to develop the skills necessary to be successful in the school/work environment, which leads to earning more money with less unemployment in adulthood. The session covers: checking the implementation of Positive Discipline; co-constructing expectations; co-constructing rules; and consequences with the use of the objective discipline procedure (ODP) break system and behavior chart (a method of recording what happens whenever an incident of noncompliance with directions occurs).

5A CHECKING THE IMPLEMENTATION OF POSITIVE DISCIPLINE

The third family meeting begins with a check-in regarding the implementation of the Positive Discipline techniques of Kay Manning (see above). This discussion begins by asking the children what happened during the last week whenever they followed the three rules of kindergarten (i.e., keep hands and feet to self, follow directions, and be respectful of others). What you're hoping to get from the children is a description of the parents providing positive attention whenever the children are behaving positively and providing an acknowledgment of their feelings and two structured choices whenever they are behaving inappropriately. If not, then ask the parents if they remember how they responded to the children when they were behaving positively or inappropriately. If necessary, review the basic concepts of Positive Discipline by Kay Manning.

5B CO-CONSTRUCTING EXPECTATIONS

After assessing the implementation of the positive discipline techniques, the next step is to work with the children and parents to "Co-construct" the expectations, rules, and consequences of how things will operate in the home. This process of "Co-constructing" is critical in order for the children to understand and "buy in" to this family plan. This process begins with a review of the three outcomes of young adulthood and the skills that are necessary in order to achieve each of these.

An example of this may involve the following:

> "Just a reminder that the focus of the family is to prepare the children to become happy and successful adults. As we discussed before, it's important for the kids to learn how to become self-maintaining, have one good friend, and to stay out of jail if they want to be happy as adults. So, it's important to talk about what skills you need to develop to achieve each of these three. Let's look at the first skill: be self-maintaining. What are some of the things you need to be able to do in order to maintain yourself?"

This should lead to a discussion of tasks such as:

- Cleaning up after yourself
- Doing your own laundry
- Cooking and cleaning for yourself
- Being able to follow specific instructions in order to obtain and keep a job in order to earn enough money
- Developing the self-control necessary to be able to budget in order to buy necessities such as food, shelter and clothing
- Prioritizing and saving for the things or experiences you most want to buy
- Taking care of your own health including eating right, exercising, and getting enough sleep.

> "Let's look at the second skill: having at least one good friend. What are some of the things you need to be able to do in order to have at least one good friend?"

This should lead to discussion of skills such as:

- Maintaining personal hygiene standards
- Listening to others and being able to express yourself clearly
- Being able to control your emotions enough so that you can talk about your feelings and be empathetic to others' feelings
- Being able to be assertive in acknowledging your needs as well as the needs of others
- Being able to respect physical and emotional interpersonal boundaries including personal space, secrets, and other social considerations

> "Last but not least, let's look at the third skill: staying out of jail. What are some of the things you need to be able to do in order to stay out of jail?"

This should lead to a discussion of skills such as:

- Being aware of and understanding the rules and consequences of society
- Learning to respect the power of authority while also learning how to effectively advocate for yourself in order to change the rules and consequences

5C CO-CONSTRUCTING RULES, AND CONSEQUENCES WITH THE OBJECTIVE DISCIPLINE PROCEDURE (ODP) BREAK SYSTEM

The next important process of this session is to co-construct with the children and parents the specific rules and consequences and specific procedures that the family will use to implement these. This co-construction process is critical in order to incorporate the child's input into the development of the behavior management system. This typically results in less resistance on the part of the children to participating in the system because of their ownership over how it was developed. This involves exploring the *current* behavior management situation in the family, and then co-developing new ways of dealing with noncompliance with parental directions.

Exploring the Current Behavior Management Situation in the Family: An example of this discussion could be as follows:

> "Now that we all have a better understanding of the skills that need to be developed in order to be happy and successful when you're older, let's talk about how the family can develop some procedures to use to help the kids learn these skills. One the most important skills necessary for learning is to be able to follow directions in a timely manner. Tell me what happens in the family when kids **do** follow directions. What happens when kids **do not** follow directions?"

This often leads to a discussion of the current consequences for both following and not following parental instructions. Families are often not aware of any positive consequences for following directions, but typically talk about parents yelling, taking away things and privileges from the children, and other negative consequences for not following directions.

Developing a New Way of Dealing With Noncompliance With Parental Directions. It is important to highlight for the family that following directions involves decision points that may not be obvious because they happen so quickly. First, parents need to be mindful of their decisions regarding the specific directions they ask of each child and the need to be reasonable in terms of the child's ability to comply. Factors such as developmental level and age-appropriate expectations are important to discuss. The parent then needs to be sure that the child is demonstrating attending behaviors (e.g., direct eye contact with the parent without attending to anything else) before giving the direction. Initially, only one direction should be given at a time and, if the child is able to comply with that direction, then other directions can be given. For example, "Joseph, please look at me … Thanks, I'd like you to take out the trash right now."

Children often complain that parents start yelling or take things away too quickly before the child realizes what's happening. In addition, parents often take away things or privileges without thinking about the difficulty in following through with these consequences in a fair manner. This is why it is so important to have pre-set consequences for negative behavior whenever possible. Therefore, one of the goals of any family plan is to slow down interactions so that these decision points are more clear. One way of doing this is to have a procedure with specific keywords and phrases that can help children and parents become more aware of these decisions that are being made and the consequences that follow. Children usually appreciate a suggestion by the counselor to insert an intermediate consequence that can occur before the restriction of things or privileges, especially if it allows the child more time to think about the more long-term negative consequences. One of the best intermediate consequences for not following directions can be to create a break, where the child sits in a chair for about five minutes to reflect on their decision. If the child refuses to take the break, then the parent can add another break period, and then, if the child refused to take the breaks, implement a restriction.

Parental restrictions of things and privileges are often problematic because they are too harsh, last too long, or allow children to substitute an equally pleasurable activity for the restricted one. These restrictions also prevent the child from being able to reduce the time of restriction even after they have learned their lesson. In order to address these difficulties, it is often more effective to restrict the child from *all* privileges (i.e., use of electronics, favorite foods, and playing with others) for a shorter duration of time that can be reduced once the child learns to follow directions. This is also consistent with the negative consequences that adults experience when they fail to follow the directions of authority figures (i.e., prison time without these privileges and the opportunity to reduce the sentence through good behavior).

This is often termed: grounding of all privileges. This essentially means that a child is not allowed to use anything involving electronics, nor allowed to eat favorite but nonessential foods, and is not allowed to play with others inside or outside the house. This "grounding" occurs *only* if the child will not take the breaks once they have earned two breaks. The child is then grounded, which lasts at least 40 minutes, but can stop as soon as the child serves the two breaks (only when it is convenient for the family) and a period of 30 minutes elapses after the serving of all the breaks.

Other Important Aspects of the Break System.   Children should never earn more than two breaks per incident of noncompliance. If the child engages in another inappropriate behavior (e.g., hitting or being disrespectful) during a noncompliant incident, then the focus needs to be on first following through with the consequences for not following directions and then addressing the additional inappropriate behavior immediately afterwards. For example, the parent would follow through with breaks and possible grounding until the child complies with the initial direction. Then the parent would provide consequences for the hitting (usually two breaks), and after those are served, provide consequences for the disrespectful behavior (usually one break).

It is also critically important to explain that it will take time for the entire family to learn how to use this system and that it may be difficult to use when in public settings or when the family is experiencing time constraints such as having to get to school in the morning or go to bed at night. It will be important for the family to be assisted in developing routines and incentives for following directions during these times. Once the family is more accustomed to using this break system, the concept of "roll-over breaks" will be able to be used. The roll-over breaks are when the parent says, "If you don't follow this direction now then you will receive a break as soon as we get home" (or when the child gets home from school that day – if it happens in the morning, or tomorrow – if it occurs during the bedtime routine). It's also important that the family understands that the breaks should not be taken close to bedtime and, in general, fewer directions should be given as bedtime nears so that the child will not get emotionally activated, which can hinder falling asleep. A specific, detailed description of this process is entitled, "The Objective Discipline Procedure for Noncompliance (with Grounding)" (M.J. Carter, 1979) (see Appendix B).

Family Role-Play of the System and Behavioral Charting of Incidents. Once the children and parents have agreed on this procedure for noncompliance (with grounding), the SBFC practitioner facilitates a specific role-play of the entire break procedure with the family. During this role-play, it is often helpful to put an older child in the role of a parent and put one of the parents in the role of a child who is not following directions. The SBFC practitioner should focus on helping the child, in the role as a parent, to follow through with the procedure, as long as the child is capable of doing this without too much trouble. This also allows both the child and parent to experience the opposite role and perhaps build a sense of empathy for each other's position.

Once this role-play has been accomplished to the point that each member of the family understands what is going to happen, the parents are instructed in how to use the Objective Discipline Behavior Chart (Carter, 1979). See Box 3.14 and Appendix B for the complete procedure. This chart is filled out each time a child earns a break and is used to provide continuous information on the date and time of each incident, which parent and child is involved, a description of the behavior (e.g., noncompliance, physical aggression, or disrespect of others), and the consequences that were earned. The last column provides an opportunity for the parent to put in comments and considerations related to the incident. This column has very little space and, because of the importance of these comments, the parent is directed to continue their discussion on the back page of the chart which is left blank. The parents are also instructed to keep this chart hidden from view, but also readily available in case an incident occurs.

It is important to impress upon the parents the critical importance of consistently filling out this chart in order to efficiently assess the success of this system.

Box 3.14 Objective Discipline Procedure for Noncompliance (with Grounding)

CARTER – INCLUDE ODP Procedure
Behavior Key:

1. _____
2. _____
3. _____
4. _____
5. _____

Date/ Time	Parent	Child	Behavior	Consequence	Comments/ Consideration

---

An example of this discussion could be as follows:

"Using this form to record every incident of a break is so important because it enables us to know all of the critical information about the incident without having to ask the family to remember details from the past week. The immediate and objective recording of these details provides an opportunity for the family to specifically discuss the incident with the counselor in order to improve family functioning. Remember, if it's not written down, it didn't happen."

Finally, and most importantly, the SBFC practitioner reminds the family that this is a learning experience for the whole family and it is expected that each child at some point will earn at least one break. So, earning a break is nothing to fear or be embarrassed about, it's just another experience to learn from in their road to a better job, less worry, and more happiness. The family is then asked to meet within one week with the SBFC practitioner and to bring the behavior chart so that progress can be assessed.

Step 6: Fourth family meeting: checking on progress and focus on family fun

The fourth family meeting provides an opportunity to check on the progress of the implementation of the objective discipline procedure including troubleshooting, problem-solving, and effective communication through dyad work. Once these are accomplished, the focus then turns to how the family experiences fun together.

6A CHECKING ON THE PROGRESS OF IMPLEMENTATION OF THE OBJECTIVE DISCIPLINE PROCEDURE

The fourth family meeting begins with a reminder that the purpose of this counseling is to help the children to be more successful and happy in their lives now and in the future. After this, the counselor reviews the behavior chart in order to better understand what has happened during the previous week. The counselor should notice behavioral trends related to the day of the week and the time of the day (e.g., Mondays, mornings or later in the day, etc.) as well as which child and parent is most noted on the chart. This may provide some direction for the family discussion of the strengths and challenges of the week. Often, an older child may be more successful in adapting to the system and have fewer incidents, and it should be pointed out that this is natural given their older age and expectation of more maturity. It's also important to remind everyone that, even if there were a lot of incidences during the week, this constitutes family progress because it allows for important learning experiences that can lead to Improvement.

6B DISCUSSION OF STRENGTHS AND POSITIVE BEHAVIOR AND CHALLENGES DURING THE PAST WEEK

The counselor then facilitates family discussion of the positive aspects of the past week, particularly those that are related to appropriate child behavior such as following directions immediately. It's important to ask the children if they can recall how they and the parents felt during these positive experiences and to remind everyone that the ability to follow directions is highly correlated with competence and future success in life. Competence is what makes us feel good about ourselves and allows us to praise ourselves, which leads to more confidence and optimism about the future.

An example of this discussion could be as follows:

> "It's always good to begin family meetings by discussing the positive things that have happened during the past week. Since you're the youngest, Jimmy, let's begin with you. How well do you think you followed your parents' directions during the past week? Did you notice what happened when you followed a parent's directions? How did that feel for you? How did your parent seem to feel? Is it something you want to continue to do?"

After discussion of the positive aspects of the past week, the discussion moves to addressing the challenges of the past week, with a primary focus on when the break procedure was used. This begins with the SBFC practitioner reviewing how many breaks occurred, with whom, and on which days of the week and during what times they most occurred. This can give the SBFC practitioner an idea of the trends and themes of the breaks and whether any of the breaks are related to parental errors or a lack of established morning, afternoon, or bedtime routines. Parental errors might include giving breaks at bedtime or in the morning when children are less available for learning and the breaks might be ineffective due to time constraints such as needing to get sleep or getting to school. Until the break system is firmly established and learned by all, these times and tasks need to have pre-established routines and incentives for completion in a timely manner. These might include earning some screen time if the child is ready for school on time or story time with parents if ready for bed on time.

The SBFC practitioner begins the discussion of challenges by discussing these trends, for example:

> "It looks like this was a good week, but also with some challenges. Some of the breaks seem to be happening during the mornings with Mom and Jimmy, especially on Mondays when it's harder to get back into the work routine after a weekend off. Perhaps we could talk together to see if we can develop a clear routine that helps Jimmy to be ready for school on time and earn something fun to do."

The discussion then turns to a focus on the most problematic of the break incidents, with a reminder that this is an opportunity for everyone to learn versus feeling bad again. It's usually best to ask the child who was involved in the incident to try to remember what happened and what they were thinking and feeling at each step of their noncompliant behavior. If the child has difficulty, then the child can be encouraged to ask other family members to help to fill out the narrative. It's also important to ask the child whether the initial direction seemed reasonable in terms of the child's ability to comply.

An example of this discussion could be as follows:

> "Jimmy, on Thursday afternoon, when your mom asked you to stop playing on the computer and start your homework, was there anything about this direction that you didn't understand or weren't able to do? When you didn't turn it off, did your mom tell you that you would get a break if you didn't follow her direction? What were you thinking when you didn't do what she asked you to do?"

Finally, the child is asked to comment on how the parent seemed during the incident. Was the parent calm or upset, did the parent speak clearly or with a raised voice? After the child comments on this, ask the parent if they agree with the child's perception or have a different view. Regardless of the answers, it's important to point out to the family that the parents are role models for how children can remain calm and positive even when upset and progress will depend upon this. It may also be useful to teach the family mindfulness of emotions and ways of calming down, including relaxed breathing. It may also be necessary to review the Objective Discipline Procedure, including further role-play of the process.

6C IMPROVING FAMILY COMMUNICATION THROUGH ACTIVE LISTENING SKILLS AND PRACTICE IN DYADS

Another important process in this session is to focus on differences of opinion between family members by using active listening skills and practice with two family members (i.e., dyad work). While it may seem simple, many family disagreements are caused by ineffective communication where neither person is really listening to what the other is saying. Active listening skills can be one of the most important things that families are taught. Briefly, active listening involves asking one person (i.e., Person 1) to express one *positive* thing about the other (Person 2), who is directed to listen carefully with the expectation that Person 2 will be asked to reflect back to Person 1 what they said and how they felt. Then, Person 1 is asked if Person 2 was correct and if not, then Person 1 corrects any misperceptions of content or feeling with Person 2 again reflecting back what was said.

Then, Person 2 gives their reaction to what Person 1 said, with Person 1 reflecting back the content and feelings of what Person 2 said. Then, Person 2 expresses one positive thing about Person 1, and the whole process is repeated.

An example of this discussion could be as follows:

> "Many family disagreements are caused by ineffective communication where neither person is really listening to what the other is saying. One of the things that often helps families is learning how to communicate as effectively as possible. We'll begin by making sure that you're able to

communicate effectively about positive things that you think about or feel about the other person."

"Mom, I'd like you to begin by telling Julie one positive thing about her, either something she's done or perhaps something you feel is good about her. Julie, after your mom finishes, I'm going to ask you to reflect back to her what she said and how she felt about it."

"Julie, please tell your mom the basics of what she told you. Please tell her how she seemed to feel about what she said."

"Mom, how accurate was Julie in her perceptions about what you said and how you felt?"

"Julie, now that your mom feels that you understood her, could you please give your reaction to what she said. Mom, be sure to listen carefully because when Julie is finished, I'll ask you to reflect back to her what she said and how she feels about it."

Once both persons are successful in actively listening to positive comments with this process, then they are each asked to tell the other person one thing that they would like the other person *to improve on*, using the same process.

An example of this discussion could be as follows:

"Julie, now I would like you to tell your mom one thing that you would like her to try to improve on during this next week. Try to pick something that you think she is able to do, but that you would like to see more of. Mom, I want you to pay close attention because I'm going to ask you to reflect back to Julie what she said and how she feels about it."

During this phase, it is critically important for the counselor to help each person to focus on the content and feelings involved in what is being said before responding to what the other person said. While this may seem somewhat laborious at times, it is an important building block in improving patience and the effectiveness of family communications.

6D ASSESSING EXISTING FAMILY FUN AND EXPLORING NEW ACTIVITIES

One of the most neglected aspects of families is the degree to which they experience having fun with each other. While it is important to address specific problems within families, it is also important to improve the quality of family functioning by focusing on how they experience fun with each other. This begins with assessing what family activities occur that cause each person to experience fun. This includes fun that happens between smaller groups of family members as well as the whole family. This discussion may seem unimportant to some families, especially those who did not have this experience in their own families of origin, but it is important to remember that having fun is an important ingredient in experiencing happiness. To a large degree, happiness depends upon experiencing positive, meaningful relationships with others, and enjoyable interactions with others often leads to these types of relationships. Also, as discussed earlier, one of the primary protective factors against the high-risk behaviors of adolescence involves a strong, open, and trusting relationship with a credible adult, preferably a parent. Experiences of fun with the parents and family often help to promote this type of relationship. In addition, experiences of family fun also create positive memories related to the family that can help maintain interpersonal connections between siblings as they grow older.

One way of assessing current aspects of family fun is to ask:

"When was the last time that you remember having fun with members of your family? Who was there and what did you do?"

After assessing current experiences of family fun, the SBFC practitioner can then facilitate discussion about other types of activities that might be fun for the family. Suggestions might include cooking a family meal together, interactive board games such as "Apples and Oranges" or card games such as "UNO." It's important to remind the family that the main purpose of family games is not to win or lose, but to enjoy an interactive experience with each other. Another suggestion might be to explore their neighboring community for free fun experiences such as visiting museums, taking a walk in a park, or hiking together to a place with a view. Larger-scale family fun trips such as camping can be an inexpensive way to spend quality family time together outside each other's usual environment.

One of the greatest challenges to family fun with each other is the almost constant use of technology in many people's lives. The constant access to smartphones often distracts family members from what is being experienced while together. At home and during family outings to restaurants, It's become more and more commonplace to see families all together, but not attending to each other because of technology. Consequently, it's often necessary for the SBFC practitioner to facilitate a family discussion about the need for specific boundaries around time spent with the family in order to create positive, lasting memories. This also requires that parents focus on activities that are fun for everyone, not just for themselves.

The fourth family meeting concludes with a summarization of the session, highlighting the positive progress and continuing challenges in using the behavior management system and communicating effectively, as well as a renewed focus on improving the amount of fun that they experience together.

Step 7: Fifth family meeting: termination, generalization, and transfer

The fifth family session is focused on assessing progress, troubleshooting and problem-solving, and beginning the process of termination by introducing the concept of "family meetings." The explanation and practicing of this important family function are used to help the family to generalize and transfer the knowledge and skills they have learned in sessions to monitor progress and address any challenges in the future. At the end of this session, a one-month follow-up appointment is made.

7A TERMINATION OF CONJOINT FAMILY COUNSELING

As the family learns to deal with crises, improve family structure and functioning, and address and resolve specific family problems, the process of termination begins. This process begins by introducing the concept of "family meetings," where the family takes more responsibility for facilitating what happens in the family counseling sessions. Conjoint family counseling often incorporates these meetings into the termination process so that the counselor can measure how well the family can work together without assistance.

7B FAMILY MEETINGS

In a few words, family meetings are an opportunity for families to get together to discuss both the positive and negative things that are happening. Family members rotate taking the role of the facilitator who helps to run the meeting and monitors the communication rules. The family counselor directs this initial family meeting to ensure maximum participation and success. The meeting usually begins with each family member having the opportunity to comment on something positive that has happened in the past week and one area where they would like to see improvement during the next week. Then, the discussion turns to how the whole family can help make this happen. As the family engages in this discussion, the counselor focuses on reminding the family to use their active listening and other effective communication skills to attend to each other and to reflect back the content and feelings of their statements. When necessary, the counselor points out mutual points of agreement and areas of difference and creating ways of compromise to resolve these. This discussion also allows the counselor to assess to what degree the family is consistently using the tools of Positive Discipline and the break system.

An example of this discussion could be as follows:

> "Today we're going to start the process of helping your family to be able to work together consistently through the use of family meetings without me being present. These meetings should follow the same format that we've been using here during our counseling sessions. These meetings will provide an opportunity for you all to get together periodically to discuss both the positive and negative things that happened during the past week (or other consistent time period). This will help the family to know about and enjoy many of the positive things that happen to each of you and will also help the family to work together so that everyone

can improve. I will help your family to learn how to conduct these family meetings over the next few sessions."

"We'll begin by giving each person a chance to comment on something positive that has happened during this past week. Julie, why don't you begin by sharing with us something positive that happened to you or that you've observed in the family over the past week. Everyone, be sure to listen closely to what Julie says so that, if you are asked, you can reflect back to her what she said and how she felt."

"Now that everyone has had a chance to share something positive about the last week, each person will get a chance to talk about one thing that they would like to see improvement in during the next week and how the family can help make this happen. Julie, would you mind going first? Again, everyone needs to listen carefully just in case you are asked to reflect back to Julie what she said and how she feels about it."

As discussed above, during this discussion of desired improvements, the SBFC practitioner can point out mutual points of agreement and areas of difference and create ways of compromise to resolve these. This discussion also allows the counselor to assess to what degree the family is consistently using the tools of Positive Discipline and the break system.

An example of how this might be discussed is the following:

"Julie, one of the things that you said you would like to see improved is for you to receive more privileges, such as having a later bedtime, because you are the eldest child and have to do more chores. You said that your parents acknowledged your feelings about this and gave you a choice of staying up 15 minutes later in your room before turning out the lights. They also said that you need to be more dependable in completing your chores without being reminded. You said that you agree to do this, but only if you can stay up one hour later than your other siblings. Your parents then said that they are concerned that you won't get enough sleep and will be harder to wake up in the morning and more irritable in the afternoon. What do you think of this?"

Okay, so Julie said that she'll try to do her chores without being asked during the next week, but that staying up 15 minutes later is not enough of a privilege. Perhaps a compromise might be that, for the next week, your parents will let you stay up a half hour later than you are now, and then you can all observe and record how well you get up in the morning and what your mood is like in the afternoon. How does that sound to all of you?

During the next session, the SBFC practitioner chooses a family member and assists them in serving as the facilitator of the family meeting.

An example of how this might be discussed is the following:

"Before we begin, I'd like Julie (the oldest child) to take my place in the role of the facilitator, who will help to run the meeting and monitor the communication rules. The main part of this role is to make sure that only one person is speaking at a time and that everyone is actively listening to what is being said. I'll help Julie until she feels comfortable doing this today and then someone else can serve as facilitator next session."

7C CRISIS PREVENTION THROUGH FAMILY LIFE CYCLE PREPARATION AND PROBLEM-SOLVING

Resilience can be enhanced when a family is able to anticipate problems that may come up in the future and learn to deal with them through a proactive family problem-solving process. As previously discussed, transitions into new stages of the family life cycle often create a great deal of stress and conflict in families. Specific explanations of family life cycle stages, especially those that are in the near future, can help a family to understand what adaptations they will need to make to be successful as their family develops. Discussion of the challenges of these transitions can provide an opportunity to explore the family's problem-solving process, of which they may not be aware. It's often useful to use the most recent family life cycle stage to explore how the family dealt with previous problems.

An example of how this might be discussed is the following:

"I know that Julie just turned 11 years old yesterday and will be starting middle school next year. Because Julie is the oldest child, this development will move your family into the next family life cycle stage: The Individuation of the Adolescent. This stage is one of the most important of the family life cycle because this is when the family needs to work together to prepare the adolescent to become an independently functioning adult. During this stage, children usually experience a remarkable change in the way that they see themselves and the world around them and this can often lead to an increase in family conflict, especially between the adolescent and parents. Can you think of the time during the past year when you and Julie had a conflict and were able to resolve it effectively? What seemed to work best and how might you be able to use that memory to help in the future? What about when Julie wanted to stay up later in exchange for taking on more responsibilities in her chores?"

Family resilience can be enhanced by integrating the above concepts into the conjoint family counseling processes of family evaluation, treatment, and termination. These can help the family to recognize and use their own resources to maintain healthy structure and communication and to solve family problems now and in the future.

Step 8: Follow-up session and identifying if another session is necessary

Lastly, a follow-up session will be scheduled within a month's time. The purpose of this follow-up session is to check in with the family regarding progress, obtain an update about how things are going in regards to the Presenting Problem and interventions put in place, and anticipate possible future obstacles or crises. During the follow-up session, psycho-educational concepts will also be revisited and reinforced as needed. Based on the information provided, additional resources and referrals may need to be provided to the family.

Another important process is helping the family to identify if and when they might need to return for continued family counseling. The counselor can help the family to understand and identify individual and family symptoms that may indicate the existence of problems. Individual symptoms may include reduced functioning in any of the areas of the "circle of life" as well as maladaptive responses to specific situations. Family symptoms may include a reduction in the frequency of family fun and time spent together or an increase in family conflict or negative mood. When these occur, the family should reactivate the processes of family meetings and problem-solving. If the family does not improve significantly following these occurrences, then the family should contact the counselor sooner rather than later in order to prevent crises.

It is also important to remind the family that the teachers, administrators, and staff will continue to monitor the student's performance in the school environment and report back to the family if any challenging situations occur. However, if the parents are seeing anything regarding the child's school functioning that they are concerned about, they should contact the counselor for a brief phone call session, or an in-person booster session if necessary.

Another important part of this process is to help the family gather the necessary referral information just in case these are necessary at a later date.

Multicultural Counseling Considerations

One of the most important aspects of effective conjoint family counseling is the specific consideration of the cultural and historical backgrounds of the family. These factors must be included in the evaluation of the family in order to improve understanding and reduce resistance. It is critical to focus on family history as well as cultural background in order to avoid making faulty generalizations that can adversely affect the success of conjoint family therapy. Counselors often make assumptions regarding cultural background, particularly regarding variations within the same ethnic group. For example, some counselors assume that Latino clients are Mexican or Spanish-speaking or that Latino cultures are essentially all the same. This often leads to misunderstandings that insult the client and cause irreparable damage to rapport and the effectiveness of conjoint family counseling. Of course, there are significant differences between all Latino cultures. There are also significant differences within each family's experience of the same culture, especially when one considers how place of birth, class, and gender intersect with ethnicity. Exploring these differences is a critical aspect of effective family evaluation, for it influences all subsequent processes of conjoint family counseling.

It is important for the counselor to create a narrative that incorporates the family's cultural and historical factors. This often includes an exploration of the family's specific cultural beliefs and family history and how these may affect individual family members' development and the presenting problem. For instance, using an example of speaking to a family about their teenage daughter's aggressiveness, the counselor might say:

> "It seems that you are having difficulty understanding how your daughter came to be so aggressive in her interactions with you. Mrs. Salazar, you have spoken of your childhood in Mexico where you felt your choices were limited because of the fact that you were a woman and how you came to this country to find a husband who respected women as equals. Since then, you and your husband have encouraged your three daughters to "speak their mind no matter what." Mr. Salazar has also said that he has raised his daughters to "be strong and don't let anyone mess with you." You both also indicate that you were never allowed to disagree openly with your own parents. Due to these factors, it would make sense that, while you want your daughter to express herself, you may also have an expectation that she will do so in a respectful fashion and not argue with you. However, many children in early adolescence, like your daughter, have not yet learned how to modulate the intensity of their voices when speaking about their feelings."

In this sense, the cultural and historical story of the family becomes the context for the daughter's present-day problems. By presenting this narrative in a compassionate way, it creates new connections and opens up a space of awareness for the family. Within this space of awareness, the SBFC practitioner should also consider the systemic issues that the family has faced and continues to face due to race, ethnicity, religion, class, immigration status, and any other cultural factor. For instance, an issue such as poverty can affect the family on a daily basis. Any family intervention must consider not only the individual and systemic functioning of the family itself, but also the way in which systemic factors in society interact with and affect the family's ability to function.

Challenges and solutions

There can be many challenges to applying the seven-step SBFC procedure for conjoint family counseling in schools. This process can be difficult and time-consuming, and requires knowledge, training, and experience in working with family systems. The following Box 3.15 provides a list of possible challenges and alternative solutions for the SBFC practitioner.

Box 3.15 Challenges and Alternative Solutions for Implementing Conjoint Family Counseling Practices in Schools

Challenge	Solution
Obtaining buy-in from administration to integrate more work with families in the schools can be a challenge.	This may take time. Align with the administration, develop a strong rapport and working relationship with the administration, provide regular updates regarding your work and outcomes to the administration, demonstrate your effective skills in working with families by volunteering or intervening in situations that lend themselves to working with parents/families, be visible in your interactions fostering family engagement with the school.
School focus is on the student and there is an unwillingness to include the family in intervention.	Provide research and studies on the importance of family engagement in the school setting. Provide information about how frequently the problems that are affecting students in the classroom are related to issues outside school.
SBFC practitioner access to a school campus.	School/district can hire counselors with training and experience in working with families and school counseling. School/district can contract or partner with local agencies that can work collaboratively with the school staff and support team.
Time management, other assigned non-counseling job responsibilities.	This is where the importance of administrator buy-in comes in. Ensuring administration and school governance understands the position, role, and responsibilities. Advocating for working with families, and explanation of the time investment. Be visible on campus in your work with families.
Billable services. This process does not involve the billing of services for remuneration and as a result is often not a focus by administration because it is not incurring a visible profit. This is a common way of thinking for administration or management, and it is frequently believed that the counselor time is better spent in other areas needed.	Review a cost benefit analysis related to assigned tasks. Another important aspect to introduce is the concept of increasing attendance which is connected to increased revenue for the school and district through Average Daily Attendance (ADA) monies. When working with families, attendance is usually increased and behavioral incidents decrease, providing an

	added value to the school that is directly observable and measurable.
Appropriate education and training level in multicultural counseling and understanding of family systems is needed.	School/district can hire counselors with training and experience in working with families and school counseling. Many more school counseling programs are integrating work with families and multicultural counseling into their degree offerings. Provide professional development at the school site.
Administrators may be reluctant to due to the fear of possible complicated family dynamics (child abuse, marital conflict, domestic violence, or underlying psychiatric issues). All of these issues can cause trauma in children.	Focus on trauma-informed practices in the schools and how counseling in the schools addresses this need. Focus on having an expert on campus who can intervene with complicated family dynamics, and provide appropriate screening, treatment, and referrals for more intensive services as needed.
Negative school climate.	Focusing on interventions that include morale-building within the school, faculty and staff. Focus on trauma-informed practices, positive school climate, student engagement, and implementing school-wide interventions. "Hurt people, hurt people."
Logistical issues (time, space, confidentiality, work times, working parents unable to come in during the day, etc.).	Allowing for flexible counselor schedules; not more time, just flexible hours. Examples of this may include weekend shifts, later start times to accommodate evening hours for seeing families, etc. This would also address space and confidentiality issues allowing for more private space to be available if this is an issue, and also help with accommodating parent work schedules.

Appendix A

SBFC Interview Procedure and Format

In implementing this SBFC Postvention procedural model, we have found that a critical component is the use of a structured interview format that provides a procedure for assessing the involvement and viewpoints of teachers, parents, and students and leads to structured interventions to be implemented by members of the school and family systems. Rather than asking the person to fill out a survey or questionnaire, we have found that a brief individual meeting using the SBFC Interview Form (below) is more effective in gaining participation from teachers and parents. This may be because they can provide more information verbally in a shorter period of time without having to write anything down. It also provides a direct interaction of a more personal nature where they have control over the specificity and confidentiality of information that they provide.

The interview format is used for two main purposes: to gather information about the respondent's view of the student and the problem, and as an initial step in the process of activating a collaborative team approach to addressing the problem. This leads to a decision tree of which interventions are most efficient for the SBFC to implement, depending on the degree of parental and teacher involvement for that particular case.

As soon as a child is referred because of academic or behavioral difficulties, the SBFC schedules a 5–10 minute meeting with the teacher or administrator who made the initial referral and then with the parent(s). In order to maximize participation, it is important to make the appointment at a time that is convenient for the respondent. The SBFC explains to the respondent that the purpose of the interview is to learn about their view of the student and the problem. The respondent is also informed that the same questions will be asked of others (e.g., parents, teachers, the student) and that this information will be used to set up a collaborative intervention between home and school to address the problem as comprehensively as possible. Again, the fostering of a sense of collaboration and of being a part of a team is critical to the success of this approach. The respondent is told that at the end of the interview, the information to be shared with others will be read back to them and if there is anything that they do not want to be included, it will be kept confidential. As mentioned above, the SBFC Interview Form can be used to record responses. The form includes space to record information about the student, respondent, scheduling process (number of telephone or direct contacts necessary to make the appointment, appointment attendance, etc.), date, and the responses to questions.

Interview Content

Exploration of Student Strengths   The respondent is first asked to comment on the student's *strengths*. This question is a critical initial step because it frames subsequent discussions within a balanced perspective of positive and challenging traits and behaviors. Helping participants to acknowledge positive aspects of the student is an important part of the process of addressing challenging behaviors. As described later, this balanced perspective also is important in reducing defensiveness on the part of parents and students. At times, it may be difficult for parents and teachers to come up with strengths, and the SBFC may need to help them define and explore these aspects. In addition, it is often necessary to reframe negative comments into positive ones. For example, a mother responded to a question about her child's strengths by saying, "Well, he's not a total slob." The SBFC then reframed this in terms of the student's ability to sometimes clean up after himself.

Exploration of Student Challenges The respondent is then asked to describe the student's challenges. These challenges are separated into challenges to the student, to those around him or her, and to the teacher or parent. Part of this discussion is to ascertain the respondent's view of how well the student is able to satisfy the three rules of kindergarten discussed earlier. While these may seem to be more applicable to the school setting, they are in fact important parts of the student's functioning in home and social environments as well.

Exploration of Previously Attempted Interventions In order to prevent redundancy and to communicate respect, the respondent is then asked to describe what attempts, if any, they have made to address the above challenges. These responses are separated into what has seemed to work and what has not seemed to work. The respondent also is asked if they know of any specific obstacles that may have hindered these interventions.

Exploration of Underlying Causes The respondent is then asked to comment on what they think might be underlying factors of the problem behavior. This information typically involves discussion of feelings, situational variables, current stressors, and other aspects that may be critical to developing strategies that address the most important issues involved in the behavior.

Interview Process One of the most important aspects of the SBFC Interview format is the *process* of how the interview is conducted. While the information obtained through the questions is vital, the process of developing a collaborative relationship between parents and teachers may be more important to the overall success of the intervention. In order to begin this process, the interviewer actively searches for any similarities in the views of the current respondent (e.g., the parent) and previous respondents (e.g., teachers), particularly in the area of student strengths. If any exist and confidentiality is not violated, the interviewer then shares this information with the respondent about the specific similarities between their responses and those of others.

For example, after a parent commented on his child's strength of keeping his room clean, the SBFC shared the teacher's comment of how well the student kept his desk organized. When the parent described his child's challenge of sitting still in church, the SBFC shared that the teacher also had mentioned that the student had some difficulty remaining in his seat during story time. This feedback showed the parent that he and the teacher shared some similar views of the child's strengths and challenges. When these interactions occur, they can have a profound effect on reducing parents' defensiveness while increasing their willingness to work together with the school to improve student success. This process is more complex than it appears, and requires the interviewer to be sufficiently competent in the active listening and reflection skills necessary to be an effective SBFC.

This interview process is conducted with as many of the important players in the child's school and family systems as possible. It is preferable for the SBFC to meet directly with these individuals, but if this is not possible, then telephone interviews can be conducted. If the SBFC is unable to obtain participation from the parents or teachers, it is critical to document all of the attempts made to contact them, any appointments made and missed, or other information about the process. While the SBFC practitioner may then be forced to work only with the teacher (or parent) and student (if old enough), the interview format can still be very useful in promoting their mutual understanding of the problem and development of effective strategies. In this scenario, the SBFC practitioner serves as both a facilitator and a motivator of the student (in place of the teacher or parent). If both the teacher and parent are resistant to participating, then the SBFC practitioner must work with the student either individually or within a group setting. The information obtained in the interview, however, will still be an important part of an efficient individual or group intervention process because it establishes a collaborative working relationship between the student and SBFC practitioner. This collaboration is critical to the success of most individual and group counseling interventions. The above process and resultant data enhances the decisions regarding the types of interventions that will be used to address the student's difficulties. While it is most effective and therefore most efficient for the SBFC practitioner to work with participants from both family and school systems, if this is not possible, the data from the SBFC Interview Form can be used to document attempts and obstacles to obtaining maximum participation.

SBFC INTERVIEW FORM

Student: _____Date: _____ Time:_____

Parent:_____Teacher(s): _____

Grade: _____ Referral Source: _____

School Support Personnel: _____

Administrator:_____

Wrote to _____Called _____Scheduled appt. When:_____attended appointment

If not, reason: _____

Attempts to contact: _____

	Strengths	Challenges	Ability to use three rules of kindergarten	Interventions tried Comments Underlying causes Previous parental contact
Teacher				
Parent/ Student				

Further Comments: _____

_____

CLASSROOM

Behavior	Strategy
	Outcomes

FAMILY

Behavior	Strategy
	Outcomes

Appendix B

Objective Discipline Procedure for Noncompliance (with Grounding)

M. J. Carter

When: When your child has not obeyed a reasonable request that you have made and it is necessary that she comply.

***Remember, only give a demand when you are prepared to follow it through to the end, whatever the consequences might be!

How:
DEMAND – Clearly and simply tell the child what you want him to do.
Example: "Name, you need to pick up your clothes and put them in the basket right now."
          Silently, count to three (1-2-3).

—If the child obeys the demand, then Give Positive Attention immediately!

***Remember when Giving Positive Attention, tell the child that you see what they're doing that's positive. Say, "I see that you're following directions. That's helpful" (or whatever positive behavior it is – e.g., keeping hands and feet to self, being respectful, etc.). Say it in a positive manner that shows how important their positive behavior is. Be sure to SHOW that you're pleased; words mean nothing without your expressions.

—If the child does not obey the demand, then: PROMPT!

PROMPT: Repeat the initial DEMAND and state the consequences if the child does not obey.

Example: "IF you don't pick up your clothes and put them in the basket right now, then you're going to have a 'BREAK'."

(NOTE: Be sure to start the Prompt with the word "IF" and put emphasis on both the specific DEMAND and the consequence for not following directions.)

Silently count to three (1-2-3).

—If the child obeys the prompt, then Give Positive Attention immediately!
—If the child does not obey the prompt, then:

Follow through with negative consequences!

Following through with negative consequences: – In as unemotional a manner as possible, follow through with the consequences (e.g., send the child to a BREAK) while making clear to the child why she is getting consequences. Begin by telling the child why she is getting the BREAK and use the word "BECAUSE" first.

Example: "BECAUSE you did not follow directions, you have to go take a BREAK."

—Once the child is sitting in the BREAK area, set the timer for five minutes and completely ignore the child for the entire BREAK period, as long as the child does not get up or move the chair or talk loudly or become a danger to self.

If the child does not GO take a BREAK, say:

"IF you do not go take a BREAK right now, then you'll have two BREAKS."

If the child does not go to the BREAK, say:

"BECAUSE you have not taken a BREAK, you have two BREAKS. IF you do not go to BREAK right now, then you will be grounded off of everything until you serve the 2 BREAKS plus 30 minutes. You will be grounded starting right now, but your 30 minutes to get off of grounding will not start until after you have served the two BREAKS."

If the child does not go take a BREAK, then begin their grounding immediately, with a reminder of the above. (Note: Remember, the child does not have to sit in the chair during grounding, but has no privileges – electronics, favorite foods, or play with others).

When the child goes to take the BREAK, set the timer for one BREAK.

When that is finished, say to the child:

"That's your first BREAK. But because you did not go take a BREAK, here is your second BREAK."

If the child violates the boundaries of the BREAK

(i.e., butt on the chair, the chair doesn't move and no loud talking),

then tell the child that the BREAK will start over and RESET the timer.

If the child refuses to return to the BREAK, then say:

"IF you do not go and take the BREAK right now, then you will be grounded off of everything until you serve the 2 BREAKs plus 30 minutes. You will be grounded starting right now, but your 30 minutes will not start until after you have served the two BREAKS."

NOTE: Remember that you must not interact with the child while she is in BREAK.

You only speak to the child to give directions.

When the break period is over, tell the child ONCE why they had to take a BREAK.

(Do not require the child to answer questions or agree with you – this will probably just lead to a power struggle.)

Then direct the child to:

A) If the situation permits, return the child to the original situation and require them to obey the original DEMAND.

—If the child obeys the demand, then Give Positive Attention immediately!

—If the child does not obey the demand, then PROMPT and FOLLOW THROUGH WITH THE CONSEQUENCES,if necessary, WITHOUT DELAY!

NOTE: Of course, you don't require the child to repeat a negative behavior such as hitting again.

B) If the situation does not permit you to return to the original situation, then repeat to the child the consequences for not following directions.

"Remember, if you don't follow directions (or whatever the demand was), then you are going to have to go to BREAK. If you do not go to BREAK, then you will have two BREAKS."

Then, if the child has earned grounding, set the timer for 30 minutes to finish the grounding. If the child earns another BREAK during this time, then the timer is stopped until they have finished the BREAK and then it is restarted.

***After this whole procedure is finished, write down what happened and the results, and then try to create situations in which the child can earn positive attention for appropriate behavior, especially those that include a lot of interaction with you – IF you're emotionally ready for giving positives.

What the child can do next time Also be sure to create time when you can talk to the child about her choosing to refuse to follow directions (or whatever behavior resulted in the BREAK) and discuss what other choices were available that would not have resulted in negative consequences (e.g., complying with your demand and then talking about it, etc.). Essentially, what can they do next time to avoid having to take a BREAK.

*****Remember, Consistency** is the most important factor of this procedure – CONSISTENCY in ALL three steps of the OBJECTIVE DISCIPLINE PROCEDURE, and just as importantly, CONSISTENCY in GIVING POSITIVE ATTENTION FOR APPROPRIATE BEHAVIOR!

LEVELS OF LEVERAGE – (to be used whenever the child refuses to go to or remain in a BREAK):

*****Remember to use the Prompt-Consequence statements with IF and BECAUSE at the beginning of each one.

Level 1. CONSEQUENCE: Another BREAK_____

Level 2. CONSEQUENCE: Immediate grounding off of all privileges (i.e., electronics, games, favorite foods, activities outside the home unless required, etc.) until the child serves the 2 BREAKS PLUS 30 minutes, with the 30 minutes beginning after the two BREAKS are completed.

Level 3. CONSEQUENCE: _____

Copyright 1979 M. J. Carter

Bibliography

Burr, W. R. (1970). Satisfaction for the various aspects of marriage over the life cycle: A random middle class sample. *Journal of Marriage and Family*, *32*(1), 29–37.

Carter, M. (1979). Objective discipline procedure for noncompliance (with grounding). In Gerrard, B. & Soriano, M. (Eds.), *School-based family counseling: Transforming family-school relationships* (pp. 195–198). Phoenix, AZ: Createspace.

Carter, M. J. & Evans, W. P. (2008). Implementing school-based family counseling: Strategies, activities, and process considerations. *International Journal for School-Based Family Counseling*, *1*(1), 1–21.

Compas, B. E., Adelman, H. S., Freundl, P. C., Nelson, P., & Taylor, L. (1982). Parental and child causal attributions during clinical interviews. *Journal of Abnormal Child Psychology*, *10*(1), 77–83.

Fraser, M. W. (2004). *Risk and resilience in childhood: An ecological perspective*. Washington, DC: NASW Press.

Glied, S. & Cuellar, A. E. (2003). Trends and issues in child and adolescent mental health. *Health Affairs*, *22*, 5.

Karpel, M. & Strauss, E. (1983). *Family evaluation* (Chapter 2, pp. 49–77). New York, NY: Gardner Press.

Manning, K. (2018). Personal communication. Positive methods of discipline and redirection.

McGoldrick, M. & Gerson, R. (1988). Genograms and the family life cycle. In Carter, E. A. & McGoldrick, M. (Eds.), *The expanded family life cycle: Individual, family, and social perspectives* (3rd Edition) (pp. 164–189). Boston, MA: Allyn and Bacon.

Minuchin, S. & Fishman, H. (1981). *Family therapy techniques*. Cambridge, MA: Harvard University Press.

Whitaker, C. A. & Keith, D. V. (1981). Symbolic-experiential family therapy. In Gurman, A. S. & Kniskern, D. P. (Eds.), *Handbook of family therapy* (pp. 187–225). New York: Brunner/Mazel.

4 Family Intervention
How to Do Family Counseling with Individuals

Brian A. Gerrard

Overview: This chapter describes how to help an individual client relate more effectively with other family members through the use of CBT techniques applied within a family systems framework.

Background

Family Counseling with Individuals (FCI) is an approach to family counseling that uses family systems theory to guide the counselor in working with an individual client who wishes to improve a relationship with another person, such as a family member, teacher, or peer. It is a mistake to think of family counseling as solely conjoint family counseling, where the counselor works with two or more family members at the same time. Conjoint family counseling is the classic form of family counseling as demonstrated in videos by many of the family counseling pioneers such as Salvadore Minuchin, Virginia Satir, Carl Whitaker, and Jay Haley. However, there is also a long family counseling tradition of working with individuals to effect family change, as exemplified by the work of Murray Bowen, Behavioral Family Therapists (e.g. Patterson) using parent consultation/behavior modification approaches, and by Strategic Family Therapists such as John Weakland, Paul Watzlawick, and Richard Fisch who emphasized that significant family change could result from effective work with a motivated family member (the "customer"):

> Consistent with that interactional view, we assume that alteration of the behavior of one member of an interactional unit – a family or some other group – can influence the behavior of other members of that unit.
> (Fisch, Weakland, & Segal, 1982, p.36)

What makes the counseling approach a family counseling approach is not the number of persons in the room with you, but whether you are using a family systems approach to guide your interventions. You can be effective doing family counseling with an individual, but you must know where to make your interventions.

Since there are many situations in SBFC in which only one person may be available for counseling, it is important to know how to do FCI. Common examples are: 1) a child is available for counseling, but the parents/guardians are unable or unwilling to participate; 2) one parent/guardian is available, but the child and other family members are not willing or able to participate; 3) the family will not give consent for counseling, but the teacher is willing to work with you to help improve a classroom situation involving the child. In each of these examples the "customer" or primary client is an individual: a child, a parent/guardian, or a teacher, but the target of change will be a relationship.

A Cautionary Note: Because working conjointly with multiple family members is generally more difficult than working with just one client, counselors who are inexperienced in doing conjoint family counseling or who are strongly introverted may prefer the "ease" of working with just one child or adult. My recommendation is that you should always make every effort to collaborate with significantly involved family members and not rely exclusively on counseling an individual. If the child's problem is related to a conflict between parents, you should be aware of the research that indicates that when there is a couple problem, counseling only one partner has a deterioration rate twice (14%) that of conjoint counseling (7%) (Gurman & Kniskern, 1978). It is likely that seeing only one partner promotes triangulation (coalitions of two against one) – if only in the mind of the absent partner. If the counselor is young and inexperienced, she or he may experience a strong preference to work alone with the child rather than deal with a "difficult" parent (who may remind the counselor of their own "difficult" parent). The problem with doing this type of counseling which I call "Parent Replacement Counseling" is that the counselor takes on the role of "Good Parent" to the child rather than helping the actual parent to become a better parent. Counselors who feel the urge to do "Parent Replacement Counseling" need to be courageous and act in the best interests of the child by helping the child and the parent to improve their relationship.

There are many different individual counseling techniques that can be used in doing FCI. In the remainder of this chapter the ways in which the following six CBT (cognitive-behavioral therapy) techniques can promote family systems change will be described:

- Behavioral Relationship Assessment
- Systematic Muscle Relaxation
- Desensitization
- Cognitive Restructuring
- Problem-solving (Decision Grid)
- Behavior Rehearsal

A useful way to think about these techniques is in terms of a developmental model that describes three basic stages to counseling:

Stage 1 – Preparing for Change
Stage 2 – Changing Cognitions
Stage 3 – Changing Behavior

Stage 1– Preparing for Change is the initial phase of counseling that typically occurs in the first session (although it may last many sessions if it takes more time for the client to develop trust for the counselor). During Stage 1 the counselor explores the client's concerns using empathy, warmth and respect, as well as questions (such as Lazarus's Multimodal Assessment). Behavioral Relationship Assessment is typically used during this phase. During this stage the counselor must earn the trust of the client and obtain sufficiently detailed information about the client's problem in order to make a family systems diagnosis.

Stage 2 – Changing Cognitions is the stage in which the counselor uses techniques that decrease stress by interrupting or replacing negative thoughts. The goal of the CBT techniques used in this stage is to shift the client's thoughts from ones like: "This is terrible; I'm a worthless person; I can't cope" to more constructive thoughts such as: "I can cope with this; I have worth; It's distressing but not dangerous." The techniques typically used in this stage are more cognitive in focus.

Stage 3 – Changing Action is the stage in which the client is encouraged to take action in improving their relationship. This stage involves having the client interact differently with a family member or other person. The techniques typically used in this stage are behavioral.

The CBT techniques described above fit into the Stage model as shown in Table 4.1

Evidence-Based Support

The CBT techniques have extensive evidence-based support and this will be referenced as each technique is presented.

Table 4.1 Relationship Between Counseling Stages and CBT Techniques

Stage 1 *Preparing for Change*	*Stage 2* *Changing Cognition*	*Stage 3* *Changing Behavior*
Behavioral Relationship Assessment	Systematic Muscle Relaxation Desensitization Cognitive Restructuring	Problem-solving Behavior Rehearsal

Procedure

To do FCI, generally follow these steps:

Step 1: Establish Stage 1 rapport with the client by using empathy, warmth, and respect. Build client trust by showing you understand the client's concerns. Obtain a detailed history of the client's problem and strengths.

Step 2: Conduct a Family Systems Assessment of the client's relationships with significant others (such as family members or friends) focusing especially on those relationships that seem linked to the client's symptoms.

Step 3: Conduct a Behavioral Relationship Assessment to determine the interpersonal behaviors (Troublesome Social Stimuli) that are most distressing to the client and which seem to block assertive action to improve the relationship.

Step 4: Identify a Relationship Change Goal acceptable to the client.

Step 5: Formulate a Treatment Plan that will help the client achieve the relationship change goal.

Step 6: Implement the Stage 2 stress reduction techniques. Have the client practice them in the counseling session, then try them out as a "homework" assignment.

Step 7: Implement the Stage 3 techniques of Problem-solving (Decision Grid) and Behavior Rehearsal when the client is ready to contemplate taking action to modify the relationship.

Step 8: Address any Additional Relationship Change Goals (as needed). As your client becomes less stressed and more assertive, review with your client whether there are additional relationship goals they would like to attain. Repeat Steps 5–7 as needed with the new goals.

Step 9: Prepare Client for Termination. An effective way to do this is to discuss termination before the session in which it actually occurs and by offering the client a follow-up session after a suitable interval so that the SBFC practitioner and client can ensure the positive changes are being maintained.

Important Point: Since there is evidence-based support for the Stage 2 (Systematic Muscle Relaxation, Desensitization, and Cognitive Restructuring) and Stage 3 (Problem-solving and Behavior Rehearsal) CBT techniques being effective when used on their own or as the primary intervention, you may wish to use them separately. However, they can also be used in concert with each other as described above. At the end of this chapter is a case study illustrating the nine-step procedure for implementing FCI.

Each of these CBT techniques will be described using the following structured format: Definition, Background, Evidence-Based Support, Procedure, Challenges and Solutions, Resources.

CBT Technique #1: Behavioral Relationship Assessment

Definition

Behavioral Relationship Assessment when working with an individual involves asking the client for specific examples of behaviors that occur between the client and the Significant Other (i.e., the person your client is in a relationship with). Troublesome Social Stimuli analysis involves asking clients to give detailed behavioral examples of their responses to seven common "troublesome" behaviors demonstrated by the Significant Other.

Background

This approach to the behavioral assessment of relationships is based on the social interactional model developed by Christensen (Christensen & Pass, 1983). It assesses for sources of client interpersonal stress called Troublesome Social Stimuli (TSS). According to Christensen most relationship stress is caused by specific behavioral triggers or TSS. The TSS Model is shown in Figure 4.1. The seven most common TSS are shown in Table 4.2.

It is important to note that the TSS is a behavior engaged in by your client's Other Person (who may be a family member, teacher, student, or any other person with whom your client is having difficulty). The seven common TSS may not all be troublesome for them. The purpose of conducting a TSS assessment is to determine which of these common interpersonal stressors are, in fact, a challenge for your client. If a TSS is troublesome your client will likely show one or more of the following responses shown in Table 4.3. Also shown in Table 4.4 are responses that indicate that the "TSS" is not, in fact, troublesome for your client.

The fundamental difference between the Tolerate responses and the responses indicating that the TSS is troublesome is that the Tolerate responses are characterized by your client being relatively calm and free to

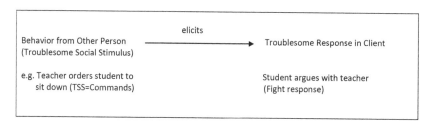

Figure 4.1 The TSS Model

Table 4.2 Seven Common Troublesome Social Stimuli (TSS)

TSS	Description from Client's Point of View
Commands	Other person gives order or strong request to client
Anger	Other person speaks to client in angry tone, yells, or gives angry look
Criticism	Other person criticizes client, points out client's mistake
Depression/Sadness	Other person is sad or depressed in presence of client
Unresponsiveness	Other person makes no response to comment or presence of client
Impulsivity	Other person acts odd or irrational in client's presence
Affection	Other person expresses warmth, caring for client

Table 4.3 Common Responses to a TSS Indicating the TSS is Troublesome

Response	Description
Tense	Client's muscles tense up Client may be silent A "freeze" response
Leave	Client removes himself/herself from the presence of the other person A "flight" response
Change	Client tries to get other person to stop engaging in the TSS through deflecting responses such as pleading, apologizing, denying, joking
Change-Fight	A change response where the client criticizes or becomes aggressive towards the other person A "fight" response

Table 4.4 Common Responses to a TSS Indicating that the TSS is **not** Troublesome

Response	Description
Tolerate	Client is able to tolerate the TSS Client does not show a Tense, Leave, or Change response
Tolerate sub-category:	
Assertive	Client chooses to make an assertive response
Ignore	Client chooses to ignore the TSS
Positive	Client chooses to respond with warmth or empathy

choose their response. The troublesome responses are compulsive and reflex-like for your clients, who may be aware that they are not responding in a way they like. Diagnosis involves systematically asking your clients about their responses to specific TSS with the Other Person. The TSS

Box 4.1 Relationship Assessment Form for Troublesome Social Stimuli

Client:_____ **Relationship with:**_____

Troublesome Social Stimuli	Stimulus	Response	Classification of Your Response
For each of the following TSS identify a recent, typical incident in which the other person demonstrated the TSS	How did the other person display the TSS? What did they say? do? What was their voice tone? facial expression?	What did you say/do in response? What was your voice tone? Did you feel tension? Breathing affected?	Troublesome: *Tense (T) Fight (F) Leave(L) Change(C)* Tolerating: *Assertive (A) Calm (C) Ignore (I) Positive (P)*
Commands			Troublesome: __Tense __ Fight __ Leave __ Change _ Tolerating: __ Assertive __ Calm __ Ignore __ Positive
Criticism			Troublesome: __Tense __ Fight __ Leave __ Change Tolerating: __ Assertive __ Calm __ Ignore __ Positive
Anger			Troublesome: __Tense __ Fight __ Leave __ Change Tolerating: __ Assertive __ Calm __ Ignore __ Positive
Depression/ Sadness			Troublesome: __Tense __ Fight __ Leave __ Change

	Tolerating:
	__ Assertive
	__ Calm
	__ Ignore
	__ Positive
Unresponsive-ness	Troublesome:
	__Tense
	__ Fight
	__ Leave
	__ Change
	Tolerating:
	__ Assertive
	__ Calm
	__ Ignore
	__ Positive
Impulsivity	Troublesome:
	__Tense
	__ Fight
	__ Leave
	__ Change
	Tolerating:
	__ Assertive
	__ Calm
	__ Ignore
	__ Positive
Affection	Troublesome:
	__Tense
	__ Fight
	__ Leave
	__ Change
	Tolerating:
	__ Assertive
	__ Calm
	__ Ignore
	__ Positive

Relationship Assessment Form shown as Box 4.1 may be used to collect this information.

What is important to note about unbalanced and extreme relationships on the Circumplex Model is that they are characterized by TSS that family members respond to by fighting, getting tense, and avoiding each other. That is, relationships that are unbalanced are characterized by aversive social stimuli. By identifying the TSS operating within a specific relationship, the SBFC practitioner can select a CBT technique that helps the family member on the receiving end of the TSS to cope more effectively with it and thus potentially transform the relationship to a more balanced type.

Summary: The strengths of using a relationship assessment of troublesome social stimuli are:

- In the absence of being able to actually view directly interaction between the client and the Other Person, focusing on the client's report of behaviors is helpful in reconstructing an interaction pattern.
- This is both a Stage 1 assessment approach and a Stage 2 insight producing technique because it helps clients to look at their relationships in a new way.
- The TSS model is easily taught to clients.
- The TSS assessment questions are straightforward and easily mastered by practitioners.
- The identification of client response patterns to TSS help motivate clients to change.
- By getting clients to focus on the trigger behaviors demonstrated by the other person, and then teaching the client new and effective ways to respond differently to the TSS, change in a relationship can be quickly introduced.

Evidence-Based Support

The reliability and validity of client self-report based on the counseling interview alone is a challenge. However, because this assessment technique is based on accounts of behavior – which is observable and tends to be concrete – it is more likely to be reliable. The SBFC practitioner can evaluate the reliability and validity of this type of behavioral assessment by: a) over several sessions looking for similar TSS from the Other Person and b) checking for consistency in the Other Person's stimulus behaviors and consistency in the client's response. For example, does the client consistently make a Tense response to different TSS of Criticism from the Other Person?

Procedure

When collecting this behavioral assessment information, follow these steps:

Step 1. Teach Your Client about TSS and Common Responses to Them

"There is a useful way to look at the things people do that cause us stress. It's called a Troublesome Social Stimulus Analysis. May I tell you about it?"
"A Troublesome Social Stimulus is_____."
"There are seven common TSS. They are_____."
When interviewing a younger client, the term "troublesome behavior" should be substituted for "troublesome social stimuli."

Step 2. Invite Your Client to Do a TSS Assessment of Their Relationship with the Other Person

"I would like to recommend that we look at your relationship with _____ (name of other person) in terms of the TSS that may be affecting you. Doing this will help me understand better what is happening between you and _____(name of other person). Clients also tell me that doing this helps them to see more clearly what the other person's behaviors are that cause problems. Would it be alright with you if we did this together?"

Step 3. Select the First TSS and Ask for a Recent, Specific, Typical Example of the TSS

Give your client a copy of the Relationship Assessment Form for Troublesome Social Stimuli (Box 4.1).

"Here is a copy for your use of the form I am going to use to record information about your TSS."

"I am going to use this form to write down some information about your TSS and your responses to them so that later you and I can look at it together and see if there is any pattern."

There are two main ways to use the Relationship Assessment Form for Troublesome Social Stimuli:

1. Ask your client for an example for each of the seven TSS with the Other Person. This approach is thorough and should be used if you are uncertain as to which TSS are the main ones for your client.
2. Ask your client to select the three TSS that the client is most concerned about and collect data on these. This approach can be used if the TSS affecting your client are obvious.

Begin by asking the client to pick the TSS that affects them the most.

"Which TSS with _____(name of other person, e.g. your father) bothers you the most?"

"Can you tell me about a recent time (Other Person) gave you a (mention TSS, e.g. Command)."

If your client gives a general example, ask if they can identify a specific incident in which the Other Person emitted the TSS behavior. Remember that the TSS behavior is always that of the Other Person, not your client. Use the behavioral assessment questions listed on the form to guide your inquiry. Make brief notes on the form to record your client's responses. Ask detailed questions about the verbal and non-verbal behavior of the Other Person.

"What exactly did he say to you?"

"What did he do?"

"What did his voice tone sound like (e.g. stern, calm, etc.)?"

"What did his face look like?"

Make brief notes of your client's descriptions.

Step 4. Ask Your Client How They Responded to the TSS

Use the behavioral assessment questions provided on the form. Be aware that the client's response may be classified in more than one category, e.g. "I tensed up, then left the room." Check to see if your client had any urges as these can indicate a response tendency. You can also assess the strength of your client's Tense responses on a 1 to 10 scale (10 = very high tension).

"When (Other Person) gave you a (e.g. Command), what did you do?"

"What did you say?"

"What did your voice sound like?"

"Did you feel tension in your body anywhere?"

"Did you have an urge to do anything?"

Ask your client to classify their response using the response categories on the form.

"Have a look at the different types of responses listed in the last column of your form. Which of these do you think fit your response?"

Step 5. Collect Information on the Next TSS and Continue with Steps 3 and 4 Until the Assessment is Complete

Step 6. Ask Your Client to Look at the TSS Assessment Form with You and Tell You If They See Any Pattern

Common patterns are a similar stress response across TSS, e.g. your client responds with a Tense response to each TSS or a unique response to one TSS, e.g. a tense response to Commands and Anger, but a Fight response to Criticism.

"Let's have a look now at the notes I wrote on the form." (Show your form to the client.)

"Do you see any pattern here?" (Wait for client to respond.)

If the client doesn't see a pattern, but you do, or the client sees a pattern but you also see an additional pattern, share your observations with the client. Always ask your client's view of your interpretation.

"What I notice is that although you get tense every time your mother criticizes you, you also show some assertiveness and try to explain yourself. What do you think?"

Step 7: Motivate the Client to Change

Point out to the client that there are some things you and the client can do to help improve the client's relationship with (Other Person).

"Can you imagine what your life would be like if whenever (Other Person) gave you a command or criticized you, instead of getting very tense, you remained relatively calm?"

If the client indicates that this would be a good thing, say:

"There are some things we could do in counseling that would help you to respond differently to your TSS with (Other Person). Would you like me to tell you about them?"

The Example of Kim

A TSS Relationship Analysis for Kim, age 14 (see Case Study below), revealed the following TSS and response patterns for key persons in her life (Table 4.5).

Goal-Setting and Intervention Plan

In Christensen's social interactional approach to counseling (called Interpersonal Coping Skills) the counseling goal for Kim would be to determine if she would like to learn to tolerate the TSS from Mother in order to be able to choose a different set of responses: for example, to be able to make requests of Mother in a way that is assertive but does not provoke upset from Mother; to be able to communicate more effectively with her mother in order to develop a closer relationship with her; and to be able to not feel tense when Kim's mother criticizes her or gives her a command. The CBT counseling techniques most typically used to promote these changes are: Desensitization to the TSS, Cognitive Restructuring to replace catastrophic thoughts triggered by the TSS, and Assertiveness Training and Behavior Rehearsal to build more effective communication skills.

Challenges and Solutions

When using this technique with younger children, use terms such as Troublesome Behavior instead of Troublesome Social Stimuli. The TSS assessment model can also be used as a conceptual model by the SBFC practitioner. For example, when a client describes a problem with another person that is causing the client a lot of stress, the Other Person's triggering behavior is invariably a TSS. By teaching the client to cope with that TSS the SBFC practitioner can introduce rapid positive change into the relationship.

Table 4.5 Summary of Kim's TSS and Responses

Other Person	TSS from this Person	Kim's Typical Response
Mother	Commands (about Kim not going to the mall)	Tense (10/10)
	Criticism (about Kim's messy room)	Leave, Tense (8/10)
Father	Unresponsiveness	Tense (9/10)

Resources

Christensen, C. & Pass, L. (1983). *The social interactional approach to counselling/psychotherapy.* Monograph Series 16, The Ontario Institute for Studies in Education, Toronto, ON: OISE Press.

CBT Technique #2: Systematic Muscle Relaxation

Definition

Systematic Muscle Relaxation (SMR), also known as Progressive Relaxation, is a stress-reduction technique that works by having the client systematically tense and relax the different muscle groups, one at a time over a period of about 20 minutes. For example, the client begins by tensing and relaxing the hands, then arms, shoulders, head and face, stomach, legs, and finally feet.

Background

This technique was first developed by Jacobson (1929) and subsequently used by Wolpe as a key ingredient in Desensitization (Wolpe, 1961). This technique induces a deep state of relaxation. As the muscles begin to relax the client experiences a decrease in anxious thoughts that induce stress. The decrease in anxious thoughts likely occurs because SMR is a distraction technique (the client is asked to focus only on following the SMR instructions) and because as the muscles begin to relax the client experiences more positive, coping thoughts ("I am relaxed" vs. "This is terrible").

Evidence-Based Support

There have been extensive studies demonstrating SMR's effectiveness. Some examples are shown in Box 4.2.

Procedure

Follow these steps to implement SMR.

Step 1: Review with the client their stress pattern

Determine their motivation to change (use 1–10 rating scale).
"Your troublesome social stimuli seem to be_____."
"Whenever your family member does_____, you tend to respond by_____."
"On a scale from 1 to 10 with 10 as very high, how stressed do you get when your family member does this?"
"How long do you experience the stress?"

> ## Box 4.2 Evidence-Based Support for Systematic Muscle Relaxation
>
> Brootha, A. & Dhir, R. (1990). Efficacy of two relaxation techniques in depression. *Journal of Personality and Clinical Studies*, 6, 83–90.
>
> Carlson, C. & Hoyle, R. (1993). Efficacy of abbreviated progressive muscle relaxation training: A quantitative review of behavioral medicine research. *Journal of Consulting and Clinical Psychology*, 61, 1059–1067.
>
> Egbochuku, E. O. & Obodo, B. O. (2005). Effects of systematic desensitization (SD) therapy on the reduction of test anxiety among adolescents in Nigerian schools. *Journal of Instructional Psychology*, 32 (4), 298–306.
>
> Kahana, S. & Feeny, N. (2005). Cognitive behavioral treatment of health-related anxiety in youth: a case example. *Cognitive and Behavioral Practice*, 12, 290–300.
>
> Lopata, C. (2003). Progressive muscle relaxation and aggression among elementary students with emotional or behavioral disorders. *Behavioral Disorders*, 28, 162–172.
>
> Margolis, H. & Pica, L. (1990). The effects of audiotaped progressive muscle relaxation training on the reading performance of emotionally disturbed adolescents. *ERIC Reports* ED331032, 16pp.
>
> Omizo, M. (1986). The effects of biofeedback and relaxation training on memory tasks among hyperactive boys. *Exceptional Child*, 33, 56–64.
>
> Rasid, Z. & Parish, T. (1998). The effects of two types of relaxation training on students' levels of anxiety. *Adolescence*, 33, 99–101.
>
> Roome, J. & Romney, D. (1985). Reducing anxiety in gifted children by inducing relaxation. *Roeper Review*, 7, 177–179.
>
> Singer, G. (1988). Stress management training for parents of children with severe handicaps. *Mental Retardation*, 26, 269–277.
>
> Walton, W. (1979). The use of a relaxation curriculum and biofeedback training in the classroom to reduce inappropriate behaviors of emotionally handicapped children. *Behavioral Disorders*, 5, 10–18.

"It sounds like this stress is having a strong effect on you."
"On a 1 to 10 scale (10 means you really want to change) how much do you want to change this pattern of you getting so stressed?"

Step 2: Describe SMR to the client and invite them to try it

"Can you imagine what your life would be like if you didn't get so stressed when your family member_____?"
"I have an exercise I can show you that would help you to lower your stress significantly. Would you like to hear about it?"
"It's called Systematic Muscle Relaxation. It works by having you tense and relax each of your muscle groups one at a time. I would start by having you

tense, then relax, your hands, then your arms, then your head, and so forth ending with your feet."

"Clients report that when they do this exercise it is very effective in reducing their stress and that it can produce a deep state of relaxation."

"It might be helpful to you in reducing your stress when your family member_____ (mention TSS) or when you know you are shortly going to be meeting your family member and you begin to get tense just thinking about it."

"Would you like to try it?"

Step 3: Implement SMR

"Do you have any sore muscles or injuries that we would have to be careful about?"

"I'd like you get relaxed in your chair and keep your eyes open or closed – whichever you prefer."

1. "Now I'd like you to take your right arm and stretch it out in front of you. Now holding your palm out with your fingers raised, I'd like you to bend your hand back at the wrist like this (SBFC practitioner should demonstrate). Now feel the tension in your hand for 1...2...3...4... seconds and now slowly relax your hand and arm. Feel the relaxation spreading through your hand."
2. Repeat #1.
3. "Now I'd like you to take your left arm and stretch it out in front of you. Now holding your palm out with your fingers raised, I'd like you to bend your hand back at the wrist like this (practitioner should demonstrate). Now feel the tension in your hand for 1...2...3...4... seconds and now slowly relax your hand and arm. Feel the relaxation spreading through your hand."
4. Repeat #3.
5. "Now I'd like you to bring your right arm up to your shoulder and make a fist. Make a tight fist and hold it...hold it...hold it... now let it go. Let your arm relax and slowly lower it to a comfortable resting position."
6. Repeat #5.
7. "Now I'd like you to bring your left arm up to your shoulder and make a fist. Make a tight fist and hold it...hold it...hold it... now let it go. Let your arm relax and slowly lower it to a comfortable resting position."
8. Repeat #7.
9. "Now I want you to imagine you are a turtle and raise your shoulders up as if to touch your ears as you pull your head into your shell. Now hold the tension...hold it.... Now relax.... Let your shoulders relax to a comfortable position."

10. Repeat #9.
11. "Now I want you to close your eyes really tight and purse your lips together really tight and hold it for four seconds ...1...2...3....4.... Now relax your face. Let your eyes and mouth just relax."
12. Repeat #11. "Just feel the relaxation spreading through your face and shoulders as you become more and more relaxed."
13. "Now I would like you to take a deep breath and hold it for four seconds ...1...2...3...4.... Now let it out slowly to a count of four ... 1...2...3...4. Now take another deep breath and hold it for 1...2... 3...4... and now let it out slowly ...1...2...3...4. For the next minute I want you to continue breathing slowly and deeply as you feel your chest muscles relax ...... as you slowly breathe in and out."
14. "Now I want you to press your knees and thighs together. Feel the tension and hold it...hold it...hold it... now let it go. Let your thighs relax."
15. Repeat #14.
16. "Now I want you to stretch your legs out in front of you and point your toes straight ahead so that you feel the tension spreading through your foot. Hold it...hold it...hold it... and now let it go."
17. Repeat #16.
18. "Now I want you to stretch your legs out in front of you and bend your feet backwards so that your toes point towards the ceiling. Hold the tension...hold it... and now let it go. Slowly let your feet relax and return to a resting position."
19. Repeat #18.
20. "Now I am going to remain silent for two minutes while you focus on relaxing your muscles. If you feel tension anywhere just focus on the area and let your muscles relax as you continue to breathe slowly and deeply".

Note: for a shorter version of this exercise you can omit the repetitions or focus on an area where the client experiences the most tension, e.g. the head and shoulders. You can also emphasize to the client that as they become more proficient at SMR they can induce a state of relaxation by tensing up multiple muscle groups at once and then letting them relax.

Step 4: Debrief the Exercise

"How was that?"
"On a scale of 1 to 10 how relaxed are you right now?"
"On the scale how relaxed were you when we began the exercise?"
"What part of the exercise gave you the most relaxation?"
"Were there any parts that were difficult to do?"

Step 5: Discuss Homework Application

"Do you think this exercise might be helpful to you in lowering your stress in dealing with_____?"

"How could you use it?"

"Would you be willing to try this out once during the next week?"

"If you used this with_____when would you use it? Before talking with them or after meeting with them?"

"I look forward to hearing how it goes."

Challenges and Solutions

When using this technique with very young children, you can make it more engaging by inviting the child to imagine they are an animal at different points.

"Now I want you to imagine you are a cat and you are going to stretch out your paw like this."

This is illustrated above in Step 3.9 (turtle example). This technique can be implemented by the SBFC practitioner reading the SMR (Step 3) steps or by playing an audio recording of the SMR instructions.

For homework assignments, clients can be given a copy of the SMR (Step 3) instructions and make their own recording to listen to. In order for a client to use SMR in a counseling session, the client must feel trust for the SBFC practitioner. This is because the SMR steps require the client to submit to the control of the practitioner who "guides" the client. If the client is reluctant to have you "guide" them, consider playing an SMR audio file from the internet (see Resources, below) while you and the client go through the SMR steps together. Clients who experience Commands as a major TSS may have difficulty letting you "guide" them in the SMR steps during a session. If this is the case consider asking them to try the SMR steps alone at home where they will feel more in control. If SMR does not work to relax your client, have them try alternative relaxation techniques such as: deep breathing and guided relaxation, guided imagery, mindfulness and meditation exercises, and soothing music.

Resources

Dartmouth College Student Wellness Center (n.d.). Progressive Muscle Relaxation audio.*

This website contains a 30-minute SMR exercise. The website also includes multiple exercises on Deep Breathing, Guided Imagery, Mindfulness and Meditation, and Soothing Music.

McKay, M. & Fanning, P. (2008). Progressive relaxation (relaxation and stress-reduction audiobook). Oakland, CA: New harbinger Publications

Progressive muscle relaxation (with background music), (n.d.) Audio.*

* See SBFC EResources for links to audio-recordings.

CBT Technique # 3: Desensitization

Definition

Desensitization (also known as Systematic Desensitization) is an anxiety-reducing technique that works by having your client repeatedly visualize the situation they fear in gradual increments.

Background and Rationale

Desensitization was developed by Joseph Wolpe (1961) and was used to treat veterans suffering from post-traumatic stress. Wolpe would develop for a client a hierarchy of anxiety-provoking scenes ranging from those that produced low anxiety to those that produced high anxiety. For example, for a client afraid of flying the scenes might be:

1. Driving to the airport
2. Having baggage screened
3. Waiting to board the airplane
4. Boarding the airplane
5. The airplane taking off
6. The airplane encountering turbulence

Wolpe would have the client visualize the first scene for a few seconds then evaluate the client's stress level using a scale from 1–10 with 1 = Relaxed and 10 = Very Tense. Next Wolpe would relax the client (who typically would experience tension from visualizing the scene) using SMR. The scene would be repeated for increasing lengths of time (alternating with SMR) until the client could visualize the scene for about a minute without experiencing strong anxiety. Then Wolpe would proceed to the next scene in the hierarchy. When the client could visualize the most anxiety-producing scene in the hierarchy without becoming very anxious, at that point there was typically a generalization of learning to the "real world" so that the client would experience much lower anxiety when encountering the actual feared situation (e.g. actually flying). Wolpe's rationale was that by pairing SMR relaxation with feared scenes the client learned a different association (relaxation) with the scene. A cognitive interpretation of why this technique works is that the client begins to have a shift from thoughts like: "Terrible things are going to happen" and "I can't cope with this" to "This is not a dangerous situation" and "I can handle this." Desensitization may be implemented in a number of different ways other than the classic Wolpe version involving a scene hierarchy and SMR. Examples of this are the EMDR (eye movement desensitization reprocessing approach) and Christensen's desensitization approach (which is presented below). However, the key ingredient in all desensitization approaches is exposing the client a little at a time to the image of the thing they fear, in increments, so that they can successfully manage the degree of anxiety produced by the scene.

Evidence-Based Support

There is a 70-year history of extensive research demonstrating the effectiveness of Desensitization for a wide variety of phobias (see Box 4.3 for examples of this research).

Box 4.3 Evidence-Based Support for Desensitization

Acierno, K., Tremont, G., Last, C., & Montgomery, D. (1994). Tripartite assessment of the efficacy of eye-movement desensitization in a multi-phobic patient. *Journal of Anxiety Disorders*, 8, 259–276.

Cox, B., Swinson, R., Morrison, B., & Lee, P. (1993). Clomipramine, fluoxetine, and behavior therapy in the treatment of obsessive-compulsive disorder: A meta-analysis. *Journal of Behavior Therapy and Experimental Psychiatry*, 24, 149–153.

Horne, D., Vatmanidis, P., & Careri, A. (1994). Preparing patients for invasive medical and surgical procedures: II Using psychological interventions with adults and children. *Behavioral Medicine*, 20, 15–21.

Menzies, R. & Clarke, J. (1993). A comparison of in vivo and vicarious exposure in the treatment of childhood water phobia. *Behaviour Research and Therapy*, 31, 9–15.

Menzies, R. & Clarke, J. (1995). Individual response patterns, treatment matching, and the effects of behavioural and cognitive interventions for acrophobia. *Anxiety, Stress, and Coping*, 8, 141–160.

Motley, M. & Molloy, J. (1994). An efficacy test of a new therapy for public speaking anxiety. *Journal of Applied Communication Research*, 22, 48–58.

Murphy, W., Yaruss, S., & Quesal, R. (2007). Enhancing treatment for school-age children who stutter: I. Reducing negative reactions through desensitization and cognitive restructuring. *Journal of Fluency Disorders*, 32 (2), 121–138.

Pitre, A. & Nicki, R. (1994). Desensitization of dietary restraint anxiety and its relationship to weight loss. *Journal of Behavioral Therapy and Experimental Psychiatry*, 25, 153–154.

Schneider, W. & Nevid, J. (1993). Overcoming math anxiety: A comparison of stress inoculation training and systematic desensitization. *Journal of College Student Development*, 34, 283–288.

Stamou, V., Clerveaux, R., Stamou, L., Le Rocheleuil, S., Berejnoi, S., & Graziani, P. (2017). The therapeutic contribution of music in music-assisted systematic desensitization for substance addiction treatment: A pilot study. *The Arts in Psychotherapy*, 56, Nov., 30–44

Strumpf, J. & Fodor, I. (1993). The treatment of test anxiety in elementary school-age children: Review and recommendations. *Child and Family Behavior Therapy*, 15, 19–42.

Tarquinio, C., Brennstuhl, M., Rydberg, J., Schmitt, A., Mouda, M., Lourel, M. & Tarquinio, P. (2012). Eye movement desensitization and reprocessing (EMDR) therapy in the treatment of victims of domestic violence: A pilot study. *European Review of Applied Psychology*, 62 (4), 205–212.

Wolpe, J. (1961). The systematic desensitization treatment of neuroses. *Journal of Nervous and Mental Disorders*, 112, 189.

Procedure

The desensitization procedure presented here was developed by Christensen and Pass (1983).

Step 1: Review the Client's Stress Pattern

"Whenever you encounter _____(refer to client's Troublesome Social Stimulus, e.g. 'Your mother giving you a Command'), it seems to cause you to be very stressed."

"Your typical stress response seems to be_____ (describe client's pattern, e.g. 'You become very tense and don't say anything')."

"On a scale from 1 to 10 how stressed do you get when this happens?"

"It sounds like this is having a very strong effect on you."

Step 2: Motivate the Client to Try the Technique

"Can you imagine what your life would be like if you didn't get so stressed when_____ (describe client's Troublesome Social Stimulus)?"

"I have an exercise that may help you to lower your stress in dealing with this. Would you like to hear about it?"

Step 3: Orientation and Invitation

"The exercise involves having you visualize the thing you fear in small doses over and over. The way it works is similar to something you may have experienced as a child. Can you remember a time when you were young and you couldn't get to sleep because there was a strange noise, like a tree brushing against a window and the sound frightened you? But after hearing it 200 more times you got used to it and it didn't bother you anymore? That's how this exercise works.

"It's like learning to swim. First we get your feet wet. Once you are used to that then we have you get in the water up to your knees. Then gradually up to your waist, and so forth, a little at a time.

"If you would like to try this it would take about 20 minutes. I would begin by having you imagine (describe the client's TSS, e.g. that you are with your father and he is yelling at you). We would do this for a few seconds, then I would have you do something relaxing, like visualize being on your favorite beach. We would alternate back and forth between your stress scene and a peaceful scene until you can visualize your stress scene without being very stressed.

"Clients report that this exercise is very helpful and that when they are able to visualize their stress scene and remain calm, the calmness transfers into their real life so that the next time they are actually with the person who triggers their stress, they remain calm.

"Would you like to try it?"

Step 4: Implement Desensitization

STEP 4.1 HAVE THE CLIENT SELECT A STRESS SCENE

"Can you identify a scene (e.g. involving your father yelling at you) that makes you anxious just thinking about it?"

STEP 4.2 OBTAIN A BASELINE ON THE DEGREE OF STRESS THE SCENE INDUCES

"Do you visualize better with your eyes open or closed?"

"Go ahead and get comfortable in your chair with your eyes open or closed as you prefer."

"I want you to visualize the scene with (e.g. your father yelling at you) for 45 seconds. As you imagine the scene I want you to notice in detail what he is saying and doing, how his face looks. But don't try to change the scene in any way. I want you to be like an anthropologist who is studying something interesting so you are just going to observe. Now go ahead and imagine the scene." (Use a watch and time 45 seconds.) After 45 seconds say: "OK, I'd like you to bring your awareness back to the room."

If the client is not able to visualize the scene because of a distraction, have the client try again. If the client appears overwhelmed by intense anxiety (10+) from visualizing the scene, chose a less intense scene involving the same person.

STEP 4.3 DEBRIEF THE SCENE

Do this after each presentation of the stress scene and the peaceful scene. Write brief notes recording the tension rating and urge.

"Were you able to focus on the scene?"

"What was your tension rating on the 1–10 scale?"

"Did you have an urge to do anything?"

STEP 4.4 HAVE THE CLIENT IMAGE A PEACEFUL SCENE

This is to counteract any strong anxiety produced by the visualization of the stress scene.

"OK, now I want you to visualize the most peaceful scene you can think of. What would that be for you?"

"Go ahead and visualize your peaceful scene for 60 seconds."

"Notice the detail in the peaceful scene and let yourself become very relaxed."

After 60 seconds say: "OK, now I'd like you to bring your awareness back to the room." You should end each scene presentation with this instruction.

Debrief (repeat Step 4.3).

STEP 4.5 DISTANCE THE STRESS SCENE

This is the technique of reducing the anxiety potency of the stress scene by moving it into the distance by projecting it onto a movie screen.

"I want you to imagine that your stress scene has been filmed and that you are alone in a movie theater sitting 100 feet from the screen. The film starts to play and you can see up on the screen a small picture of (e.g. your father yelling at you), but it's a film and you are not in the film. Go ahead and visualize that for 30 seconds, but don't do anything to change the image."

After 30 seconds, "OK, I'd like you to bring your awareness back to the room."

Debrief (repeat Step 4.3).

This distancing technique generally results in a lower stress rating. If it does, proceed to the next step. However, if the stress rating is very high (9+ or 10 +) repeat the scene but move the client in the image back to say 200 feet in the theater and emphasize that the image of the stressful person is now much smaller. That is, distance the scene so that the client can experience a lower level of anxiety. As the tension rating comes down, move the client closer to the screen.

STEP 4.6 REPEAT VISUALIZATION OF THE PEACEFUL SCENE

Debrief (Step 4.3).

If visualizing the peaceful scene is sufficient to lower your client's tension rating to 2 or less, continue using it. If the client still appears tense after the peaceful visualization, consider adding an additional relaxation component such as deep breathing or muscle relaxation. You can also extend the length of the peaceful scene to two minutes. Remember to debrief after each peaceful scene.

STEP 4.7 DISTANCE THE STRESS SCENE

Repeat Step 4.5, the movie presentation, but have the client imagine they are now sitting 50 feet from the screen. The goal here is to begin building up the client's tolerance for visualizing the scene in a more potent form.

"OK, now I want you to return to the movie theater and this time imagine you are only 50 feet from the screen. Go ahead and visualize that for 30 seconds, but don't do anything to change the image."
Debrief (Step 4.3).

STEP 4.8 REPEAT VISUALIZATION OF THE PEACEFUL SCENE

Debrief (Step 4.3).
Repeat this distancing of the stress scene until the client reports a diminished stress rating (e.g. below 4).

STEP 4.9 DIRECT SCENE PRESENTATION 1

This time you distance the scene by shortening the presentation time. Do not extend the presentation time until the client reports a lower stress rating.
"Now I would like you to imagine you are right there with the other person. Again don't try to change them. Focus on what they are saying and the way their face looks. Go ahead now and visualize that for 20 seconds."
Debrief (Step 4.3).

STEP 4.10 REPEAT VISUALIZATION OF THE PEACEFUL SCENE

Debrief (Step 4.3).

STEP 4.11 DIRECT SCENE PRESENTATION 2

"Now I would like you to imagine being right there with_____ but again don't try to change the scene. Go ahead and imagine that for 30 seconds."
Debrief (Step 4.3).

STEP 4.12 REPEAT VISUALIZATION OF THE PEACEFUL SCENE

Debrief (Step 4.3).

STEP 4.13 DIRECT SCENE PRESENTATION 3

"One last time I would like you to imagine you are right there with_____. Go ahead and visualize that scene for 45 seconds."
Debrief (Step 4.3).

Step 5: Debriefing and Review of Client Improvement

Point out to the client any improvements that occurred in the tension ratings for the stress scenes.

"So how did you experience doing this exercise?"

"Did you notice a change in how you felt from the beginning to the end?"

"On the first presentation of the stressful scene you gave it a rating of___.
In the movie theater it then went down to a ___ then to a ____.
Finally, in the direct scene presentations, your ratings went from a ____
down to a ____.
That's a significant drop from ____ in the beginning to a ____ at the end."

"What this means is that you are becoming desensitized to your stressor."

"The next time you are with the other person and they_____ (describe
TSS behavior: e.g. criticize you) it will not have as strong an effect on you.
This will free you up so that you will feel calmer and more able to choose
a different response."

Step 6: Discuss Homework

"This is an exercise that helps to build up your ability to remain calm during
a stressful encounter."

"Would you be interested in a special assignment in which you practice this
during the next week?"

"OK, the next time the other person_____(describe TSS behavior, e.g.
your father yells at you), before you respond just look at him and pay
attention to the way his face looks and the sound of his voice. Do this for
about 10 seconds then go ahead and respond as you normally would." (This
is an example of in vivo desensitization).

Challenges and Solutions

If the client is unable to visualize the troublesome scene (TSS) because it is
too potent, the SBFC practitioner can "paint" the scene for the client using
guided visualization. To do this have the client describe the scene to you,
then ask the client to try to image the scene as you briefly describe it. For
example:

"Your father comes into the room and says: 'What is the matter with you?
Why can't you come home on time like a normal person?' His face looks
tense and his voice is firm, but not angry. He continues to look at you
waiting for an answer."

Resources

Bjerkness, T. (2014, December 7). *Systematic desensitization example.**
   *This Youtube video illustrates the introduction of systematic desensitization in
a counseling session.*
   Christensen, C. & Pass, L. (1983). *The social interactional approach to counsel-
ling/psychotherapy.* Monograph Series 16, The Ontario Institute for Studies in
Education, Toronto, ON: OISE Press.

An example of desensitization is provided on pages 115–118.

Cormier, S. & Nurius, S. (2016). Chapter 14: Exposure therapy for anxiety, fear and trauma. In Cormier, S. & Nurius, S. (2016). *Interviewing and change strategies for helpers*. New York, NY: Brooks Cole.

This chapter gives detailed guidelines, along with model dialogue between helper and client, for the application of systematic desensitization.

Marich, J. (2017, March 28). EMDR therapy demonstration, Phases 1–8.*

EMDR therapist Jamie Marich demonstrates the EMDR approach to desensitization.

Smethalls, J. (2012, December 5). *Snake Phobia Behavioral (Exposure) Therapy.**

This video illustrates an actual in vivo desensitization session with a client with a severe snake phobia. Although imagery is not used in the desensitization process, the principle of gradual exposure (whether in imagery or real life) is the same.

Wolpe, J. (1973). *The practice of behavior therapy*. Elmsford, NY: Pergamon Press.

This text contains instructions on how to implement classic systematic desensitization.

Young, S. (2015, January 24). *Systematic desensitization role play.**

This counselling session role play demonstrates construction of an anxiety hierarchy for systematic desensitization.

*See SBFC EResources for links to videos.

CBT technique #4: Cognitive Restructuring

Definition

Cognitive Restructuring refers to a group of cognitive therapy techniques that focus on helping clients to shift from having negative, pessimistic thoughts to having positive, optimistic thoughts.

Background

The phrase: "Thinking makes it so" taken from Shakespeare's play Hamlet reveals the essence of Cognitive Restructuring. Aaron Beck's Cognitive Therapy and Albert Ellis's Rational Emotive Behavior Therapy are the most popular current forms of cognitive restructuring. Other approaches to Cognitive Restructuring include Stress Inoculation and Thought-stopping. However, important precursors in the modern era are Alfred Adler's belief in the importance of correcting mistaken beliefs and Abraham Low's approach to Will training and its emphasis on having clients use recovery language.

Most approaches to Cognitive Restructuring emphasize helping the client to: a) recognize their pessimistic thoughts and b) replace these with optimistic thoughts. An important assumption in this approach is that clients frequently catastrophize and exaggerate the dangers and consequences of interpersonal incidents (e.g. "Because she rejected me I am therefore worthless and will never find love"). The SBFC practitioner helps clients to test the validity of their irrational beliefs and replace these with more valid, generally more positive beliefs (e.g. "The fact that she rejected me does not mean I have no worth or that I will never find someone to love").

Evidence-Based Support

There is an extensive body of research demonstrating the effectiveness of Cognitive Restructuring techniques with children, adults, and diverse populations (see Box 4.4).

Box 4.4 Evidence-Based Support for Cognitive Restructuring

Cunningham, R. & Turner, M. (2016). Using rational emotive behavior therapy (REBT) with mixed martial arts (MMA) athletes to reduce irrational beliefs and increase unconditional self-acceptance. *Journal of Rational-Emotive & Cognitive-Behavior Therapy*, 34 (4), 289–309.

David, D., Szentagotai, A., Eva, K., & Macavei, B. (2005). A synopsis of rational-emotive behavior therapy (REBT): Fundamental and applied research. *Journal of Rational-Emotive & Cognitive- Behavior Therapy*, 23 (3), 174–221.

Eseadi, C., Anyanwu, J., Ogbuabor, S., & Ikechukwu-Ilomuanya, A. (2016). Effects of cognitive restructuring intervention program of rational-emotive behavior therapy on adverse childhood stress in Nigeria. *Journal of Rational-Emotive & Cognitive-Behavior Therapy*, 34 (1), 51–72.

Eseadi, C., Onwuka, G., Otu, M., Umoke, P., Onyechi, K., Okere, A. & Edeh, N. (2017). Effects of rational emotive cognitive behavioral coaching on depression among type 2 diabetic inpatients. *Journal of Rational-Emotive & Cognitive-Behavior Therapy*, 35 (4), 363–382.

Hains, A. (1992). Comparison of cognitive-behavioral stress management techniques with adolescent boys. *Journal of Counseling and Development*, 70, 600–605.

Haley, W., Roth, D., Coleton, M., & Ford, G. (1996). Appraisal, coping and social support as mediators of well-being in Black and White family caregivers of patients with Alzheimer's disease. *Journal of Consulting and Clinical Psychology*, 64, 121–129.

Hajzler, D. & Bernard, M. (1991). A review of rational-emotive outcome studies. *School Psychology Studies*, 6 (1), 27–49.

Heard, P., Dadds, M., & Conrad, P. (1992). Assessment and treatment of simple phobias in children: Effects on family and marital relationships. *Behaviour Change*, 9, 73–82.

Iwamasa, G. (1993) Asian Americans and cognitive behavioral therapy. *The Behavior Therapist*, 16, 223–235.

Lyons, L. & Woods, P. (1991). The efficacy of rational-emotive therapy: A quantitative review of the outcome research. *Clinical Psychology Review*, 11, 357–369.

Organista, K., Dwyer, E., & Azocar, F. (1993). Cognitive behavioral therapy with Latino outpatients. *The Behavior Therapist*, 16, 229–232.

Podina, I., Mogoase, C., David, D., Szentagotai, A., & Dobrean, A. (2016). A meta-analysis on the efficacy of technology mediated CBT for anxious children and adolescents. *Journal of Rational-Emotive & Cognitive-Behavior Therapy*, 34 (1), 31–50.

Renfrey, G. (1992). Cognitive-behavior therapy and the Native American client. *Behavior Therapy*, 23, 321–340.

Scheeringa, M., Weems, C., & Cohen, J. (2011).Trauma-focused cognitive-behavioral therapy for posttraumatic stress disorder in three-through-six year-old children: A randomized clinical trial. *Journal of Child Psychology and Psychiatry*, 52 (8).

Shannon, H. & Allen, T. (1998). The effectiveness of a REBT training program in increasing the performance of high school students in mathematics. *Journal of Rational-Emotive and Cognitive-Behavior Therapy*. 16 (3), 197–209.

Silverman, M., McCarthy, M., & McGovern, T. (1992). A review of outcome studies of rational-emotive therapy from 1982–1989. *Journal of Rational-Emotive & Cognitive-Behavior Therapy*, 10 (3), 111–186.

Wilde, J. (1996). The efficacy of short-term rational-emotive education with fourth-grade students. *Elementary School Guidance and Counselling*, 31, 131–138.

Procedure

A cognitive restructuring approach based mainly on Ellis's ABC approach to Cognitive Restructuring is shown below. I like this approach because of its strong research base and because it is relatively easy for practitioners to learn and teach to clients.

Step 1: Orientation and Invitation

Briefly review your client's stress pattern, describe the technique and how it could be useful, and invite the client to try it.

Describe your client's Troublesome Social Stimulus and typical response: e.g. "Whenever your teacher points out your mistakes, you get very tense and give the teacher an angry reply."

"Would you like to learn a way to be calmer in that situation?"

"I have an exercise called the ABC approach to looking at stressful situations. It was developed by a psychologist called Albert Ellis and many clients have found it very helpful in reducing their stress. Would you like to hear about it?"

"In the ABC approach, A refers to an Activating Event; for example, your friend criticizes you. C refers to the Consequences, which in this example might be you feel hurt and criticize your friend back. According to Dr. Ellis most people think that A causes C. If someone criticizes you it makes you upset. However, Dr. Ellis believes A does not cause C. C is caused by B which is what you Believe. If you have a negative or pessimistic belief like: 'This is terrible' or 'I can't stand it' then you are going to have a stressful emotional Consequence. However, if you can focus on more positive and optimistic beliefs, like: 'My friend is just upset: she'll get over it' or 'It's unpleasant that she is criticizing me but I can stand it' then you are not going to get so upset. Clients report that when they are able to focus on these more positive thoughts they feel calmer and less stressed. Does this make sense?"

In implementing this step it is helpful to make a simple table that illustrates what you are talking about (see Table 4.6).

"If you would like to try this, here is what we would do. First we would do an ABC analysis of what happened between you and the other person. Then I would ask you some questions to help you identify more positive thoughts to lower your stress. Would you like to try it?"

Step 2: Draw an ABC Table for Your Client's Situation

In this step teach your client how the ABC model applies specifically to them.

"Let's look at your situation with_____ using the ABC model."

"What was the Activating Event that resulted in you becoming stressed?"

"How would you describe your stressful Consequences? What emotions did you experience? What did you do?"

"What thoughts did you have about the Activating Event?"

"Some common pessimistic thoughts that are normal to have are:

- Making mistakes is terrible
- If someone doesn't approve of me it's awful
- Terrible things are going to happen to me
- I can't stand it
- They should be punished
- I am a bad person

Is it possible you had any of these thoughts?"

Table 4.6 Ellis's ABC Model

	causes	
A	B ————————➤	C
ACTIVATING EVENT	BELIEF	CONSEQUENCES
Your friend criticizes you.	Negative: "I can't stand it!"	Hurt, angry
	Positive: "I can handle this"	Concerned, less stressed

Step 3: Teach the Connection Between Beliefs and Consequences

"According to Dr. Ellis, your negative emotions at C were not caused by your Activating Event of_____, but were caused by your pessimistic belief at B."

"If instead of having the pessimistic thought you did of_____, you instead had more positive, coping thoughts like: 'It's not so bad, I can handle this,' how do you think you would have felt?"

"If you have a pessimistic belief like _____ (refer to client's pessimistic belief), it is normal to have a negative emotional Consequence and feel stressed."

Step 4: Help Your Client Identify More Positive Coping Thoughts

This step is implemented by asking the client questions to elicit coping thoughts and by your suggesting coping thoughts and images the client could use. The following sub-steps illustrate different ways you can implement Cognitive Restructuring. You may find it useful to use several and then explore with your client which ones seemed more helpful. These could be assigned as homework.

STEP 4.1 ASK THE CLIENT TO EVALUATE THEIR PESSIMISTIC THOUGHT

"Your pessimistic thought is_____."
"Does that thought help you or hurt you?"
"How does it hurt you?"

STEP 4.2 ASK THE CLIENT TO IDENTIFY A COPING THOUGHT

"What would be a more positive coping thought that would help you?"
If the client comes up with one, encourage them to try it.

STEP 4.3 GENTLY CHALLENGE THE IDEA THAT THE CLIENT'S ACTIVATING EVENT WAS CATASTROPHIC

"Why was the _____(refer to Activating Event) so awful?"
"I understand that your Activating Event was unpleasant, but why do you think it is catastrophic?"

STEP 4.4 USE A CATASTROPHE SCALE

Ask your client to place their Activating Event onto a Catastrophe Scale.
"I'd like you to imagine a Catastrophe Scale that goes from 1 to 100. One hundred would represent the worst catastrophe that could happen to you. For many persons 100 might involve death of a loved one."
"What would be an example of 100 on your scale?"

"What would be a 25?"
"What would be a 75?"
"What would be a 50?"
"Now where on the scale would you put your Activating Event (e.g. your father criticizing you)?" Most clients will place their Activating Event at the lower end of the scale.
"So your Activating Event is not that catastrophic."

STEP 4.5 ASK FOR A SIMILAR SITUATION WHEN YOUR CLIENT COPED WELL

"Can you think of a time your (refer to Activating Event, e.g. father criticized you) and you didn't get so upset?"
"What coping thoughts did you have at that time?"
"Are those coping thoughts you could use if (refer to Activating Event) occurs again?"

STEP 4.6 ASK YOUR CLIENT IF THEY CAN IDENTIFY ANY POSITIVES RESULTING FROM THIS TYPE OF ACTIVATING EVENT

"Can you think of anything good that can come from your having to deal with _____(refer to the Activating Event, e.g. your father criticizing you)?"
If your client cannot think of anything, make a suggestion – if you have one.
"Could this be an opportunity for you to improve the relationship?"
"Could this be an opportunity for you to learn some coping skills to make you a stronger person?"

STEP 4.7 HAVE YOUR CLIENT PRACTICE USING COPING IMAGERY

"Can you think of a positive image that would contradict your pessimistic thought?"
For example, if your client's pessimistic thought is: "I am not approved of" ask them for an image where they are approved of or loved. If the pessimistic thought is: "I made a mistake and it's terrible" ask them for an image of a situation in which they were very competent. That is, try to help the client find an image that is not just positive, but which contradicts the pessimistic image.
"That sounds excellent. Would you be willing to try it out?"
"Go ahead and imagine you are encountering your Activating Event and then switch your focus to your positive image for a minute."
"How was that?"

Step 5: Debrief the Exercise and Negotiate Homework

"How did you experience doing this exercise?"

"What coping thoughts approach did we use today that you think would be most helpful to you when you begin to feel stressed by_____ (refer to Activating Event)?"

"Would you be willing to try out your coping thoughts during the next week?"

Challenges and Solutions

Effective use of this technique requires the practitioner to take charge of the session and move sequentially through the CBT steps. This technique is best used when Stage 1 has been established. Clients may be embarrassed that they have irrational thoughts. The way to handle this is to normalize the client's irrational beliefs. That is, you emphasize that it is common for people to hold these beliefs, but that something can be done to reduce their grip.

Resources

Australian Association of Professional Counsellors (2013, September 5). *Role play: Cognitive-behavior therapy*.*

  This role play with a university student demonstrates use of the REBT ABC model and disputation.

Bernard, M. & Joyce, M. (1993). *Rational-emotive therapy with children and adolescents*. New York, NY: Wiley.

Duncan, S. (2013, May 3). *Albert Ellis and Gloria – Counselling (1965) Full Session – Rational Emotive Therapy*.*

  This is the full length interview by Albert Ellis with Gloria from the film Three Approaches to Psychotherapy (in which client Gloria was interviewed by Carl Rogers, Fritz Perls, and Albert Ellis). Ellis has a blunt style that turns some beginning practitioners off. However, the REBT approach can be used in a more gentle fashion as illustrated in the Australian Association of Professional Counsellors' role play (see above).

Ellis, A. & Bernard, M. (2006). *Rational emotive behavioral approaches to childhood disorders: Theory, practice and research*. Kindle book. New York, NY: Springer.

Ellis, A. & McLaren, C. (2005). *Rational emotive behavior therapy: A therapist's guide*. 2nd Edition. Santa Claria, CA: Impact Publishers.

Neenan, M. & Dryden, W. (2013). *Rational emotive behavior therapy in a nutshell*. Thousand Oaks, CA: Sage.

*See SBFC EResources for links to videos.

CBT Technique #5: Problem-Solving (Decision Grid)

Definition

The Decision Grid is a problem-solving technique developed by Carkhuff (2009). The technique involves having the client systematically generate alternatives and then evaluate the alternatives in a table format.

Background

This technique works by guiding the client to first generate alternatives rather than moving prematurely to evaluating the first alternative selected. It also emphasizes systematically identifying advantages and disadvantages of each alternative. A refinement to the Carkhuff technique involves use of a rating scale to indicate the strength of each advantage and disadvantage. This technique is especially useful when a client is conflicted about which alternative to use or is having difficulty finding alternatives. The use of a table allows the client to view all the alternatives and strengths and weaknesses simultaneously.

Evidence-Based Support

There is strong support in the literature generally for various forms of problem-solving used with a wide variety of clients. Some examples are shown in Box 4.5.

Box 4.5 Evidence-Based Support for Problem Solving

Bedford, L., Dietch, J., Taylor, D., Boals, A., & Zayfert, C. (2017). Computer-guided problem-solving treatment for depression, PTSD, and insomnia symptoms in student veterans: A pilot randomized controlled trial. *Behavior Therapy*, 48 (3), 100–120.

Erwin, P. & Ruane, G. (1993). The effects of a short-term social problem solving programme with children. *Counseling Psychology Quarterly*, 6, 317–323.

Foxx, R., Kyle, M., Faw, G., & Bittle, R. (1989). Teaching a problem solving strategy to inpatient adolescents: Social validation, maintenance, and generalization. *Child and Family Behavior Therapy*, 11, 71–88.

Guervremont, D. & Foster, S. (1993). Impact of social problem-solving training on aggressive boys: Skill acquisition, behavior change, and generalization. *Journal of Abnormal Child Psychology*, 21, 13–27.

Hains, A. & Fouad, N. (1994). The best laid plans .... assessment in an inner-city high school. Special issue: Multicultural assessment. *Measurement and Evaluation in Counseling and Development*, 27, 116–124.

Hammond, R. & Yung, B. (1991). Preventing violence in at-risk African American youth. *Journal of Health Care for the Poor and Underserved*, 2, 359–373.

Jafee, W. & D'Zurilla, T. (2009). Personality, problem solving, and adolescent substance use. *Behavior Therapy*, 40 (1), 93–101.

Moncher, M. & Schinke, S. (1994). Group intervention to prevent tobacco use among Native American youth. *Research on Social Work Practice*, 4, 160–171.

Nagle, D., Carr-Nagle, R., & Hansen, D. (1994). Enhancing generalization of a contingency-management intervention through the use of family problem-solving training: Evaluation with a severely conduct-disordered adolescent. *Child and Family Behavior Therapy*, 16, 65–76.

Nezu, A. (2004). Problem solving and behavior therapy revisited. *Behavior Therapy*, 35 (1), 1–33.

Pfiffner, L., Jouriles, E., Brown, M., & Etscheidt, M. (1990). Effects of problem-solving therapy on outcomes of parent training for single-parent families. *Child and Family Behavior Therapy*, 12, 1–11.

Sandoval, L., Buckey, J., Ainslie, R., Tombari, M., & Hegel, M. (2017). Randomized controlled trial of a computerized interactive media-based problem solving treatment for depression. *Behavior Therapy*, 48 (3), 413–425.

Shure, M. (1993). I can problem solve (ICPS): Interpersonal cognitive problem solving for young children. Special issue: Enhancing young children's lives. *Early Child Development and Care*, 96, 49–64.

Yang, B. & Clum, G. (1994). Life stress, social support, and problem-solving skills predictive of depression symptoms, hopelessness, and suicidal ideation in an Asian student population: A test of a model. *Suicide and Life Threatening Behavior*, 24, 127–139.

Procedure

Step 1: Describe the Decision Grid Technique

Describe the technique to the client and invite the client to try it.

"You've been struggling with what to do in this situation. I have an exercise called the Decision Grid that you might find helpful. Would you like to hear about it?"

"The Decision Grid involves making a list of all the alternatives you can think of for handling your situation with_____ and then carefully reviewing each alternative to list its advantages and disadvantages. Clients who have done this exercise report that it often helps them to figure out a clear course of action. Would you like to try it?"

Step 2: Draw a Decision Grid

Draw a decision grid like that shown in Table 4.7.

Table 4.7 The Decision Grid

ALTERNATIVES	ADVANTAGES	DISADVANTAGES
1.		
2.		
3.		
4.		

Step 3: Have the Client Generate Alternatives

Try to generate from two to four alternatives.
"What do you see as your alternatives for handling this situation?"
"What is one thing you could do to deal with this situation with_____?"
"What would be another thing you could do?"

Step 4: If the Client is Having Difficulty, Suggest Alternatives

"I have an idea about an alternative. Would you like to hear it?"
"Another alternative would be to_____. What do you think about that?"
"Sometimes people in this type of situation will _____ (mention alternative). What do you think of that?"
"Would you like to add it to your list?"

Step 5: Generate Advantages and Disadvantages

During this step encourage your client to take their time. If the client has difficulty thinking of an advantage or disadvantage, or there is an advantage/disadvantage that you think may be relevant, suggest it to the client. Make clear that placing your suggested advantage/disadvantage on the grid is strictly up to them.
"OK let's take your first alternative which is_____. What do you see as the advantages of doing this?"
"Can you think of any more advantages?"
"OK, now what do you think are the disadvantages of this alternative?"
"Would you consider_____ to be an advantage?"
"Would you like to add that to your advantage list?"
"Are there any changes you would like to make to your list of advantages and disadvantages for your first alternative?"
"Now let's look at the advantages and disadvantages for your second alternative."

Step: 6 Have the Client Rate the Strength of Each Advantage or Disadvantage Using a +10 to −10 Scale

The purpose of this step is to give you and the client a clearer picture of the degree to which the client regards something as an advantage or disadvantage.
Advantages are rated on a scale from +1 to +10.

+10 Very strong advantage
+8 Strong advantage

+6 Moderate advantage
+4 Mild advantage
+2 Slight advantage

Disadvantages are rated on a scale from -1 to -10.

−10 Very strong disadvantage
−8 Strong disadvantage
−6 Moderate disadvantage
−4 Mild disadvantage
−2 Slight disadvantage

As your client rates each advantage/disadvantage you should write the rating beside the item being rated.

"Let's rate each advantage and disadvantage for how strong it is using a scale from −10 to +10."

"Starting with your first alternative, the first advantage you listed was_____. How strong an advantage is that on your +1 to +10 scale, with +10 being a very strong advantage and +2 being a slight advantage?"

"How would you rate the second advantage which is_____?"

Continue until all the advantages for Alternative #1 have been rated.

"Now let's rate the disadvantages for Alternative #1. We will use a scale from −1 to −10, with −10 being a very strong disadvantage and −2 being a slight disadvantage."

"How would you rate the first disadvantage?"

Continue until all the disadvantages for Alternative 1 have been rated.

Repeat Step 6 for each Alternative.

Step 7: Compute the overall advantage and disadvantage scores

Total the ratings for the advantages and then the disadvantages for each alternative. Subtract the disadvantage total from the advantage total and place this summary total beside the alternative.

Example: A Decision Grid for a client in Grade 9 deciding whether to cut class to hang out with friends who are skipping school to skateboard is shown in Table 4.8.

Step 8: Review the totals with the client

Summarize the total scores for each alternative and then ask the client to comment on this. Review whether the result matches the client's view of what the best alternative is. Check to see if there are any changes the client wants to make in the ratings or in the alternatives, advantages, or disadvantages. Be flexible in accommodating any changes the client might like.

Table 4.8 Example of a Completed Decision Grid

ALTERNATIVES	ADVANTAGES	DISADVANTAGES
1. Skip school	• Fun with friends +10	• May get caught −10 • Grounded by parents −9 • Get detention −10
Total: −19	Total: +10	Total: −29
2. Don't skip school	• Stay out of trouble +8 • Get better grades +7	• Miss fun with friends −10
Total: +5	Total: +15	Total: −10
3. Don't skip school and ask parents for more weekend time with friends	• Stay out of trouble +8 • Get better grades +7 • Fun with friends on Weekend +10	• No fun with friends during weekdays −10
Total: +15	Total: +25	Total: −10

"When you look at your total scores for your alternatives, what do you conclude?"

"Based on your total scores, your alternative with the most advantages and least disadvantages appears to be_____. Does this fit how you feel?"

"Now that we are looking at your overall evaluations for your alternatives, are there any changes you think you should make in your ratings or any of your advantages or disadvantages?"

"Based on this exercise, what alternative do you think would be best for you?"

Challenges and Solutions

Clients commonly have difficulty thinking of alternatives. If this is the case, it is important to suggest – in a tentative manner – any alternatives you may see. For example, for a client who sees the alternatives for dealing with a friend who has been spreading gossip about the client being: a) ignore the gossiping or b) end the friendship, you might suggest a third alternative c) confront the friend about the gossip. Some clients who are math phobic will prefer to not use the rating scale to evaluate the advantages and disadvantages. An alternative with these clients is to have them evaluate each alternative using the following words:

Strong advantage (SA)
Moderate advantage (MA)
Slight advantage (SLA)
Strong disadvantage (SD)
Moderate disadvantage (MD)
Slight disadvantage (SLD)

Resources

Carkhuff, R. (2009). *The art of helping*. 9th Edition. Amherst, MA: HRD press.
This book describes the Decision Grid approach to problem-solving.
Gordon, T. (2000). P.E.T. parent effectiveness training: The proven program for raising responsible children. New York, NY: Harmony Books.
Chapter 11. The "No Lose" Method for Solving Conflicts describes how a parent can use Method III problem-solving to handle a power struggle with a child.
Greene, R. & Ablon, S. (2005). Treating explosive kids: The collaborative problem-solving approach. New York, NY: Guilford.
This book describes a problem solving approach to working with highly oppositional children and their families.

CBT technique #6: Behavior Rehearsal

Definition

Behavior Rehearsal is the technique of having the client role play in session a new social skill (e.g. an assertive behavior).

Background and rationale

The key ingredients of Behavior Rehearsal are: instruction in assertive and socially skilled communication, role playing, coaching, modeling, and use of scenarios involving a gradually increasing level of difficulty. By practicing a new social skill in the safety of the session with the SBFC practitioner, the client develops increased self-efficacy. The client sees that they are successful in role playing (e.g.) an assertion skill with the SBFC practitioner and begins to think: "I did it with my SBFC practitioner; I think I can do it with my family member." Behavior Rehearsal is traditionally used in situations where the client has a skill deficit. That is, it is used in situations where the client doesn't know what to say or do to deal with the other person. The SBFC practitioner teaches the client a social skill and then has the client practice it. If the client already knows what to say and do, but is blocked from doing it by anxiety, then a more appropriate starting point is to begin with an anxiety-reducing technique (one of the Stage 2 techniques, such as SMR, Desensitization, or Cognitive Restructuring, discussed above). However, even if the client already has the social skill, Behavior Rehearsal may be useful if the client is anxious about implementing it. Role playing the social skill in session has the effect of desensitizing the client to possible challenging and unexpected responses from the family member.

Evidence-based support

Evidence-based support for behavior rehearsal is shown in Box 4.6.

Box 4.6 Evidence-Based Support for Behavior Rehearsal

Anderson, S. & Swiatowy, C. (2008). *Bullying prevention in the elementary classroom using social skills.* Master of Arts Action Research Project, Saint Xavier University.

Hijazi, A., Tavakoli, S., Slavin-Spenny, O., & Lumley, M. (2011). Targeting interventions: Moderators of expressive writing and assertiveness training on the adjustment of international university students. *International Journal for the Advancement of Counselling*, 33, 2, 101–112.

Kim, Y. (2003). The effects of assertiveness training on enhancing the social skills of adolescents with visual impairments. *Journal of Visual Impairment & Blindness*, 97, 5, 285–297.

Klug, W. (2000). Nonassertive mothers, aggressive teens: Toughlove as a community intervention. ERIC ED Report 448395.

Koglin, U. & Petermann, F. (2011). The effectiveness of the behavioural training for preschool children. *European Early Childhood Education Research Journal*, 19, 1, 97–111.

Moore, R. (1995). The effects of social skill instruction and self-monitoring on game-related behaviors of adolescents with emotional or behavioral disorders. *Behavioral Disorders*, 20, 4, 253–266.

Polansky, J., Buki, L., Horan, J., Ceperich, S., & Burows, D. (1999) The effectiveness of substance abuse prevention videotapes with Mexican American adolescents. *Hispanic Journal of Behavioral Sciences*, 21, 2, 186–198.

Scharfstein, L., Beidel, D., Rendon Fennell, L., Distler, A., & Carter, N. (2011). Do pharmacological and behavioral interventions differentially affect treatment outcomes for children with social phobia? *Behavior Modification*, 35, 5, 451–467.

Sukhodolsky, D., Golub, A., Stone, E., & Orban, L. (2005). Dismantling anger control training for children: A randomized pilot study of social problem-solving versus social skills training components. *Behavior Therapy*, 36, 1, 15–23.

Tavakoli, S., Lumley, M., Hijazi, A., Slavin-Spenny, O., & Paris, G. (2009). Effects of assertiveness training and expressive writing on acculturative stress in international students: A randomized trial. *Journal of Counseling Psychology*, 56, 4, 590–596.

Vaughn, S., Kim, A., Sloan, C., Hughes, M., Elbaum, B., & Sridhar, D. (2003). Social skills interventions for young children with disabilities. *Remedial and Special Education*, 24, 1, 2–15.

Procedure

Step 1: Assess the Degree to Which Your Client Has a Skill Deficit

Ask the client what they would like to say or do in dealing with their Troublesome Social Stimulus with the other person. For example:

"What would you like to say when your father criticizes you?"

"What would you like to do when your mother gives you a command?"

Step 2: Orientation and Invitation

"There is an exercise we can do that could help you to relate more effectively to _____ (refer to the other person). Would you like to hear about it?"

"It's called role playing. We would identify together an assertive response which is appropriate for your situation and then we would role play it here in the session. You would practice with me and I would play the role of the person you find it challenging to deal with."

"This is what actors do when they rehearse their lines for a play. By rehearsing it builds up their confidence so that they can get their lines right on opening night."

"Would you like to try it?"

Step 3: Help the Client Select an Assertive Response

STEP 3.1 TEACH THE CLIENT ABOUT ASSERTION

"Being assertive means standing up for your rights without violating the rights of the other person. Being assertive means being socially skilled. There are many different categories of assertive behavior:

1. Being Confrontive
2. Saying No
3. Making Requests
4. Expressing Opinions
5. Initiating Conversations
6. Maintaining Conversations
7. Active Listening
8. Self-disclosure
9. Expressing Affection

The alternatives to being assertive are being submissive (giving in or saying nothing) or being aggressive (criticizing, yelling, blaming)."

STEP 3.2 TOGETHER WITH THE CLIENT SELECT AN APPROPRIATE ASSERTIVE RESPONSE

"Do you have some thoughts about what sort of assertive behavior you would like to use in this situation?"

"My impression from what you have been saying is that you would like to_____. What do you think?"

"If you like, something we could do is to practice having you develop your skills in_____."

Step 4: Discuss With the Client the Desired Assertive Response

"Let's talk about some different ways you could_____(be confrontive, say no, initiate a conversation, etc.)."

Consider using the Decision Grid to generate alternatives. For clients requiring confrontation skills, consider teaching DESC Confrontation (see Box 4.7).

Box 4.7 DESC Confrontation

Definition: DESC Confrontation is an assertion skill developed by Bower & Bower (2004) for constructively confronting someone who has violated your rights in some way. DESC is an acronym for **D**escribe, **E**xpress, **S**pecify, **C**onsequences.

Describe: This is a behavior description of the other person's behavior that caused you stress. "You" messages that involve blaming, criticizing, yelling, commands, or swearing are omitted.

Express: This is a description of your feelings in response to the other person's behavior and the way in which their behavior is having a tangible negative effect on you.

Specify: This is a specific request for the other person to change their behavior in some way.

Consequences: This is a description of the positive consequences for the other person and the relationship if the other person grants the request.

In some situations it may be necessary to use negative consequences if the other person refuses to grant a reasonable request. Negative consequences refer to the negative effects that will result for the relationship or for the other person.

Background: Confronting another person can be very difficult and anxiety-provoking for a client. The value of the DESC Confrontation is that the acronym helps the client to remain focused on assertive communication during the discussion. Helping a client write out and practice a DESC Confrontation is a valuable form of assertion training.

Procedure:
Step 1: Teach the Client about the DESC Confrontation

Step 2: Have the Client Write a DESC Confrontation Using the DESC Confrontation Worksheet
This could be done in the counseling session or assigned as homework, to be brought to the next session.

Step 3: Review the Client's DESC Confrontation

Have the client read the DESC Confrontation to you as though you were the person being confronted. As the client completes reading each section, stop and give the client coaching on how to improve the response, especially if there are "You" messages present.

"I really liked the way you began by describing word for word what your father said that upset you. However, I got a little tense when you said: 'It's all your fault.' If I were your father I think I might get defensive and start arguing with you here. What do you think?"

"Would you be willing to take that phrase out?"

Step 4: Continue with Behavior Rehearsal

Reference:

Bower, S. & Bower, G. (2004). *Asserting yourself: A practical guide for positive change.* Lebanon, IN: Da Capo Lifelong Books.

DESC Confrontation Worksheet
Briefly describe the incident that caused you stress:

_____

_____

Write a DESC Confrontation for this situation:
Describe:
"When you_____

_____ "

Express:
I felt_____

"Because_____

_____ "

Specify:
"I would like you to_____

_____ "

Consequences:
Positive: "If you will do that it will be helpful in _____

_____ "

Negative: "If you are not willing to do that, then _____ "

_____

Step 5: Have the client covert rehearse the assertive behavior

The purpose of this covert rehearsal is to increase the client's self-efficacy by creating an expectation of a positive outcome. The covert rehearsal also helps to weaken any images of failing which clients commonly have.

"I'd like you to imagine using your (refer to assertion skill, e.g. DESC Confrontation, conversational skills, active listening, etc.) with your family member. Go ahead and visualize this for a minute and imagine having a positive outcome with the family member responding positively to you."

"How was that?"

Step 6: Have the Client Role Play the Assertive Behavior

STEP 6.1 PREPARE FOR THE ROLE PLAY

"Let's try role-playing it."

"I will play the role of_____ (e.g. your father). Now how would they typically react in this situation." (get your client's suggestions).

STEP 6.2 DO AN EASY ROLE PLAY

"This first time I'm going to role play the other person as being very cooperative."

"Go ahead now and use the assertive skills we discussed."

Do the role play for about one minute.

STEP 6.3 DEBRIEF THE ROLE PLAY AND PROVIDE COACHING

"How did you experience doing that?"

"You did an excellent job of_____."

"Here's one area for improvement:_____."

Note: If your client has a strong skill deficit and you think they would benefit from seeing a model response, trade roles: you take their role and have them take the role of the family member. Do the role play again and model for your client an effective response. Then repeat Step 6.2 with the client role playing herself. If your client does well in the initial role play, move directly to the advanced role play in Step 6.5.

STEP 6.4 REPEAT THE EASY ROLE PLAY TO ASSESS FOR IMPROVED CLIENT RESPONSE

Repeat Steps 6.2 and 6.3. If the client demonstrates improved performance, then move to Step 6.5.

STEP 6.5 DO AN ADVANCED ROLE PLAY

"You are now ready to do a more challenging role play. This time we will go longer and I will be slightly more challenging (e.g. by interrupting you, criticizing you, talking a lot, etc.)."
Do the role play for about two minutes. Be sure to moderate your difficult response near the end if necessary so that your client experiences success.

STEP 6.6 DEBRIEF THE ROLE PLAY AND PROVIDE COACHING

"How did you experience doing that?"
"You did an excellent job of_____."
"Here's one area for improvement:_____."

STEP 6.7 DEBRIEF THE EXERCISE

"How did you find doing this?"
"You did_____ really well."

Step 7: Discuss Homework Applications

"Do you feel ready to try this with your family member?"
If your client doesn't feel ready, or if you think your client isn't ready yet, indicate that more practice is needed.
"You have made an excellent start. I recommend we practice this some more in our next session. An actor usually rehearses lines several times before opening night."
If your client feels ready:
"During the next week, when do you think you might try this?"
"I look forward to hearing how it goes."

Step 8: Debrief Homework in the Next Session

At the next session, if your client reports having a successful assertion with the family member, congratulate them.
"That's great. You must feel very proud of yourself!"

Challenges and Solutions

If the client becomes very anxious while doing the Behavior Rehearsal, stop using this technique and return to a Stage 2 technique (SMR, Desensitization, or Cognitive Restructuring) to lower the client's anxiety. If the client has difficulty practicing the assertive response, consider doing a reverse role play where you model an assertive response while the client role plays the person they are having difficulty with.

If your client for homework attempts being assertive and at the next session reports having an unsuccessful assertion, normalize this and engage in further Behavior Rehearsal incorporating into the role plays any challenging responses the family member demonstrated. This is the principle of successive approximation. If necessary, review with your client their Stage 2 anxiety-reduction skills as the difficulty they are having may be due to anxiety rather than a skill deficit.

"You showed courage in attempting this."

"It's important to remember that there are three stages to change. The first stage is where you realize a week later that you handled things wrong with the other person. The second stage is where you are talking with the person and you realize that you are not acting the way you want. The third stage is where you are right on target and say and do exactly what you want."

"So it's important to be patient and realize that change comes in steps."

"Your new skill is like a muscle: the more you exercise it the stronger it gets."

Resources

Bower, S. & Bower, G. (2004). *Asserting yourself: A practical guide for positive change*. Lebanon, IN: Da Capo Lifelong Books.
   This book gives a detailed description of how to make a DESC confrontation.
   Michael, D. (2007, February 17). *Assertiveness training demonstration.**
   In this brief demonstration Dr. Diane Michael coaches a "client" in how to make an assertive response.
   Lauercm11 (2014. November 9*). Behavior rehearsal.**
   This student role play demonstrates behavioral rehearsal with a pregnant student. The "therapist" does a reverse role play in which she models an assertive response demonstrating how the "client" can tell her parents about the pregnancy.
   * See SBFC EResources for links to videos.

Case Study

The following hypothetical case study illustrates how the six CBT techniques could be used in FCI using the nine-step approach described at the beginning of the chapter.

Kim, age 14, is having difficulty concentrating in school because of conflict she is having with her mother Alicia. Kim, who self-refers for counseling, reports to the SBFC counselor Elena that Alicia is very strict and makes Kim do three hours of homework every day, including weekends. Kim is not allowed to spend any after-school times with her friends. Kim's teacher reports that Kim has difficulty concentrating in class and that she is sometimes tearful. Kim has only occasional weekend visits with her father Dan, who she says is very busy. Elena's phone messages to Dan are not returned and Kim says her father is too busy to come to counseling. Elena invites Alicia to meet with her to discuss Kim's performance at school, but Alicia says that she is overwhelmed as a working single parent and cannot afford the time to come to the school. However, she consents to her daughter receiving counseling.

Session 1

Step 1: Establish Stage 1 Rapport

During the first session with Kim, Elena alternates between using empathic listening (active listening) and asking questions to build trust with Kim while obtaining information about Kim's problems.

Step 2: Conduct a Family Systems Assessment

After gathering a more detailed history Elena used the Circumplex Model to diagnose Kim's relationship with the significant people in her life: her mother, her father, her friend Beth (age 14), and her teacher (see Figure 4.2).

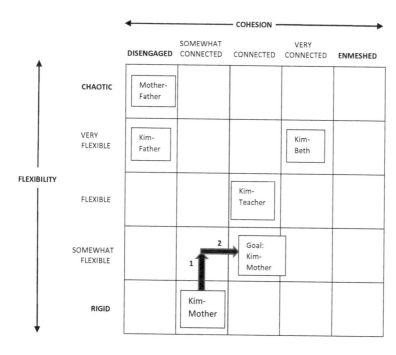

Figure 4.2 Circumplex Model for Kim

The Circumplex diagnosis for Kim's relationship with these four persons was as follows:

Kim-Mother: *Rigid-Somewhat Connected*
Kim-Father: *Flexible-Disengaged*
Kim-Beth: *Very Flexible-Very Connected*
Kim-Teacher: *Flexible-Connected*

Kim described her relationships with her friend, Beth, and with her teacher as positive. She expressed upset with her relationship with her mother because her mother is too strict. She also expressed a wish to be closer to her mother (who seemed preoccupied with problems at work and with Kim's father). Kim described her father as "very busy with work." Elena notes that Kim's parents have a Chaotic-Disengaged relationship. Elena hopes to develop a closer relationship with Kim's parents so that she can eventually address the marital conflict that affects Kim as well. However, in the absence of this parental cooperation, Elena decides to initiate FCI with Kim to improve Kim's relationship with her mother.

Session 2

Step 3: Conduct a Behavioral Relationship Assessment

Using the Behavioral Relationship Assessment Form Elena identified that Kim had two main TSS with her mother: Commands and Criticism. The behavioral data that Elena gathered on Kim's TSS is shown in Table 4.9.

Table 4.9 Kim's Troublesome Social Stimuli with her Mother and Father

Troublesome Social Stimulus	Example of TSS from Parent	Response to TSS by Kim
Commands	Mother: "You are not going to the mall."	Tenses and says nothing. Has an urge to argue her point of view.
Criticism	Mother: "You are lazy just like your father."	Becomes very tense, starts to argue: "No, I'm not" then becomes silent.
Unresponsiveness	Father: Does not respond to Kim's phone calls	Becomes tense.

As can be seen, Criticism and Commands from her mother are TSS for Kim producing a typical response of tension and withdrawal. Nevertheless, Kim in both situations has an urge to assert herself.

Step 4: Identify a Relationship Change Goal

In this step Elena discusses further with Kim her goals and helps Kim to identify a relationship change goal. Elena helps motivate Kim by pointing out some possible positive results of counseling.

Step 5: Formulate a Treatment Plan

Based on her first two sessions with Kim, Elena decided on the following treatment goals for Kim:

Overall Treatment Plan: Move Kim's relationship with her mother from Rigid-Somewhat Connected to Somewhat Flexible-Connected. Elena planned to achieve this Circumplex goal by increasing Kim's ability to tolerate the TSS of Commands and Criticism from her mother in order for Kim to remain calm enough to make a more appropriate assertive response that would promote the shift to a Somewhat Flexible-Connected relationship.

Circumplex Model Goal #1: Move Kim's relationship with her mother from Rigid-Somewhat Connected to Rigid-Connected. The purpose of this initial goal was to increase cohesion in the mother-daughter relationship, since Elena detected in Kim a wish for a warmer, closer relationship with her mother. Elena felt that this would be a more attainable goal than trying to get mother to be initially more flexible with discipline. In addition, Elena believed that if mother felt closer to Kim, she might be more willing to be less strict.

CBT strategy: To achieve this goal Elena decided to teach Kim SMR to lower her stress so that she could tolerate any likely initial resistance from her mother in spending mother-daughter time together. Problem-solving was selected to help Kim identify suitable mother-daughter activities to present to her mother.

Circumplex Model Goal #2: Move Kim's relationship with her mother from Rigid to Somewhat Flexible. This second goal was meant to follow the first.

CBT Strategy: Because Kim was very anxious about asking her mother to be less strict with her, Elena decided to use a combination of Desensitization and Cognitive Restructuring to lower Kim's stress. Assertion Training and Behavior Rehearsal were used to develop positive social skills Kim could use to negotiate with her mother.

Session 3

Step 6: Implement the Stage 2 Stress Reduction Techniques

Because her mother's Criticism has a strong controlling effect on Kim and produces a tense and leave response in Kim, Elena decided to help Kim address lowering anxiety before working with Kim on request skills related to spending more time with friends. As an initial step Elena chose to teach Kim SMR as a way to remain calmer when her mother criticized her.

Session 4

Kim reported that during the previous week she had practiced SMR and that this had really helped her to remain calmer around her mother. During this session Elena taught Kim an additional stress reduction approach: Cognitive Restructuring. After implementing Step 1: Orientation and Invitation, Elena helped Kim do an ABC analysis of her situation with her mother. Kim decided that the coping thought that helped her the most was to remind herself that her mother was under a lot of stress because of marital tension and that her mother wanted only what was best for Kim. Elena asked Kim to practice using this coping thought during the next week, and also to continue using her SMR.

Session 5

Step 7: Implement the Stage 3 Techniques

During Session 5 Elena determined that Kim's relationship with her mother had become more cohesive and had moved from Structured to more Connected. She decided to explore with Kim whether Kim was ready to try to move her relationship with her mother from Rigid to Structured. Elena implemented problem-solving using the Decision Grid and this helped Kim to decide she wanted to use a constructive way to confront her mother about giving Kim more freedom to spend time with friends.

Session 6

In this session Elena introduced Behavior Rehearsal to help Kim negotiate a less Rigid relationship with her mother. Elena next taught Kim about DESC Confrontation and then had Kim write out a DESC Confrontation she could make to her mother concerning her mother's statement that she was lazy. Elena and Kim then role played Kim's DESC Confrontation with Elena playing the role of Kim's mother. Because Kim was still nervous about actually using the DESC Confrontation with her mother, Elena asked Kim to postpone confronting her mother for now. For homework Elena asked Kim to practice visualizing her DESC Confrontation.

Session 7

During Session 7 Elena and Kim continued using Behavior Rehearsal with Elena playing the role of Kim's mother. Elena did a reverse role play with Kim in the role of mother, in order to show Kim how to use active listening with her mother. This use of empathy in the context of making a confrontation reduces the defensiveness of the person being confronted.

Session 8

Step 8: Address Any Additional Relationship Change Goals

In Session 8 Kim reported that she had spoken to her mother on Sunday using her DESC Confrontation and that her mother had – to Kim's surprise – apologized. In this session Elena used the Decision Grid – this time to help Kim generate alternatives in asking her mother to let Kim spend more time with her friends. Kim also reported that instead of phoning her father she wrote him a letter. Also, to her surprise, he wrote back and suggested they met for lunch sometime soon.

Session 9

Step 9: Prepare the Client for Termination

During this session Elena and Kim agree that Kim's counseling goal has been met and that they will take a break in counseling for three weeks and then have a follow-up session to ensure that the positive changes are being maintained. Kim reports that her mother is very pleased with her relationship with Kim and has commented: "Perhaps Elena can help me be a better parent with Dan."

Multicultural Counseling Issues

The CBT counseling techniques have many studies demonstrating their evidence-based support; however, most of these studies (about 80%) have been conducted with Caucasian clients (Hays & Iwamasa, 2006). There is, however, a growing literature that suggests CBT techniques can be effectively used with diverse clients, such as Native Americans, Asian Americans, Latinos, African Americans, gays and lesbians, the elderly, and low socioeconomic status clients, provided the practitioner adapts the CBT techniques to the cultural situation of the client (see Box 4.8).

Box 4.8 Evidence-Based Support for the Use of CBT with Diverse Clients

Arean, P. (1993). Cognitive behavioral therapy with older adults. *The Behavior Therapist*, 16, 236–239.

Hays, P. (1995). Multicultural applications of cognitive-behavior therapy. *Professional Psychology*, 26, 309–315.

Iwamasa, G. (1993). Asian Americans and cognitive behavioral therapy. *The Behavior Therapist*, 16, 233–235.

Kamimura, E. & SaSaki, Y. (1991). Fear and anxiety reduction in systematic desensitization and imaging strategies: A comparison of response and stimulus oriented imaging. *Japanese Journal of Behavior Therapy*, 17, 29–38.

Kuchlwein, K. (1992). Working with gay men. In A. Freeman & F. Dattillio (Eds.). *Comprehensive casebook of cognitive therapy* (pp. 249–255). New York, NY: Plenum.

Miranda, J. & Dwyer, E. (1993). Cognitive behavioral therapy for disadvantaged medical patients. *The Behavior Therapist*, 16, 226–228.

Miranda, J., Green, B., Krupnick, J., Chung, J., Siddique, J., Belin, T., & Revicki, D. (2006). One-year outcomes of a randomized clinical trial treating depression in low-income minority women. *Journal of Consulting and Clinical Psychology*, 74, 1, 99–111.

Organista, K., Dwyer, E., & Azocar, F. (1993). Cognitive behavioral therapy with Latino outpatients. *The Behavior Therapist*, 16, 229–232.

Renfrey, G. (1992). Cognitive-behavior therapy and the Native American client. *Behavior Therapy*, 23, 321–340.

Scheeringa, M., Wems, C., Cohen, J., Amaya-Jackson, L., & Guthrie, D. (2011). Trauma-focused cognitive-behavioral therapy for posttraumatic stress disorder in three-through six year-old children: A randomized clinical trial. *Journal of Child Psychology and Psychiatry*, 52, 8, 853–860.

Waldron, H. & Turner, C. (2008). Evidence-based psychosocial treatments for adolescent substance abuse. *Journal of Clinical Child and Adolescent Psychology*, 37, 1, 238–261.

Webb, M., de Ybarra, D., Baker, E., Isilinha, M., & Carey, M. (2010). Cognitive-behavioral therapy to promote smoking cessation among African American smokers. *Journal of Consulting and Clinical Psychology*, 78, 1, 24–33.

Weisz, J., Southam-Gerow, M., Gordis, E., Connor-Smith, J., Chu, B., Langer, D., McLeod, B., Jensen-Doss, A., Updegraff, A., & Weiss, B. (2009). Cognitive-behavioral therapy versus usual clinical care for youth depression: An initial test of transportability to community clinics and clinicians. *Journal of Consulting and Clinical Psychology*, 77, 3, 383–396.

Wolfe, J. (1992). Working with gay women. In A. Freeman & F. Dattillio (Eds.). *Comprehensive casebook of cognitive therapy* (pp. 249–255). New York, NY: Plenum.

Wu, C., Lo, Y., Feng, H., & Lo, Y. (2010). Social skills training for Taiwanese students at risk for emotional and behavioral disorders. *Journal of Emotional and Behavioral Disorders*, 18, 3, 162–177.

Traditional CBT techniques have often been used to promote traditional Euro-centric values such as assertiveness and independence. Promoting assertiveness with an abused woman can lead to further abuse if the assertion is prematurely directed to the abusive partner. Promoting assertiveness with an Asian American client having difficulty with their parents can lead to a violation of cultural and family norms and worsen a client's condition. However, assertiveness training in both these cases can promote client empowerment, if applied with multicultural sensitivity by the SBFC practitioner. For example, in the case of the abused woman client an appropriate focus for assertion training would be helping the client to expand her social network. This requires the development of social skills for making friends (an important assertion skill). Social support is an important buffer for stress, plus one of the problems faced by many battered women is that they often lack any support network beyond the abuser. In the case of the Asian American client wanting to deal differently with their parents, it would be very important that the SBFC practitioner emphasize the importance of showing respect towards the parents in making requests for change. That is, you can request someone to modify their behavior in a polite, even gentle way, without resorting to blunt confrontation. The issue isn't whether to use assertion training with diverse clients, but what specific assertion skills to teach and how to demonstrate them with caring and sensitivity.

A social justice approach to using CBT techniques takes into account the client's sociopolitical circumstances. For example, if your client is an African American student who is being bullied at school, and the teacher is turning a blind eye to the racist behavior of the bully, you need to go beyond teaching the victim stress-coping and assertive responses and make additional interventions with the teacher, the class, and possibly the entire school, as well as the bully, the bully's parents, and the victim's parents. This kind of broad-based intervention is the hallmark of SBFC. In a social justice intervention, CBT constitutes just one of several counseling strategies.

Challenges and Solutions

To be effective at using FCI it is essential that the SBFC practitioner understand how the use of a CBT technique can help a client change their relationship with another person. In other words, the SBFC practitioner must maintain a family systems focus while working with an individual client. This requires frequent checking with the client about the Other Person's behavior in response to the client's behavior. Because the CBT techniques are highly goal-focused, it is essential that the SBFC practitioner have successfully established Stage 1: Preparing for Change with the client such that the client is ready for what Prochasa, DiClemente, and Norcross (1992) call the Action stage of therapy, which involves Stage 2: Changing Cognitions and Stage 3: Changing Behavior. If clients become anxious while practicing a Stage 3 behavior change technique, it is important to do further Stage 2 work using CBT stress reduction techniques to prepare the client for behavior change. Some SBFC practitioners will need to use all five of the above-mentioned CBT techniques to help a client improve a family relationship. However, with some clients (especially with clients ready for Stage 3: Changing Behavior) the use of only one or two techniques may be necessary to bring about relationship change. These FCI CBT techniques can also be used to help a client deal with any relationship (e.g. peers, teachers, etc.).

Resources

Cormier, S., Nurius, P., & Osborn, C. (2016). *Interviewing and change strategies for helpers.* 8th Edition. New York, NY: Cengage Learning.
This is a comprehensive, practical text on how to do CBT, containing many detailed examples of mental health practitioner-client dialogue.
McKay, M., Davis, M., & Fanning, P. (2001). *Thoughts and feelings: Taking control of your moods and your life.* Oakland, CA: New Harbinger.
This self-help book contains many useful CBT techniques and worksheets that clients will find useful.

Bibliography

Carkhuff, R. (2009) *The art of helping* (9th Edition.). Amherst, MA: HRD Press.
Christensen, C. & Pass, L. (1983). *The social interactional approach to counselling/psychotherapy.* Monograph Series 16, The Ontario Institute for Studies in Education, Toronto, ON: OISE Press.
Fisch, R., Weakland, J., & Segal, L. (1982). *The tactics of change: Doing therapy briefly.* San Francisco, CA: Jossey-Bass.
Gurman, A. & Kniskern, D. (1978). Deterioration in marital and family therapy: Empirical, clinical, and conceptual Issues. *Family Process*, 17(1), 3–20.
Hays, P. & Iwamasa, G. (2006). *Culturally responsive cognitive-behavioral therapy: Assessment, practice, and supervision.* Washington, DC: American Psychological Association.
Prochasa, J., DiClemente, C., & Norcross, J. (1992). In search of how people change: Applications to addictive behaviors. *American Psychologist*, 47, 1102–1114.
Wolpe, J. (1961). The systematic desensitization treatment of neuroses. *Journal of Nervous and Mental Disorders*, 112, 189.

5 School Intervention

How to Consult with Teachers Using A Functional Behavior Assessment Model and Process Consultation

Margaret Garcia and Michele D. Wallace

Overview: This chapter illustrates how the SBFC practitioner can engage a teacher in process consultation integrated with a functional behavior assessment model to address specific student problems manifested in the classroom.

Background

Teacher Consultation

The direct services provided by an SBFC practitioner can yield significant improvements in students' social and emotional development as well as academic performance. Such improvements are evident in the classroom as well as in the home setting. But it isn't feasible for the SBFC practitioner to work directly with every student demonstrating problem behaviors in the classroom employing a dyadic model as illustrated in Figure 5.1. Nor is it best practice given that it is the teacher who will most directly work with students on a daily basis. Yet teachers should not be expected to address problem behaviors without additional support. One of the best aspects of a profession is the access one has to other professionals. For this reason, the consultation relationship between the SBFC practitioner and teachers is critical to the effective functioning of a school. The consulant relationship with the student is indirect in the triad illustrated in Figure 5.2. This allows the teacher to gain knowledge, skills, or perspective that can yield results for other students in addition to the current student with challenging behaviors.

There are many models of consultation as well as models for addressing problem behavior, but this chapter will focus on integrating a specific consultation model while conducting a functional behavior assessment to address problem behavior within the classroom. process consultation (PC) (Schein, 1999) alongside a functional behavior assessment (FBA) model (Asmus, Vollmer, & Borrero, 2002) will provide an opportunity to demonstrate expert consultation reined in by a process of inquiry that places the teacher in the driver's seat.

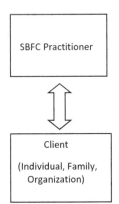

Figure 5.1 SBFC Practitioner – Client Dyadic Relationship

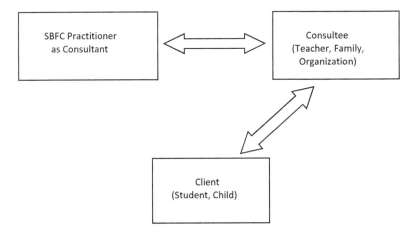

Figure 5.2 Consultant – Consultee – Client Triad

This chapter will demonstrate how the integration of two models can improve the consultation experience for the teacher. This in turn will lead to improved outcomes for the teacher's current students as well as for future students. It will be key to establishing an ongoing relationship so that when problems do arise that require additional support for the teacher, he or she will more likely consider reaching out to the SBFC practitioner for that support. At the same time, the SBFC practitioner avoids fostering dependence so that the teacher improves his or her skill set in order to prevent similar problems in the future. Before beginning the consultation relationship, consider the concept of One Downsmanship as presented in Box 5.1.

Box 5.1 One-Downsmanship

An important aspect of the PC and FBA integrative consultation model is the non-hierarchical relationship. The SBFC practitioner holds expertise but the teacher is the expert in the classroom and knows his or her students best in the context of that classroom. Nonetheless, the teacher may turn to the consultant as the expert. This is fine when the teacher does so in recognition of the SBFC practitioner's specific knowledge and skills (e.g., family systems, social and emotional development, conducting assessments, and running group therapy sessions). However, it is up to the SBFC practitioner to maintain the balance with respect to the current case. This may be accomplished by engaging in subtle acts of one-downsmanship to maintain the balance.

For example, the teacher might say "I am so glad you are here to help since you are the expert in this area." To which the SBFC would benefit from responding "Actually, you are the expert in the classroom and with this student" rather than "Great, I'm glad to offer my expertise."

Please note that SBFC practitioners who have backgrounds and experience in teaching should avoid calling in their expertise as teachers when they are being consulted for their expertise as SBFC practitioners. If teachers want to consult with other teachers – as they often do – then they will reach out to current teachers. It's an especially poor demonstration of one-upmanship to give a teacher advice based on your teaching experience when the teacher is the expert on teaching in this current relationship. Please use restraint even if the teacher is new to teaching and has a lot to learn. He or she will have plenty of opportunity to learn on the job and to seek mentoring from professionals currently teaching. Moreover, teachers will have greater appreciation for what they learn on their own based on their own mistakes and regrets. Your contributions will be significant as the SBFC practitioner.

The Case of Justice

PC will be presented with an FBA model using the case of Justice to illustrate each level.

Justice is a 13-year-old seventh grade student at Hoover Middle School. The Department of Social Services indicates that he is biracial (African American and Caucasian) and has lived at his current foster home for the last three years with two other foster children. He has a younger sister (age 9) and a brother (age 8), who are in a separate foster placement. Both of his biological parents are incarcerated. Justice moved around a lot during his elementary school years and the school records are incomplete. However, standardized testing has him below the 25th percentile in most areas. He has a typical schedule including Math, Language Arts, Social Studies, Science, P.E., and Computer Science. His math teacher Mrs. Hart sends Justice to the Assistant Principal frequently because of his "lack of respect and insubordination." The SBFC practitioner Linda has been asked to intervene.

Functional Behavior Assessment Model Overview

The purpose of an FBA is to determine the environmental reasons why an individual is engaging in problematic behavior. It is not to say that past experiences, emotional statuses, or feelings are not important, it is just that those are not easily observed or changed. Thus the focus of the FBA model is to determine what is currently reinforcing the behavior (i.e., maintaining it), to modify the triggers and to support the consultee to eliminate the problem behavior while promoting an acceptable replacement behavior.

There are three steps included in an evidence-based FBA:

Step 1   Indirect Assessment
Step 2   Descriptive Assessment
Step 3   Functional Analysis

It is beyond the scope of this chapter to debate the merits of an FBA or teach these assessments comprehensively; however, a brief overview will be provided. For a more detailed description of an FBA see Mayer, Sulzer-Azaroff, and Wallace (2018). It should be noted that by combining PC within this model, the SBFC practitioner is consulting with the teacher rather than serving as an expert; this can lead to better treatment integrity as well as behavioral improvements (Ringdahl & Sellers, 2013).

Indirect Assessment

The purpose of the indirect assessment is to start framing the case and get some insight into why the behavior is occurring. This step is a great step to start to understand what the actual behavior of concern is, making sure everyone is on the same page, and identifying possible triggers and supports for the problem behavior. Indirect assessment can either be unstructured, where the consultant asks the consultee open-ended questions (e.g., Hanley et al., 2014), or can have structured questionnaires (e.g., Christensen et al., 2002; Iwata, 1995, Matson & Vollmer, 1995). Indirect assessment is illustrated below in Boxes 5.5 and 5.7.

Descriptive Assessment

After getting some ideas about the triggers and supports related to the behavior problem from the consultee, it is time to see what actually happens before and after the behavior occurs in the classroom. Thus, this assessment is usually accomplished by having the practitioner conduct a direct observation in the classroom and record what triggers the behavior and what happens after the behavior occurs. The most straightforward descriptive assessment is to just list these events as they happen (Bijou, Peterson, & Ault, 1968). After recording the triggers and supports, the practitioner must analyze the results to determine which variables are correlated with the problem behavior and then hypothesize why the behavior is occurring: to get something (social positive reinforcement), to get out of something (social negative reinforcement), or because it feels good (automatic reinforcement). This is Illustrated in Box 5.6.

Functional Analysis

The purpose of this step is to verify the hypothesis developed after the indirect and descriptive assessments. It should be noted that only individuals with explicit training in this technique conduct this assessment. Generally, to verify the hypothesis the triggers and supports are manipulated in such a way as to turn them off and on and see the results with respect to if the behavior occurs. For example, if you suspect the student engages in problem behavior to get attention, you would compare at least two conditions: 1) Attention TEST: deprive the individual of attention and provide attention contingent on the display of problem behavior and 2) Attention CONTROL: provide attention freely for a specified amount of time (Iwata et al., 1982/1994).

After verifying the reason the individual engages in problem behavior, this information is used to create a function-based behavior intervention plan. The behavior intervention plan should consist of multiple components targeting the triggers and the support of the problem behavior as well as prompts and supports for a replacement behavior. This is Illustrated in Box 5.8.

Behavior Intervention Plan

The Behavior Intervention Plan (BIP) should include at least three components: 1) antecedent manipulations for both the problem behavior as well as replacement behavior, 2) reduction of the support for the problem behavior (extinction), and 3) reinforcement. Again, it is beyond the scope of this chapter to provide a detailed instruction on these procedures; however, a brief overview will be provided (for more detailed description see Mayer et al., 2018).

Antecedent (trigger) Manipulations

It is important to view this category of intervention as ways to prevent problem behavior and promote replacement behavior. In other words, how can you remove the triggers for the problem behavior and replace them with prompts for the replacement behavior?

Extinction

We know if a problem behavior is occurring the person is getting something, getting out of something, or that it feels good to them. Thus, if we want them to stop engaging in that problem behavior we must interfere with them getting what they want by engaging in that problem behavior. In other words, we need to switch the contingencies so that they do not get what they want for engaging in problem behavior and get it only when they engage in acceptable replacement behavior.

Reinforcement

If we want someone to not engage in problem behavior and to engage in the replacement behavior, we *must* provide reinforcement for doing so. We can also give them reinforcement for not engaging in the problem behavior for an extended period of time. But remember: If they are used to engaging in the problem behavior daily to get what they want and you offer them reinforcement for not engaging in the problem behavior for a month, the likelihood they will switch is very low. It is also important to take into consideration the reason they engage in the problem behavior: Is it to get something or get out of something? For example, if Johnny engages in problem behavior to get out of work, giving him attention when he engages in appropriate work behavior probably will not have an effect. Instead, give him some free time away from work for engaging in the appropriate behavior, since we know he likes to get away. In addition, you must ensure the individual engages in the replacement behavior. If they never engage in the behavior they will never receive reinforcement. Thus, it is important to teach and/or prompt the replacement behavior initially so that the response comes into contact with reinforcement.

Evidence-Based Support

Cholewa, Thomas, and Cook (2016) looked at teacher perceptions of school counselors in consultation. They found that teachers report a greater likelihood for seeking consultation when the school counselor is visible and available and has made deliberate efforts to initiate contact. The SBFC practitioner should not expect to have a successful consultation experience when they are available only by appointment. The consultation relationship is only a subset of a larger relationship among school professionals. If teachers perceive the SBFC practitioner as someone who primarily meets with students and families only to offer direct services, then the teacher is less likely to see the SBFC practitioner as a collaborative colleague.

Most teacher training programs do not involve student teachers in consultation with support personnel such as SBFC practitioners. They learn to make referrals to special education staff for students with learning problems or refer students to the school administration if they are very disruptive in the classroom. Alderman and Gimpel (1996) found that teachers are most likely to seek consultation from the school-based professonal for aggressive behaviors, but tend to address disruptive behavior on their own. They also found that teachers first prefer to address problem behaviors on their own followed by consulting with other teachers, then the principal, followed by taking classes on behavior interventions. This may be due to perceptions of greater access to fellow teachers and the principal than to the SBFC practitioner.

There is a growing appreciation for the role of SBFC practitioners as teacher consultants. Many schools and school districts have implemented Response to Intervention (RTI) models of identifying and addressing students at risk. These are tiered approaches that provide basic preventive interventions at the primary level for all students, including screening for academic and mental health risk factors. At the next tier, research-based interventions are provided for students who have been identified to be at risk due to low performance on progress-monitoring measures (secondary prevention). Finally, the third tier addresses students at highest risk in need of individualized interventions (tertiary prevention). There is less emphasis on identifying students for special education in a "wait-to-fail" approach and more emphasis on providing classroom consultation at the preventive level (Sugai & Horner, 2009). Katsiyannis, Conroy, and Zhang (2008) conducted a survey of district level administrators in two southern states and generally found that FBAs were thought to be successful at addressing the problem behaviors. They tended to support the use of FBAs using a team approach.

Meta-analyses looking at the application of FBAs in school settings find general success with FBA versus non-FBA models (Anderson, Rodriguez, & Campbell, 2015; Bruni et al., 2017).

Procedure

Process Consultation

Based on ten principles, PC as described by Schein (1999) offers a good structure for SBFC practitioners to conduct school-based consultation, including FBAs. The ten principles will be briefly reiterated here as applied to Justice in the classroom.

Ten Principles of Process Consultation

1　*Always try to be helpful.* At times, teachers will ask quite directly for ideas about what to do. We caution consultants to avoid providing quick answers. It may seem helpful to provide quick answers to an eager teacher, especially when you are providing evidence-based strategies. But unless the teacher has a very good handle on defining and analyzing the problem, a more helpful approach is to engage in active inquiry and problem-solving. In addition, without understanding the reason(s) the student is engaging in the problem behavior, your evidence-based suggestion is merely a guess.

2　*Always stay in touch with the current reality.* When a teacher asks you "Have you ever taught before?" that is a good indication that you are demonstrating a lack of empathy for the teacher's current reality. Sometimes consultants offers suggestions that require the teacher to engage in an inordinate amount of data collection and responding when he or she has over 20 other students in her classroom demanding her attention. What works in an ideal setting will not always be feasible for the large-class setting.

3　*Access your ignorance.* Don't be eager to demonstrate how much you know about behavioral terminology, attention deficits, hyperactivity, relational aggression, etc. Instead, be willing to spend time clarifying statements and making sure your understanding of the teacher's view of the problem is clear. Don't make assumptions about the principal just because you already know the principal, for instance. Many times teachers will expect that you already know aspects of the case because you work with the same people and have worked with many students in their classrooms. Don't let this stop you from learning more about the case from the teacher's point of view. There are many times we have an impression of certain students in our graduate programs and we are surprised to find out how rude they may be when interacting with staff or adjunct faculty. People present themselves differently in different settings and under varying circumstances.

4　*Everything you do is an intervention.* Through PC the SBFC practitioner will serve as a model for how to think about the case. This is going to extend beyond your immediate role in a consultation session to how you present yourself overall as an SBFC practitioner. Then of course, your inquiry and ability to demonstrate an understanding about the present-ing problem first from the teacher's perspective and then from an objective framework that redirects the teacher's attention is very power-ful as an intervention tool.

5　*It is the consultee who owns the problem and the solution.* Leave your ego at the door when serving as a consultant. The teacher is the expert on his or her classroom. Mrs. Hart knows her students, their strengths and weaknesses, her support staff, her own abilities and competencies, etc. She may not reveal all the relevant details to the consultant, especially one whose time is difficult to access. Consider the media regarding student achievement. Whose reputations are really on the line? When measuring student success, it's the teachers who are held most directly accountable. Don't forget this, and appreciate your role in supporting their success without trying to gain commendations when things go well. If teachers associate success in their classrooms with consultation sessions with you, your value will be recognized.

6 *Go with the flow.* As an SBFC practitioner your time will be tightly scheduled and your days will go by quickly before you've managed to complete everything on your to-do list. You may often feel overwhelmed with putting out fires, dealing with crises, meeting with teachers and administrators, holding regular counseling groups, and seeing students for individual counseling as well as families in their homes. But with all that, you may have more flexibility than the classroom teacher. Mrs. Hart cannot just schedule meetings throughout the day, she can't even leave her classroom to go to the bathroom when needed without getting someone to cover for her. She has many students who demand her attention before, during, and after class. When you schedule meetings with the teacher, go with the flow.

7 *Timing is crucial.* Don't blurt out a question the moment it enters your mind. Take note and ask the question when the time is right. Remember the fourth principle, *everything is an intervention.* Your questions are most effective when asked at the right time. Be deliberate and patient so that the teacher can gain the most from your inquiry. PC involves phases of inquiry that we will present in the next section. The phases are sequential and should be timed to serve their purpose before moving to the next phase.

8 *Be constructively opportunistic with confrontive interventions.* One of the most difficult skills to learn as a consultant is recognizing when one is being confrontive. Consultants need to realize that questions such as "Did you talk to his parents?" or "Did you try ignoring him when he talks out of turn?" are confrontive and should be avoided until one has fully gone through Exploratory Diagnostic Inquiry.

9 *Everything is data. Errors will always be observed and are the prime source for learning.* You won't always say and do the exact right thing during consultation and in response to what a teacher has told you. There doesn't exist an exact protocol to spell out the most correct line of questioning and responding to the consultee. Use your client observation skills to gauge reactions and learn from mistakes.

10 *When in doubt, share the problem.* A good consultant should recognize the value of consultation and seek it out as a consultee when appropriate. While respecting FERPA (Family Educational Rights to Privacy Act) and HIPAA (Health Insurance Portability and Accountability) laws and confidentiality, an SBFC practitioner can share a case with a colleague who can offer a different problem-solving perspective. When seeking out

consultation, the SBFC practitioner should reach out to other SBFCs or counseling professionals who are knowledgeable about relevant ethics codes and any institutional policies or regulations surrounding privacy and confidentiality.

Three Stages of Process Consultation and Active Inquiry

It is critical to follow each stage in sequence. This process differs from doctor-patient models in which the consultee knows exactly what the problem is and contacts an expert to resolve the issue. The SBFC practitioner will use active inquiry to follow the ten principles listed above. The consultee (the teacher) is allowed to share the narrative with minimal direction from the consultant. The consultee has a very active rather than passive role in consultation.

INITIATING CONSULTATION

The consultation process begins before Stage 1 when the consultation agreement is established or at the first moment of contact when setting up the first meeting. Avoid engaging in a discussion of the case during this brief conversation to arrange a meeting time. Recognize that teachers have very restrictive schedules and it may be more feasible for the SBFC to accommodate the teacher's time. It is also important for the SBFC to be ready to recognize any possible attempt to avoid formal consultation. While the teacher is motivated to see the situation improve, avoidance may come as teachers will quickly, if not immediately, realize that they will be expected to make changes in how they do things in order to support change in students' behaviors. Initiating consultation is illustrated in Box 5.2.

Box 5.2 Initiating Consultation

- Keep in mind that consultation begins at the first moment of contact.
- Contact the teacher to set up the first meeting.
- Avoid engaging in a discussion of the case during this brief conversation to arrange a meeting time.
- Recognize that teachers have very restrictive schedules.
- Accommodate the teacher's time while also being aware of a possible attempt to avoid formal consultation. While the teacher is motivated to see the situation improve, avoidance may come as teachers will quickly, if not immediately, realize that they will be expected to make changes in how they do things in order to support change in students' behaviors.

Step 1: Initiating the Consultation

Linda, the SBFC practitioner, contacts Mrs. Hart to set up a meeting. "Hi Mrs. Hart, my name is Linda and the assistant principal has asked me to contact you regarding Justice. Could we meet so that you can tell me about what is going on?" Mrs. Hart says that she is really busy but can meet for about 10 minutes during her conference period at the end of the week. Linda tells Mrs. Hart she needs at least 30 minutes of her time because she really wants to understand what is going on. Mrs. Hart. says "How about I just send him to you so you can handle the situation?" Linda says "I would really like to know what is going on from your perspective, do you have any time later in the week?" Mrs. Hart. reluctantly agrees to meet on Friday from 1:00–1:30 pm.

STAGE 1 PURE INQUIRY

During Pure Inquiry, the consultee controls both the process and the content of the conversation. The role of the consultant is to prompt the story and listen carefully and neutrally. It takes great restraint to avoid asking leading questions. Do not underestimate how difficult it will be to ask open questions and not closed questions that suggest an answer. Pure Inquiry is illustrated in Box 5.3.

Box 5.3 Pure Inquiry and Identifying the Problem

PC Phases of Inquiry	*FBA Model*	*Case of Justice*
Pure Inquiry:	*Identifying the problem:*	
Ask questions that allow the consultee to provide his or her own perspective. This should be uncensored and the consultant should avoid redirecting the discussion unless the consultee wanders far from the presenting problem. While taking care not to direct the conversation, make every effort to bring the focus back to the primary student of concern.	Allow the consultee to provide an overview of the problem. Consultee presents the story from his or her own perspective with minimal directing from the consultant. However, the beginnings of identifying the problem will emerge. Refocus on current problem and student.	Linda allows Mrs. Hart to discuss her views of Justice's behavior. Mrs. Hart uses terms such as "always" but Linda does not confront Mrs. Hart at this stage. She asks open questions to learn more about Justice. Linda redirects when Mrs. Hart tries to include Charlie along with Justice.
Summarize along the way, taking care to	Summarize the problem concern objectively.	Linda: So Justice is always late and

demonstrate to the teacher that you captured the main points of her concerns and observations. Allow for clarification.

unprepared for class, he uses foul language towards his peers, the other students get riled up in response, and there is another student, Charlie, who is causing just as much of a disruption in your class. Do I have that right?

It is typical that multiple behaviors will be mentioned as problematic. Ask the teacher to prioritize the behaviors and select one to focus on for the next session.

If multiple behavioral concerns are identified, make sure to have the teacher prioritize the behaviors and select one to focus on for the FBA.

Linda: Thank you Mrs H, this is really helpful and you have really painted a picture of what is going on. There is so much going on with Justice, as we prepare to address some of his behaviors, which would you prioritize to start with; coming to class late, his homework, or the foul language?
Mrs. Hart: Well, they are all related. so how can you separate them?
Linda: They may be all related, but I'd like to focus on one at a time.
Mrs. Hart: OK then, I just can't have him saying those foul things in my class. If he came in late and just sat there I could handle it. You know, if I let him use foul language, the next thing I know the whole class will be calling each other names.
Linda: Great, let's focus on the foul language.

End the session by arranging for the next session. This must be done without giving premature advice even if such input is solicited by the teacher. Rather than give premature advice, acknowledge the complexity of the problem and how more information is needed

Make sure to not give any advice regarding quick fixes, even if you think you know why the student is engaging in the behavior.

Linda: So, before we can develop a plan, I still have more questions and would like to set up another meeting.
Mrs. Hart: You know I'm just so busy, I don't know about another meeting. How long will it take?

prior to problem-solving.
Set up the next meeting.

Linda: We should plan
for about 30–45 minutes
for our next meeting.
Mrs. Hart: Well, what
should I do in the
meantime?
Linda: At this moment
I'm not ready to suggest
anything differently than
you have been doing.

STAGE 2 EXPLORATORY DIAGNOSTIC INQUIRY

The consultant begins to manage the process of how the content is analyzed and elaborated but does not insert content ideas, suggestions, advice, or options. There are three areas of redirection during the Exploratory Diagnostic stage of inquiry. The SBFC practitioner may choose to address each area of focus or just one, depending on the case. When using PC integrated with an FBA model, it is helpful to address all areas, but please note that the FBA model will look at reactions, not feelings. Exploratory Inquiry is illustrated in Box 5.4.

Box 5.4 Exploratory Diagnostic Inquiry and Operationally Defining the Target Behavior

PC *Phases of Inquiry*	*FBA Model*	*Case of Justice*
Exploratory Diagnostic Inquiry:	*Operationally defining the target behavior.*	
In this phase the consultant approaches the presenting problem with a specific model in mind. The questions asked serve to gather more information and to direct the consultee's attention to specific aspects of the case.	The consultant will ask questions that allow the consultee to more operationally define the problem and/or target behavior.	Linda starts off the second meeting by asking Mrs. Hart to help define the behavior so that they are both on the same page when talking about Justice's problem. Linda provides the following operational definition: Linda: So, in order to get some more information about how you react and why you think Justice engages in foul language, I think

we should first start off by coming up with an operational definition that is objective and complete so we both are on the same page. How would you like to describe the behavior?

Mrs. Hart: I would like to define the behavior as any time Justice uses foul language or calls people names.

Linda: Can you give me examples of what will count and not count as foul language?

Mrs. Hart: Well, expletives should count. I also can't have him yelling in class, so that should count. And being disrespectful towards me should also count.

Linda: What do you mean by expletives, can you give some examples?

Mrs. Hart: You know words like b*tch and f*ck, words like that.

Linda then asks if Mrs. Hart wants to include these words regardless of whether they are directed at anyone specifically, and Mrs. Hart states that it doesn't matter, they should all be included.

Linda then summarizes and says: So far we have Justice's problem behavior defined as any time he uses bad words regardless of whether they are directed at anyone in particular, is that right?

Mrs. Hart: Yes.

Linda: Will that defini-
tion capture Justice's
use of foul language?
Mrs. Hart: Well, what
about him yelling in
class that he hates me,
I can't have that either.
Linda: OK, let's add
any yelling to the definition, how does that
sound?
Mrs. Hart and Linda
agree on the definition.

- *Feelings and Reactions* – Ask questions that will get at how the teacher reacted when the student engaged in the target behavior such as "How did you react when …?" (illustrated in Box 5.5).

Box 5.5 Exploring Reactions and Indirect Assessments

PC Phases of Inquiry	FBA Model	Case of Justice
Exploring reactions:	*Indirect Assessment*:	
Ask questions that bring out the details of a specific case. Be sure to have the consultee talk about a specific incident of the problem behavior. While acceptable during Pure Inquiry, in this phase, do not allow the consultee to explain the problem in generalities such as "He always …" or "He never …."	Consultant asking questions that address the antecedents and consequences of the target behaviors. More specifically, the consultant asks about the consultee's actions around the target behavior.	Linda: Mrs. Hart, when Justice called Cassidy a "brown nose bitch" the other day, what did you do? Mrs. Hart: I told you, I always tell him he can't act that way in my class and then I sent him to the AP's office.
Use this step of the exploratory phase to ask the consultee how he or she responds to client's behavior.		
As the teacher elaborates, the consultant will need to continue to probe for details. Unlike Pure Inquiry, the exploration is guided by	Specifically ask about the antecedents and consequences related to the behavior, but make sure you are not attributing function.	Linda: Can you tell me what you said to Justice and how you got him to leave the classroom? Mrs. Hart: I told him that he was being disrespectful

a specific model and the details relevant based on that model, which in this case is an FBA model. The consultant provides more structure for discussing the problem but must avoid offering suggestions.

Note that questions are suggestive when they imply what should have or could have happened. Avoid any questions that make suggestions such as "Have you considered that it might be to escape math?" This is a good question but not until Confrontive Inquiry.

Ongoing inquiry about what happened in response to the student's actions will help in the understanding of the behavior and relevant environmental factors.

Prior to taking the opportunity to directly observe a classroom to note teacher and student behavior, the next best thing is to get the teacher to describe specific incidents in detail rather than accept notions of what "typically" or "usually" happens. Without returning to a very specific incident, the teacher may inadvertently cobble together a narrative that does not accurately reflect actual antecedents and consequences of target behaviors.

and that I will not put up with it and then I told him to go to the AP's office.
Linda: What happened then?
Mrs. Hart: Then he kept yelling and using foul language and eventually got up out of his seat and left the room.
Linda: What did you do then?
Mrs. Hart: Well, I usually tell the other students how I am not going to put up with that kind of behavior and then I start my lesson.

Linda: What exactly did you do the other day?
Mrs. Hart: I told Cassidy how sorry I was and then I started teaching my lesson.
Linda asks about how other students responded as well; remember she is trying to get as much information about the incident as she can.
Linda: Mrs. Hart, how did the other students and Cassidy respond to Justice?
Mrs. Hart had to think about it and then she said:
They really didn't do anything except for Charlie who started mocking Cassidy.
Linda: OK, Mrs. Hart, when you told him to leave, what did you actually tell him and did you give any further instructions on where he should go?
Mrs. Hart: I told him to go directly to the AP's office and then I followed up with the AP to make sure he went to his office.
Linda: Mrs. Hart, when you send Justice to the

AP's office do you give any other directions?

Mrs. Hart: No, I just send him. He is pretty good at leaving the classroom and just going and sitting in the AP's office for the remainder of the class.

Linda: Mrs. Hart, how does Justice make up the work he misses or the instruction when he gets sent to the AP's office?

Mrs. Hart: Oh, that is the other problem, Justice never does any work and doesn't pass tests either.

Formal Indirect Functional Assessment:

Choose a formal indirect assessment and conduct it with the consultee.

Linda: Mrs. Hart, I would like us to fill out the Indirect Functional Assessment to help us make sure when are talking about the same problem behavior and to help us look at things in the environment that may be related to Justice engaging in this behavior. So let's start off by labeling the problem behavior as **Inappropriate Verbal Behavior** and defining it as: *Any time Justice raises his voice above a conversation level or says inappropriate words (such as B*tch, F*ck, or "I hate you") either directed at someone or not*. Does that sound right?

Mrs. Hart: Yes, that is exactly what I'm dealing with.

Linda: Good, let's start the assessment. I'm going to ask you some questions and I want you to respond with either a yes/always, maybe/sometimes, or no/never. I can't explain the questions so just try to answer them as best you can. Ready?

- *Hypotheses about causes* – This is an important opportunity to allow the teacher to provide his or her own hypotheses for why the student acts the way he does. The SBFC practitioner may have very different views about the hypotheses, but it is critical to learn what the teacher believes. When the teacher has been engaged in hypothesizing, he or she is more receptive to alternative ideas later in the consultation process. This is Illustrated in Box 5.6.

Box 5.6 Exploring Hypotheses and Indirect and Descriptive Assessments

PC Phases of Inquiry	*FBA Model*	*Case of Justice*
Exploring hypotheses:	*Indirect Assessment continued:*	
At this step, ask questions such as "Why do you think he responded that way?" or "What purpose do you think that behavior is serving for him?" "What does he get out of that behavior?" "Why did you respond the way you did?"	Ask the teacher to hypothesize the function of the client's behavior giving him or her the choices of Attention, Escape, Tangible, Automatic.	Linda: Why do you think Justice uses foul language in your class? Before you respond, I'd like you to decide whether he does it to gain attention, escape a task or situation, access some type of tangible, or because it's an automatic, sensory response. Mrs. Hart: Well, I think he likes getting the other students in class to give him attention even if he is mean to them. He probably doesn't get enough attention at home, so he tries to get it in my classroom. I know what you are thinking … I am giving him a lot of attention too because I have to keep scolding him. Bad attention is better than no attention, right? Linda: I'd like us to consider only what happens in the classroom rather than what might be happening at home for now. So you believe that Justice engages in foul language because he gets attention

| Conduct a classroom observation. | *Descriptive Assessment:* Conduct an ABC assessment recording the antecedents and consequences for a minimum of five instances of the problem behavior.

Even if the consultant has already formed a hypothesis, that result is not to be shared until Confrontive Inquiry. It is best to allow the teacher to offer his or her own insights before providing him or her with your results. | from his peers and from you. Is that correct?

Mrs. Hart: Yes, it could be for other reasons too, but I think that is the main reason.
Linda: Great, Mrs. Hart. Would it be OK if I did a classroom observation tomorrow?
Mrs. Hart: Sure, I would love for you to help.
Linda: Well I'm not going to intervene, I just want to observe if that is ok with you.

Linda conducts an ABC assessment recording the antecedents and consequences related to Justice yelling and saying bad words.

A=Mrs. Hart tells the class to do their one-minute math warm up.
B=Justice tells Mrs. Hart that there is no f*cking way he is going to do the warm-up.
C=Mrs. Hart tells him he can't talk like that and that he needs to do his work.

A=Justice tries to copy from Melissa and she covers her paper.
B=Justice starts calling Mrs. Hart a b*tch.
C=Mrs. Hart goes over to Melissa and asks what is going on.

A=Mrs. Hart tells the class to open their books to page 79 and to follow along with the lesson.
B=Justice says that the lesson is a f*cking joke and so is Mrs. Hart.
C= Mrs. Hart ignores Justice and focuses on the |

other students in the class.

A=Mrs. Hart asks Justice to come up to the board and do a problem.
B=Justice tells Mrs. Hart there is no way in hell he is going to do the problem and she can go f*ck herself.
C= Mrs. Hart tells Justice he cannot speak to her that way and he needs to leave and go to the AP's office.

• *Actions taken or contemplated* – This is where the SBFC practitioner would ask the teacher about what he or she has already tried to do to address the problem. It is also a good idea to ask the teacher what he or she has thought about trying but has not had the chance to do so, or hasn't made the decision to do so. This helps to avoid giving the teacher that annoying feeling one gets when a suggestion is made later, but one doesn't get credit for thinking of it first. This is Illustrated in Box 5.7.

Box 5.7 Exploring Actions Taken or Contemplated and Indirect Assessment

PC Phases of Inquiry	*FBA Model*	*Case of Justice*
Exploring actions taken or contemplated:	*Indirect Assessment continued*:	
Be certain to ask the consultee what he or she has already tried to do to address the problem. This helps the consultee to understand the perception of resources including his or her own knowledge and skills.	Have the consultee discuss the strategies that have been tried to address the challenging behavior in the past. Try to probe why the outcomes did or did not work.	After the observation, Linda starts asking Mrs. Hart about what she has tried in the past to address the issue. Linda: So Mrs. Hart, when Justice is frustrated and engages in inappropriate verbal behavior, you send him to the AP's office. What else have you tried to either prevent or eliminate that behavior?
The consultant provides enough opportunity for the consultee to discuss what has already been tried along with how well		

it worked or didn't work
and the reasons behind
the outcomes.

Mrs. Hart: Well, of
course I have tried talk-
ing to him and telling
him he cannot act that
way in my class.
Linda: OK, so you have
tried talking to him about
his behavior; did that
have any effect on him?
Mrs. Hart: No, it is just
like it went in one ear and
out the other.
Linda: What else have
you tried?
Mrs. Hart: Well, I tried
ignoring him and putting
his seat in the back corner
of the classroom.
Linda: So you put his seat
in the back corner away
from his peers and tried
to ignore him; how did
that work?
Mrs. Hart: Actually, when
I sat him in the back
corner he just sat there but
he didn't do any work.
Linda: Did you try any-
thing else?
Mrs. Hart: No, I think
that those are all the
things I have tried.
That's why he just needs
to be removed from my
class. I have tried everything in my ability to
make him stop being
disrespectful.
Linda: Let me make sure
I got everything; you
have tried talking to him,
telling him the rules of
your class, and putting
his seat away from the
other students, but none
of these interventions
have worked in getting
him to stop engaging in
inappropriate verbal
behavior which we have
defined as *any time Justice
raises his voice above a conversation level or says*

> *inappropriate words (such as b*tch, f*ck, or "I hate You") either directed at someone or not.*
>
> Linda: Mrs. Hart, you have clearly tried multiple things to help Justice. Can you think of why talking to him, telling him the rules, or putting him at the back of the class did not work?

This is a difficult stage for the SBFC practitioner to navigate. While there is more direction provided and the SBFC practitioner does not have to be so careful not to prematurely impose a structure such as during Pure Inquiry, there still needs to be caution not to inadvertently enter into Confrontive Inquiry. For example, the SBFC practitioner can ask: "What have you tried?" but should not ask "Have you tried calling his parents?" or "Have you considered ignoring him when he acts like that?" These questions would be confrontive and would be fine if they were asked deliberately during the Confrontive stage of Inquiry.

STAGE 3 CONFRONTIVE INQUIRY

The consultant shares his or her own ideas and reactions about the process and the content of the story. By sharing one's own ideas, the consultant forces the consultee to think about the situation from a new perspective, hence these questions are by definition confrontive. This is illustrated in Box 5.8.

Box 5.8 Confrontive Inquiry and Analysis of Assessments and Functional Analysis

PC Phases of Inquiry	*FBA Model*	*Case of Justice*
Confrontive:	*Analysis of assessments:*	
	During this part of the consultation the consultant goes over the results of the Indirect and Descriptive Assessment and then has the consultee identify why the	Linda: Mrs. Hart, I would like to go over the results of the Indirect and Descriptive Assessment at this time. The conclusion from the Indirect Assessment indicates that

former interventions were not effective. It's at this stage that the consultant offers a great deal of direct feedback about the details of an effective treatment plan. If the consultee lacks the appropriate skills, the consultant may take the opportunity to teach the skill.

Justice engages in inappropriate verbal behavior to escape aversive tasks. Likewise, the Descriptive Assessment yields more information regarding the fact that Justice keeps engaging in inappropriate verbal behavior until he is sent out of class because that is when the demand to engage in an aversive task is removed. Let's go over what you have done in the past and why it might not have worked: When Justice has gotten frustrated with math and just wants to get out of doing his work, what have you done? Mrs. Hart: Well, when I told him the rules and talked to him, he remained in my class and I had to keep telling him to get to work before he would blow up. And when I put him at the back of the class, he just sat there with his head down until I told him to get to work and then he would blow up. So I guess, when I tell him to get to work he still gets frustrated and then he wastes the period arguing with me or just sitting there not doing anything. Linda: That is great, Mrs. Hart. Let me try to summarize what we have talked about this time. So by doing our assessments we have identified that Justice is behind in math, that math frustrates him, and that he wants to get out of doing math work. You have tried talking to him, which didn't work.

You have also tried moving his chair, which somewhat worked except when you would tell him to pick up his head and do work. So could we say that we know three things: 1) Justice needs help academically with math, 2) sending him out of the class is giving him what he wants, and 3) that talking to him and letting him sit out doesn't work.

Mrs. Hart: Wow, Linda, that is it.

Linda: Great, I know you have already given me so much of your time, but I think we are really ready to come up with a constructive approach that will not only help you but will also help Justice. What do you say about scheduling a brainstorming session for the end of the week? In the meantime, I would like to bring Justice to my office so I can make sure we have hit the nail on the head for why he engages in the problem behavior and to get a better idea of where he is at academically with math.

Mrs. Hart: So the next time we will meet, you will tell me what to do and how to handle Justice?

Linda: No, Mrs. Hart, we will work together to come up with a plan to help Justice as well as have him be more successful and appropriate in your class. But we need to have a plan for what you can do if he does engage in problem behavior.

Functional Analysis:

Consultant validates the hypothesized function of the problem behavior by manipulating suspected variables and conducts any academic assessments.

Consultant conducts assessments with Justice and determines he is not at grade level in math and that his problem behavior functions to escape from doing math work.

It's at this phase of inquiry that the process consultant asks about specific strategies to consider and will offer his or her expert perspective on the problem and why it is occurring.

In the Confrontive phase, the consultee can be direct about addressing the evidence that supports an intervention and the knowledge and skills that need to be developed to implement the plan effectively.

Consultant relays information from assessments and discusses evidence-based strategies related to the function of the problem behavior and the teacher's feasibility of implementing interventions.

Linda: Thanks for meeting with me, Mrs. Hart. As we suspected, the assessments indicate that Justice is below grade level in math and that he engages in problem behavior to get out of class. I would like for us to take a look at some evidence-based interventions for escape-maintained behavior. One thing we know is that when Justice is frustrated he will react with inappropriate verbal behavior and that he is likely to get frustrated given he is so far behind in his math skills. Generally, Justice starts engaging in problem behavior when you ask the class to start their math warm-up. Can you think of a way based on some antecedent manipulations that we can ensure that Justice does not get frustrated during this time?

Mrs. Hart: Well, I never knew he was so far behind academically, so I guess he really needs some help in catching up. Maybe I can spend the warm-up time working directly with him where he is at academically and try to bring in real-life examples that he may be interested in.

Linda: Great idea Mrs. Hart! We also know that when you sit him in the back of the class or send him to the AP's office, he gets out of doing math, which is what he wants. What do you think we could do instead?

Mrs. Hart: Well, I guess I could commit to not sending him out of class, but how will I make sure the other kids don't start doing the same thing?

Linda: Great, Mrs. Hart. Yes, let's make the commitment that you will keep Justice in class no matter what. And if you are worried about the other kids, why not give them a break or attention when they are doing their work?

Mrs. Hart: Oh, I get it, teach Justice how to act to get a break.

Linda: Exactly! Maybe we could even schedule some breaks in after he has done some work for a specific amount of time; what do you think?

Mrs. Hart: Yeah, I guess we could all use a break every now and then.

During this stage, the SBFC practitioner who is new to PC might find that new information is shared by the teacher at this time. This can be evidence that Pure or Exploratory Inquiry were not completed as thoroughly as they should have been. Chalk it up as lessons learned to improve your skills set for future applications of PC. But when the teacher shares new information, this can also be a form of resistance, changing the narrative deliberately to avoid reaching the stage where changes are discussed. Teachers often appreciate Pure Inquiry and Exploratory Inquiry as being quite engaging and stimulating. But Confrontive Inquiry, for some teachers, brings about suggestions for change. Strategies for monitoring and follow-up are shown in Box 5.9.

Box 5.9 Follow-up and Monitoring Intervention

PC Phases of Inquiry	*FBA M7odel*	*Case of Justice*
Follow-up:	*Monitoring Intervention:*	
It is important to check in with the teacher to determine if any of the developed interventions are working to improve the behavior. This will serve to reinforce the elements that can be applied in similar situations in the future.	Consultant should have teacher take data on the number of inappropriate verbal behaviors that occur per day. In addition, consultant should do a treatment integrity check. If the behavior is not improving, but the intervention is being implemented, then a more complex analysis needs to be done. If the behavior is not improving and the intervention is not being implemented appropriately, the SBFC needs to use his or her PC skills to address.	Linda: Hi Mrs. Hart, how are things going with Justice? Mrs. Hart: Linda, you would be amazed. Since I started helping him first thing when he comes to class he has really made a lot of improvements both in his academic level as well as in the way he talks to me. Linda: Great, how is the not sending him out of class going? Mrs. Hart: Well ... that is a little harder, but since he doesn't start off saying bad words it has been easier for me to ignore what he says and just try to get him back on task. Linda: I'm so glad to hear that things are going well. Would you mind if I come in and do an observation? Mrs. Hart: No, not at all.

Multicultural Counseling Considerations

SBFC practitioners may recognize that FBAs and the treatment plans that result when done well have significant support in the literature, but may at times seem quite prescriptive. During treatment implementation and treatment evaluation the SBFC practitioner should consider cultural issues that could affect treatment integrity. For example, if a child sasses back to a teacher, the teacher may not ignore the behavior as this may appear to condone such displays of disrespect to elders. So rather than ignore the backtalk or outburst, the teacher may try to punish the student. Consultants shouldn't disregard the importance of displaying respect for elders and should accept that tolerating certain behaviors (cussing, threatening) is unacceptable. Another consideration is that the details elicited by the FBA involve a scrutiny of behavior that may feel too invasive within certain cultural groups.

Rogers (2000) identifies six cross-cultural consultation competencies, many of which go beyond consultation and apply to all roles of the SBFC practitioner:

1   Understanding one's own and others' culture
2   Developing cross-cultural communication and interpersonal skills
3   Examining cultural embeddedness of consultation
4   Using qualitative methodologies
5   Acquiring culture-specific knowledge
6   Developing knowledge and skill in use of interpreters

Sheridan (2000) notes that although behavioral consultation and conjoint behavioral consultation, which both apply FBAs, have significant support in the literature for their effectiveness in addressing challenging behaviors, little research has been done on their applications in multicultural settings. Sheridan points out that the structural elements of behavioral consultation and conjoint behavioral consultation are often the focus of research, but that consultation itself is relational in nature and this is an area that needs further study among behavioral bonsultants. We have partially addressed this through the use of PC along with the FBA model, but Howethe effectiveness of this proposed framework is yet to be investigated. Nonetheless, even within the structural features of the FBA model, consultants can address cultural values and issues through improved relational skills and better awareness of how problems are identified, analyzed, and treated from different cultural viewpoints (Holcomb-McCoy, 2009). Sheridan, Eagle, and Doll (2006) found that over an eight-year study of graduate students in school psychology training programs, conjoint behavioral consultation was perceived to be effective in settings both with and without diversity. They looked at behavioral change, goal attainment, and acceptability, and reported satisfaction with the elements of conjoint behavioral consultation.

Generally speaking, behavioral consultation is typically based on single-case research design, thus it offers excellent opportunity for addressing the specific cultural aspects of the problem in the setting in which it occurs. The difficulty arises when either consultants fail to recognize cultural variables or when the behavior occurs across settings such as at home and in the classroom.

Challenges and Solutions

From our experience working with graduate students in SBFC at California State University, Los Angeles, we find that one challenge in preparing them to conduct an integrated approach using PC and especially FBAs is that it tends to be inconsistent with their general skill repertoire when conducting family counseling. Our SBFC graduate students will often hold less value for an approach that limits focus to measureable, tightly operationalized behaviors than they do for methods that invite consideration of thoughts and feelings of the client. There is a tendency to believe that behavior analysts are too sterile in their approach to the presenting problem because there is a greater emphasis on structure than on relationships during the problem-solving process. Some behavioral consultants may come across as too dogmatic or pay minimal attention to building relationships in the consultation process and the criticism is often deserved. Many have complained about the high level of jargon that behaviorists use in working with non-behavioral clients, consultees, and colleagues. However, the FBA model has strength in its evidence of effective outcomes and goal attainment, leaving no doubt that the approach is quite effective at reducing unwanted behaviors and increasing desired behaviors. We find that one way to improve the FBA model is to align it with PC and have provided this as a way to address the shortcomings of an FBA approach, especially as applied by SBFC practitioners.

As indicated in the previous section, FBA can be applied in multicultural settings, but very little research has been done in this area. We hope to address this as we study the effectiveness of our PC/FBA framework. Integrating these two models holds promise for modeling problem-solving for the consultee in a manner that will promote better skill development and improved functioning in face of current and future problems.

Another challenge that is important to point out to the SBFC practitioner comes up with the concept of "assessment" in school settings. If assessments are conducted in order to consider placement in special education settings or services for any given student, then a written assessment plan must be obtained. This is not the intent of this chapter. Instead, the FBA is described in consultation to help the teacher gather information that will lead to appropriate, evidence-based interventions. This is certainly allowable as long as it is understood that this is not a formal assessment for special education.

Summary

SBFC practitioners are in a good position to engage parents in consultation that allows them to implement their own treatment plans. With practice and experience, SBFC practitioners can learn to differentiate their direct intervention skills such as family counseling from their indirect intervention skills such as in consultation. We know we may have complicated this chapter by introducing the SBFC practitioner not only to behavioral consultation but also to process consultation. We encourage the use of PC with any model of consultation including Mental Health Consultation and Adlerian Consultation. It allows the consultant to more fully involve the consultee in problem-solving through active inquiry. Consultees first present the problem from their own perspectives, and that helps to improve cultural awareness for the consultant. It also makes it more palatable for the consultee to discuss solutions as they are not simply being "prescribed" by the expert.

Resources

Center for Effective Collaboration and Practice

This website offers descriptions of FBAs and offers tools and examples that support understanding of its applications.

Intervention Central

This site offers many resources for behavior interventions and ready-to-use forms that can be helpful in developing plans.

The Iris Center

This site offers excellent resources and tutorials in many areas pertaining to students with disabilities including culturally relevant classroom management strategies.

NICHCY National Dissemination Center for Children with Disabilities

This site is specifically intended as a resource for parents and provides many articles and resources regarding behavior for children with disabilities that can be applied to all children.

OSEP Technical Assistance Center on Positive Behavior Interventions and Supports

This site has excellent resources for positive behavioral, school-wide interventions.

PENT Positive Environments, Network of Trainers

This site is offered by the California Department of Education and is filled with useful materials including PowerPoint presentations of various topics relating to behavior.
See SBFC EResources for links to these sites.

Bibliography

Alderman, G.L. & Gimpel, G.A. (1996). The interaction between type of behavior problem and type of consultant: Teachers' preferences for professional assistance. *Journal of Educational & Psychological Consultation*, 7(4), 305–313.

Andersen, M.N., Hofstadter, K.L., Kupzyk, S., Daly III, E., Bleck, A.A., Collaro, A.L., & Jones, K.E. (2010). A guiding framework for integrating the consultation process and behavior analytic practice in schools: The treatment validation consultation model. *Journal of Behavior Assessment and Intervention in Children*, 1(1), 53–84.

Anderson, C.M., Rodriguez, B.J., & Campbell, A. (2015). Functional behavior assessment in schools: Current status and future directions. *Journal of Behavioral Education*, 24, 338–371.

Ashbaugh, R. & Pecks, S.M. (1998). Treatment of sleep problems in a toddler: A replication of the faded bedtime with response cost protocol. *Journal of Applied Behavior Analysis*, 31, 127–129.

Asmus, J.M., Vollmer, T.R., & Borrero, J.C. (2002). Functional behavior assessment: A school-based model. *Education and Treatment of Children*, 25, 67–90.

Bijou, S.W., Peterson, R.F., & Ault, M.H. (1968). A method to integrate descriptive and experimental field studies at the level of data and empirical concepts. *Journal of Applied Behavior Analysis*, 1, 175–191.

Bruni, T.P., Drevon, D., Hixson, M., Wyse, R., Corcoran, S., & Fursa, S. (2017). The effect of functional behavior assessment on school-based interventions: A meta-analysis of single-case research. *Psychology in the Schools*, 54(4), 351–369.

Butler, T.S., Weaver, A.D., Doggett, R.A., & Watson, T.S. (2002). Countering teacher resistance in behavioral consultation: Recommendations for the school-based consultant. *The Behavior Analyst Today*, 3(3). Retrieved from www.biomedsearch. com/ article/Countering-teacher-resistance-in-behavioral/170020731.html

Caplan, G. & Caplan, R.B. (1998). *Mental health consultation and collaboration.* San Francisco, CA: Jossey Bass.

Cholewa, B., Thomas, A., & Cook, J. (2016). Teachers' perceptions and experiences consulting with school counselors: A qualitative study. *Professional School Counseling*, 20(1), 77–88.

Christensen, A., Wallace, M.D., Romick, K., Houchins, N., Landaburu, H., Tarbox, J., & Tarbox, R. (2002, February). The systematic development of an indirect assessment: Indirect functional behavioral assessment. Presented at the annual meeting of the California Association of Behavior Analysis, San Francisco, CA.

Gortmaker, V.J., Daly III, E.J., McCurdy, M., Persampieri, M.J., & Hergenrader, M. (2007). Improving reading outcomes for children with learning disabilities: Using brief experimental analysis to develop parent-tutoring interventions. *Journal of Applied Behavior Analysis*, 42, 659–664.

Guli, L.A. (2005). Evidence-based parent consultation with school-related outcomes. *School Psychology Quarterly*, 20(4), 455–472.

Hanley, G.P., Jin, C.S., Vanselau, N.R., & Hanratty, L.A. (2014). Producing meaningful improvements in problem behavior of children with autism via synthesized analysis and treatments. *Journal of Applied Behavior Analysis*, 47, 16–36.

Holcomb-McCoy, C. (2009). Cultural considerations in parent consultation. *Professional Counseling Digest* (ACAPCD-25). Alexandria, VA: American Counseling Association.

Ingraham, C.L. (2000). Consultation through a multicultural lens: Multicultural and cross-cultural consultation in schools. *School Psychology Review*, 29(3), 320–343.

Iwata, B. (1995). *Functional analysis screening tool*. Gainseville, FL: The Florida Center on Self-Injury.

Iwata, B.A., Dorsey, M.F., Slifer, K.J., Bauman, K.E., & Richman, G.S. (1994). Toward a functional analysis of self-injury. *Journal of Applied Behavior Analysis*, 27, 197–209. doi: 10.1901/jaba.1994.27-197 (reprinted from *Analysis and Intervention in Developmental Disabilities*, 2, 3-20, 1982).

Kampwirth, T.J. & Powers, K.M. (2012). *Collaborative consultation in the schools: Effective practices for students with learning and behavior problems* (4th ed.). Boston, MA: Pearson.

Katsiyannis, A., Conroy, M., & Zhang, D. (2008). District-level administrators' perspectives on implementation of functional behavior assessment in schools. *Behavioral Disorders*, 34(1), 14–26.

Kratochwill, T.R. & Bergan, J.R. (1990). *Behavioral consultation in applied settings: An Individual guide*. New York, NY: Plenum.

Kratochwill, T.R., Bergan, J.R., Sheridan, S.M., & Elliott, S.N. (1998). Assumptions of behavioral consultation: After all is said and done more has been done than said. *School Psychology Quarterly*, 13(1), 63–80.

Matson, J. L., & Vollmer, T. R. (1995). *The Questions About Behavioral Function (QABF) user's guide*. Baton Rouge, LA: Scientific Publishers.

Mayer, G.R., Sulzer-Azaroff, B., & Wallace, M.D. (2018). *Behavior analysis for lasting change* (4th ed.). Cornwall-on-Hudson, NY: Sloane.

McKenna, S.A., Rosenfield, S., & Gravois, T.A. (2009). Measuring the behavioral indicators of instructional consultation: A preliminary validity study. *School Psychology Review*, 38(4), 496–509.

Mueller, M.M., Piazza, C.C., Moore, J.W., Kelley, M.E., Bethke, S.A., Pruett, A.E., Oberdorff, A.J., & Layer, S.A. (2003). Training parents to implement pediatric feeding protocols. *Journal of Applied Behavior Analysis*, 36, 545–562.

Ringdahl, J.E. & Sellers, J.A. (2013). The effects of different adults as therapists during functional analysis. *Journal of Applied Behavior Analysis*, 33, 247–250.

Rogers, M. (2000). Examining the cultural context of consultation. *School Psychology Review*, 29(3), 414–418.

Schein, E. (1999). *Process consultation revisited: Building the helping relationship*. Reading, MA: Addison-Wesley.

Sheridan, S.M. (2000). Considerations of multiculturalism and diversity in behavioral consultation with parents and teachers. *School Psychology Review*, 29(3), 344–353.

Sheridan, S.M., Eagle, J.W., & Doll, B. (2006). An examination of the efficacy of conjoint behavioral consultation with diverse clients. *School Psychology Quarterly*, 21(4), 396–417.

Sheridan, S.M. & Elliott, S.N. (1991). Behavioral consultation as a process for linking the assessment and treatment of social skills. *Journal of Educational and Psychological Consultation*, 2(2), 151–173.

Skinner, M.E. & Hales, M.R. (1992). Classroom teachers' "explanations" of student behavior: One possible barrier to the acceptance and use of applied behavior analysis procedures in the schools. *Journal of Educational & Psychological Consultation*, 3(3), 219–233.

Sugai, G. & Horner, R. (2009). Responsiveness-to-intervention and school-wide positive behavior supports: Integration of multi-tiered system approaches. *Exceptionality*, 17, 223–237. DOI: 10.1080/09362830903235375.

Tarver Behring, S. & Ingraham, C.L. (1998). Culture as a central component to consultation: A call to the field. *Journal of Educational and Psychological Consultation*, 9, 57–72.

6 School Intervention

How to Facilitate Classroom Meetings

Gema Macias and Deborah Ribera

Overview: *In this chapter, SBFC practioners will learn how classroom meetings can benefit students of all levels. The components and format of classroom meetings are identified as well as the specific procedural steps one should follow in order to successfully implement classroom meetings at their school site.*

Background

Classroom meetings are a period of structured time in a school classroom during which all students are led in a discussion and/or lesson related to a specific topic that is important or relevant to the group (Emmett & Monsour, 1996). The classroom meeting may be facilitated or co-facilitated by a School-Based Family Counseling (SBFC) practitioner within a classroom setting.

Classroom meetings act as a vehicle to teach conflict resolution skills, effective communication skills, critical thinking skills, and decision-making skills (Edwards & Mullis, 2003). They are an ideal strategy for the SBFC practitioner because they provide the learning experiences missing in skills-based programs by modeling equality, inclusiveness, and relationship-building (Frey & Doyle, 2001). Students become skilled at identifying problems, seeking possible solutions, entering discussions, and holding each other accountable for implementing solutions (Knapp, 2010). Classroom meetings carry the potential of preventing classroom problems from arising.

Classroom meetings can be used to provide psychoeducation regarding a variety of topics such as conflict resolution skills, effective communication skills, perspective taking, and the resolution of interpersonal problems such as bullying and harassment. They can also help the teacher develop a sense of belonging and community in the classroom (Curran, 2003). The classroom meeting can help students learn to hold civil, respectful discussions, the cornerstone of the democratic process.

If held on a regular basis, classroom meetings can help build a community of learners within the classroom by teaching new skills, increasing communication, and providing an environment where problems and conflict can be resolved (Kriete, 2003). Students are known by name, thereby reducing the sense of isolation and alienation. The participants develop a common understanding of the language used in the classroom. During classroom meetings the group members (students) identify causes of problems and can see the results of their actions by hearing reports from other group members.

Alfred Adler is widely cited at the first practitioner to make the connection between child psychology and the classroom, establishing child guidance centers in Austrian schools in the 1920s (Adler, 1930; Gerrard, 2008; Utay & Utay, 1996). In the 1930s, Adler's contemporary, Rudolf Dreikurs, popularized these ideas in the United States (Dreikurs, 1958). The application of Adlerian psychology in school programs persists today largely through the philosophies that underlie classroom management strategies (Soheili et al., 2015). Various counseling theories inform current classroom interventions, however. For instance, there has been success in using an integrative approach to children's school behavior that incorporates theory and technique from both Adler and psychiatrist William Glasser (Gamble & Watkins, 1983).

In *Schools Without Failure* (1969), Glasser conceptualized the procedural foundations of a classroom meeting. Glasser believed that, in order to help students take responsibility for their learning, particularly their choices, schools must avoid stimulus response programs that control student behavior and instead help develop programs that increase intrinsic student motivation and improve student achievement. Classroom meetings can help students make better choices and can have a positive impact upon the participant's sense of belonging, power, freedom, and enjoyment. Such constructs are the foundation of Glasser's choice theory (1988).

In a climate of reduced resources and increased accountability, the SBFC practitioner must find effective methods to address student needs that reach the largest number of students in an efficient manner. These methods must also have a positive and lasting impact on school culture and community. Classroom meetings, then, are an ideal and essential strategy for an SBFC practitioner.

Evidence-based Support

Research conducted using Glasser's classroom meeting model shows positive change with primary school students (Emmett & Monsour, 1996) and students with learning disabilities who show behavioral disturbances (Marandola & Imber, 1979). Sisco (1992) reported elementary students who participated in classroom meetings exhibited fewer referrals for disciplinaries to the main office. Feldhusen and Feldhusen (2004) studied the effects of the classroom meeting on students identified as gifted. The results suggest classroom management can be enhanced via weekly class meetings in which gifted and talented students have the opportunity to offer ideas, solutions, and creative insights. Angell (2004) studied the minutes from classroom meetings held over two years in a private school and concluded that classroom meetings appeared to allow students the opportunity for collective problem-solving, in turn contributing to a peaceful classroom environment.

In 1993, Walsh and McCarroll recommended the school counselor move to a group focus, providing services such as teaching skills to groups, serving in the role of consultant to teachers and parents, and serving as a link to community services agencies. Dreikurs and Cassel (1972) specifically mention the classroom meeting as a vehicle for modeling the democratic process of group problem-solving through developing empathy and group membership. Halaby (2000) found that students benefit from classroom meetings because they can see cause and effect of their actions since conflicts are named and the repercussions of actions are publicly discussed.

Classroom meetings are a common tenet of positive discipline approaches to classroom management (Nelsen, Lott, & Glenn, 2013). As a standardized format for the classroom meeting does not exist, its level of effectiveness as an evidence-based intervention is not yet widely understood (Edwards & Mullis, 2003). More research is still needed on the effectiveness of classroom meetings; however, it is important to understand that while the lack of standardization may make the method resistant to replication, it is the inherent flexibility and adaptability of the method that makes it so effective across diverse classroom settings.

Procedure

Definition

Classroom meetings are short-term or long-term psychoeducational topic and discussion sessions that are led by an SBFC practitioner and/or the classroom teacher. A basic classroom meeting has four components:

a) *A regular meeting time:* The ideal time to meet is in a homeroom or advisement period, immediately before a release time such as recess or lunch, dismissal to another class, or at the end of the school day. This prevents the meeting from spilling into time scheduled for a lesson or classroom change.
b) *A regular meeting location:* The location for the meeting should remain the same. This builds familiarity and predictability for the group.
c) *An agenda:* An agenda should be posted. The agenda should be short and fit into the time frame set aside for the meeting. The facilitator should make the agenda; however, group member input should be included. Sometimes group members may not want to discuss an issue in public; it may be too personal to a group member. The SBFC practitioner should clarify how and when students can discuss private matters with them or the teacher.
d) *A circle for seating arrangement:* A critical element is the use of the circle in a classroom meeting. It may be tempting to hold the meeting with

students seated in their usual seating arrangement and the facilitator in a central location. This arrangement is convenient and avoids the brief disorganization of moving furniture to accommodate a circle. But the typical seating arrangement defeats the purpose of the classroom meeting: to include all group members. In a circle every group member is visible and is included in the group process. It may be cumbersome to move furniture, but with continued practice students will quickly learn to move furniture with little disturbance and time.

The content discussed in a classroom meeting will change; however, the format remains the same and includes the following:

a) *An opening:* The opening may be a greeting, reviewing group norms or reviewing the agenda for the meeting.
b) *A time for discussion:* The discussion centers around the agenda item(s) posted.
c) *A closing:* The closing may be a review of the lesson, a closing activity, agreements made, and/or announcements relevant to the group.

Implementing classroom meetings as an SBFC method requires three distinct stages: planning, implementation, and evaluation. Each of these stages requires their own steps.

Step 1: Planning

This first step, planning, can be organized into three substeps: consultation, needs assessment, and logistics. The planning stage is extremely important for the success of classroom meetings, as it lays a strong foundation for introducing a new practice to the school.

Step 1a: Needs Assessment

During the needs assessment, the SBFC practitioner must determine and develop the reason for the classroom meetings: How could classroom meetings benefit the students, the teachers, and the school as a whole? The SBFC practitioner should seek information from administrators, counselors, and teachers about student needs. Students and families should also be included in the planning stage. As trained professionals we often think we know what our students need, but once we discuss our point of view with students and parents, they can make us aware of an aspect of the problem that we did not see before. This can broaden or narrow the original scope of the project. Centering the student voice in the development of interventions is an essential step to creating culturally responsive programming. Common classroom meeting purposes are shown in Box 6.1.

Box 6.1 Common Classroom Meeting Purposes

Develop classroom routines

Teach prosocial skills

Prevent or intervene in teasing/bullying

Teach conflict resolution skills with subsequent application in a safe
environment

Solve classroom disagreements

Discuss issues relevant to students

Develop leadership skills

Step 1b: Consultation

If the SBFC practitioner has established during the needs assessment that classroom meetings would be an appropriate intervention, he/she should continue by
discussing the method of classroom meetings with school administrators, counselors, and teachers. In this step, it is important to clearly define what classroom
meetings are, to present evidence that supports the use of classroom meetings, and
to tie all of this in with the information you gleaned from your needs assessment. If
your school is implementing School-wide Positive Behavioral Intervention and
Supports (PBIS), then it will be helpful to discuss with all the stakeholders how
classroom meetings can support this framework.

Identifying and collaborating with teachers who are willing to implement
the classroom meeting is a key aspect of establishing buy-in. Some teachers
may want to hold regular meetings on their own. In this case, the SBFC
practitioner may initially lead meetings serving as a model while the teacher
serves as co-facilitator. The SBFC practitioner eventually cedes the role of
lead facilitator to the teacher and may remain for a short time as co-
facilitator or leave altogether. The SBFC practitioner's role changes at this
point to that of a consultant. The SBFC practitioner may meet with
participating teachers to debrief, identify problem areas in facilitating meetings, and propose solutions to address difficulties.

When working with teachers it is important for the SBFC practitioner to help
the teacher understand the purpose of the classroom meeting. The skills of
unconditional acceptance, attention to nonverbal communication, active listening,
open-ended questioning, and group facilitation are the skills of the SBFC practitioner and not necessarily part of a teacher's repertoire of responses. For this
reason, it is important that the SBFC practitioner collaborate with teachers to plan
meetings or co-lead them, and serve as the model for the skills of facilitation. The
SBFC practitioner's role may be to assist the teacher in understanding that his/her
role changes from that of managing a class and serving as disciplinarian to that of

a facilitator. As a consultant, the SBFC practitioner helps teachers become mindful of their responses to student participation during classroom meetings.

Step 1c: Logistics

The best time to implement the classroom meeting is at the start of school year. The classroom meeting can be used to build cohesion among students for successful classroom instruction. The SBFC practitioner can serve as consultant to teachers to identify issues that need attention in order to prevent problems from developing. Intervening early in the year will prevent escalation and identify students who may need intensive intervention outside the classroom. Classroom meetings may be short term with a particular goal such as teaching conflict resolution skills or communication skills, or long term with the goal of having students eventually take responsibility for and lead the meetings.

Step 2: Implementation

Once you have conducted a needs assessment, consulted with key stakeholders, and planned the logistics of the classroom meeting, the meetings can be implemented. This second step of the process involves laying the groundwork for classroom meetings and implementing the basic classroom meeting format. Laying the groundwork refers to teaching the students what a classroom meeting is and clarifying how they should behave and participate during this time. If the students are not aware of the expectations the SBFC practitioner and teacher have for the classroom meeting, it is unlikely they will be able to fulfill them. In order to ensure successful implementation then, the SBFC practitioner must complete the following substeps:

Step 2a: Develop and Teach Norms

Norms are positively stated rules and expectations that students will be asked to follow in the meetings. An example of a norm could be: "Show respect to the speaker." A discussion around this norm would need to include how we show respect to the speaker (e.g., by not talking over them, by listening closely, by not having side conversations while they are talking). The SBFC practitioner should develop and pre-teach norms prior to the initial meeting. Including students in the development of norms is ideal, as it will ensure that students understand the norms and will give them more ownership over the meetings. Norms should number five or fewer so that students have no trouble remembering them. More than five norms becomes difficult to consistently implement. Norms should be stated in positive terms, i.e., stated in terms of what group members should do rather than what they should not do. This allows students to aspire to enact positive behaviors through the group. Sample norms are listed in Box 6.2.

Box 6.2 Sample Classroom Meeting Norms

1. Respect others (the idea that no person is belittled)
2. Maintain confidentiality (all information discussed in the meeting remains in the meeting)
3. Freedom to pass (no one is pressured to speak)
4. One person speaks at a time
5. Listen with an open mind

Step 2b: Teach and Rehearse Group Discussion Skills

It is important to teach and rehearse group discussion skills before the class meetings begin. Skills such as taking turns speaking, how to address group participants, active listening, and how to respond when a group member disagrees should be modeled and practiced. These skills are basic to effective communication and help students develop a repertoire of responses useful in a variety of situations.

Step 2c: Hold A Practice Meeting

This initial meeting may be short: 15 or 20 minutes. This meeting allows students to experience the meeting without the pressure of having to participate. The first meeting provides an opportunity for the students to practice the norms and group discussion skills they have learned. The facilitator should serve as a model of the norms and skills. At the end of the meeting the students should be encouraged to evaluate how they did on following norms and practicing good discussion skills. The basic classroom meeting format and components should be followed so that students and teachers can familiarize themselves with the procedure.

Step 3: Evaluation

Ensuring that you are continuously monitoring the implementation of the classroom meetings is key to their sustainability, as all stakeholders will want to know if this intervention is "working." Any evaluative inquiries you make will reflect the information that you collected during the needs assessment. That is, everyone will have slightly different reasons why they are implementing classroom meetings based on the particular student population at their particular school, so evaluation methods should be designed to address the intentions of the intervention. The suggested questions here are only meant to serve as an impetus for thinking about your own evaluation design.

Step 3a: In-meeting Evaluation

The facilitator should incorporate a simple evaluation into the meeting itself. Simply asking students during the closing how they felt the meeting went and if they have any feedback reinforces the democratic aspect of the meeting.

Step 3b: Student Surveys

The SBFC practitioner should also design a more formal evaluation method. A short survey that is administered to the students halfway through the semester as well as at the end of the semester would provide excellent data that can be presented to administrators, teachers, counselors, and parents. Sample evaluative survey questions for students are included in Box 6.3. Note that the design of the questions should be based on the age of the students you are surveying. You should also always give students space where they can respond freely (as in question number 11).

Box 6.3 Sample Student Evaluative Survey Questions

Instructions: Circle your preferred response for each item

1. I enjoy our classroom meetings.
   Definitely Yes   Kind of   Not really   Definitely No

2. I have learned to be a better communicator through our meetings.
   Definitely Yes   Kind of   Not really   Definitely No

3. I feel like our classroom is more of a community thanks to these meetings.
   Definitely Yes   Kind of   Not really   Definitely No

4. I feel like I can learn better because of our meetings.
   Definitely Yes   Kind of   Not really   Definitely No

5. I like how my facilitator leads the meetings.
   Definitely Yes   Kind of   Not really   Definitely No

6. I have learned new things about myself because of the meetings.
   Definitely Yes   Kind of   Not really   Definitely No

7. I have learned new things about my classmates because of the meetings.
   Definitely Yes   Kind of   Not really   Definitely No

8. I talk to my family about the things I learned in the meetings.
   Definitely Yes   Kind of   Not really   Definitely No

9. I talk to my friends about the things I learned in the meetings.
   Definitely Yes   Kind of   Not really   Definitely No

10. I would like to have meetings next year.
    Definitely Yes   Kind of   Not really   Definitely No

11. Is there anything else you would like to say about the meetings?
    Write it below:

Step 3c: Facilitator Feedback

A feedback form should be given to facilitators in order to understand how they have experienced the groups. Depending on how comfortable the SBFC practitioner is with qualitative research methods, they can also interview the facilitators. Sample feedback form questions for facilitators are included in Box 6.4.

Box 6.4 Sample Facilitator Feedback Questions

Instructions: Circle your preferred response for each item

1. I enjoy facilitating our classroom meetings.
   Strongly Agree   Agree   Undecided   Disagree   Strongly Disagree

2. I feel my training prepared me well to lead classroom meetings.
   Strongly Agree   Agree   Undecided   Disagree   Strongly Disagree

3. The classroom meetings are a useful way to spend in-class time.
   Strongly Agree   Agree   Undecided   Disagree   Strongly Disagree

4. I feel my class is a community of learners.
   Strongly Agree   Agree   Undecided   Disagree   Strongly Disagree

5. My students are more inclusive with each other because of classroom meetings.
   Strongly Agree   Agree   Undecided   Disagree   Strongly Disagree

6. I need more training in order to facilitate our classroom meetings.
   Strongly Agree   Agree   Undecided   Disagree   Strongly Disagree

7. I believe more classes should be holding classroom meetings.
   Strongly Agree   Agree   Undecided   Disagree   Strongly Disagree

8. I feel my students have fewer behavioral problems because of classroom meetings.
   Strongly Agree   Agree   Undecided   Disagree   Strongly Disagree

9. Please write any successes and challenges you have had with classroom meetings below:

10. Please write any questions you have about classroom meetings below:

Case Studies

The three case studies provided here are meant to familiarize you with the format of classroom meetings as well as highlight common challenges that a facilitator may face when leading a meeting. The three challenges are: handling peer conflict, the role of silence, and navigating emotion. A discussion follows each dialogue.

Case Study 1: Handling Peer Conflict

Classroom meetings can be held in a variety of classroom settings. The following is a sample dialogue from one of a series of classroom meetings in an eighth-grade special education day class with the goal of helping Albert and his classmates develop communication and conflict resolution skills. The dialogue begins after the opening and the facilitator has opened up the discussion portion of the meeting.

Facilitator:	(reviewing notes from the previous meeting) Last week the group agreed to practice asking before joining an individual or group in an activity. How did it go?
Group:	(silence)
Jason:	Albert won't leave me alone. I stay away from him but he follows me and never asks. I am trying to stay out of trouble.
Albert:	(shaking his head) No, no, that's not true. I don't follow him.
Marco:	(to Albert) I saw you.
Facilitator:	Jason, what do you want to say to Albert?
Jason:	I want Albert to leave me alone.
Facilitator:	Tell Albert what you would like him to do if he wants to join you. (silence)
Marco:	Albert has to ask if he could be with us at lunch but he never asks.
Albert:	(shaking his head) I ask.
Jason:	No, you don't, you just come up to us and last time you started calling Andrew names and Andrew didn't do nothing to you. You never ask. You have to ask.
Albert:	I didn't call Andrew names.
Facilitator:	(to the group) Let's help each other out. When anyone wants to join a group, what does the new person need to do?
Group:	Ask to see if it's ok to join the group.
Facilitator:	Albert, what do you need to do if you want to join any group?
Albert:	Ask.
Facilitator:	Jason, tell Albert what you need from him if he wants to join your group.
Jason:	(looking at Albert) You have to ask first and you can't call people names.
Albert:	(looking down) I'll ask.

Sara: I ask.
Tiffany: Me too.
Facilitator: (to the group) How can you help each other out?
Tiffany: We could remind each other to ask like we practiced.

In this sample dialogue, the facilitator kept the conversation focused on the agreed-upon skill of asking before joining a group and facilitated dialogue that addressed the skill. Note that the facilitator avoided turning the subject to the accusation of Albert's name-calling. The facilitator further avoided having a third party make the request for Jason, thereby allowing Jason the opportunity to rehearse and develop the communication skill of making a direct request to fulfill a need. The facilitator also used the group dynamic to reinforce the skill, thereby supporting all students in learning to apply the skill. The facilitator may privately discuss the name-calling accusation with Jason and Albert to determine whether intervention is required.

The teacher's use of "Let's help each other out" indicates that "Help each other out" may perhaps be a norm of that group. It seems that the students in the group had an understanding of what that meant and were able to take the facilitator's cue to stay focused on conflict resolution. This model dialogue shows how establishing and teaching norms that are related to conflict resolution can be helpful for group facilitation.

Case Study 2: The Role of Silence

The following model dialogue is from a classroom meeting facilitated by an SBFC practitioner in an eighth grade social studies course. The social studies course was selected following conversations with faculty on issues impacting instruction and exploring methods of reaching the largest number of students in an efficient and effective manner. Due to the nature of its content (people, ideas, communication, and their impact on the evolution of civilization and societies), the social studies department agreed to allow classroom meetings on a monthly basis. The topic for the meeting is cyberbullying.

Opening

Facilitator: Good morning all. On a scale of 1–5, with 5 meaning "great" and 1 meaning "not good at all," think for 30 seconds where you would rate yourself.
Group: (silence for 30 seconds)
Facilitator: Okay, how about you turn to someone beside you and tell that person your rating and one reason you gave yourself the rating.
(Facilitator(s) scan the room and monitor for level of participation and then participate in the activity.)
Group: (talking heard throughout group)

| Facilitator: | Good. Anyone willing to share your rating? |
| Group: | (silence) |

Discussion

Facilitator:	Okay. Well, I heard a lot of people sharing with their partner and I saw a lot of partners listening, so that's wonderful. Let's move on. Today's topic is about cyberbullying. I saw several requests for that topic. I have a video clip I would like to share with you. It is about a 14-year-old girl talking about her real-life experiences with being bullied on her cell phone.
Group:	(students watch video clip)
Facilitator:	How was this student bullied?
Amy:	Some people sent her messages telling her mean things like she was ugly and stupid.
Frankie:	She *was* ugly.
Group:	(snickering heard)
Amy:	That is mean Frankie.
Staci:	Yeah, it's like the bullying she was talking about. You're doing the same thing.
Jessica:	I know kids who get bullied on their cell phone. And nobody does anything about it.
Facilitator:	Why do you think that is, Jessica?
Jessica:	(shrugs): They're afraid to tell anybody. They're afraid if they tell, they'll get beat up.
William:	A lot of kids get bullied. Sometimes their parents find out and they take away their cell phone.
Facilitator:	So it sounds like cyberbullying happens frequently; kids are scared not only because they are afraid of what the bully or bullies may do but they are afraid their parents will take away their cell phones. And cell phones and messaging are very important to you.
Group:	(heads nodding ... discussion continues)

Closing

| Facilitator: | You all brought up some important points today about cyberbullying. We learned that (short summary of the discussion). We're approaching the end of our meeting time and I want to thank you so much for participating. Whether you talked or listened, you were an important part of this meeting. I also want to thank you all for following our group norms of speaking from the heart, listening from the heart, and minding the time. You did a great job. Would someone like to suggest a closing activity? |
| Julissa: | Let's do One Word. |

Facilitator: Great idea! So remember One Word is our closing activity where you think of one word that describes how you felt about group today and then we go around the circle so everyone has a chance to say your word. If you don't have a word you can just say "Thanks." Okay?
(activity …)

Facilitator: Thank you everyone. See you next month for our classroom meeting!

The facilitator opened the meeting by using a simple rating scale to gauge student level of preparedness to participate. The facilitator used "wait time" and then, rather than limit the number of students who respond aloud, allowed the opportunity for all to participate by reporting their rating to their peers, thereby preparing them for participation in the meeting. Since no volunteers stepped forward in response to the facilitator's invitation to report to the group, the facilitator was left with the option of pressing for a response or moving forward with the agenda. Using the results from the visual scan of student engagement, the facilitator elected to move forward with the agenda.

This model dialogue highlights the unavoidable and essential role of silence in a classroom meeting. Silence is unavoidable because students will inevitably have moments of shyness, fear, or fatigue either for whole class meetings or at various points during them. This is absolutely understandable, so students should not be castigated for their silence. Silence is essential because, if the facilitator is comfortable with it, it can actually be used to encourage conversation. If the facilitator allows for silence, students will have time to consider the topic and often will eventually speak up. However, if the facilitator moves on too quickly, potential opportunities for discussion will be lost. Further, students will respond to any nervousness or frustration the facilitator has about silence – often with more silence! So it is important that the facilitator become comfortable understanding silence as a natural and useful aspect of communication.

Note that the facilitator refrains from lecturing, giving advice, or correcting perceptions during the dialogue. Rather, participants in this scenario are taking the lead in verbalizing their knowledge: cyberbullying is common, the nature of the messages instills fear, and the fear leads to inaction on the part of the target. The participants also call out their peer for the comment regarding the targeted student in the video clip. In successful groups, peers will regulate each other and hold each other accountable for adhering to the norms of the group. This is an ideal dynamic, creating a more democratic group that relieves the facilitator of the need to take on the role of disciplinarian.

Case Study 3: Navigating Emotion

A common fear among administrators and teachers is that too much emotion will arise in classroom meetings and that such group discussions are better left to trained mental health professionals. SBFC practitioners do have the skills to navigate emotional content and can be helpful co-facilitators in this sense. However, if the meeting is run well and the facilitator understands their role, the emotion that arises should be something that the teacher or facilitator can handle. The key to dealing with emotion in classroom meetings is to let go of the need to act as a "fixer" for the students' problems. The facilitator's role is to encourage the students to share and to create a safe environment in which they will be heard. The facilitator's role is not to ameliorate or resolve emotions during the meeting time, but rather to create a space in which those emotions can be expressed and acknowledged. In the following dialogue, a teacher navigates an emotional discussion.

Teacher:	We are talking today about our family traditions. Many families have traditions that they pass down from generation to generation. Can you think of any traditions that your family has?
Tasha:	When my family sits down for dinner we always say grace. Now, even when I'm at a friend's house for dinner, I always say grace before I eat.
Lucas:	Yeah, I do that too!
Group:	(murmurs of agreement, then silence)
Teacher:	That's a great example of a tradition you learned from your family that you still do today. Anyone else learn something from your family that you still do today?
Angel:	How to mess someone up! (laughs)
Teacher:	What do you mean by that, Angel?
Angel:	I didn't learn anything from my parents except how to fight. Everyone was always fighting.
Raya:	At least you have parents. I didn't learn anything from my parents because I lived with my grandma. And other places. I didn't learn anything good from most of the places I lived growing up.
Teacher:	Thank you both for sharing. Angel brings up an important point, which is that what we learn from our families isn't always good. And Raya, you're pointing out that not everyone has the guidance of a family growing up. Can anyone relate to Angel and Raya?
Group:	(silence)
Teacher:	Has anyone else learned something from their families that they realize now is probably not a good behavior? Or were any of you brought up in a way that maybe didn't feel "normal" compared to other kids?
Louis:	I have a dad, but I don't have a mom because she died.
Chloe:	Same. It sucks. (begins to cry)
Tasha:	I don't like this topic, it's sad.
Lucas:	Yeah, let's stop talking about this.
Teacher:	I hear you that talking about difficult topics can make you feel uncomfortable. But I think we're learning something here so let's

	stick with it. What are we seeing here in this group today? Remember our norm of "Point out the positive." What behaviors have we seen in the group today that are positive?
Nellie:	People are sharing things that are hard to share. That's brave.
Robert:	Everyone is here in school trying to be better even if they learned bad stuff from their family.
Chloe:	I didn't know that Louis didn't have a mom, too. I thought I was the only one, so I'm glad I know that now.
Raya:	I'm always embarrassed to talk about how I don't have a family really. But I talked about it today.
Naya:	We all listened well.
Teacher:	That's amazing. Yes. Today we wanted to talk about our family traditions. If each of you thought about it long enough, you could probably come up with things that are both positive and negative that you learned from your families. The important thing to remember is that you have a choice over how you act in any given moment. And today we see people making the choice to be brave by sharing, to be respectful by listening, and to be open to growth by allowing yourselves to connect with each other through your shared experiences. These are incredible skills and I want to thank you for bringing them to our group today. At the end of the day, we get to decide what traditions we carry on and what traditions we leave behind. And we can also create new traditions for ourselves. If you could make a new tradition in your life right now that you might want to pass on to your future family, what would it be?
Group:	(discussion continues)
Teacher:	Before we do our closing, I want to remind all of you that if you feel sad or uncomfortable after our meetings you can always let me know or let the counselor, Mr. Morinaga, know. Remember he came in for our first two meetings? Great. I'm also going to do my regular check-ups after the meeting, okay? And just a reminder, is it okay if someone is hurting us or hurting someone close to us?
Group:	No!
Teacher:	And what do we do if someone is hurting us or someone close to us?
Group:	Tell the teacher or counselor!
Teacher:	Exactly! Great memory, everyone. Does anyone have an idea for a closing?
	(meeting continues)

In this dialogue, we see that a seemingly innocuous meeting topic on family traditions turned into an emotional session that illuminated feelings of violence, loss, and trauma in the students' families. Corresponding feelings of sadness, anger, and fear were exhibited by the group members. The anticipation of having to navigate these issues is often enough to turn many administrators and teachers off from allowing classroom meetings; however, it is important to point out that there are several easily learned structural strategies that allowed the teacher to successfully facilitate this discussion.

First, we can assume that this teacher understood that the topic of family has the potential to bring up complex and difficult emotions. It is safe to assume this because the teacher references having brought the school mental health professional in for the first two meetings. By front-loading the students with information about the services that the school mental health professional provides, the teacher was able to make sure that she was not left scrambling to address emotions that might linger after the meeting. The teacher also indicates that she has an "after-care" plan for her students, as she references doing her "regular check-ups" after the meeting. Establishing a plan for checking in with students who exhibit concerning behavior or speak about concerning content during the meeting allows teachers to follow up in a way that will not embarrass or single-out students. If the follow-up is normalized, the additional attention will hopefully encourage students to keep speaking up in the group.

Second, the teacher did not act as a "fixer" for her students' problems. Rather, in the role of facilitator, she simply repeated what the students said and thanked them for sharing. She also raised some new questions based on what they shared in order to create connections amongst the students. The teacher did not avoid emotional content. She provided a space where the students were assured that their contributions were accepted. Learning how to do this does not take specific skills so much as a shift in perspective. We often believe that it is our job as adults, teachers, and mental health professionals to solve problems. And at times we do have to be problem solvers. However, the point of classroom meetings is to empower our students to solve their own problems. Our role is to create the structured, supportive environment within which they can do that. The work comes in creating the container for the meeting process rather than having the perfect response to every situation or emotion the students bring up. The teacher's norm of "Point out the Positive" shows that the teacher was possibly anticipating that a group can sometimes focus on difficult emotions. This norm encourages students to look for the lesson in every interaction, a practice which encourages a growth mindset.

Third, the teacher understood her legal and ethical obligations as a mandated reporter. Angel's comment that he learned how to "mess someone up" from his family should raise a red flag for potential child abuse or domestic violence in the home. It is clear that the teacher anticipated that the meetings had the potential to elicit such stories as she asks the students in the end to repeat what they learned about what to do when someone is hurting them or someone else. This was potentially discussed when the school counselor attended the first two meetings. It is important that this is reinforced often in the group so that students remember it is okay to discuss such issues.

Ethically, even though the teacher was naturally concerned about Angel, it would have been inappropriate to ask him leading questions within the group in order to ascertain then and there if he were in an abusive home environment. This is an ethical because: a) the teacher is not trained in the mental health professional skills necessary to navigate the potential trauma of Angel's situation, and b) even if this group were being led by a mental health professional, Angel's privacy should be respected and he should not be put into a position where he feels forced to share details of his life. The teacher acknowledged his comment and allowed him to clarify and share, but did not dig deeper into the details. Certainly, though, Angel will be one of her "check-ups" after the meeting, and depending on what he shares she may need to report suspected child abuse to child protective services. Consulting with the school mental health professional about this discussion would also be wise, as it sounds as if other children in the group could benefit from counseling groups or individual therapy: two students may be suffering from grief and loss and one student appears to be in foster care. These students should be offered supplementary support services. For this reason, it is important that the students know from the first meeting that what they say in the group may be shared with the school mental health professional.

Lastly, the teacher used the norms of the group and a focus on the present to wrap up the discussion in a positive way. The students were sharing difficulties they encountered outside the group. By focusing on the actions the students were exhibiting in the present moment within the group, the teacher was able to highlight the students' strengths. By "Pointing out the Positive," the teacher was able to help the students focus on what they can control and what types of traditions they can create and carry forward in their lives. This allows the students to leave the group feeling empowered. It is important to note though that the teacher did not indicate that discussing "negative" emotions was unacceptable, which would have left students feeling unheard. Rather, she allowed for the negative emotions to be shared, and then tried to reframe the topic of the day given the feedback she was getting from the students. So now, instead of exclusively exploring the family traditions they grew up with, she is also exploring the family traditions they hope to create for themselves.

The subjects that the students brought up are incredibly common, so it is important for classroom meeting facilitators to expect them to come up and not be afraid of them. This teacher exhibited flexibility and was not afraid to address difficult subjects. The teacher had done the planning work necessary to create a safe container for the students' emotions. The strong structure of the group helped the teacher to navigate this emotional conversation even though the teacher was not trained in the mental health field.

Multicultural Counseling Considerations

Multicultural considerations in the application of the classroom meeting may cover a broad range of factors because the term "culture" is itself a broad term that may include, but is not limited to, the history, values, experiences, expectations, and lifestyles of particular groups of people. Groups may be based on religion, race, sexual identity, ethnicity, disability, national affiliation, and age, to name a few. The inclusive nature of the classroom meeting suggests the facilitator(s) may do well by gaining an awareness and understanding first of his/her own values and biases and how these may impact their work in the school setting. Understanding one's own identity may help, in turn, in becoming aware of and understanding and appreciating differences between and among groups of people, and may reduce the likelihood of influencing outcomes in a biased manner.

In preparation for classroom meetings the SBFC practitioner is encouraged to gain multicultural information on the groups represented within the school setting in which they are working. This information includes the cultural expectations within the age group; i.e., high school students have a different culture compared to middle school students. Understanding the lifestyles and circumstances that influence children and youths place the culturally sensitive SBFC practitioner in a position to guide young people toward the development of skills that can be applied to a range of situations, thereby increasing the likelihood of successful interactions.

The SBFC practitioner should also be sensitive to the indigenous origins of classroom meetings. Indigenous (Native American) talking circles are widely believed to be the first known example of this practice in North America (Wolf & Rickard, 2003). The African tradition of *Ubuntu* also uses talking circles as a form of dialogue and conflict resolution (Bremer, 2015). It is important to properly locate the concept of the talking circle with your students. Doing so will help all students understand the historical nature of the classroom meeting. It will also help indigenous students and students of color understand how people in their ancestry have contributed to today's classroom practices. The impact of recognizing this history cannot be overestimated, as the contributions of indigenous peoples and students of color to society have been erased and undervalued due to institutional and personal racism. Acknowledging the roots of this practice is one way to begin to undo the dire material consequences of racism.

Challenges and Solutions

Many of the challenges and solutions you will face facilitating classroom meetings are addressed in our case study examples; however, it is important to be aware that the systemic implementation of classroom meetings will also present its own challenges. Middle school and high school contexts pose unique challenges for implementation. Multiple teachers, rigid bell schedules, inflexible groupings, and even staff perception can be obstacles to the implementation of the classroom meeting. In the departmentalized setting, staff may believe the classroom meeting to be appropriate for the elementary-aged child and ineffective for older youth. It is precisely at the middle school and high school levels that the classroom meeting can be most beneficial. The preteen/teen years are a time of developing independence, and students at these ages increasingly look to their peers for inclusion, guidance, and acceptance. During the teen years students begin to form intimate relationships and need to have the skills necessary to develop empathy, the cornerstone of caring about others. The skills developed in the classroom meeting can help students develop and practice these skills in the context of the supportive environment of the classroom meeting.

Beginning with a pilot group rather than jumping directly to whole-school implementation can be beneficial. If adminstrators are supportive of classroom meeting implementation, but you are finding it difficult to recruit teachers and counselors as facilitators, a pilot year can give you time to generate interest. Professional developments, data presentations on your evaluation results, and word of mouth will go a long way towards influencing how staff members feel about classroom meetings. As a reminder, indivdiual student data should be anonymized; however, class level identification can be helpful.

Listed below are several resources that will help broaden your understanding of the importance of classroom meetings. Many of the videos and handouts are appropriate to be shared at professional development meetings. The more prepared you are to discuss the development, implementation, and impact of classroom meetings, the more likely you will receive buy-in from stakeholders.

Resources

There are several free, online resources available that will help you to further conceptualize what a classroom meeting is and how to implement it.

Videos

Positive Discipline Class Meeting: Compliments & Appreciations, Problem Solving
This video demonstrates a classroom meeting with second graders. The opener is "Compliments and Appreciations" and the discussion centers around problem-solving. Notice the norms posted on the wall, the talking piece used, and the various ways the facilitator gently corrects behavior through nonverbals.

Class Meeting: A Management Tool
Produced by the Center for the Collaborative Classroom, this video shows snippets from various classroom meetings and also includes interviews with teachers and administrators explaining classroom meetings. This particular video would be helpful to show to stakeholders at your school as it demonstates the versatility of the classroom meeting.

The Classroom of Choice: Problem-Solving Class Meetings
Produced by QEP Video Courses for Teachers, this is a 26-minute video that shows almost an entire classroom meeting with fifth graders from

beginning to end. The meeting explores the topic of self-control and demonstrates many of the techniques shared in this chapter.

The Class Meeting: Building an Inclusive Community
Produced by the Center for the Collaborative Classroom, this video shows a second grade classroom demonstrating partner sharing.

William Glasser: Don't Lose Your Child
In this 18-minute video, Dr. William Glasser discusses Choice Theory and how the field of psychology affects the mental health of children.

Websites

Positive Behavioral Intervention and Supports
This website offers research and tools related to Positive Behavioral Intervention and Supports.

Positive Discipline
This website contains various resources locating class meetings within the framework of positive discipline. Much of the information is based on the book Positive Discipine in the Classroom by Jane Nelsen and Lynn Lott (available for purchase on the website).

Ways of Council
This website describes the practice of council, based on indigenous talking circles. The site links to numerous other websites around the world, of people who are using talking circles to build community. There are several organizations that train professionals to implement council in schools.

Books and Articles

Edwards, D. & Mullis, F. (2003). Classroom meetings: Encouraging a climate of cooperation. *Professional School Counseling*, 7(1), 20–28.

Emmett, J.D. & Monsour, F. (1996). Open classroom meetings: Promoting peaceful schools. *Elementary School Guidance and Counseling*, 31(1), 3–10.

Frey, A. & Doyle, H.D. (2001). Classroom meetings: A program model. *Children and Schools*, 23(4), 212.

Nelsen, J. (1996). *Positive discipline*. Revised edition. New York, NY: Ballantine Books.

Videos

See SBFC EResources for links to videos.

Bibliography

Adler, A. (1930). *The education of children*. Chicago, IL: Gateway.

Angell, A.V. (2004). Making peace in elementary classrooms: A case for class meetings. *Theory and Research in Social Education*, 32(1), 98–104.

Bandura, A. (1969). *Principles of behavior modification*. New York, NY: Holt, Rinehart and Winston.

Bremer, M. (2015, November 5). How to co-create change in an Ubuntu circle. Retrieved from www.leadershipandchangemagazine.com/how-to-co-create-change-in-an-ubuntu-circle/

Curran, K. (2003). Thinking hats in the classroom. *Primary and Middle Years Educator*, 1 (3), 11–13.

Dreikurs, R. (1958). *Children: The challenge*. New York, NY: Norton.

Dreikurs, R. & Cassel, P. (1972). *Discipline without tears*. New York, NY: Hawthorne Books.

Edwards, D. & Mullis, F. (2003). Classroom meetings: Encouraging a climate of cooperation. *Professional School Counseling*, 7(1), 20–28.

Emmett, J.D. & Monsour, F. (1996). Open classroom meetings: Promoting peaceful school. *Elementary School Guidance and Counseling*, 31(1), 3–10.

Feldhusen, J. & Feldhusen, H. (2004). The room meeting for gifted and talented students in an inclusion classroom. *Gifted Child Today*, 27(2), 54–57.

Frey, A. & Doyle, H.D. (2001). Classroom meetings: A program model. *Children and Schools*, 23(4), 212.

Gamble, C. & Watkins, E. (1983). Combining the child discipline approaches of Alfred Adler and William Glasser: A case study. *Individual Psychology*. 39(2), 156–164.

Gerrard, B. (2008). School-based family counseling: Overview, trends, and recommendations for future research. *International Journal for School-Based Family Counseling*, 1(1), 1–30.

Glasser, W. (1969). *Schools without failure*. New York, NY: Harper and Row.

Glasser, W. (1988). *Choice theory in the classroom*. New York, NY: Harper Perennial.

Glasser, W. (2000). School violence from the perspective of William Glasser. *Professional School Counseling*, 4(2), 77–80.

Halaby, M.H. (2000). *Belonging*. Boston, MA: Brookline Books, Inc.

Hess, D. (2011). Discussions that drive democracy. *Educational Leadership*, 69(1), 69–73.

Knapp, J.R. (2010). Bully prevention through classroom meetings. Retrieved from www.articlesbase.com/childhood-educationarticles

Kriete, R. (2003). Start the day with community. *Educational Leadership*, 61(1), 68–70.

Leachman, G. & Victor, D. (2003). Student-led classroom meetings. *Eductional Leadership*, 60(6), 64–68.

Marandola, P. & Imber, S. (1979). Glasser's classroom meeting: A humanistic approach to behavior change with preadolescent inner-city learning disabled children. *Journal of Learning Disabilities*, 12(6), 30–35.

National Center for Education Statistics. (2011). Indicators of school crime and safety (Data file). Retrieved from www.nces.ed.gov/programs/crimeindicators

Nelsen, J. (1996). *Positive discipline*. Revised edition. New York, NY: Ballantine Books.

Nelsen, J., Lott, L., & Glenn, S. (2013) *Positive discipine in the classroom*. 4th Edition. New York, NY: Harmony.

Sisco, S.C. (1992). Using goal setting to enhance self-esteem and create an internal locus of control in the at risk elementary student. (ERIC ED 355017).

Soheili, F., Alizadeh, H., Murphy, J.M., Bajestani, H.S., & Ferguson, E.D. (2015). Teachers as leaders: The impact of Adler-Dreikurs classroom management techniques on students' perceptions of the classroom environment and on academic achievement. *The Journal of Individual Psychology*, 71(4), 440–461.

Utay, J. & Utay, C. (1996). Applications of Adler's theory in counseling and education. *Journal of Instructional Psychology*, 23(4), 251.

Walsh, I.D. & McCarroll, L. (1993). The future role of the school counselor. *The School Counselor*, 41, 48–53.

White, J. (2009). *Budget cuts will hurt students*. Association of California School Administrators. Retrieved from www.acsa.org.

Wolf, R. & Rickard, J. (2003). Talking circles: A Native American approach to experiential learning. *Journal of Multicultural Counseling and Development*, 31(1), 39–43.

7 Family Prevention

How to Facilitate A Parent Education Workshop

Nancy Rosenbledt and Deborah Ribera

Overview: *This chapter helps SBFC pratitioners understand why parent education workshops are important to a comprehensive school counseling program and how to implement them. A four-step approach to designing a parent education program is detailed. Five essential aspects of a parent education workshop are also explored.*

Background

The SBFC practitioner and parent partnership is a vital one. When SBFC practitioners work collaboratively with parents in targeting emotional, behavioral, and academic concerns, the home and school success of children is far more likely. SBFC practitioners are in an optimal position to form an alliance with families. Although schools cannot usurp the parenting process, they can position themselves as a resource to parents by providing parent education. Parent education workshops are an excellent method to help families access and develop interventions that will remediate and prevent problems at school and at home.

Offering educational programming for parents is paramount to the SBFC model. Parent education workshops take a preventive-family focus. Through these workshops, SBFC practitioners teach, coach, and guide parents in how to reduce problematic behaviors as well as how to increase positive, pro-social behaviors that youth are exhibiting in home and/or school. Parents are instructed in the use and application of behavioral principles and methods that have been found to be effective in reducing problematic child behaviors. Parents can also learn about common issues that both parents and children face during the life span. Parent empowerment is emphasized, as the parents' feelings of self-efficacy are viewed as key to the process.

Whether implemented in a one-time workshop format or a series of classes, a typical parent workshop would include the SBFC practitioner teaching parents how to attend to, praise, and encourage positive behaviors that the child exhibits, and education about how to address common problems that arise in childhood. Parents are taught to effectively use discipline skills appropriate to the developmental level of their child (Eisenstadt, Eyberg, McNeil, Newcomb, & Funderbun, 1993; Hanf, 1969).

Evidence-based Support

In a meta-analysis of studies examining the effects of behavioral parent training, Maughan, Christiansen, Jenson, Olympia, and Clark (2005) concluded that behavioral training was effective in reducing behavior problems in children. In an earlier meta-analysis, Serketich and Dumas (1996) also found support for the effectiveness of parent training in reducing problematic child behaviors, specifically citing its effectiveness with older children. Although behavioral parent training has shown empirical support in effectiveness, it does not work for all families and can end up alienating parents who interpret this approach as authoritarian, imposition of the parent's will, and conducted through a rigid process.

Researchers have evaluated other interventions that involve working with parents as partners on the school team. In particular, Greene and Ablon (2006) provide a collaborative problem-solving (CPS) model that initially focuses on the antecedents of the child's problem behaviors. By learning what predicts the targeted behavior, parents, children, and school staff can engage in a CPS process to resolve the problem. The CPS intervention process has empirical support.

The Parent Management Training-Oregon Model (PMTO) was designed to use family interventions to treat and prevent antisocial behavior problems in children and adolescents (Patterson & Forgatch, 1985; Patterson, Reid, & Dishion, 1992; Patterson, Reid, Jones, & Conger, 1975). Both the shape and the contexts in which the model has been applied evolved since the early work of Patterson and his associates in the 1960s and 1970s. Several studies using the PMTO model have shown that intervention benefits to parenting and reductions in deviant peer association have led to immediate and long-term reductions in negative youth outcomes. Furthermore, reciprocity in outcome effects help parents improve depression, decrease financial stress, and decrease police arrests (DeGarmo, Patterson, & Forgatch, 2004; Forgatch & DeGarmo, 2007).

Parent-Child Interaction Therapy (PCIT), a program based on parent training, is aimed at parents of young children. In this program, parents are taught to use child-directed interaction, in which parents use play skills to implement positive attending and communication skills, including praise, reflection, imitation, description, and enthusiasm. Parents are then instructed on implementation of parent-directed interaction skills, including clear, effective command and time-out procedure (Brinkmeyer & Eyberg, 2003). In studies of the effectiveness of PCIT, parents reported a decrease in child behavior problems and parenting stress, more internal locus of control, and an increase in positive interactions with their children, i.e., praises, reflections, behavior descriptions, and decreases in negative parenting behavior during child-led play, i.e., questions, commands, and criticisms (Bagner & Eyberg, 2007; Schuhmann, Foote, Eyberg, Boggs, & Algina, 1998). Outcomes have been noted by researchers to have positive long-term effects even with an abbreviated form of PCIT (Hood & Eyberg, 2003; Nixon, Sweeney, Erickson, & Touyz, 2003).

Multisystemic therapy (MST), developed by Henggeler & Lee in 2003, combines family, peer, school, and individual interventions to assist children with serious mental health issues and those who are involved in the juvenile justice system. MST necessitates a time-intensive family system, team-based approach. Parent education workshops can be a part of this approach. Studies have demonstrated many favorable effects for MST with juvenile offenders and their families, such as decreases in substance use and recidivism, externalization of problems, and improvement in family functioning (Borduin, Henggeler, Blaske, & Stein, 1990; Borduin et al., 1995; Brunk, Henggeler, & Whelan, 1987; Henggeler et al., 1986).

Procedure

Parent education training can be done individually, in groups, or through a combination of both, as often happens in a workshop setting. What follows are common elements of effective principles that can be used when designing and presenting parent education workshops. This procedure consists of four basic steps: Research, Needs Assessment, Recruitment, Planning and Implementation.

Step 1: Research

An important first step is for the SBFC practitioner to research what, if any, parent education program has been used at their site in the past and to what degree that program was successful. To do this, the SBFC practitioner will need to talk to administrators, teachers, and parents. If there is a parent center at the school, it is essential to communicate with them at this point. School districts often recommend using a specific parent training program. Calling district administrators to ask if the district provides resources for these types of workshops would be essential. An SBFC practitioner at a clinical site that provides court-ordered parenting classes will need to become familiar with the curriculum beforehand.

Parent education programs typically consist not only of a written curriculum, but also a literature review that details the research used to prove the effectiveness of the program. The SBFC practitioner should read this research before they decide whether or not they would like to adopt that specific program. If the foundations of the approach do not resonate with the training of the SBFC practitioner, a different program should be used.

Step 2: Needs Assessment

Capuzzi and Gross (2008) state that "Prevention programming should always be designed to address needs and concerns identified by recipients of future services" (p. 34). In other words, parents must be involved when designing a parent education program at the site. It is essential that the SBFC practitioner reach out to parents in order to assess what issues parents are struggling with, what they need help with, and how the school or clinical site could best support them. It is not enough to base your assessment on research or your own personal opinion. Parent voices must be at the heart of your programming. Such outreach can be done through documented individual meetings, survey administration, and/or volunteer focus groups.

The needs assessment is when parent buy-in begins. Adopting a collaborative approach is key to the success of any prevention program. A good technique is to solicit parent participation in this stage by consulting with them as "co-counselors" – conveying to parents that while the SBFC practitioner may have expertise in certain behavioral interventions, it is the parents who have the expertise in their children's behavior. By working together to improve the child's behavior both at home and at school, a mutually beneficial partnership is formed where the combined efforts of each party becomes greater than the sum of its parts.

Step 3: Recruitment

The desired scale of your workshop depends on space availability, demand, and the SBFC practitoner's comfort level. Choose to have open enrollment or specifically target parents of certain children. To recruit the latter population, consider doing parent and student interviews and/or student observations in order to identify which parents would benefit the most from the parent education workshop. Interviews are frequently conducted as the first step in the assessment process. Interviews should generally cover the following areas (Merrell, 2008):

Intrapersonal functioning: including information on feelings, eating/sleeping habits, understanding of reason for referral/interview.

Family relationships: including information regarding relationships with siblings and extended family, perceived family conflict/support, family routines.

Peer relationships: including report of friendships, activities enjoyed with friends, problems experienced in social situations.

School adjustment: including information on academic achievement, favored/ less favored teachers and academic subjects, involvement in extracurricular activities.

Community involvement: including information on community-based activities (sports, clubs, religious organizations) and relationships with others in these contexts.

Observations are commonly used in school settings to obtain a direct picture of the behaviors in question. The SBFC practitioner can conduct observations in the classroom setting. Gathering observational data from both home and school can provide useful information and a picture of the problem across settings, but it is important to keep in mind that parents and teachers cannot always devote their full attention to the observational process and may need to be trained by the SBFC practitioner on remaining objective through functional behavioral analysis techniques. Comprehensive assessments can include self-report measures and rating scales in which the SBFC practitioner has achieved competency. By obtaining data on the problem behaviors and the function that these behaviors serve, the SBFC practitioner will be in a better position to develop the most effective parent training intervention that is most likely to lead to a reduction of the problematic behaviors children are exhibiting.

Step 4: Planning and Implementation

In planning for program support, regular communication and/or meetings with appropriate staff and personnel are key. The best prevention efforts have been based on collaborative, interdisciplinary teams including members of the population to be served. A detailed description of the program should be presented to the administration and staff for further review, revision, and refinement. Staff professional development meetings can provide opportunities for announcing the class and for questions and concerns to be addressed.

The logistics of the program should emerge naturally based on the data you have gathered from your initial research, needs assessment, observations, and interviews that took place during recruitment. Will your workshop be a one-time event or a series? The day and time of the workshops is often a main factor determining program success. Oftentimes parents need workshops to be held in evening hours or on weekends in order to attend. They may also need child care for school aged-children or younger. It is important that the SBFC practitioner negotiate with their administrator so that they can arrange the workshops based on the parents' schedules, not the school's. This is an aspect of delivering culturally responsive services. Another essential part of logistics is refreshments. Advertising that there is free childcare and food is a wonderful way to entice parents to attend workshops.

SBFC professionals can choose between using a packaged program (see Resources below) or creating their own curriculum for parents based on their research and the needs assessment. The SBFC practitioner may also combine these two options, using a packaged program for broad topics and activity ideas, but tailoring the content to reflect the needs of the specific population.

Evaluation procedures should be planned prior to program implementation. A packaged curriculum will often come with pre- and post-tests. If you are using your own curriculum, evaluation is an important part of the design. Baseline functioning of parents will need to be assessed in the first meeting or before. Outcomes will need to be assessed during the last meeting. Ideally, a six-month follow-up assessment can also be administered. To elicit the richest data, both quantitative (e.g., through a Likert scale) and qualitative (e.g., through answering open-ended questions) methods should be used. The more thoughtful your evaluation process, the more likely you will be able to prove the effectiveness of the program, and thus the more sustainable and impactful your parent education program will be.

Example of A Parent Education Program

The following sample training program format offers a diverse approach, yet provides for personalizing the material presented and for transfer of learning (Brigman, Mullis, Webb, & White, 2005). The program consists of five steps, or aspects of a parent education program: warm-up, ask before telling, introduce information and practice skills, process and summarize, and evaluate. For the beginning SBFC practitioner, we have also included model dialogue in order to further illustrate the steps.

Step 1: Warm-up

Begin the training session with an activity or brief sharing of something positive tied to the theme of the session. Involve parents by having them think, write, and share their ideas in dyads, which is a safe way to introduce them to the topic. Ask for two or three volunteers to share their ideas with the larger group. This provides an opportunity for the SBFC practitioner to tie experiences back into the theme of the session, creating a rationale for parent involvement.

Facilitator: Welcome, everyone, to "What to Know About …," our parent education program that explores what you need to know about the topics affecting your life and your child's life. This week's topic is "What to Know About … College!" We are going to begin with a warm-up exercise to help us get to know each other better. Please find someone you don't know to be your partner and sit with them. Take three minutes to share with your partner the questions or concerns you have about college entrance requirements for your child. I will time you for three minutes while the first person shares, then you will switch and I will time you for another three minutes while the second person shares.
(Parents complete activity)

Facilitator: Thank you for participating. Would anyone like to share their questions or concerns with the group? I encourage you to share to we can make sure we address all of your questions and concerns in our presentation.

Step 2: Ask Before Telling

Before offering information at any stage of the training, ask for parents' ideas and experiences first. The more SBFC professionals use parents' input, the more it becomes their program.

Facilitator: You all shared some really good and important questions from your share-out and the good news is that we address all of them in our presentation. Before I go on, however, I know we have parents in the group today who already have children in college. Would any of you like to briefly share for a minute or two about what the process was like for you?
(Later in the meeting)

Facilitator: Now we're going to talk about the feelings we can expect to have in the college application process. How are you all feeling right now?

Participant A: A little overwhelmed with information.

Participant B: Yes, I'm excited for my child, but nervous at the same time.

Facilitator: Absolutely normal feelings. Yes, the process of determining whether or not your child will be attending college, what college they can realistically attend, completing the applications for those colleges, and then waiting to see if they get accepted can produce a lot of nervousness, pressure, and worry for both parents and children. Has anyone else already experienced some of these feelings? Would any of you like to share about your experience?

Step 3: Introduce Information and Practice Skills

In order to introduce information, it is best to use a slide presentation and handouts so that parents can follow along and take the information with them for further reference. The "Model, Rehearse, and Practice" method can help when providing information and introducing new ideas or skills.

Step 3a: Model

In this step, the SBFC practitioner explains the skill, discusses it with the parents, then performs the desired skill while the parents observe. The SBFC practioner might call the parents' attention to specific aspects of the modeled performance (e.g., "Did you notice how I was _____(name the modeled behavior)?"

Facilitator: Often parents don't know what to say when their child receives a rejection letter from a college. If you have a partner, it's also possible that you might not be on the same page with them. Does anyone have experience with talking their child through a rejection? How did it work out? (Ask before telling).
(Sharing)

Facilitator: Thank you for sharing those experiences! If you look here at the slide, you'll see some suggestions for how you can support your child through rejection. And this does not just apply to college rejection letters, but really to any rejection. The first skill we see up there is "Meet your child where they are at." This skill reminds us that our child may not deal with rejection the same way we do. And we should not force them to deal with it the way we do. Some people may react to rejection by minimizing how much they care. Others may cry and feel the rejection says something about their own self-worth. Still others might react positively and believe that particular option was not meant to be. What's important is to allow your child the space to tell you how they feel, then accept that in that moment instead of forcing them to feel another way. Let them know that it's normal for their feelings to change and that you are still here to talk about that. So let's say my child got rejected from one of their back-up schools and they are extremely upset, weeping. If I were to go into their room and say, "Listen, you didn't even want to go to that school. Who cares that you got rejected? Get it together!" would that be meeting my child where they are at?

Group:	No.
Facilitator:	Right. My child is sad. So in meeting my child where they are at, I'm going to acknowledge they are sad and accept that. So I might say something like, "I see how sad you are. I'm so sorry you're hurting. Tell me what thoughts are going through your head about this." The goal is always to open up communication with your children, and meeting them where they're at makes this more likely. Any questions about that?

Step 3b: Rehearse

Behavior rehearsal is synonymous with role playing. Often, in the behavior rehearsal, the SBFC practitioner or other parent participants will take the role of the child or another family member in the parent's life. Depending on the skill, Modeling and Rehearsing may be combined into one role play. Role plays should be brief (less than two minutes), so that the SBFC practitioner and parent participants can provide feedback immediately. The role play should be as close as possible to real-world situations to maximize generalization. The goal is for the parent to generalize the new skill they are learning in the workshop to their own lives.

Facilitator:	Let's practice this skill of meeting your child where they are at. Would anyone like to volunteer to do a quick two-minute role play with me? I am the parent and you are the child. You have just been rejected from your top school choice, but you are acting like you don't care.
	(A parent volunteers to role play their son.)
Facilitator>:	Hey, son, do you want to talk about the letter you got from USC?

"Son":	Not really.
Facilitator:	How are you feeling right now?
"Son":	I don't know. Fine. Whatever, I don't really care.
Facilitator:	Okay, that's okay. You might feel something different in a few minutes or a few days. I'm here for you if your feelings change and you want to talk, okay?
"Son":	Yeah, fine, whatever.
Facilitator:	I also just want to remind you that I'm proud of you no matter what school you end up going to and that I love you. I'm going to keep checking in with you to see if you're doing okay, but let me know if it's too much. Okay?
"Son":	I just don't want to make a big deal out of it.
Facilitator:	That's fine. What does that look like to you though so I know?
"Son":	I don't, like, want to talk about it at Grandma's party tonight. I don't want everyone asking me about it.
Facilitator:	No problem, I won't bring it up with them. If anyone asks let's just say you're focused on the physics test you have Monday, not college.
"Son":	Yeah, that's a good idea.
Facilitator:	Good. And if you end up feeling like sharing with them what happened, you can do that, too. I think you'd be surprised at the amount of support you would get. They all love you no matter what, just like me. In fact they'll probably hate USC now for rejecting you.
"Son":	Yeah, maybe. (Small smile.)

Step 3c: Practice

After information is presented, allow time for personalizing and practice by asking parents to think, write, share, and/or role play in small groups. This kind of learning is essential for understanding to occur. Small groups then report their experience to the large group. Encouraging the parents to role play with each other can help everyone in the workshop practice the skills that have been modeled. Homework can also help with this. The SBFC practioner and parent(s) can collaboratively develop opportunities for the parent to transfer the workshop practice into a range of situations where the parent(s) can practice and master behavioral skills (Tolin, 2016).

This approach keeps parents involved and leads to application of workshop skills and information. It is important for the SBFC practitioner to understand and appreciate real obstacles a parent may face before implementing the training program. As skills are being introduced, you should anticipate, prepare, and problem-solve with parents as much as possible. For example, when discussing spending one-on-one quality time with each of their children, parents should think about when they can commit to this quality time, what they will do with their other children, and what problems they may encounter. There are typically multiple solutions to any given situation, so it is important that SBFC practitioners be flexible in finding solutions that best fit for the family while still ensuring effective behavioral methods.

Facilitator: Great job, thank you for helping with that role play! So how did this parent meet her child where he was at in this role play? (Discussion continues)

Facilitator: Now that we've gone over five ways that you can support your child through rejection and I have role played the skills for you, let's all practice! Split into pairs and come up with a scenario of your own. Each of you take a turn playing the parent and practicing one of the skills we've gone over. We'll come back together as a group and talk about what you learned after.

Step 4: Process and Summarize

Help parents summarize the workshop by providing time at the end to reflect on process questions.

What did I learn or relearn?

How can I use what I learned?

What questions do I still have about the topic?

How involved was I in the activities and discussions?

How did I feel during the activities and discussions?

It is important to ask each parent to share with a partner or small group what they learned. Allow volunteers to share ideas with the larger group about how they can apply what they've learned. This provides the SBFC practitioner an opportunity for encouragement, coaching, and reinforcement of key concepts.

Facilitator: I would like you now to get into groups of four and share with your group your responses to these questions on the handout. What did you learn or relearn today? How can you use what you learned? And what do you still have questions about? I'd also like you to reflect on how involved you were with the activities and discussion and discuss with your group how you felt during the those times. Were you uncomforable or interested or bored ... however you felt! Each group should select a volunteer who will give a brief summary of the group's responses. You'll have about five to seven minutes to discuss with your group.

Step 6: Evaluate

Have simple written evaluations at the end of the workshop/training session. These evaluations can be content-specific, which would mean you would design a different one for each session (e.g., How comfortable do you feel helping your child deal with rejection from the college of their choice?). General questions can also yield helpful info, though. (e.g., How comfortable do you feel using the skills that were taught in today's workshop?). How you design your evaluation depends on the results of your needs assessment and what your goals are for your own prgram and population. What do you want your parents to take away from these meetings and how can you measure that? You should also include at least one free response question (e.g., Is there any other feedback you have about today's workshop? Do you have any suggestions for how we can improve future workshops?). You can use the results of evaluations to improve your next parent training workshop. You can also use them to communicate to your school adminstrators about how the parents are learning and growing due to the workshops and what their continued needs are.

Multicultural Counseling Considerations

Multicultural counseling competence refers to the SBFC practitioner's attitudes, beliefs, knowledge, and skills in working with people from cultural groups different from their own, including racial, ethnic, gender, social class, and sexual orientation (Arredondo et al., 1996). The SBFC practitioner is responsible for understanding and generating awareness of specific cultural factors relevant to particular cultural groups. This includes knowledge to assess factors such as acculturation, language proficiency, and sociocultural history that are critical concerns for children's development in the schools (Paniagua, 1994; Vasquez-Nuthall, DeLeon, & Valle, 1990). Strategies that support multicultural competence within the context of family involvement consist of three components: parent education and support, school-family curriculum activities, and school staff-parent partnership efforts (Banks, 1993). SBFC practitioners must use their knowledge of counseling diverse populations to apply counseling skills, techniques, and interventions within the context of the parent education program.

In order to provide culturally competent services, it is important that the SBFC practitioner critically reflect on how they understand the concept of parenting. Many homes have other adults besides parents who are involved in parenting children. Therefore, it is important that such trainings should be open to anyone involved in parenting, raising, and managing the behavior of students, not just legal parents. Conversely, in some homes there is only one adult involved in raising the children. Further, gender should not be implied when discussing parents. That is, the SBFC practitioner should not assume that if there are two parents in the household that they are a man and a woman. The SBFC practitioner should be mindful and intentional in their acknowledgement of this diversity, and change their language and examples to provide the most inclusivity possible.

A related multicultural aspect to consider is one of essentialism. Service providers can slip into language that reinforces damaging gender roles by separating parenting discussions into "mom" and "dad." For instance, they may imply that "mom" is more naturally nurturing while "dad" is the natural disciplinarian. There are no inherent personality characteristics that accompany biological sex. Rather, humans are socialized from birth to take on gender roles that are reinforced in society and therefore seem "natural." The SBFC practitioner should be careful not to reinscribe any of these gender roles. In the example above, for instance, reinscribing the idea that the mother is more naturally nurturing can rob a father of the opportunity to be nurturing, or lead him to believe it is not his responsibility as a parent to nurture his child. Reinscribing the idea that the father is the natural disciplinarian can lead a mother to believe that it is not her responsibility as a parent to discipline her child. In both instances, essentializing gender roles according to the biological sex of the parent can result in negative consequences for the children. Ideally, the child should have caregivers who support each other and fulfill their parental duties regardless of their gender and biological sex.

That being said, cultural elements such as race, ethnicity, religion, sexuality, socio-economic class, and gender do need to be taken into account when developing and delivering parent education workshops. Professionals cannot assume that treatment developed primarily for one cultural group will be applicable to other groups without modification. Many parent-child interactions and child-rearing practices are deeply woven into religious teachings and cultural beliefs and customs. For example, types of punishment, the demands made on children, and educational expectations are all culture-bound issues. It is reasonable, therefore, to expect various aspects of culture to moderate intervention effects (Weisz & Kazdin, 2010).

Challenges and Solutions

Although parent training can be a very effective intervention, it is not uncommon to encounter certain obstacles in implementing this intervention. One of the first obstacles frequently observed involves parent expectations, or an unawareness of what to expect when they seek assistance for their children. Frequently, parents view the problem as the child's and do not understand the need for their involvement. Alternatively, some parents may believe that it is not their responsibility, but the responsibility of the school to "fix" any problems their child is having.

Another obstacle encountered with parent training involves parents who view the training program as potentially negative and believe that the use of regular discipline may negatively impact their relationship with their child. The SBFC practitioner must emphasize the importance and appreciation children actually have for consistency and structure. The positive part of the parent training program is designed so that parents can lay a positive foundation of interacting with their child before beginning the discipline component.

Lastly, a significant challenge to participation may arise if the parent feels alienated from the school system itself. Parents who are receiving constant contact from the school about negative behaviors their child is exhibiting may feel overwhelmed and blamed. They may not have previously engaged with the school due to time conflicts between work and school schedules, cultural and language barriers, feeling uncomfortable or unwelcome in their child's school, lack of community support and transportation, and/or lack of understanding and support in the workplace (Thompson, 2002).

The above reasons demonstrate why parent buy-in is the most effective method in modifying a child's behaviors. The SBFC practitioner must anticipate all of the above and think carefully about how they will address each challenge and each barrier. In order to truly involve and engage challenging parents as key players and partners in their children's education, SBFC practitioners need to be oriented to a positive psychology perspective and belief system (Wilde, 2005). The beliefs listed in Box 7.1 are key for adopting a positive psychology perspective.

Box 7.1 Positive Psychology Beliefs

Belief #1: Parents love their kids in the best way they know how. Most people raise their children as their parents raised them, and most challenging parents did not have good role models as children.

Belief #2: Parents' inability to believe negative behaviors attributed to their children is biologically/evolutionary rooted. That's how parents protect their progeny and keep their line of DNA moving forward in the next generation.

Belief #3: Carefully consider the requests made of parents as they have the skills, understanding, self-discipline, and organization to be successful in the implementation of plans.

Belief #4: With the exception of parents who have mental health issues, most of their behaviors would be predictable if professionals had access to the complex patterns that have been ingrained in their life histories. Keeping this in mind while unraveling these complex patterns will most likely engender successful engagement of challenging parents.

Belief #5: Imagining sitting in the parent's chair as if an SBFC practitioner were talking about your child will dramatically increase your empathic understanding of parents.

Resources

Documents

Stephen Small and Rebecca Mather, University of Wisconsin-Madison. Evidence-Based Parenting Programs

This is an extremely thorough and well-researched directory of evidence-based parenting programs.

Child Welfare Information Gateway. *Parent Education to Strengthen Families and Reduce the Risk of Maltreatment*

An excellent directory of evidence-based and evidence-informed programs that also discusses the research related to parenting programs as well as considerations for implemetation.

Article

A Review and Critique of 16 Major Parent Education Programs by Christina Collins and Robert Fetsch.

The authors use three review criteria – program readiness, strength of scientific base, and empirical evidence of program effectiveness – to rate parent education programs.

Collins, C.L. & Fetsch, Robert. (2012). A review and critique of 16 major parent education programs. *Journal of Extension, 50(4). Retrieved from* https://www.joe.org/joe/2012august/a8.php

Videos

Boys and Girls Club of Canada. *Engaging Families through Parent Education Workshops*

This webinar is specific to the Boys and Girls Club. However, if you are considering implementation of parent education workshops at your school site, it will give you a good overview of all the logistical aspects you should consider in implementation.

Oregon Social Learning Center *Supporting Children's First Teachers: Promoting school readiness through parent education*

This is another specific implementation webinar; however, it features good information that connects parent education to student educational outcomes.

See SBFC EResources for links to the above documents, articles and videos.

Bibliography

Arredondo, P., Toporek, R., Brown, S.P., Jones, J., Locke, D.C., Sanchez, J., & Stadler, H. (1996). Operationalization of the multicultural counseling competencies. *Journal of Multicultural Counseling and Development*, 70, 477–486.

Bagner, D.M. & Eyberg, S.M. (2007). Parent-child interaction therapy for disruptive behavior in children with mental retardation: A randomized controlled trial. *Journal of Clinical Child and Adolescent Psychology*, 36, 418–429.

Banks, J. (1993). Multicultural education for young children: Racial and ethnic attitudes and their modifications. In Spodek, B. (Ed.). *Handbook of Research on the Education of Young Children* (pp. 246–258). New York, NY: Macmillan.

Borduin, C.M., Henggeler, S.W., Blaske, D.M., & Stein, R. (1990). Multisystemic treatment of adolescent sexual offenders. *International Journal of Offender Therapy and Comparative Criminology*, 35, 105–114.

Borduin, C.M., Mann, B.J., Cone, L.T., Hengggeler, S.W., Fucci, B.R., Blaske, D.M., et al., (1995). Multisystemic treatment of serious juvenile offenders: Long-term prevention of criminality and violence. *Journal of Consulting and Clinical Psychology*, 63, 569–578.

Brigman, G., Mullis, F., Webb, L., & White, J. (2005). *School counselor consultation: Skills for working effectively with parents, teachers, and other school personnel.* Hoboken, NJ: John Wiley and Sons.

Brinkmeyer, M. & Eyberg, S.M. (2003). Parent-child interaction therapy for oppositional children. In Kazdin, A.E. & Weisz, J.R. (Eds.). *Evidence-based psychotherapies for children and adolescents* (pp. 204–223). New York, NY: Guilford Press.

Brunk, M., Henggeler, S.W., & Whelan, J.P. (1987). A comparison of multisystemic therapy and parent training in the brief treatment of child abuse and neglect. *Journal of Consulting and Clinical Psychology*, 55, 311–318.

Capuzzi, D. & Gross, D. (Eds.). (2008). *Youth at risk: A prevention resource for counselors, teachers, and parents* (5th ed., p. 34). Alexandria, VA: American Counseling Association.

DeGarmo, D.S., Patterson, G.R., & Forgatch, M.S. (2004). How do outcomes in a specified parent training intervention maintain or wane over time? *Prevention Science*, 5, 75–89.

Eisenstadt, T.H., Eyberg, S., McNeil, C.B., Newcomb, K., & Funderbunk, B. (1993). Parent-child interaction therapy with behavior problem children: Relative effectiveness of two stages and overall treatment outcome. *Journal of Clinical Child Psychology*, 22, 42–51.

Forgatch, M.S. & DeGarmo, D.S. (2007). Accelerating recovery from poverty: Prevention effects for recently separated mothers. *Journal of Early and Intensive Behavioral Intervention*, 4, 681–702.

Greene, R.W. & Ablon, J.S. (2006). *Treating explosive kids.* New York, NY: Guilford Press.

Hanf, C. (1969). A two-stage program for modifying maternal controlling during mother-child (M-C) instruction. Paper presented at the meeting of the Western Psychological Association, Vancouver, British Columbia, Canada.

Henggeler, S.W. & Lee, T. (2003). Multisystemic treatment of serious conduct problems. In Kazdin, A.E. & Weisz, J.R. (Eds.). *Evidence-based psychotherapies for children and adolescents* (pp. 301–322). New York, NY: Guilford Press.

Henggeler, S.W., Rodick, J.D., Borduin, C.M., Hanson, C.L., Watson, S.M., & Urey, J.R. (1986). Multisystemic treatment of juvenile offenders: Effects on adolescent behavior and family interactions. *Developmental Psychology*, 22, 132–141.

Hood, K. & Eyberg, S.M. (2003). Outcomes of parent-child interaction therapy: Mothers' reports on maintenance three to six years after treatment. *Journal of Clinical Child and Adolescent Psychology*, 32, 419–429.

Maughan, D.R., Christiansen, E., Jenson, W.R., Olympia, D., & Clark, E. (2005). Behavioral parent training as a treatment for externalizing behaviors and disruptive behavior disorders: A meta-analysis. *School Psychology Review*, 34, 267–286.

Merrell, K. (2008). *Helping students overcome depression and anxiety: A practical guide.* New York, NY: Guilford.

Nixon, R.D., Sweeney, L., Erickson, D.B., & Touyz, S.W. (2003). Parent-child interaction therapy: A comparison of standard and abbreviated treatments for oppositional defiant pre-schoolers. *Journal of Counseling and Clinical Psychology*, 71, 251–260.

Paniagua, F.A. (1994). *Assessing and treating culturally diverse clients: A practical guide.* Thousand Oaks, CA: Sage.

Patterson, G.R., & Forgatch, M.S. (1985). Therapist behavior as a determinant for client noncompliance: A paradox for the behavior modifier. *Journal of Consulting and Clinical Psychology*, 53, 846–851.

Patterson, G.R., Reid, J.B., & Dishion, T.J. (1992). *A social transactional approach: Vol. 4. Antisocial boys.* Eugene, OR: Castalia.

Patterson, G.R., Reid, J.B., Jones, R.R., & Conger, R. (1975). *A social learning approach to family intervention: Families and aggressive children.* Eugene, OR: Castalia.

Schuhmann, E.M., Foote, R., Eyberg, S.M., Boggs, S., & Algina, J. (1998). Parent-child interaction therapy: Interim report of a randomized trial with short-term maintenance. *Journal of Clinical Psychology*, 27, 34–45.

Serketich, W.J. & Dumas, J.E. (1996). The effectiveness of behavioral parent training to modify antisocial behavior in children: A meta-analysis. *Behavior Therapy*, 27, 171–186.

Thompson, R.A. (2002). *School counseling: Best practices for working in the schools* (2nd ed.). New York, NY: Routledge.

Tolin, D. (2016). *Doing CBT: A comprehensive guide to working with behaviors, thoughts, and emotions.* New York, NY: Guilford Press.

Vasquez-Nuthall, E., DeLeon, B., & Valle, M. (1990). Best practices in considering cultural factors. In Thomas, A. & Grimes, J. (Eds.). *Best practices in School Psychology II* (pp. 219–235). Washington, DC: National Association of School Psychologists.

Weisz, J.R. & Kazdin, A.E. (Eds.). (2010). *Evidence-based psychotherapies for children and Adolescents* (2nd ed.). New York, NY: Guilford Press.

Wilde, J. (2005). *80 creative strategies for working with challenging parents: A resource for elementary, middle & high school professional educators.* Chapin, SC: Youthlight.

8   Family Prevention

How to Facilitate A Parent Support Group

Allan A. Morotti

Overview: *The chapter's focus is on how to develop and facilitate parent support groups. It will define the term "parent support groups," discuss how these groups are developed and function, and provide a short list of resources. The chapter will use the Systematic Training for Effective Parenting (STEP) program by Dinkmeyer, McKay, and Dinkmeyer, Jr. (1997) as a model for illustrating the common elements found in these types of programs.*

Background

There is often confusion nowadays when one hears the term "support group." As originally conceived by Alfred Adler (Ansbacher & Ansbacher, 1956), this type of group was to be based on principles of child development and guidance. Its purpose was to educate the group's participants. Today, many groups employ the term "support" when naming themselves. For example, Alcoholics Anonymous offers weekly support groups for individuals in recovery from alcohol addiction. However, this type of group is primarily therapeutic in scope. Parenting groups, which focus on a single subject, such as childhood trauma, parenting the autistic child, or the divorced parent may or may not be more therapeutic than educational. However, within the SBFC paradigm, parent support groups are placed in the prevention quadrant; therefore, when the SBFC practitioner facilitates this type of group the primary goal of the group is to educate the participants on how to implement specific parenting strategies for the benefit of the child. Most of these programs utilize some type of book (e.g. *Active Parenting Today* or *Positive Discipline*), which provides a ready-made curriculum for the SBFC practitioner to follow.

> Parenting programs appear to have considerable potential to affect one or more aspects of parental psychosocial functioning. Group-based parenting programs are typically manualized and structured interventions, underpinned by a range of theoretical approaches (including behaviorism and cognitive behavioral therapy). Although the content and delivery of such programs can and do vary

(Hutchings, Lane, & Kelly, 2004; Sanders & McFarland, 2000), the programs typically use a range of strategies—including discussions, activities, videotaped demonstrations, and modeling of parenting behaviors—which are delivered in 2-hour sessions ... that range from 4 to 12 weeks.

(Bennett, Barlow, Huband, Smailagic, & Roloff, 2013, p. 301)

A parent support group provides the SBFC practitioner with a way to provide prevention services on a range of topics tailored to the needs of specific parent populations. Additionally, a parent support group can be a bridge, linking school and community. Since these groups are usually offered as an extension of a school's guidance program, they are primarily psycho-educational in scope and most often have a preset curriculum to follow. For example, the program for Systematic Training for Effective Parenting (Dinkmeyer, McKay, & Dinkmeyer, Jr.1997) comprises three curriculums each focusing on a specific age group (i.e. birth to 5; 6–12 year olds; teens) (Collins & Fetsch, 2012). When using this type of a program, the program curriculum is the source of training and the SBFC practitioner is the group facilitator. Nevertheless, all parent support groups provide participants with opportunities to share their thoughts and experiences, and ask questions about the topics being presented. This implies that the SBFC practitioner assumes the expert role when interpreting the psychological principles the curriculum is based on. When functioning in this role it is imperative for the SBFC practitioner to stay focused on the psycho-educational purpose of the group and not allow group process moments to evolve into a set of individual therapeutic encounters.

However, a potential drawback of these planned parenting curriculums is that some participants may think that if they do not parent like the examples in these books and achieve the same results, then they are failing as parents. The SBFC practitioner needs to remind the group's participants that the examples in the text always are portrayed as working and it would be nice if the same held true for all real time parent-child interactions. It is important for parent support group participants to realize that the more strategies they possess to effectively guide their child towards making positive choices the better for parent and child. Furthermore, no one intervention strategy will work in every situation. Additionally, programs like STEP (1997) draw on Adlerian principles of democratic parenting (Adler, 1931) that are based on mutual respect between parent and child. In this paradigm, parenting decisions are based on the maturity of the child with the child's input being considered on matters affecting the child. This is a Euro-American approach to parenting, which may or may not be deemed acceptable in some cultures or family systems.

Parent support groups that focus on a single topic such as autism or attention deficit hyperactivity disorder and do not rely on a planned curriculum are by their very nature more open-ended. The SBFC practitioner facilitating this type of group will want to make available to the group members current research on the topic from a variety of different perspectives. For the SBFC practitioners this means synthesizing the key points of each research article, translating those ideas into common, everyday language, developing discussion questions around the articles' key points, and ideally developing group activities to reinforce those points. Furthermore, they will also want to define the group's purpose before the initial group meeting. For example, "Parenting the Autistic Child: A Parent's Journey" tells prospective members that parenting autistic children is one focus of the group and the participants' parenting experiences are the other. This type of parent support group is likely to be more process-oriented than traditional parenting programs. Nevertheless, by giving voice to the participants' experiences, the participants become better able to understand how those experiences have impacted them. It is in the sharing of their story that begins this process.

Parenting children today is a challenging endeavor made even more so by the rapidly expanding world of social media, which children find themselves exposed to once they enter the school system. Like their children, parents also need support to be better able to face these challenges. The SBFC practitioner is the ideal professional to help assist parents and children in finding the support they need to better navigate successfully their respective worlds.

Evidence-based Support

Bennett, Barlow, Huband, Smailagic, and Roloff (2013) write, "Parental psychosocial functioning (e.g. mental health, interparental conflict, confidence) has been shown to be a significant predictor of the later psychological health of children" (p. 300). Their research reviewed 46 studies evaluating the effectiveness of various parent education programs. In addition, they examined the psychosocial benefits to the parents participating in these programs. They found:

> Parenting programs appear to be effective in the short-term in improving a range of aspects of parental psychosocial functioning. Although there is insufficient evidence to demonstrate a strong and consistent effect on paternal psychosocial functioning, the limited available evidence suggests that parenting programs have the potential to improve the psychosocial functioning of fathers as well as mothers.
>
> (p. 317)

Studies providing evidence-based support for parent support programs are shown in Box 8.1.

Box 8.1 Research Articles on Parent Support Groups

Banach, M., Iudice, J., Conway, L., & Couse, L. (2010). Family support and empowerment: Post autism diagnosis support group for parents. *Social Work with Groups*, 33, 69–83.

Bennett, C., Barlow, J., Huband, N., Smailagic, N., & Roloff, V. (2013). Group-based parenting programs for improving parenting and psychosocial functioning: A systematic review. *Journal of the Society for Social Work and Research*, 4(4), 300–332.

Chacko, A., Wymbs, B., Wymbs, F., Pelham, W., Swanger-Gagne, M., Girio, E., Pirvics, L., Herbst, L., Guzzo, J., Phillips, C. & O'Connor, Briannon. (2009). Enhancing traditional behavioral parent training for single mothers of children with ADHD. *Journal of Clinical Child & Adolescent Psychology*, 38(2), 206–218.

Chrispeels, J. & Gonzalez, M. (2006). No parent left behind: The role of parent education programs in assisting families to actively engage in their children's education. Retrieved on December 28, 2017 at: www.bridgingworlds.org/mod elsand metrics/Chrispeels_Gonzalez_PIQE2006.pdf

DeGraaf, I., Speetjens, P., Smit, F., deWolff, M., & Tavecchio, L. (2008). Effectiveness of the Triple P Positive Parenting Program on parenting: A meta-analysis. *Family Relations*, 57, 553–566.

Farooq, D., Jefferson, J., & Fleming, J. (2005). The effect of an Adlerian video-based parent education program on parent's perception of children's behavior: A study of African American parents. *Journal of Professional Counseling*, 33(1), 21–34.

Gonzalez, L., Borders, L., Hines, E., Villalba, J., & Henderson, A., (2013). Parental involvement in children's education: Considerations for school counselors working with Latino immigrant families. *ASCA: Professional School Counseling*, 16(3), 185–193.

Hill, N. & Craft, S. (2003). Parent-school involvement and school Performance: Mediated pathways among socioeconomically comparable African American and Euro-American families. *Journal of Educational Psychology*, 95(1), 74–83.

Kratochwill, T., McDonald, L., Levin, J., Young Bear Tibbetts, H., Demaray, M. (2004). Families and Schools Together: An experimental analysis of a parent-mediated multi-family group program for American Indian children. *Journal of School Psychology*, 42 (2004), 359–383.

Lundahl, B., Risser, H., & Lovejoy, M. (2006). A meta-analysis of parent training: Moderators and follow-up effects. *Clinical Psychology Review*, 26, 86–104.

McVittie, J. & Best, A. (2009). The impact of Adlerian-based parenting classes on self-reported parental behavior. *The Journal of Individual Psychology*, 65(3), 264–285.

Prinz, J. Arkin, S., & Gelkopf. (2008). Hadarim: A description and evaluation of a school-based Adlerian parenting program in Israel. *The Journal of Individual Psychology*, 64(1), 37–54.

Sanders, M. R., Cann, W., & Markie-Dadds, C. (2003). The Triple P-Positive Parenting Program: A universal population-level approach to the prevention of child abuse. *Child Abuse Review*, 12, 155–171.

Schultz, T., Schmidt, C., & Stichter, J. (2011). A review of parent education programs for parents of children with Autism Spectrum Disorder: Focus on Autism and Other Developmental Disabilities. 26(2), 96–104.26(2), 96–104.

Turner, K., Richards, M., & Sanders, M. (2007). Randomised clinical trial of a group parent education program for Australian indigenous families. *Journal of Paediatrics and Child Health*, 43, 429–437.

Turner, K. M. T., & Sanders, M. R. (2006). Dissemination of evidence-based parenting and family support strategies: Learning from the Triple-P Positive Parenting Program system approach. *Violent Behavior*, 11, 176–193.

Procedure

Definition

A parent support group is educational in scope, based on principles of child development, and facilitated by a group leader. Since these groups have a set curriculum, participants usually have homework assignments (e.g. chapter reading) to complete before each meeting. Nevertheless, all groups whether educational or therapeutic draw on the same principles of group leadership and undergo similar stages of group development (Yalom, 2005).

The three STEP (1997) programs examine common themes central to the parent-child or parent-teen dyad. These programs offer parents a variety of strategies to better achieve the behaviors they desire to see in their children and teens. For example, the STEP program for parents with children aged 6–12 uses *The Parenting Handbook* (1997) that addresses the following topics:

- Understanding Yourself and Your Child
- Understanding Beliefs and Feelings
- Encouraging Your Child and Yourself
- Listening and Talking to Your Child
- Helping Children Learn to Cooperate
- Discipline that Makes Sense
- Choosing Your Approach

The STEP programs usually consist of a set number of meetings (six to eight), lasting approximately two hours each. Group members are asked to practice the various techniques highlighted in the text. Good communication skills are identified as an important factor for all healthy relationships. Some examples of communication exercises commonly used in these types of support groups follow.

Background / Rationale

SBFC practitioners may utilize a wide range of techniques when conducting a parent support group. There are multiple examples of "how to" scenarios included in these programs. For example, the use of "I" statements: "I" statements are specific to the speaker's perceptions of what has occurred or is occurring. In using this technique the speaker assumes responsibility for the message being sent, his or her corresponding feelings about what is being said, a desired outcome, and an implied request for a response from the person who is being addressed. Participants practice with one another completing the model:

> I feel _____ (Insert feeling word)
> when _____ (identify what caused the feeling)
> I would like _____ (state what you would like to happen instead).

For example:

> "I feel upset and anxious
> when you don't come home for dinner.
> From now on I'd like you to let me know when you're not going to be home for dinner."

Another "I" statement model uses four steps:

> When you _____ (state observation)
> I feel _____ (state feeling)
> Because _____ (state need)
> I would prefer that _____ (state preference)

For example:

> "I feel angry
> about the way he spoke to me
> because it embarrassed me in front of my friends.
> I would prefer that we discuss these things in private." (Montemurro, 2014, Retrieved May 28, 2018)

Whichever model is used, the goal is the same, which is to resolve a conflict through a more constructive dialogue. Another popular communication technique is changing words like *can't*, which implies helplessness, to *won't*, which implies choice. For example, "I can't cook dinner and watch the kids at the same time." This sentence implies it is not humanly possible to do these two tasks simultaneously. Whereas, "I won't cook dinner and watch the kids at the same time" states that you will do one or the other but not both.

A common challenge for parents with school-aged children is getting their children to turn in their homework assignments at school. It is not uncommon to hear a child say, "I'll try to do better next time." The word "try" gives the child permission to fail again, whereas if the child is encouraged to use the word "will" (I will do better next time) he/she assumes responsibility for his/her actions and the subsequent consequences of the choices made.

However, communication is much more than merely the words spoken by one person to another. Body language, facial expressions, eye contact, tone of voice, rate of speech, physical distance between the two individuals are other factors that affect communication interchanges. Also, one's culture can also be a factor affecting communication interchanges. In parenting groups, how to discipline a child is a common topic of discussion. To help parents better understand the importance of the relationship between discipline and how it is communicated, it is always good to have the participants engage in some activities that help them remember what it is like to be a child.

For example, the SBFC practitioner can ask the group participants to get into pairs. The pairs are asked to face each other. One individual is then asked to stand on a chair, assuming a parental role, while the other is identified as the child and asked to kneel down. The person standing on the chair is told to act like a parent scolding their child for misbehaving. The exercise lasts for approximately a minute with the pairs reversing roles. The pairs debrief first and then members of the group are asked to share their impressions of what it was like being the child.

Glenn and Nelsen (1989) write:

> The suffix *ism* has a negative connotation in our culture. We tend to tack *isms* onto painful problems and/or sicknesses—as in alcoholism ....
> In this book, *isming* refers to our bad habit of requiring others to read our minds and think as we do.
>
> An *adultism* occurs any time an adult forgets what it is like to be a child and then expects, demands, and requires of the child ... to think, act, understand ... and do things as an adult. These unrealistic expectations from adults ... undercut the value of expressions of love ... [and] destroy children's belief in their own capabilities, their sense of their own significance, and their influence over events.
>
> (91)

Awareness is the first step towards change. It is imperative that the SBFC practitioner when facilitating a parent support group model behaviors, which reinforce the principles the particular parenting program espouses. For example, STEP programs use encouragement rather than praise to reinforce desired behaviors in the child; the reason being, encouragement recognizes the effort regardless of outcome, while praise underscores that only when the child achieves a specific outcome (e.g. A+ or 1st place) is her value recognized.

Effective parenting requires parents to be mindful of the fact that children are social animals just like themselves and the primary goal of their behaviors is to belong (Dreikurs & Soltz, 1964). However, "children are expert observers but make many mistakes in interpreting what they observe" (p. 15). This is why parents must be willing to see the world through their child's eyes, taking the time to understand their child's logic and ultimately provide corrective measures where needed. The cornerstone of these countless interactions between parent and child is the belief that healthy relationships are built on mutual respect and that democratic parenting is the key to raising happy, self-reliant children.

Procedural Steps

Set-up

Parent support group members are seated in a circle. The SBFC practitioner is seated in the circle, also. Ideally, this individual sits next to a different person at each group meeting. By changing seats at each meeting the SBFC practitioner changes the power dynamics present in the group. The message being sent to the participants is that the SBFC practitioner is a member of the group collaborating with everyone (Psychology Today, 2012).

Model Dialogue

SBFC Practitioner: We're now going to practice making "I" statements, using the model shown in your manual, which is:

I feel _____(Insert feeling word)

when _____(identify what caused the feeling)

I would like _____(state what you would like to happen instead).

You can refer to your manual for a list of feeling words if that helps.
I'd like you to find someone in the group you haven't worked with yet and partner with that individual. I want you to take turns making "I" statements to one another. When I ask you to stop (activity lasts approximately five minutes) I want you to debrief with one another and talk about what the activity was like for you (allow approximately five minutes for debriefing), then we'll come back together as a group and discuss the activity.

SBFC practitioner:	All right everyone, I'd like you to finish up sharing and come back together as a group. It sounded like there were a lot of good discussions going on. Who would like to share what the experience was like for them?
Michael:	The way you and the book described it made it sound so easy. But, it was hard.
SBFC practitioner:	Can you tell me how it was hard?
Michael:	I'm not used to talking that way.
Diane:	I'm not either. When the kids are driving me crazy, I just want the fighting to stop now!
SBFC practitioner:	So, how do you get the children to stop fighting?
Diane:	I'm usually in another room, so I raise my voice loud enough to be heard.
Michael:	Me, too. I let them know that there will be hell to pay if they don't knock it off.
SBFC practitioner:	I can understand your frustration. I hear it in your voices. My own kids drive me crazy sometimes. But, they're just kids and according to Adler those misbehaviors are telling us what they want. Does anyone remember what those are?
Maya:	Attention, power, revenge, and I always forget the last one.
Jackson:	Helplessness.
SBFC practitioner:	That's right. Children want to belong and feel love more than anything else from their parents. Maybe, one way you can practice integrating "I" statements into your conversations with your children is acknowledging them when they do something good. For example,

I feel happy

when you pick up your toys without me asking you

because it helps me keep the house neat.

Thanks!

Too often parents and teachers respond to a child only when they see the child acting out. One of the key tenets of Adlerian-Dreikursian child guidance principles is to catch the child being good. If a child's ultimate goal is to belong and experience parental love, what better way to encourage a child's positive behaviors than a parent's acknowledgement of the child's positive efforts to do so.

Multicultural Counseling Considerations

When conducting parent support groups it is helpful if the SBFC practitioner is familiar with the parenting practices commonly exercised in various cultures, especially those represented by the group's participants. Depending on the parents' level of acculturation to American norms and values, parenting practices may differ markedly from one familial group to another. In addition, the SBFC practitioner must be sensitive to how the information on parenting is shared with the group members, so as not to unintentionally insult a member. For example, in traditional Chinese culture the male is considered the head of the household. It would be an insult to the family if when discussing various parenting practices the SBFC practitioner encouraged a Chinese mother to question her husband's parenting decisions.

Culture is transmitted through language. The nuances associated with a word in one culture may be lost when translated from one language to another. Many of today's parenting programs are now made available in Spanish. The STEP (1997) program has been translated not only into Spanish, but also French, German, and Japanese.

Diaz (as cited in Quiocho & Daoud, 2006, p. 255) writes:

> Culturally diverse communities have been told through overt and covert avenues that they are not as good as White students and will not do as well because of their background. They overhear teachers say things like, "Well, you can't expect anything from these children. Their parents don't care and they come from transient families."

It is imperative for the SBFC practitioner to be cognizant of the possibility that some of the group's participants may have encountered varying degrees of racial or social denigration in the past, making them acutely sensitive to how you interact with them. Demonstrating respect in your interactions with them and validating their experiences are critical to forming a strong working relationship with all parents.

> Multicultural counseling [including group counseling] challenges the notion that problems are found exclusively within the person. Going beyond this stance of "blaming the victim," the multicultural approach emphasizes the social and cultural context of human behavior and deals with the self-in-relation. It is essential that group workers recognize that many problems reside outside the person.
>
> (Corey, 2012, p. 11)

Additionally, every parent who walks through the school doors brings with them their own personal history of what school life was like for them. For ethnic minority individuals, the school may represent an institution that is attempting to instill in their child ideas and values contrary to parental beliefs. It may be a place where as a child they first encountered prejudice and racial slurs. SBFC practitioners need to realize this and demonstrate through word and deed that they respect and celebrate the differences defining our humanity.

The importance of respecting and acknowledging the socio-historical factors that have shaped the worldviews of the group's participants cannot be over-emphasized (Sue & Sue, 2008). Often ethnic minority children are considered being at-risk for academic failure simply because of their ethnicity. Not only do these children have to navigate the typical developmental milestones of childhood and adolescence, but also factors like poverty, limited employment opportunities for family members, and societal stereotypes can all negatively impact the child's sense of being a valued member of society. Cardenas (cited in Montemayor, 2004, p. 1) explains:

> In successful programs for the education of at-risk school populations, there is a valuing of the students in ways in which they are not valued in regular and traditional school programs. In successful school programs, the student is valued, his language is valued, his heritage is valued, his family is valued, and, most important, the student is valued as a person.

Parent and child must feel welcomed at the school. The challenge for the SBFC practitioner is to demonstrate to these individuals his or her willingness to learn their cultural language from them, to embrace the narrative that frames each family's everyday life. The SBFC practitioner must be an active participant in advocating for the children's educational needs to ensure they have the opportunity to experience life at its fullest potential. For this to happen, there must be honest communication between all parties involved with the child's well-being.

Challenges and Solutions

A common challenge for SBFC practitioners when conducting a parent support group is the participants' regular attendance at weekly meetings. Since these groups are outreach efforts by the school and offered at no cost to the participants, the incentive for getting one's money's worth out of the group is non-existent. Additionally, today's families may have two working parents or be headed by a single parent or guardian, thereby creating child-care issues for some parents in attendance. Other challenges the SBFC practitioner must address include: scheduling meetings at a time most beneficial to a majority of the school's parent population, providing healthy snacks, getting permission from teachers for the use of their classrooms as a meeting place or childcare facility. Eliminating as many of these potential obstacles as possible can be critical to the success of your parent support group.

One of the first steps the SBFC practitioner can take is sampling the parent population to determine what meeting times would be best for a majority of the individuals. Most SBFC practitioners have a variety of avenues for sampling a school's parent population. The use of newsletters, attendance at PTA meetings, having teachers hand out a survey at parent-teacher conferences, posting the survey on the school's website, or providing students with a handout to give to their parents about the group are just some of the ways a sampling can be taken. Regardless of the method used this initial contact sets the tone for how participants will perceive the group. This is why the SBFC practitioner's letter introducing the survey, as well as the survey itself, must be written in positive terms. No parent or guardian wants to feel they are doing poorly in raising their child or that their child is ill-behaved and willful.

Also, asking what parenting issues most concern parents can aid the SBFC practitioner in modifying the topics to be addressed in the group. It is suggested that the parents be provided with a list of topics and asked to rank order them from most to least important. It is also recommended that the list provide the participants with the option of identifying two or three other areas of concern not listed. As noted previously, discipline is a common topic of discussion in most programed curriculums. However, issues like bullying, internet safety, and sexting are concerns many parents have today.

Once a meeting time has been set and the group's topics identified, the SBFC practitioner can then set about addressing other pre-group tasks. These include: finding rooms appropriate for both meeting with the parents and another suitable for childcare, funding for purchasing healthy snacks, and contacting local service groups (e.g. Boy Scouts or Girl Scouts) as potential childcare providers. Funding for these types of activities can often be attained through the school's PTA organization. If there are no school or district funding sources available, the SBFC practitioner can choose to use their own funds for financing the group or ask the group participants to each donate five to ten dollars to offset the costs of food and the stipend for the service group providing childcare.

Having navigated the mechanics of developing a parent support group the SBFC practitioner must decide whether the group will be open or closed, meaning will others be allowed to join the group after the first meeting. Secondly, how large will the group be? Most groups limit their membership from 8 to 12 individuals. However, it is not uncommon for a school parent support group to have as many as 20 to 25 participants. This is why it is recommended to have a co-facilitator, who can either be another SBFC practitioner or a member of the school community. It is understood that whoever agrees to act as a co-facilitator is bound by the same ethical guidelines as the SBFC practitioner.

Confidentiality is always a crucial issue for all group experiences. Even though parent support groups are primarily psycho-educational in scope, group participants must know that what they share in the group stays in the group. It is the very safety that confidentiality provides, which encourages group participants to offer candid evaluations of self and honest feedback to others. Confidentiality is one of the first topics always discussed at an initial parent support group meeting and many practitioners recommend starting subsequent meetings with a confidentiality reminder. One of the challenges for the SBFC practitioner leading this type of group in school settings is the fact that schools put on many social events throughout the academic year, creating the possibility of group members coming into contact with one another outside the parent support group setting. In addition, it is likely that some group members will already know one another from other venues.

When discussing confidentiality it is important for the SBFC practitioner to share with the group the limits of confidentiality. All school personnel and licensed mental health professionals (i.e. SBFC practitioners) are state-mandated reporters, meaning if an individual discloses information about harm to self (e.g. suicide) or others (e.g. child abuse) the SBFC practitioner must report that information to the appropriate authorities. While confidentiality protects parent support group members from sharing information about other members outside the group, no such protection is allotted to the SBFC practitioner. A leader's self-disclosures can be effective tools for building trust with group members; however, those individuals are free to share with others whatever you have shared with them.

In summary, SBFC practitioners who utilize parent support groups have a valuable tool for reaching out to their school community. Through these groups, SBFC practitioners can assist parents in developing new strategies for helping their children learn how to make better choices for themselves. Additionally, practitioners can discuss what resources are available in the community for parents dealing with a specific set of concerns. Most importantly though, parent support groups provide their members with the opportunity to share their parenting concerns in a safe, non-judgmental environment. Parents need to know other parents also have parenting concerns. Through this sharing, the SBFC practitioner can help build a nurturing community of support for parents and children, the ultimate goal of which is the development of a happy, responsible child living in a healthy family system.

Resources

"I" messages and positive parenting practices

Good Therapy.org. (2018). "I" message. Retrieved on April 21, 2018 at: www.goodtherapy.org/blog/psychpedia/I-message

Johnson, J. (2012). Are "I" statements better than "you" statements? *Psychology Today*. Retrieved on April 14, 2018 at: www.psychologytoday.com/us/blog/cui-bono/201211/are-i-statements-better-you-statements

KidsHealth. (2015). 9 steps to more effective parenting. Retrieved on April 21, 2018 at: https://kidshealth.org/en/parents/nine-steps.html

LifeMatters. (1996). STEP and positive discipline series. Retrieved on December 16, 2017 at: www.lifematters.com/step.asp

Peaceful Parent Institute. (n.d.). "I" statements—Expressing limits non-aggressively. Retrieved on April 14, 2018 at: www.peacefulparent.com/expressing-limits/assertively-yet-non-aggressively/

The Center for Parenting Education. (n.d.). Healthy communication: The skill of active listening. Retrieved on April 14,2018 at: https://centerforparenteducation.org/library-of-articles/healthy-communication/the-skill-of-listening

Van der Linden, N. (n.d.). 8 psychologist-backed tips for improving communication with kids. Retrieved on May 8, 2014 at: www.mother.ly/child/8-expert-tips-talk-effectively-kids

Positive discipline

Nelson, J. (2011). *Positive discipline.* New York: Ballantine Books.

Glenn, H. S. & Nelsen, J. (1989). *Raising self-reliant children in a self-indulgent world.* Rocklin, CA: Prima Publishing.

Active parenting

Popkin, M. (1989). Active parenting: A video-based program. In M. Fine (Ed.), *The second handbook on parent education: Contemporary perspectives* (pp. 77–98). San Diego, CA: Academic Press.

Mullis, F. (1999). Active Parenting: An evaluation of two Adlerian parent education programs. *The Journal of Individual Psychology*, 55, 225–232.

STEP (Systematic Training for Effective Parenting)

Dinkmeyer, D., McKay, G., & Dinkmeyer, Jr., D. (1997). *The parent's handbook: Systematic training for effective parenting.* Circle Pines, MN: American Guidance Service.

Parent effectiveness training

Gordon, T. (2000). *Parent effectiveness training: The proven program for raising responsible children.* New York: Three Rivers Press.

Second time around: grandparents raising grandchildren

Fetsch, R. J. & Lester, S. (2004, May). Review of *Second time around: Grandparents raising grandchildren* curriculum: A curriculum guide for group leaders. *The Forum for Family and Consumer Issues*, 9(1). Retrieved from: www.ces.ncsu.edu/depts/fcs/pub/9_1/fetsch.html.

Triple P-Positive Parenting Program

Sanders, M. R., Markie-Dadds, C., & Tully, L. A. (2000). The Triple P-Positive Parenting Program: A comparison of enhanced, standard, and self-directed behavioral family intervention for parents of children with early onset conduct problems. *Journal of Consulting and Clinical Psychology*, 68, 624–640.

Sanders, M. R., Turner, K. M. T., & Markie-Dadds, C. (2002). The development and dissemination of the Triple P-Positive Parenting Program: A multilevel evidence-based system of parenting and family support. *Prevention Science*, 3, 173–198.

Partners in parenting

Wilson, K., Hahn, L., Gonzalez, P., Henry, K., & Carbena, C. (2011). An evaluation of partners in parenting: A parent education curriculum implemented by county extension agents in Colorado. *Journal of Extension*, 49(4), Article 4RIB3.

Bibliography

Adler, A. (1931). *What life should mean to you.* New York: Putman.

Ansbacher, H. L. & Ansbacher, R. R. (1956). *The individual psychology of Alfred Adler.* New York: Harper Perennial.

Bennett, C., Barlow, J., Huband, N., Smailagic, N., & Roloff, V. (2013). Group-based parenting programs for improving parenting and psychosocial functioning: A systematic review. *Journal of the Society for Social Work and Research*, 4(4), 300–332.

Collins, C. & Fetsch, R. (2012). A review and critique of 16 major parent education programs. *Journal of Extension*, 50(4). Retrieved on December 20, 2017 at: www.joe.org/joe/2012august/a8.php

Corey, G. (2012). *Theory and practice of group counseling* (8th ed.). Belmont, CA: Thomson Brooks/Cole.

Dinkmeyer, D., McKay, G., & Dinkmeyer, Jr., D. (1997). *The parent's handbook: Systematic training for effective parenting.* Circle Pines, MN: American Guidance Service.

Dreikurs, R. & Soltz, V. (1964). *Children: The challenge.* New York: Hawthorne Books.

Glenn, H. S. & Nelsen, J. (1989). *Raising self-reliant children in a self-indulgent world.* Rocklin, CA: Prima Publishing.

Hutchings, J., Lane, E., & Kelly, J. (2004). Comparison of two treatments for children with severely disruptive behaviours: A four-year follow-up. *Behavioural and Cognitive Psychotherapy*, 32(1), 15–30.

Lundahl, B., Risser, H., & Lovejoy, C. (2006). A meta-analysis of parent training: Moderators and follow-up effects. *Clinical Psychology Review*, 26, 86–104.

Montemayor, A. (2004). Excellent bilingual early childhood programs: A parents guide. Retrieved April 15, 2012 from: http://www.eric.ed.gov/PDFS/ED484908.pdf

Montemurro, F. (2014). I messages. *Boston University Ombuds.* Retrieved on May, 28, 2018 at: www.bu.edu/ombuds/files/2014/11/IMessages.pdf

Oryan, S. & Gastil, J. (2013). Democratic parenting: Paradoxical messages in democratic parent education theories. *International Review of Education*, 59, 113–129.

Psychology Today. (2012). The power seat: Where you sit matters. Retrieved on June 26, 2018 at: www.psychologyttoday.com/us/blog/digital-leaders/201210/the-power-seat-where-you-sit-matters

Quiocho, A. & Daoud, A. (2006). Dispelling myths about Latino parent participation in Schools. *The Educational Forum*, 70, 255–267.

RAND Corporation. (2011). *Promising practices network on children, families, and communities.* Retrieved on December 28, 2017 at: www.promisingpractices.net/

Reide, M. (2009). *A review of parent education curriculums and models.* Retrieved on March 22, 2018 at: www.parentinged.msu.edu/Home/AboutThisSite/tabid/71/Default.aspx

Sanders, M. R. & McFarland, M. (2000). Treatment of depressed mothers with disruptive children: A controlled evaluation of cognitive behavioral family intervention. *Behavior Therapy*, 31(1), 89–112.

Shulruf, B. (2005). Parent support and education programmes: A systematic review. *NZ Research in Early Childhood Education*, 8, 81–102.

Small, S. A., Cooney, S. M., & O'Connor, C. (2009, February). Evidence-informed program improvement: Using principles of effectiveness to enhance the quality and impact of family-based prevention programs. *Family Relations*, 58, 1–13.

Stiener, A. (2011). A strengths-based approach to parent education for children with autism. *Journal of Positive Behavior Interventions*, 13(3), 178–190.

Sue, D. W. & Sue, D. (2008). *Counseling the culturally diverse: Theory and practice* (5th ed.). Hoboken, NJ: Wiley & Sons.

Wilson, K., Hahn, L., Gonzalez, P., Henry, K., & Carbena, C. (2011). An evaluation of partners in parenting: A parent education curriculum implemented by county extension agents in Colorado. *Journal of Extension*, 49(4), Article 4RIB3.

Yalom, I. (2005). *The theory and practice of group psychotherapy* (5th ed.). New York: Basic Books.

Ziomek-Daigle, J., McMahon, H., & Paisley, P. (2008). Adlerian-based interventions for professional school counselors: Serving as both counselors and educational leaders. *The Journal of Individual Psychology*, 64(40), 450–467.

9 School Prevention

How to Increase Student Engagement

Emily J. Hernandez

Overview: This chapter describes how to increase student engagement in a school setting as an SBFC practitioner. While there are many aspects to student engagement, this chapter will focus on cultivating a positive school climate, establishing school organization and infrastructure, and fostering student interactions.

Background

Student Engagement

Student engagement has been widely studied in educational research and is a term that is used to measure a student's relationship to school. Finn (1989) was among the first to define school engagement as the extent to which a student is invested in school and participates in school-related activities. Common terms in health and education literature include school engagement, school attachment, school bonding, school climate, school involvement, teacher support, and school connectedness. The term "school engagement" refers to a student's relationship or connection to school (Libbey, 2004). While there are many terms used to describe student engagement, there are consistent themes found by Libbey (2004) that relate to student engagement: sense of belonging and being a part of a school; whether or not students like school; level of teacher supportiveness and caring; presence of good friends in school; engagement in current and future academic progress; fair and effective discipline; and participation in extracurricular activities (Libbey, 2004). These themes are listed in Box 9.1.

Student engagement and the factors described above have been found to be highly associated with student outcomes. Student engagement has been repeatedly demonstrated to be a robust predictor of achievement and behavior in schools (Appleton, Christenson, & Furlong, 2008; Shernoff & Schmidt, 2008). Student engagement has been found to be linked to multiple educational outcomes such as achievement; attendance; behavior; and dropout/completion (Finn, 1989; Jimerson, Campos, & Greif, 2003; Jimerson et al., 2009). Researchers have identified that effective interventions to promote student engagement also enhance the probability of high school completion (Reschly, Appleton, &

Box 9.1 Consistent Themes Related to Student Engagement

- Sense of belonging and being a part of a school
- Whether or not students like school
- Level of teacher supportiveness and caring
- Presence of good friends in school
- Engagement in current and future academic progress
- Fair and effective discipline
- Participation in extracurricular activities

(Libbey, 2004)

Christenson, 2007). Studies show that student engagement is considered the main theoretical model in understanding student dropout (Christenson et al., 2008; Finn & Owings, 2006; Reschly & Christenson, 2006).

Student engagement is a complex construct that is important in promoting positive outcomes for students. Challenges exist in the measurement of this construct due to its many indicators such as affective engagement, behavioral engagement, cognitive engagement, and academic engagement (Hart, Stewart, & Jimerson, 2011). Hart, Stewart, and Jimerson (2011) recommend that student engagement interventions be a part of the key to promoting school completion and academic outcomes. They describe measures of student engagement that can be used as an assessment tool to target interventions for students who are at risk, or used as prevention efforts at the school-wide level. Furthermore, health and education literature suggests that student engagement contributes significantly to student success in school (Hart, Stewart, & Jimerson, 2011; Libbey, 2004). Reschly and Christenson (2012) refer to student engagement as the "glue, or mediator" that links the various important contexts (life, home, school peers, and community) to students which in turn has an effect on the outcome of interest and connection to school (p. 3).

Student engagement has become an important topic in the field of education. Over the past 25 years, research on student engagement has increased, vastly advancing the field. As research has expanded the information we know about student engagement, there are still unresolved questions and issues related to the research in terms of definition, theory, and measurement that require additional study. Despite this, there is a general consensus about what we do know. In general, the research points to the following widely known facts about student engagement outlined from the Handbook of Research on Student Engagement (Christenson, Reschly, & Wylie, 2012). The Handbook of Research on Student Engagement is an excellent resource to review for a more comprehensive understanding of the research on student engagement. Some common known facts about student engagement are reviewed in Box 9.2.

Box 9.2 Known Facts About Student Engagement

- Student engagement is crucial to understanding student dropout.
- Engagement behavior is complex and much more than just attending school, or doing well academically.
- Student engagement is associated positively with academic, social, and emotional learning outcomes.
- Student engagement is a multi-dimensional construct that requires an awareness and understanding of affective connections within the academic environment and student behavior.
- Context is important. Engagement is inextricably linked and influenced by the context of the student's life (school, peers, family, community). Focusing on the individual alone is not enough.
- Student engagement and motivation must be a component of effective instruction for positive learning outcomes.
- Measuring student engagement is a powerful tool to drive data-driven decision making in schools.
- There are evidence-based practices and interventions that are known to increase student engagement.

(Christenson, Reschly, & Wylie, 2012)

The student engagement construct is vast in terms of areas of study. There are multiple facets integrated into student engagement that are important including definition, theoretical models, motivational variables, contextual influences, student outcomes, and measurement. While the research shows that engagement is particularly important for students who may be at risk of dropping out of school, the beauty of this construct is that implementing student engagement interventions, and fully integrating them into existing systems and structures within a school site, will be relevant for all students, making it a universal and targeted intervention simultaneously (Christenson, Reschly, & Wylie, 2012)

School-based Family Counseling Meta-model and Framework

Student engagement can be viewed and applied through the lens of the SBFC meta-model and framework. Box 9.3 below lists the eight main strengths of the SBFC meta-model (see Chapter 1).

Using the strength areas of the SBFC model provides a way for collaborative and systems-oriented approaches to prevention and intervention. The SBFC meta-model, as described by Soriano and Gerrard (2013), illustrates the primary focus of SBFC to be on the school and the family in the area of prevention and intervention. The model consists of four quadrants: school prevention; school intervention; family prevention; and family intervention. It provides a framework to help SBFC professionals stay focused on working

---

Box 9.3 Eight Main Strengths of the SBFC Meta-Model

- School and Family Focus
- Systems Orientation
- Educational Focus
- Parent Partnership
- Multicultural Sensitivity
- Child Advocacy
- Promotion of School Transformation
- Interdisciplinary Focus

---

systemically within a school structure which is at the heart of the SBFC approach. The SBFC meta-model is shown below in Figure 9.1 (Soriano & Gerrard, 2013).

Student engagement falls largely in the area of the prevention quadrants if you are viewing it through the SBFC meta-model and framework. In order to increase student engagement within a school system, it is best to begin with a prevention-focused, systems-oriented approach. A specific focus on prevention within a systems perspective reduces the need for intervention-related services. The focus on prevention shifts the balance from a reactive model to a more proactive one. The need for school and family interventions will always exist and is a definite need within school systems. The development of a school system that is heavily prevention-focused will allow for more time and use of deliberate and intentional interventions for youth and families by SBFC professionals (Hernandez, 2016).

There are a myriad of school-related issues that are important and require attention. School officials are constantly looking for programs that address

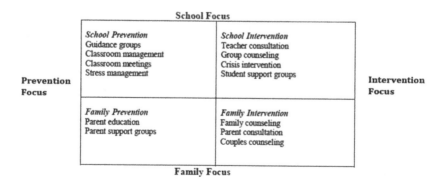

Figure 9.1 The SBFC Meta-Model

these particular issues that can be integrated into their existing programs or school infrastructure. Examples may include anti-bullying prevention programs, dropout prevention programs, violence prevention programs, mentoring programs, etc. Addressing the important issues of bullying and student dropout are common areas of immediate focus for school personnel. Student engagement can be considered a vital construct to be used in prevention and intervention efforts in both dropout and bullying prevention.

Utilizing Student Engagement As An Intervention in School-wide Problems: Dropout Prevention and Bullying

Student Engagement and Student Dropout

This section will review the connection between student engagement and dropout, and will review multiple theories of student dropout that identify student engagement as an important fluid process that leads to school dropout. Dropping out of school is a process of disengagement and is identifiable early on in the student's academic career. Disengagement from school is a key element in this process. Signs of disengagement are prevalent and can be observed in students as early as elementary school. Warning signs include poor attendance, behavior problems, and low grades in middle and early high school. Attendance is often a key barometer of a student's connection with school. Failing in school was reported as a major factor (Balfanz et al., 2010). Boys are more likely to drop out because of behavior problems, while girls are more likely to slowly disengage from school by skipping class or being absent (Rumberger & Rotermund, 2012). Dropping out is more of a process than an event (Rumberger & Rotermund, 2012); and the eventual act of dropping out involves a slow process of disengagement that begins early on in a student's academic career. The level of a student's engagement to school has been found to be an important precursor to student dropout.

Student engagement is a central construct in student dropout. The long-term effects of school disengagement on problem behaviors have been identified (Henry, Knight, & Thornberry, 2012), and the construct of student engagement is central to most theories of school dropout (Finn, 1989). Henry, Knight, and Thornberry (2012) argue that indicators of school disengagement measured during the eighth and ninth grades are robustly related to school dropout and later involvement in crime and problem substance use. Students who evidence multiple school-risk factors during middle school are prime candidates for interventions designed to enhance school engagement. Henry, Knight, and Thornberry (2012) further argued the importance of employing early warning systems and intervention strategies to enhance school engagement early on. As an example, a screening tool such as the School Disengagement Warning Index can be used and is a robust predictor of high school dropout (Henry, Knight, & Thornberry, 2012). The implementation of early warning systems and corresponding interventions should prove to be an efficient strategy for decreasing dropout and related problem behaviors in the short and long term (Henry, Knight, & Thornberry, 2012). Student disengagement in school contributes to the likelihood of those students' dropping out. Therefore, it is suggested to not wait until students are dropping out, or have dropped out, of school to intervene.

There are multiple theories of school dropout that identify student engagement as a key construct (Archambault, Janosz, Fallu, & Pagani, 2009). One of the earliest of these is Social Control Theory, which places an emphasis on attachment and belongingness to social institutions (Hirschi, 1969). This theory asserts that disengagement results from the breakdown of weakened relationships between the individual and the school. The bonds in social control theory are characterized by commitment, beliefs, attachment, and engagement (Hirschi, 1969). A second theory is Tinto's (1975) Mediation Model of school dropout. In this model, students interact with the academic and social system of a school. Goals and institutional commitment set the course for student engagement and are believed to influence a youth's academic and social experience at school, and, in unfavorable conditions, can play a role in the decision to leave the system altogether. Thirdly, Finn's (1989) Participation-identification Model of school withdrawal views engagement by identification and participation in school. Within this model, students are expected to identify more with school as they increase their participation. Conversely, low or absent participation predicts gradual disengagement and eventual school withdrawal (Archambault, Janosz, Fallu, & Pagani, 2009). Fourth, the Dropout Prevention Model of Wehlage et al. (1989) introduces the concepts of educational engagement and school membership as intermediate steps that contribute to individual and social development at school. From this perspective, students who fail to achieve these two goals present higher risks of dropping out of school. Lastly, in Rumber and Larson's (1998) model, engagement is distinguished by two components, social and academic, which contribute to academic adjustment. Social and academic engagement in this model are defined and seen as essential for understanding the process that underlies school dropout (Archambault, Janosz, Fallu, & Pagani, 2009).

There are two major similarities that emerge within these theories. First, engagement is conceived as a process that changes over the course of the school experience. Student engagement is fluid and based on the dynamics of the student and the school environment and systems; the level of engagement can change. Second, the importance of behavioral and motivational aspects of engagement is a focus (Archambault, Janosz, Morizot, & Pagani, 2009). The behavioral and motivational factors related to dynamics involving school, peers, academics, attendance, and identification and participation with school are important. All the theories are based on the notion that student engagement is important in the process that leads to school dropout (Archambault, Janosz, Fallu, & Pagani, 2009). These theories suggest that student engagement is a central component in the process of student dropout.

Student Engagement and Bullying

Bullying is not a new phenomenon. Some researchers contend that this problem has been around forever, but that school bullying probably looked different than it does today (Daniels & Bradley, 2011). At one point, bullying behaviors were considered to be a normal part of growing up and not a serious concern (Daniels & Bradley, 2011). Some parents and educators considered bullying to be a rite of passage or a normal part of building one's character. Today, however, bullying has become a serious concern among students, parents, educators, and the community at large (Lederman, 2012). Bullying has intensified in schools. A national study among 16,000 American schoolchildren found that nearly 30% of students reported moderate or frequent involvement in bullying (Nansel et al., 2001). Eleven years later, Robers et al. (2012) conducted a national study and found that 28% of students reported being bullied at school. Olweus (1994) conducted the first systematic investigation of bullying in the early 1970s in Norway, and has researched bullying behaviors in hundreds of thousands of Norwegian and Swedish primary and secondary school students over the last 30 years. Similar research has been conducted internationally with consistent findings (Chapell et al., 2004). Bullying is a common worldwide phenomenon, and students in multiple countries report being involved in bullying (Harris & Petrie, 2002; Smith et al., 1999). A study of over 7,000 students in the United States found that bullying and victimization is prevalent among urban, low socioeconomic, African American and Latino middle and high school youth (Flescher-Peskin et al., 2007). One in five children and adolescents is a victim of bullying (Limber, 2002) and one in three is involved as bully, victim or both (Nansel et al., 2001). Bullying behavior has been studied for over 30 years, and significant numbers of students continue to report being involved in bullying.

The prevalence of bullying is increasing at all school levels (Gastic, 2008). Nationally, a third of sixth through tenth grade students reported moderate or frequent involvement in bullying, as a victim or bully (Dinkes, Kemp, & Baum, 2009; Nansel et al., 2001; Nishioka et al., 2011). A study by the Kaiser Family Foundation (2001) found that 74% of students ages 8 to 11 reported being teased or bullied and 55% perceived bullying as a big problem in their school. The numbers were even higher in secondary schools (Nishioka et al., 2011). In 2009, nearly 20% of high school students who completed the U.S. Department of Health National Youth Risk Behavior Survey, a nationally representative survey on the prevalence of victimization and bullying, reported being bullied on school property during the previous 12 months (Nishioka et al., 2011). In 2010, 32% of students reported being bullied at school, according to the School Crime Supplement of the National Crime Victimization Survey administered to almost 9,000 students 12 to 18 years old (Dinkes, Kemp, & Baum, 2009). Another survey of over 7,000 elementary students found that more than a third, 34%, of students reported being victims of bullying and almost two-thirds, 65% of students, reported witnessing bully incidents at their school (Bradshaw, O'Brennan, & Sawyer, 2008). Using real-time observations, one study found that bullying episodes occurred at an average of twice per hour in participating classrooms and involved bystanders in 85% of occurrences (Atlas & Pepler, 1998). Despite the research, bullying continues to take place at schools and is on the rise.

Bullying has an impact on a student's feeling of connectedness to school. Bullying and peer aggression generally have negative long-term effects on a student's level of engagement with school. Bullying has been found to affect student engagement, attendance, behavior, and academic outcomes, and has been linked to the dropout rate of students (Gastic, 2008; Morrison, 2002). In their study of over 11,000 secondary students surveyed nationally, Hutzell and Payne (2012) clearly showed an association between bullying victimization and avoidance behaviors in school. They also found support for the concept of bully-prone locations in schools that students who are bullied frequently avoid (Hutzell & Payne, 2012). The development of avoidance behaviors in students involved in bullying has an impact on their level of connectedness to school.

Bullying has an impact on a student's overall adjustment to school, which affects their level of engagement. Research has shown that victims of bullying exhibit poor social and emotional adjustment, lower social skills and abilities to make friends, poor relationships with classmates, and higher levels of loneliness and anxiety (Harris & Petrie, 2002). Further, students who perceive high levels of bullying in their school may become less engaged in school and, consequently, be less motivated to learn. This disengagement contributes to problems with school attendance, including truancy and dropout (Gastic, 2008; Klein, Cornell, & Konold, 2012). To illustrate, Soriano (1999) reported that 160,000 students miss school daily in the United States because of bullying and threats. Suh and Suh (2007) found that poor attendance and disciplinary problems are significantly more likely for victims of bullying and are associated with increased risk for dropping out of school. According to the National Research Council and Institute of Medicine (2004), improving school engagement is crucial to addressing national problems with high school completion and academic performance. Students involved in bullying experience difficulty in adjusting to the school environment, which further results in their disengagement to school.

Dropout prevention and bullying are major educational issues at the center of school reform. All educators – school administrators, teachers, counselors, and specialized support staff – are charged with ensuring positive educational outcomes and a safe learning environment for students. The focus of this chapter will be on systemic and direct service student engagement interventions that can be put in place by a SBFC practitioner at a school site.

The procedure presented is based on a research study of a model utilizing student engagement as a promising practice in dropout prevention and bullying (Hernandez, 2014). This study focused specifically on student engagement,

Table 9.1 Findings: 3 Emerging Themes and Supporting Strategies

Theme	Supporting Strategies		
Positive School Climate	Leadership	Whole-School Approach	
School Organization and Infrastructure	Student Safety and Learning	Campus Supervision	Student Groupings/ Cohort Model
Student Interactions	Cooperative Learning Model	Character Building and Social Skills	

(Hernandez, 2014)

a key contributor to student dropout, as a promising practice in preventing bullying in K-12 schools (from kindergarten to twelfth grade) and fostering an anti-bullying culture. Three prevalent themes emerged from the data and clear, observable, concrete strategies were found to be in place within each theme. The first theme was positive school climate. There were two main findings related to this theme: leadership, which involves collective team-building, and use of a whole-school approach involving all stakeholders. The second theme was school organization and infrastructure. There were three findings related to this theme: student safety and learning involving the physical organization and layout of the school, a campus supervision plan, and use of student groupings or a cohort model. The last theme was student interactions. There were two findings related to this theme: use of a cooperative learning model, and teaching character building and social skills. The themes with their supporting strategies are depicted in Table 9.1.

Figure 9.2 below shows how the findings, consistent themes, and support-ing strategies are aligned with the Prevention Focus quadrants of the SBFC meta-model.

Implications for Practice and Policy

These findings have direct implications that may be helpful for districts, schools, educators, and SBFC professionals in improving how schools can effectively develop school-wide, wholistic approaches, specific to their school communities, which foster an anti-bullying and dropout prevention culture focused on engaging students. Implications for school-based practice are described in Box 9.4.

For the purposes of this chapter, a review of each of the promising practice themes for increasing student engagement in preventing student dropout and bullying will be provided below. Each theme and strategy will be introduced with a background and procedural steps for implementing each strategy.

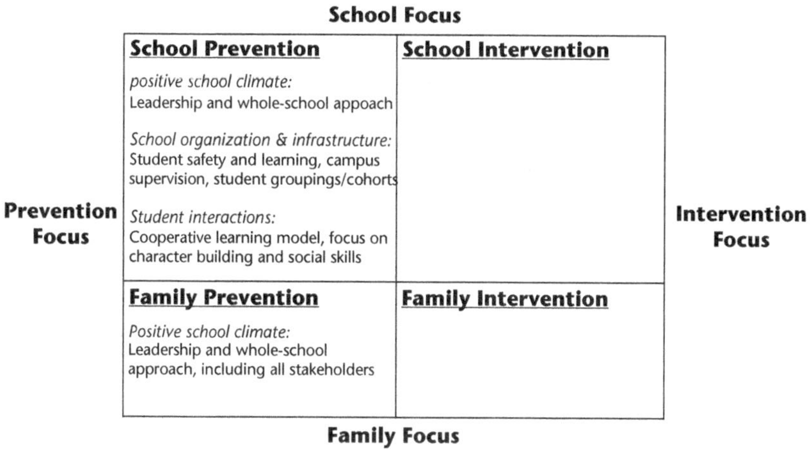

School Focus

School Prevention	School Intervention
positive school climate: Leadership and whole-school appoach *School organization & infrastructure:* Student safety and learning, campus supervision, student groupings/cohorts *Student interactions:* Cooperative learning model, focus on character building and social skills	
Family Prevention	**Family Intervention**
Positive school climate: Leadership and whole-school approach, including all stakeholders	

Prevention Focus (left) **Intervention Focus** (right)

Family Focus

Figure 9.2 Findings Aligned with the SBFC Meta-model

Evidence-based Support

Student engagement and the factors described above have been found to be highly associated with student outcomes. Student engagement has repeatedly demonstrated to be a robust predictor of achievement and behavior in schools (Appleton, Christenson, & Furlong, 2008; Shernoff & Schmidt, 2008). Student engagement has been found to be linked to multiple educational outcomes such

---

Box 9.4 Implications for Practice and Policy

1. A whole-school approach is recommended.
2. Impacting belief systems and creating a shared vision is the main foundation for an integrated whole-school approach.
3. Consider leadership styles that engage all systems levels when tasked with the complete transformation of an institution.
4. A systems-level approach is needed that includes all stakeholders to effectively create an anti-bullying culture.
5. Consider an infrastructure conducive to a focus on student interactions and relationships, such as a student grouping or cohort model.
6. Consider incorporating a cooperative learning model to increase student engagement, and focus on student interactions within their schools.
7. Consider effective systems and structures to put in place that will aid in creating this sense of safety for students when they are outside the classroom.
8. A detailed protocol for campus supervision is important to maintaining safety.

(Hernandez, 2016)

as achievement, attendance, behavior and dropout/completion (Finn, 1989; Jimerson, Campos, & Greif, 2003; Jimerson et al., 2009). Researchers have identified that effective interventions to promote student engagement also enhance the probability of high school completion (Reschly, Appleton, & Christenson, 2007). Studies show that student engagement is considered the main theoretical model in understanding student dropout (Christenson et al., 2008; Finn & Owings, 2006; Reschly & Christenson, 2006).

Procedure

The following three-step procedure addresses integrating student engagement practices through three important aspects of the school environment: positive school climate, school organization and infrastructure, and student interactions. The procedure involves fostering a positive school climate through focusing on effective leadership and a whole-school approach, strengthening the school organization and infrastructure through focusing on student safety and learning, campus supervision, and adopting a student grouping/cohort model, and creating an emphasis on student interactions by way of cooperative learning models, and implementing character building and social skills programs. The three-step procedure is broken down by thematic category and detailed in each step.

Step 1. Positive School Climate

The first step in the process is to cultivate a positive school climate. There are many aspects to cultivating a school climate. For the purposes of this paper, leadership and a whole-school approach are focused on (Table 9.2).

Leadership

In order to build a positive school climate, leadership must be involved and a whole-school approach must be taken. Effective leadership is critical in fostering an anti-bullying culture. School leaders are responsible for determining the systems and structures in place that make up the adopted model for the prevention of bullying. School leadership must work collaboratively with the same goals in mind. The leadership style of the principal and administrative team transforms and empowers the entire school and community. School leadership is the integral component to developing, implementing and

Table 9.2 Supporting Strategies for Facilitating a Positive School Climate

Theme	Supporting Strategies	
Positive School Climate	Leadership	Whole-School Approach

sustaining a systems-level, whole-school approach. The fact that administrators, teachers, counselors, staff, and volunteers all share the same beliefs about the school and the potential of students becomes a powerful message.

Examples of effective school leadership practices to foster a positive school climate include:

- Envision a plan for the school community together.
- Build a school team around shared educational values and belief systems.
- Foster the belief system that all students can learn if they feel safe and cared about.
- Create a school team of cohesive group of educators that are committed and accountable to their mission.
- The team should be supported, guided, and empowered to become change agents for students.
- Internalize the idea "it all starts in the classroom" to cultivate the sense that the students are "theirs" (teachers') and that the teachers are responsible for students as human beings, their learning, their behavior, and their social-emotional growth. This can change the dynamics at the school between students, teachers, and administrators.

Whole-school Approach

This approach requires involving all stakeholders with the school vision, mission, and operations as a main priority, along with formulating partnerships with, and involving, parents. Effective school leaders involve all their stakeholders and integrate them into the leadership team. Consistent and transparent communication and engagement with stakeholders increases cohesiveness and will have a positive effect on school climate.

Examples of involving all stakeholders include:

- Stakeholders (students, parents, teachers, staff, and community members) should be treated as partners, welcomed, respected, and given the message that they are a necessary component to the school family.
- Clear visual images and displays around the school should communicate a welcoming message to all stakeholders and set a positive tone with high expectations for all.
- Teachers at the school should be highly regarded, celebrated, respected, and seen as major change agents.
- Teachers should be provided training and guidance towards the mission and vision of the school.
- Teachers and administrators should work together as partners, a team, in collaboration towards the same goal.
- The school should support and invest in a robust parent and community center, hiring parent representatives who are an important part of the school community, to engage families.

Table 9.3 Supporting Strategies for Facilitating School Organization and
            Infrastructure

Theme	*Supporting Strategies*		
School Organization and Infrastructure	Student Safety and Learning	Campus Supervision	Student Groupings/ Cohort Model

Step 2. School Organization and Infrastructure

The second step in the procedure is to focus on the organization and infrastructure of the school. While there are many aspects to school organization and
infrastructure, this chapter will focus on student safety and learning, campus
supervision, and student groupings/cohort model (Table 9.3).

Student Safety and Learning

The organization and infrastructure at a school has an indirect impact on
the school climate. Developing internal school policies related to daily school
operations and infrastructure creates a school system that flows well and
creates a positive school climate thus fostering an anti-bullying culture at the
school. The flow and consistency of daily school operations set the tone for
the campus. School operations should be clear, consistent, and demonstrated
by the administrators and leadership team. After focusing on Step 1, this
procedural step should be easier to implement as it requires buy-in from
school staff and stakeholders. All school organization and infrastucture must
have an underlying focus on student safety and learning.

Physical Organization and Layout of the School

The main school organization and infrastructure issue related to student
safety and learning is focusing on key operational issues to do with the
physical organization and layout of the school. The physical organization
and layout of the school should be critically evaluated and incorporated into
the school plan. This plan can include strategic, but simple, logical solutions
to common problems in schools that affect student safety and learning.
These common problems include traffic in hallways, stairwells, lunch areas,
entry and exit areas, and the routine trash and cleanliness problems that
many schools deal with. These problems are often seen by schools as
uncontrollable realities that, in effect, contribute towards a chaotic feeling,
especially in larger schools. Spending time gathering information and understanding the intricacies of the school plant and operational issues is key to
making strategic improvements that will directly impact how the school
"feels," which will impact school climate.

Examples of school changes focused on the physical organization and layout of the school include:

- Gather information using observation, interviews with teachers and school staff, and surveys with students and parents to understand the main issues related to safety at the school.
- Gather and analyze school data related to office referrals and begin tracking location of incidents to gain a better understanding of where behavioral incidents may be frequently occurring.
- Have a good understanding of the flow of traffic in the school during key transition times: school arrival, transition periods, nutrition, lunch, and school dismissal.
- Implement a stairwell system to control the flow of student traffic during transition times. The stairwell system should identify one stairwell for going up only, and the opposite stairwell for going down.
- Use line dividers to teach students where to stand in lines and use painted walk paths to follow when going to certain areas of the school.
- Implement specific entry and exit doors from the buildings.
- Develop school norms for lunch and nutrition related to food consumption and disposal. A simple strategy for lunch and nutrition is teaching and reinforcing students to keep their food on their trays while they eat and to lift the tray to throw their meal away, resulting in the absence of any food remnants or wrappers on the tables. This simple norm implemented keeps the campus clean.
- Revitalize the physical look of the school and spaces. Make efforts to "beautify" the school campus. Examples may include the use of murals, planted gardens, art, benches or gathering spaces, painted lines for basketball courts and sports areas, etc. Adding color to spaces, classrooms, and hallways has a positive effect on school climate.

Campus Supervision

The second finding within the theme of school organization and infrastructure is an effective campus supervision protocol. Campus supervision is a simplified concept that all schools utilize. While all schools have a form of campus supervision, not all schools utilize an organized, effective plan for campus supervision. Campus supervision should be an organized, structured, and goal-directed active form of supervision. Members of the team should be trained and held accountable for quality supervision of students. The campus supervision system at the school is a major consistent daily function of the school staff, including the administrators. Everyone works together for the safety and structure of the whole. This "active" form of supervision requires staff to be visible regularly and provides consistency and ample opportunities for interactions with students. The campus supervision plan should have documented guidelines, norms, and regular meetings to monitor

---

Box 9.5 School Campus Supervision Guidelines and Norms

"The more effectively we supervise, the fewer problems we will have."

1. Be on active supervision.

2. Move from group to group.

3. Remind students to throw their trash in a trash can.

4. Separate from other adults.

5. Spread out.

6. If you are out, it is your responsibility to get coverage.

7. Be on time.

8. Talk to kids.

9. Enforce no personal displays of affection (PDAs).

10. Take pride in your work and area.

11. Have students keep their areas clean.

12. Students are not allowed to cross the yellow lines.

13. No food beyond ramp yellow lines.

14. Only students with a pass can enter the building.

15. Ask for help.

16. We are a team.

17. Follow radio protocol (learn codes).

18. This is our school, our students, and our job.

---

the effectiveness of supervision. Once the system is in place, it can become so embedded into the school culture that teachers may voluntarily supervise their hallways during transition periods without being asked because they want to do their part. Monitoring the hallways becomes an integral part of being visible and interacting with students. The table below provides basic guidelines and norms for a school to adopt (Box 9.5)

Student Groupings/Cohort Model

The way in which students are grouped together is a central component to the intricate infrastructure of the school. Developing a grouping system, or cohort model, keeps students and teachers together in contiguous space areas. This grouping system of students to teachers allows for a multiplicity of things to happen. Firstly, it allows for a large school to feel like a relatively small school for a student, as they becomes a part of a smaller community within their group. This creates a sense of "smallness" and increased opportunities for the development of friendships, which increases the cohesiveness of the groups. Secondly, it directly addresses safety in that students travel together from class to class in groups, although they do not travel very far as their classes are right next to each other in the same hallway. This, with the addition of their teachers outside in the halls during transition times, can create a safe and positive climate in the hallways. This has also had a tremendous impact on tardy behavior.

Due to the groupings, the teachers are able to have closer relationships with students, know them all by names and, since teacher teams work together, they have a sense of the needs of the different students. Further, all teacher teams for the entire grade should follow the same curriculum down to the detail and to the day. Lastly, implementing advisory periods can serve as a "school family" and teachers take ownership of those students. They take responsibility for their students' academic and social/emotional well-being. This advisory period allows time for students and teachers to develop relationships together and focus on non-academic content such as life skills, character development, and growing together as a class community. This time is also used to provide guidance as needed when they are struggling with academic or home issues. Implementing a grouping system at a school creates a sense of safety, community, equity, and access for all students.

Examples of how to implement a student grouping/cohort system can include:

- Review student data and create an academic program that includes heterogeneous grouping of students.
- Student cohorts, or teams, are developed based on a balance of high- and low-performing students, inclusive of all students: English Language Learners, English Only, Gifted, and Students with Disabilities. The classes are equally balanced so that each class has students who represent all areas.
- Student groups are matched with a group, or team, of teachers who all work together with the same students. The classrooms for these teams are set up next to each other, so teachers are logistically close to each other to be able to communicate frequently. In addition, this physical arrangement allows students to not have to travel much between their classes.
- The teacher teams work together to develop their curriculum uniformly and deliver the same content to all students. All teacher teams follow the same curriculum and content consistently from class to class and grade to grade.
- Implement a daily advisory class period with students every morning to cover a multitude of topics and focus on developing relationships and engaging with students.
- The advisory teacher stays with the same group of students for the duration of their stay at the school, allowing multiple years of a consistent, stable relationship with students and families. This advisor period can become somewhat of a "school family" in that it is where the students develop strong

and meaningful connections with each other and their teachers. The advisory teacher also serves as a case manager of sorts, reviewing their students' grades, attendance, and behavior, and works with the teacher team in communicating regarding students.

- The SBFC team also can adopt a grouping model and travel with their students in the same way. They remain with their students until they leave the school and transition to the next school. This allows SBFC practitioners to develop strong bonds with their students and have enough time to work with students and families before the year is over and they need to get to know an entire new group of students.

Step 3. Student Interactions

The third step in the procedure is to focus on interactions with students. This step is developed last because there will be great difficulty in implementing these components without the foundational pieces of positive school climate and school organization and infrastructure implemented. Focusing on student interactions requires the shared educational belief that student engagement with school begins in the classroom. This step requires a sincere look at what is happening in the classroom and understanding how, and if, students are interacting with their teachers and with each other. In order to increase student interactions in the classroom, two main components can be focused on: implementing a consistent cooperative learning model in every classroom with a focus on student and teacher interactions and relationships, and teaching character building and social skills to all students. Table 9.4 depicts this theme.

Cooperative Learning Model

Cooperative learning is a good instructional tool to use when focusing on how to increase student interaction in the classroom. This model allows for a strategic focus on student interactions. Cooperative learning is a teaching method that refers to small, heterogeneous groups of students working together to achieve a common goal. The students work together to learn and are responsible for their teammates' learning as well as their own. Basic elements of cooperative learning include: positive interdependence, individual accountability, equal participation, and simultaneous interaction between students (Murie, 2004). The various structures utilized in the

Table 9.4 Supporting Strategies for Facilitating Student Interactions

Theme	Supporting Strategies	
Student Interactions	Cooperative Learning Model	Character Building and Social Skills

cooperative learning model increase the interactions between students and teachers in the classroom which has an overall positive effect on academic and social outcomes because students learn and practice communicating with each other in a positive, proactive manner (Murie, 2004). The cooperative learning model allows for consistent integration of student inquiry, dialogue, and interaction. When students are exposed to this model all day, every day, consistently in every class, student engagement increases. The view is that students spend most of their time in the classroom, and any efforts at increasing student engagement must begin in the classroom. Teaching and creating opportunities for students to interact and communicate with each other in appropriate ways fosters this engagement. Once engagement in the classroom is established with their teachers, with the academic content, and with their class group, then other aspects of engagement with the larger school, such as clubs or sports, would follow. Teachers are the first and most integral factor in the process of student engagement.

Examples of how to begin implementing cooperative learning methods in a classroom/school:

- Work with the administration, counseling team, and school staff to focus on belief systems about students.
- The view taken by the school is that increasing positive interactions and communication among students will increase engagement to school.
- Research and invest in quality training and provide professional development time for school staff to learn and implement cooperative learning structures in the classroom.
- Adopt a goal that there should be "at least 50% student talking" in every classroom.
- Physically organize classrooms into spaces that encourage cooperative learning, such as desks arranged in pods of four so that students can work together.
- Encourage student talk time in the classroom.
- Encourage the development of relationships among students and teachers and staff in the classroom and during transition times. The campus supervision team is a central component to developing relationships with students outside the classroom.

Character Building and Social Skills

Teaching character and social skills is a necessary component that supports the theme of student interactions. These skills should be infused into the culture in multiple dimensions, beginning with the classroom, the daily school environment and culture, as well as with specific programs used. Social skills are modeled and taught beginning in the classroom and reinforced through cooperative learning structures. It is important to create opportunities for meaningful interaction between students, which allows for many teaching opportunities about "how" to interact with each other. Character building and social skills are taught on multiple levels from indirect messaging to very direct curriculum in the classroom. They can also be infused into issues related to counseling, discipline, and conflicts that may arise in the classroom. Various curricula are available that focus on the integration of character building and social skills teaching into schools. If adopting a curriculum, it is important to determine when and how this curriculum will be implemented. Student clubs, student leadership, and partnerships are other ways to integrate character building and social skills training into school environments. Providing opportunities for students to increase their skills in character building and socialization increases positive student interactions and contributes towards academic and social/ emotional engagement of students with school.

Examples of how to begin implementing character building and social skills into a classroom/school:

- Research with your school team and come to a consensus on the main character-building traits and social skills to focus on.
- Develop school messaging regarding what you would like to focus on and how it will be taught and communicated to students. For example, "Remember the six Ps: Prompt, Prepared, Productive, Polite, Participate and Proficient" (Hernandez, 2014).
- These concepts should be infused throughout the school by way of visual displays, posters, signage, bulletin boards, etc., in classrooms and hallways.
- Use other messaging such as newsletters, websites, social media, and assemblies to communicate, teach, and remind students and families.
- Use the school messaging whenever opportunities arise to teach these skills. Examples include in the classroom, during campus supervision, in the SBFC office, discipline, assemblies.
- Utilize student leadership to develop activities related to the character-building program and engage students. Examples can include: lunchtime games, poster competitions, visual and performing arts activities, etc.
- Research and invest in a social skills training curriculum for the school. Identify an administrator, an SBFC practitioner, and a teacher team to be responsible for the training and implementation.
- Utilize a course period, homeroom, advisor, or study period, to implement social skills training curriculum by grade.
- Use technology to deliver the curriculum through the computer lab, or through student discipline use modules on relevant social skills training specific to the situation.
- Use a positive reinforcement method program to highlight positive social skills and character building.
- Integrate active school clubs onto campus that focus on character building and social skills training. Examples can include: friendship clubs, peer mentoring and conflict resolution programs, peer leaders, student government, student ambassadors, mentoring, etc.

Multicultural Counseling Considerations

Culture is a powerful and pervasive influence on students, families, stakeholders, and attitudes and behaviors. For that reason, multicultural counseling issues should be taken into consideration by the school as a whole. Being aware of issues related to the context and histories of the students and families that we serve as educators and SBFC practitioners is an ethical requirement of the profession. In order to increase student engagement in schools, students and families must feel safe and trust their school environments. First and foremost, educators must be aware of multicultural education and relevant issues in the schools and communities that they serve. Educators and practitioners need to take a step back to listen to and understand their students and families – where they are at, where they are coming from, and what they have to say – before moving forward with any agenda. The model presented in this chapter creates a school as a safe place for community and learning that is inclusive of all stakeholders. It provides safety, learning, structure, and opportunities for meaningful communication, engagement, and sustained relationships between students and with students. The model works to create a school and community climate that embraces cultural diversity and helps to promote students' academic, career, and social/emotional success because it begins and ends with students.

Challenges and Solutions

The model described presents challenges that should be considered and anticipated prior to implementation. The biggest challenges are related to time, support/buy-in, and funding. The model is focused largely on prevention and macro-level systemic changes that will impact school climate. This type of work takes a considerable amount of time and does not happen overnight. The model does not offer a quick change or packaged solution with immediate effects, frequently sought after by schools because of the time pressures and demands on them for immediate outcomes. Contrastingly, it requires time, buy-in, and effective leadership to steer the change. The solution is to focus on one aspect of the model at a time, with leadership being first and most important. Without effective leadership in place or utilizing the whole-school approach, achieving buy-in from the school community will be very difficult. The focus of this model should be considered as a school transformation, rather than as implementing a "program." Transformational processes take time and planning, but frequently yield more positive and sustainable outcomes. Establishing the first step can take up to one year. Steps 1 and 2 will require planning by the leadership and school team in advance of the beginning of the new school year. This work is frequently done in the summer while students are not in school. Implementing Steps 2 and 3 will also require funding for school staff to receive training/professional development and/or attend school retreats throughout the year. Solutions to the issue of funding can be to streamline resources allocated for staff professional development to focus on the implementation of the model, and to engage in community partnerships to provide training. Also, additional sources of funding, such as grants, can be used to supplement funding and be utilized solely for the purposes of the model implementation. Fortunately, the core of the model does not require substantial amounts of additional funding, but rather a reorganization of existing funding, school structures, and operations.

Resources

This section lists useful organizations and internet resources.

Social Skill/Character Building

Webpages

Character Education … Our Shared Responsibility (U.S. Department of Education)

The Role of Character Education in Public Schools (California Department of Education)

Character Education Interventions Evidence Review Protocol (Institute of Educational Science, What Works Clearinghouse)

Social Skills Training (Institute of Educational Science, What Works Clearinghouse)

Social and Emotional Development and Social Skills

UCLA Center for Mental Health in Schools & Student/Learning Supports
The Center's website provides a list of information, tools, and resources related to social and emotional development and social skills.

Second Step Curriculum
Second Step is a program rooted in social-emotional learning (SEL) that helps transform schools into supportive, successful learning environments uniquely equipped to encourage children to thrive.

Character Education
The character.org website provides an array of information, resources, and tools on character education, and can help with assisting in the development of a character education program at a school.

Edutopia
In particular see the webpage Schools Cultivate the Character Development of their Students.

Cooperative Learning
Kagen cooperative learning structures are now used worldwide from kindergarten to adult education, in all academic subject areas, to boost student engagement and learning.

Student Advisory Programs

The Association for Middle Level Education's website provides information on the following characteristics of effective advisors and advisory programs:

- Strong advisory programs address issues of community.
- Strong advisories promote open communication.
- Strong advisors know and care about their advisees.
- Strong advisors closely supervise their advisees' academic progress.
- Strong advisors are problem solvers and advice givers.
- Students and advisors perceive that advisory directly improves academic performance.
- Students and advisors perceive that advisory functions as a community of learners.

Webpages

Can school structures improve teacher-student relationships? The relationship between advisory programs, personalization and students' academic achievement
   Secondary School Advisors as mentors and secondary attachment figures
   Making Connections with Advisory: Relationships are among the most important elements of student success
   Creating and Sustaining and Effective Advisory Program
   Example provided by Thomaston High School
   Five Tips for Teaching Advisory Classes at Your School

Video

The Teaching Channel. *Advisory: Check in and Support*
   See SBFC EResources for links to the above websites.

Bibliography

Appleton, J. J., Christenson, S. L., & Furlong, M. J. (2008). Student engagement with school: Critical conceptual and methodological issues of the construct. *Psychology in the Schools*, 45(5), 369–386.
Archambault, I., Janosz, M., Fallu, J. S., & Pagani, L. S. (2009). Student engagement and its relationship with early high school dropout. *Journal of Adolescence*, 32(3), 651–670.
Archambault, I., Janosz, M., Morizot, J., & Pagani, L. (2009). Adolescent behavioral, affective, and cognitive engagement in school: Relationship to dropout. *Journal of School Health*, 79(9), 408–415.

Atlas, R. S., & Pepler, D. J. (1998). Observations of bullying in the classroom. *The Journal of Educational Research*, 92(2), 86–99.

Balfanz, R., Bridgeland, J. M., Moore, L. A., Fox, J. H. (2010). *Building a grad nation: Progress and Challenge in Ending the High School Dropout Epidemic*. Washington, DC: Civic Enterprises, LLC.

Bradshaw, C. P., O'Brennan, L. M., & Sawyer, A. L. (2008). Examining variation in attitudes toward aggressive retaliation and perceptions of safety among bullies, victims, and bully/victims. *Professional School Counseling*, 12(1), 10–21.

Chapell, M., Casey, D., De la Cruz, C., Ferrell, J., Forman, J., Lipkin, R., & Whittaker, S. (2004). Bullying in college by students and teachers. *Adolescence San Diego*, 39(153), 53.

Christenson, S. L., Reschly, A. L., Appleton, J. J., Berman, S., Spanjers, D., & Varro, P. (2008). Best practices in fostering student engagement. In A. Thomas & J. Grimes (Eds.), *Best practices in school psychology* (5th ed.) (pp. 1099–1120). Bethesda, MD: National Association of School Psychologists.

Christenson, S. L., Reschly, A. L., & Wylie, C. (Eds.). (2012). *Handbook of research on student engagement*. New York, NY: Springer Science & Business Media.

Daniels, J. A., & Bradley, M. C. (2011). *Preventing lethal school violence*. New York, NY: Springer.

Dinkes, R., Kemp, J., & Baum, K. (2009). *Indicators of school crime and safety: 2009*. Washington, DC: National Center for Education Statistics, Institute of Education Sciences, U.S. Department of Education, and Bureau of Justice Statistics, Office of Justice Programs, U.S. Department of Justice.

Finn, J. D. (1989). Withdrawing from school. *Review of Educational Research*, 59(2), 117–142.

Finn, J. D., & Owings, J. (2006). The adult lives of at-risk students: The roles of attainment and engagement in high school. Statistical analysis report. NCES 2006-328. National Center for Education Statistics.

Flescher-Peskin, M., Tortolero, S. R., Markham, C. M., Addy, R. C., & Baumler, E. R. (2007). Bullying and victimization and internalizing symptoms among low-income Black and Hispanic students. *Journal of Adolescent Health*, 40, 372–375.

Gastic, B. (2008). School truancy and the disciplinary problems of bullying victims. *Educational Review*, 60(4), 391–404.

Gerrard, B., & Soriano, M. (Eds.). (2013). *School-based family counseling: Transforming family-school relationships*. Phoenix, AZ: Createspace.

Harris, S., & Petrie, G. (2002). A study of bullying in the middle school. *National Association of Secondary School Principals Bulletin*, 86(633), 42–53.

Hart, S. R., Stewart, K., & Jimerson, S. R. (2011). The Student Engagement in Schools Questionnaire (SESQ) and the Teacher Engagement Report Form-New (TERF-N): Examining the preliminary evidence. *Contemporary School Psychology*, 15, 67–79.

Henry, K. L., Knight, K. E., & Thornberry, T. P. (2012). School disengagement as a predictor of dropout, delinquency, and problem substance use during adolescence and early adulthood. *Journal of Youth and Adolescence*, 41(2), 156–166.

Hernandez, E. J. (2014). *Promising practices for preventing bullying in K-12 schools: Student engagement*. Los Angeles, CA: University of Southern California.

Hernandez, E. J. (2016). Reducing bullying and preventing dropout through student engagement: A prevention-focused lens for school-based family counselors. *International Journal for School-Based Family Counseling*, 7, 1–13.

Hirschi, T. (1969). A control theory of delinquency. In G. Eccleston, E. A. Shipp, & M. C. Braswell (Eds.), *Criminology theory: Selected classic readings* (pp. 289–305). Cincinnati, OH: Anderson.

Hutzell, K. L., & Payne, A. A. (2012). The impact of bullying victimization on school avoidance. *Youth Violence and Juvenile Justice*, 10(4), 370–385.

Jimerson, S. R., Campos, E., & Greif, J. L. (2003). Toward an understanding of definitions and measures of school engagement and related terms. *The California School Psychologist*, 8(1), 7–27.

Jimerson, S. R., Renshaw, T. L., Stewart, K., Hart, S., & O'Malley, M. (2009). Promoting school completion through understanding school failure: A multi-factorial model of dropping out as a developmental process. *Romanian Journal of School Psychology*, 2, 12–29.

Klein, J., Cornell, D., & Konold, T. (2012). Relationships between bullying, school climate, and student risk behaviors. *School Psychology Quarterly*, 27(3), 154–169.

Lederman, J. (2012). Anti-bullying ad campaign targets parents, Obama administration vows to a make it a "National Priority." Retrieved from www.huffingtonpost.com /2012/08/06/anti-bullying-adcampaign_n_1749158.html?view=print&comm_ref=false

Libbey, H. P. (2004). Measuring student relationships to school: Attachment, bonding, connectedness, and engagement. *Journal of School Health*, 74(7), 274–283.

Limber, S. P. (2002, May). Addressing youth bullying behaviors. In *Proceedings from the American Medical Association Educational Forum on Adolescent Health: Youth Bullying*. Chicago, IL: American Medical Association.

Morrison B. (2002). *Bullying and victimisation in schools: A restorative justice approach*. Trends & issues in crime and criminal justice No. 219. Canberra: Australian Institute of Criminology. Retrieved from https://aic.gov.au/publications/tandi/tandi219.

Murie, C. R. (2004). Effects of communication on student learning. *Kagan Online Magazine*, 1-11.

Nansel, T. R., Overpeck, M., Pilla, R. S., Ruan, W. J., Simons-Morton, B., & Scheidt, P. (2001). Bullying behaviors among US youth. *JAMA: The Journal of the American Medical Association*, 285(16), 2094–2100.

National Research Council and the Institute of Medicine. (2004). *Engaging schools: Fostering high school students' motivation to learn*. Washington, DC: The National Academies Press.

Nishioka, V., Coe, M., Burke, A., Hanita, M., & Sprague, J. (2011). *Student reported overt and relational aggression and victimization in grades 3–8*. Issues and Answers Report, REL, (114).

Olweus, D. (1994). Bullying at school: Basic facts and effects of a school based intervention program. *Journal of Child Psychology and Psychiatry*, 35(7), 1171–1190.

Reschly, A. L., Appleton, J. J., & Christenson, S. L. (2007). Student engagement at school and with learning: Theory and interventions. *NASP Communiqué*, 35(8), 18–20.

Reschly, A. L., & Christenson, S. L. (2012). Jingle, jangle, and conceptual haziness: Evolution and future directions of the engagement construct. In S. L. Christenson, A. L. Reschly, & C. Wylie, (Eds.), *Handbook of research on student engagement* (pp. 3–19). New York, NY: Springer Science & Business Media.

Robers, S., Zhang, J., Truman, J., & Snyder, T. D. (2012). *Indicators of school crime and safety, 2011*. Washington, DC: National Center for Education Statistics, U.S. Department of Education, and Bureau of Justice Statistics.

Rumberger, R. W., & Larson, K. A. (1998). Student mobility and the increased risk of high school drop out. *American Journal of Education*, 107, 1–35.

Rumberger, R. W., & Rotermund, S. (2012). The relationship between engagement and high school dropout. In S. L. Christenson, A. L. Reschly, & C. Wylie, (Eds.), *Handbook of research on student engagement* (pp. 491–513). New York, NY: Springer Science & Business Media.

Shernoff, D. J., & Schmidt, J. A. (2008). Further evidence of an engagement-achievement paradox among US high school students. *Journal of Youth and Adolescence*, 37(5), 564–580.

Smith, P. K., Slee, P., Morita, Y., Catalano, R., Junger-Tas, J., & Olweus, D. (Eds.). (1999). *The nature of school bullying: A cross-national perspective*. New York, NY: Routledge.

Soriano, M. (1999). The family role in violence precaution and response. *School Safety*, 12–16.

Soriano, M., & Gerrard, B. (2013). School-based family counseling: An overview. In B. Gerrard & M. Soriano (Eds.), *School-based family counseling: Transforming family-school relationships* (pp. 2–15). Phoenix, AZ: Createspace.

Suh, S., & Suh, J. (2007). Risk factors and levels of risk for high school dropouts. *Professional School Counseling*, 10(3), 297–306.

Tinto, V. (1975). Dropout from higher education: A theoretical synthesis of recent research. *Review of Educational Research*, 45, 89–-125.

Wehlage, G. G., Rutter, R. A., Smith, G. A., Lesko, N., & Fernandez, R. R. (1989). *Reducing the risk: Schools as communities of support*. New York, NY: Falmer Press.

10 School Prevention

How to Develop an Anti-bullying Program

Phillip Slee

Overview: *Within recent years there has been an increasing global concern with school bullying and violence. In Australia, the issue of school bullying has been the focus of research and policy development for over 25 years. There is no doubt that school bullying is an all too prevalent feature of society that needs to be seriously addressed. Views on the issue range from rather idealistic, overly optimistic claims to 'bullyproof' schools and students, to the idea that the problematizing and sensationalizing of child/youth violence is simply a symptom of a "ephebiphobia", or fear and loathing of young people. In this chapter a school and classroom intervention to address school bullying developed in Australia and implemented in several other countries will be described and illustrated with a case study of a school.*

Background

What Students Say

The human misery of bullying is strongly conveyed in this story of an 11-year-old boy referred to me by his doctor for counseling. As the boy described it:

> One thing that happened to me was that I was bashed up at school by one of the kids in my class. This kid kicked me in my legs and body. The teasing and bullying started in the first week of term one. It started with name-calling – Idiot, Carrot Head, Freckle-face, Stuff-head, Dick-head, Loser. The kids excluded me from groups. ... If I tried to play basket ball with them at school they would tell me to "get lost". I hated that so much I spent more and more time in the library.

What Parents Say

> If I were to find out that my child was being 'bullied' by others at school and that the staff/teachers were aware of this but hadn't intervened – I would be both angry and disappointed and also disillusioned with the school.

What Teachers Say

> Fairness, consistency, and transparency in policy and practice are needed to address school bullying effectively.

Bullying: International Research

The early pioneering research of Dan Olweus in Norway and Peter Smith in England and the outcomes of their practical intervention programs in the 1980s heralded an international focus on the problem of school bullying. Further international efforts to understand the nature of school bullying have been described in early publications such as that by Smith et al. (1999) who edited and drew together the findings of research into bullying from over 22 countries. More recently Smith, Kwak, and Toda (2016) have published international research relating to bullying and cyberbullying from eastern and western perspectives. As the authors note 'School bullying is a universal phenomenon, but most research in the last thirty years has been in western countries' (p. xv). Smith, Kwak, and Toda (2016) in their book provide an in-depth analysis of the nature of school bullying from eastern and western perspectives providing fascinating insight into how bullying is defined cross-culturally. It also would appear that bullying is as old as civilization itself.

Slee (2017) in his book *School Bullying: Teachers Helping Students Cope* draws attention to the myths and stories present in Australian Aboriginal culture (a culture that has existed for over 64,000 years). Aboriginal Dreamtime Stories are used by Aborigines to explain the beginning of life and how the world and its environment came about. The existence of Aborigines, their lifestyle and culture is centered on this concept. It is also important as it establishes their values and beliefs and the relationship they are to maintain with the land and its living creatures. One significant component of the stories includes rules and laws for living and the difference between right and wrong. In the story of 'Why the Emu Can't Fly' the Wongutha stories tell us that in the beginning emus could fly but became boastful and arrogant and began to bully other members of the bush. While the other animals tried many things to prevent the bullying it continued until an intervention by a tribal elder who reduced the power of the emus enabling victimized denizens of the bushland to live in harmony once again.

Bullying: Definitions & New Understandings

It is important to note that the matter of definition is a contested one. For example, it has been argued that a one-off incident can also constitute bullying. As we shall touch upon later in this chapter, the phenomenon of cyberbullying brings with it a range of other issues. For example, if a young person has a negative message posted on the internet once but it goes viral is it bullying? Generally agreed upon facets that distinguish bullying as a particular form of aggression include (i) a power imbalance (ii) an intention to hurt (iii) the point that the victim generally feels unable to stop the behavior and (iv) repetition of one kind or another.

Bullying has been conceived broadly as the systematic abuse of power (Smith et al., 1999). It is a deliberate form of aggressive behavior, perpetrated by a more powerful individual or group, that is unfair or unjustified and is typically repeated. The severity of bullying extends along a continuum from acts that are comparatively mild, as in insensitive teasing or taunting, to extremely severe, as in repeated violent physical assaults or deliberate and unjustifiable total exclusion by peers. Bullying may be classified as direct, as in face-to-face physical and verbal harassment, or indirect as in unfair exclusion, rumor-spreading. Slee, Ma, et al. (2003) reviewed the matter of definition in five countries in the Asia-Pacific region noting considerable differences in whether countries had a word for "bullying" and how it was defined. Slee and Skrzypiec (2016) have overviewed cross-cultural definitions of bullying noting that different cultures have different words (e.g. In Japan it is 'ijime' and in Korea it is 'wang ta') and that different meanings are attached to the word. For example, in Japan the word "ijime" refers to the indirect and exclusionary features of the behavior rather than emphasizing the physical aspects.

Young people may be involved in bullying as victims of bullying, as persons who bully others, or both, although bystanders also play an indirect role. Noting that bullying occurs in relatively permanent social groups (Slee & Skrzypiec, 2016) have identified a number of roles undertaken by young people in the bullying circle. These researchers highlighted the role that "others" who are not the bully or victim play in bullying scenarios and that holds equally true for teachers who fail to respond to bullying situations. The roles in the bullying circle include being a victim of bullying, a defender of the victim, a bully, an assistant of the bully, a reinforcer of the bully, and an outsider. Bully assistants are described as active followers of a bully, while bully reinforcers behave in a manner that reinforces the bullying behavior, such as laughing and encouraging the bully. By contrast, defenders of the victim side with the victim and are supportive and consoling, and take action to stop the bullying. Students who are not involved in bullying as assistants, reinforcers or defenders are viewed as "outsiders" or bystanders.

Most recently, the latest iteration of bullying, cyberbullying, involves the deliberate (mis)use of technology to target another person, e.g. the sending of anonymous and abusive messages by email. Researchers (e.g. Campbell & Bauman, 2017) have drawn attention to the emergent forms of cyberbullying and the new understandings regarding definitional issues that have arisen as a result. For example, the notion that the act must be "repeated" is called into question when, as part of cyberbullying, one incident can go viral. Power differentials now operate across and through technologies, and deliberate intent can now be demonstrated both privately (between individuals) and publicly (via the world wide web and social networking sites), verbally and non-verbally (through images), covertly and overtly (through deliberate stalking overtly or anonymously). Indeed, the latest technologies have shifted cyberbullying from computers in rooms, to a totally integrated, mobile platform. In terms of how students cope with traditional forms of bullying and cyberbullying, it is relevant to consider how theory attempts to explain it. These matters raise the contentious issue of whether there is a legal remedy for cyberbullying, and some countries have proceeded down this path (Slee, 2017).

Bullying and the Risk of Labeling

It is recognized that there are very real risks associated with labeling in the context of bullying. Unless we stop and think about it, we often don't recognize the labeling we are doing, and how it is affects us and others. In this chapter, consistent with systemic thinking, every attempt is made to distance the behavior from the person, e.g. perhaps talk about the "bullying behavior" and not label the individual as a "bully" or "victim".

How Commonly Cited Theory Explains Bullying

A range of theories are employed to try to explain the phenomenon of school bullying, and some of the more commonly cited theories are described below. As noted by Slee, Campbell, and Spears (2012) a theory, in the simplest sense of the term, helps to explain facts, where facts are observations. That is, theory is a way of organizing the raw data – the facts – to provide a more complete picture of what the data mean. Such organization helps an individual to better understand the portion of the world being investigated. In psychology, theories are used to provide us with future direction to set up further hypotheses.

A criticism directed at research relating to school bullying is that it is essentially atheoretical. In fact, various approaches addressing the matter of interventions are generally underpinned by some theoretical understanding that that can be identified in terms of social learning theory, humanistic theory, or systems-based models (Shute & Slee, 2015). The position adopted in the present chapter is that schools are "relationship-saturated" environments and school bullying is a relationship issue. The pivotal role of relationships in the student's learning points to the need for schools to not only have policies and procedures for dealing with aggressive behavior, but to also include a positive relationship-building dimension to the interactions among teachers and students and between students at school.

The Extent of School Bullying

As noted earlier in this chapter school bullying is an international issue and in relation to the frequency of bullying Craig et al. (2009) in a study of 40 countries noted that exposure to bullying varied across countries, with estimates ranging from 8.6% to 45.2% among boys, and from 4.8% to 35.8% among girls. Adolescents in Baltic countries reported higher rates of bullying and victimization, whereas northern European countries reported the lowest prevalence. Boys reported higher rates of bullying in all countries.

Research into Bullying in Australian Schools

In 1991 Rigby & Slee published the first Australian research on the incidence of bullying among students sample of South Australian schools. In 1994 an Australian Federal Government Senate inquiry into school bullying resulted in the publication of an influential paper "Sticks and Stones: A report on violence in Schools" (see Slee, 2017). This inquiry heralded a nationwide movement to address the issue of school violence, particularly bullying. As reported, Australian research based on our sample of 25,000 indicates that over 20% of males and 15% of females report being bullied "once a week or more often" (Slee, 2017). Involvement in bullying may be as a perpetrator, a victim, or a bully-victim. There is some evidence that bullying and being a victim of bullying are roles that remain relatively stable for students as they transition from primary to middle school. Skrzypiec et al. (2017) report that although the likelihood of onset of bullying others during high school is relatively low, new bullies emerge during each high school year. For victims, while it is known that victimization is likely to continue, new victims also emerged in each year in our sample. Our study has shown that overall the likelihood that a student will become of victim of bullying at some point in high school was 36%.

Bullying and Gender

As noted earlier there is an apparent relationship between bullying and gender with males in western countries reporting higher incidences of bullying than females. Males engage in more aggression than females and females receive more verbal aggression than males. The findings generally indicate that males both perpetrate and receive more physical and verbal aggression than females and females receive more social aggression than males. In terms of cross-gender aggression an interesting picture emerges with females directing more physical aggression to males than males to females but males directing more verbal and social aggression to females than vice versa.

In devising interventions to reduce the harmful effects of cross-gender aggression, it is vital to understand why boys engage in higher rates of verbal and social aggression towards girls.. As noted in Slee (2017), cross-gender social contact becomes more prominent during adolescence than in childhood, providing more opportunities not only for cross-gender friendships and romantic relationships, but also for cross-gender victimization. Boys' perspectives, as well as those of girls, must therefore be sought. That boys' and girls' views differ is already apparent from the fact that girls report a higher prevalence of boy-to-girl aggression than do boys. Some behaviors which girls view as bullying are seen as harmless fun by boys. Understanding such differing perspectives is crucial for prevention/intervention programs.

In Australia, research within sociological and feminist frameworks and in the educational literature has highlighted the importance of broad cultural influences, such as male-female power differentials, on boys' victimization of girls, especially through sexual harassment. Boys may bully to impress girls; it is also possible that they aim to impress other boys. In considering victimization of girls by boys, sexual harassment may seem an obvious issue, especially in the early high school years, when girls may be particularly sensitive to victimization based on their developing bodies and sexuality; indeed, even in preadolescence, a relationship has been found between girls' perceptions of sexual harassment and their body esteem. One suggestion is that boys are socialized to believe they have power over females, and even young boys sometimes use sexual aggression against girls and women.

In some societies such as Australia, adolescent boys may have status conferred by peers on boys who display a particular type of heterosexual masculinity which involves denigrating "anything that smacks of femininity". The sexual harassment literature is a separate one and, in stark contrast to the individualistic approach of the aggression/bullying literature, broad societal influences are seen as central. The importance of gaining an understanding of boys' perspectives is essential since male attitudes towards violence contribute to resistance to preventive initiatives.

The Family Environment and Bullying

The family and primary caregivers and family life are a considerable influence shaping young people's development (Slee, Campbell, & Spears, 2012). Infants are born directing behaviors such as crying, clinging, smiling (preliminary attachment behaviors) to human figures which in turn elicits responsive behaviors from the caregivers. The outcome of these precursory attachment behaviors is to bring the caregiver in close proximity to the infant helping ensure care, safety, and protection. The essential argument put forward regarding attachment is that the emotional bonds established in infancy form the basis of attitudes and behavior patterns in later adult life, particularly in terms of relationship with others. Infant attachment is generally assessed by means of a standardized "strange situation" assessment method whereby infants' behavior is observed following two brief separations from their caregivers in a familiar but pleasant room. Maternal sensitivity is defined as the mother's ability to read and respond appropriately to her infant's non-verbal behavior. Three types of attachment behavior are typically identified:

Type A, avoidant
Type B, secure
Type C, ambivalent

Types A and C reflect insecure attachment.

Generally the research suggests that the quality of attachment is related to the extent to which children will later attempt to explore and master their world. Securely attached infants will engage in more active exploration than will those who are less securely attached. Similarly, the degree of attachment also influences the emergence of the child's sense of self (self-concept). More securely attached infants appear to be more effective help-seekers, more cooperative and more able to relate to others emotionally than their less securely attached counterparts.

As reported in Slee (2017), Troy and Sroufe (1987) have published a very interesting study concerning the relationship between a child's attachment history and a tendency to "victimize" others at 4 to 5 years of age. They found that at 5 to 6 years of age children with an avoidant attachment history were more likely to be victimizers than securely attached infants. They were "hostile, anti-social and socially and emotionally isolated from others". Monks, Smith, and Swettenham (2005) in their examination of young children aged 4–6 years reported that pre-school victims did not have insecure attachment qualities, as found with middle school victims, and were mostly securely attached (p. 14); but that nearly two-thirds of aggressors were insecurely attached.

Quality of Parenting

In a review of the literature Slee, Campbell, and Spears (2012) identified that three features of parenting have been acknowledged and identified as promoting positive outcomes in young children, namely:

Sensitivity
Cognitive stimulation
Warmth

Parenting sensitivity refers to parents' awareness of their children's cues, emotions, interests, and capabilities in ways that balance children's needs for support with their needs for autonomy. Cognitive stimulation refers to parents' didactic efforts to enrich their children's cognitive and language development by engaging children in activities that promote learning and by offering language-rich environments to their children. Parents' warmth refers to parents' expressions of affection and respect towards their children.

Types of Parenting Styles

In early research as noted in Slee, Campbell, and Spears (2012), Baumrind (1966) identified three different types of parenting style, namely authoritarian, authoritative, and permissive. According to Baumrind, both authoritarian and authoritative parents are directive and have clear expectations about how their children should behave, but authoritarian parents are dictatorial and unbending. Such parents have rules that they expect their children to follow. Permissive parents, on the other hand, exercise little control over their children. Simply put the characteristics of the three types of parenting style are as follows:

Authoritarian parents. The parents' word is law. Misconduct is punished.
Permissive parents. They make few demands on their children.
Authoritative parents. They favor a democratic style of child-rearing.

Relationship Between Parenting Styles and Aggression in Children

There is a strong association between authoritarian parenting style and the tendency to bully, while the tendency to be victimized was associated with an "intrusive" parenting style. It appears that positive and warm family relationships and home environments help to buffer children from the negative outcomes associated with bullying victimization. Warm parent-child relationships can exert an environmentally mediated effect on children's behavioral adjustment following bullying victimization. A calm, well-structured environment at home may help to alleviate symptoms of stress and provide security to children experiencing stressful events outside the home environment, e.g. through bullying.

School Bullying: A Physically Harmful, Emotionally Hurtful and Socially Isolating Experience

Internationally the issue of school bullying is a significant concern of educators and students. As already noted Australian research indicates that bullying is an all too frequent facet of young people's lives. As reported by Slee (2017) research with over 9,000 students (aged 7–17 years) from around Australia indicates that 23% report being victimized on a weekly basis and 7% indicate they could definitely join in bullying another child. Incidence of bullying rates are self-reported as highest in the primary years and in the early years of secondary school. As noted by the author (Slee, 2017) reviews of research indicate that bullying is physically harmful, emotionally hurtful, and socially isolating.

The consequences of being involved in bullying vary and range from minor annoyance to suicide. In a comprehensive review of the literature Slee (2017) notes that although not all young people who are bullied develop internalizing difficulties, various studies have found that being a victim of bullying is associated with suicide ideation, increased mental health, anxiety, depression, psychosomatic symptoms, and peer problems. A study by Skrzypiec et al. (2012) found that bullies, victims, and bully-victims were more likely to score in the abnormal range of the Strengths and Difficulties Questionnaire (SDQ) (Goodman, 1997), which is a screening instrument for mental health difficulties. Over one quarter of bullies showed abnormal conduct problems and hyperactivity as well as problems with being pro-social, although a smaller proportion (7.3%) than victims (20.0%) or bully-victims (25.7%) had overall SDQ scores indicating that they required further attention for mental health difficulties. Bully-victims, i.e. young people who bully others and are also victims of bullying, fared the worst. Approximately one-third of students in the bully-victim group showed signs of having problems with being pro-social (34.3%), hyperactivity (33.9%), and conduct (36.7%), and about one quarter (25.7%) had total scores in the abnormal range, suggesting that they required assistance with mental health difficulties. One-fifth (20.0%) of students in the victim group also showed mental health difficulties, particularly in terms of emotional symptoms (14.6%).

Cyberbullying

Defined as repeated, harmful interactions which are deliberately offensive, humiliating, threatening, and power-assertive, cyberbullying interactions are enacted using electronic equipment, such as cell (mobile) phones or the Internet, by one or more individuals towards another. Cyberbullying can take the form of instant or email messages, images, videos, calls, excluding or preventing someone to be part of a group or an online community. Scientific research into the prevalence and consequences associated with cyberbullying is increasing each year and, as such, we are beginning to understand more about these behaviors. It appears that the risk of being exposed to these behaviors is greatest during the school years with particular risk associated with transition years.

In contrast to face-to-face bullying, the limits of cyberbullying are difficult to define. For instance, a single image can be forwarded countless times to innumerable people, a message can be pervasive and difficult to stop, an aggressor can remain unidentified hiding through multiple profiles, maintaining anonymity and making it harder for the victim to defend, escape or identify (and as a result, act to stop the behaviors). Furthermore, cyberbullying behaviors can change and assume new forms according to different interactional settings, highlighting both the overt and covert nature of these behaviors For example, the happy slapping phenomenon often targets the most vulnerable; trolling and flaming in forums and chats are used to disturb and harass; social image is often manipulated and exploited in social networks; while abrupt and violent threats are often made using instant messages or malicious calls.

It is important to note that while young people are often considered the masters of the cyber-world (especially the socializing aspects of it) they are the ones that are at greatest risk of being exposed to cyberbullying behaviors Spears et al. (2015). In addition, they are often the ones responsible for engaging in cyberbullying and other inappropriate behaviors. Furthermore, there is evidence that a large proportion of those who engage in cyberbullying behaviors do so against those individuals who are considered friends.

Bullying behaviors cycle between school and online (cyber) and back again, suggesting a clear link with existing relationships. In addition, research evidence at the present time is a little conflicting with some evidence suggesting that although there is an overlap between those who engage in face-to-face and cyberbullying, a large number of those who engage in cyberbullying behaviors or are victimized are not involved in face-to-face bullying. Furthermore, the impact of cyberbullying on mental health and emotional response is only just beginning to be understood, though it has been posited that it will be greater, possibly due to the 24/7 nature of it, the anonymity aspects, and the broader audience available, not to mention the power that written and visual electronic media can have.

Risky Business: Risk-taking and Well-being in Social Networking Sites

The internet has fundamentally changed the way young people spend their time and the way they communicate with peers. For example, in the Joint Select Committee on Cyber-Safety (2011) it was noted that Australia now has a generation of young people who have never been without online access and as such it is fully integrated into their lives. Australia Communication & Media Authority (ACMA) reports (2011) that over 95% of young Australians use the internet regularly. Almost daily internet use is common for children as young as 8 or 9. This rapidly changes in the "tween" years with many 10–12-year-olds using the internet from one to three hours per day. By 13 years of age, social media use has become the norm; and by 15, the internet and its use has become an "organic integrated part" of the everyday lives of Australian children.

The general suggestion is that the generation born roughly between 1980 and 1994 could be characterized as the "digital natives" because of their familiarity with and reliance on ICT. In a four-year collaborative European Co-operation of Science & Technology (COST) report involving 28 European countries and Australia (Slee, Cross, Campbell, & Spears, 2012) it was recognized that "New Media and technology are the latest vehicles for the complex range of human behaviors and interactions" (Spears et al., 2013, p. 1). As Spears et al. (2013) note:

> They (young people) have a digital footprint that has grown with them: which is intertwined in and around their relationships; and which will follow them into the future. They use media to communicate directly and indirectly, through sharing videos and images as well as text, and this has enabled young people to represent themselves and see others in ways which were not foreseeable prior to the advent of the internet.
>
> (p. 178)

It is now apparent that the very language of social relationships is being reframed: today, young people construct their "profile", make it "public" or "private", they "tweet", "Instagram", photoblog, and so forth. It seems that for many, creating and networking online content is becoming an integral means of managing one's identity, lifestyle, and social relations. This explosive growth in internet use by young people has been mirrored by an increasing awareness of its potential positive and negative impacts.

Mental Health in an Online Environment

There is growing understanding that serious online problems may be indicative of a broader pattern of problem behaviors and/or underlying emotional issues for youth, and vice versa. For example, research (e.g. Campbell & Bauman, 2018) has determined that young people engaging in bullying others online and being victimized online experience wide-ranging social and emotional problems.

Bullying and harassment in cyberspace has wide-ranging and potentially severe consequences. Of concern are those related to mental health, which include depression, lowered self-esteem, school refusal, poor psychosocial quality of life, and suicidal ideation. The limitless boundaries of online harassment pose a daunting challenge not just for the victims themselves, but also for educators and policymakers in formulating policies about online harassment. It is important to note that there are positive and beneficial aspects of the internet and how integrated it is with young people's lives. All too often the moral panics induced by incidents on the internet overwhelm the positive aspects.

Internet Use and Risk-Taking: A Challenge to Well-being!

In their text Slee, Campbell, and Spears (2012) have reviewed the research evidence, concluding that the evidence is that young people take more risks than children or adults do but understanding why this should be has been challenging. Unlike logical-reasoning abilities, which appear to be more or less fully developed by age 15, psychosocial capacities that improve decision making and moderate risk taking – such as impulse control, emotion regulation, delay of gratification, and resistance to peer influence – continue to mature well into young adulthood. Research as reviewed by (Slee, Campbell, & Spears, 2012) shows that parts of the prefrontal cortex are not fully developed until early adulthood. This apparently influences rational thinking and consequently increases the likelihood of engaging in risk-taking behavior. The rise of the internet may provide adolescents with many new outlets to engage in risky behaviors. That is, adolescents may be particularly prone to behaviors such as online bullying and harassment as compared to adults, due to significantly different mechanisms in their decision-making process.

There are hidden risks for adolescents that many are unaware of after they have left their digital footprints, e.g. profile information and personal photographs, on social networking services. However, it would be erroneous to suggest that young people comprise a homogenous group in this regard and research would suggest that certain groups may be particularly "at risk" for engaging in risky internet behavior. Online bullying/harassment can occur in a few ways: for example, through the disclosure of information to strangers who abuse the trust given by the victims, or through the posting of personal information on social networking sites without much thought given to privacy and security settings available (Ybarra & Mitchell, 2008).

School Climate and Bullying

In an overview of the field Slee and Skrzypiec (2016) noted that school climate is generally defined as the quality interpersonal interactions within the school community impacting on children's cognitive, social, and psychological development. Shortcomings with this definition have been addressed in relation to expanding it to include safety (Slee & Skrzypiec, 2016) and the physical environment. It is generally understood that school climate refers to key elements of:

Safety, e.g. safety from bullying
School Environment, e.g. rules and consequences
Engagement e.g. student connectedness

One of the salient school climate factors involved in bullying behavior is the social support individuals receive from both adults and peers at school. Students who feel disconnected from significant others (e.g. teachers, peers) may be less likely to act in a cooperative and pro-social manner. In particular, the researchers discovered that victims and bully-victims attached more importance to social support than bullies and perceived that they received less of such support from their school. This all leads to a negative perception of school climate.

Schools as 'settings' for Interventions and Health Promotion

Schools have ready-made populations of students that can be identified for general, as well as specific, health promotion initiatives such as school bullying. The focus of such initiatives in schools has moved, in accordance with World Health Organization recommendations, towards a "settings" approach, which is reflected in the concept of the health-promoting school. As reported in Slee (2017) such initiatives include the Australian KidsMatter Primary and KidsMatter Early Childhood (Slee, Lawson, et al., 2009). Evaluation of KidsMatter Primary and KidsMatter Early Childhood confirms the value of a "whole school" approach for school-based interventions.

Schools are complex organizations that pose significant challenges for the delivery and evaluation of health promotion initiatives (Slee & Skrzypiec, 2016). There are facilitators and barriers to educational change played out in the successful implementation of initiatives, such as whole-school approaches to bullying. Even within a cluster of settings that may be structurally alike in some ways (such as schools within the same educational system), conditions can vary widely. These include a range of personal and social conditions, such as students' and teachers' background knowledge, existing programs, availability of resources, and leadership commitment to the aims of the initiatives, that vary across schools. In considering schools as sites for mental health promotion initiatives such as school bullying, the matter of how an intervention developed outside the school is taken up and enacted in the "messy and busy" world of the classroom is significant. The question of how an intervention program is conducted faithfully in the classroom is a vitally important issue because it reflects on the outcomes of the programme.

Kinds of Interventions

Interventions may be categorized broadly according to whether their purpose is primarily to prevent bullying from happening or alternatively to deal with cases of bullying if and when they occur. However, a rigid distinction cannot be made; for instance, disciplinary actions taken when a case of bullying is identified may impact not only upon the person being treated but may also make it less likely that others will bully; that is, it may also have a preventative function. Some interventions are not primarily directed towards changing the behavior of individuals who become involved in bullying, but are concerned rather with establishing an environment or ethos in which bullying is less likely, for instance by developing in members of the school community (including both teachers and parents) a better understanding of the problem and promoting more pro-social attitudes and empathic feelings towards others; or alternatively by reducing the motivation to bully by involving students more deeply in school-related study. These may be described as preventative measures. Many programs include both preventative and interventive elements.

As described in Slee (2017) adapting a model described by Mrazek and Haggerty (1994), interventions may be targeted:

Universally at whole populations
Selectively at a population at risk
Indicatively at "high-risk" individuals

Universal programs: These are focused on the general public or a whole population group that has not been identified on the basis of individual risk, e.g. childhood immunization.

Populations at risk: Here the interventions are directed towards individuals or sub-groups of a population known to be at risk of developing problems, e.g. literacy programs directed towards children from economically depressed areas.

"High-risk" individuals: Programs are directed specifically towards high-risk individuals who may already be presenting with signs or symptoms, e.g. programs to prevent depression in children who have one or both clinically depressed parents.

A "whole school approach" to Bullying Prevention

A widely used phrase in anti-bullying research is that of a "whole- school approach" – what exactly does this mean? Perhaps initially, it was a reaction to "one-off" efforts to address school bullying e.g. showing students an anti-bullying video or a principal's anti-bullying announcement at a school assembly. As generally understood a "whole-school" approach incorporates activities at the school and classroom level for the purpose of changing students' behavior and perhaps their attitudes towards bullying. Described in Slee (2017), Dan Olweus (1993) developed an intervention program (The Olweus Bullying Prevention Program – OBPP) frequently referred to as using a "whole-school" approach. The core components of this program include: raising parent awareness of the issue, administering a student bullying questionnaire, holding an anti-bullying conference day, providing effective supervision during recess and lunchtime, creating a bully prevention committee, creating classroom rules against bullying, holding regular classroom meetings with students to discuss bullying, facilitating serious talks with bullies and victims, and holding talks with parents of students involved in bullying episodes. The Olweus Bullying Prevention Program was the first comprehensive whole-school intervention implemented on a large scale and systematically evaluated.

Typically a "whole school" approach focuses on a universal program directed at the entire school population. A "whole school" approach involves a systems approach to interventions whereby multiple players are involved (students, peers, parents, teachers, etc.), and an advantage is that it avoids "stigmatizing" students as perpetrators, victims, or bystanders. An issue with the approach is that it risks (particularly with older students) evincing reactions such as: "we have heard all this before" or "I am not a bully so why waste my time with these issues?" Certainly it is argued that while any incident involves bullies and victims, others are bystanders and so are aware of it, but the actual numbers may still be relatively small. It is also true that the "bystander effect" increases across primary to secondary school resulting in older students feeling less inclined to step in and intervene.

One Size Does Not Fit All

It is suggested then that school-based interventions to address bullying should be nuanced to account for developmental appropriateness and individual, social, and cultural factors. For example, one high school that the author worked with for over five years had developed a program that was differentiated across age groups and year levels beginning with a transition day where primary school students were introduced to the school and running through for three years of secondary school. The program was differentiated across year levels (Slee, 2017). The school had adopted a "whole-school" approach that was delivered in different forms across the year levels.

Evidence-based Support

We now turn to a consideration of the evaluations that have been made of anti-bullying interventions in terms of their effectiveness. Slee (2017) reviewed the literature noting that Vreeman and Carroll (2007) investigated the effectiveness of 26 school anti-bullying programs. Classifying the studies into type of intervention, categories of curriculum interventions, multidisciplinary or whole-school interventions, targeted social and behavioral skills groups, mentoring, and increased social work support, Vreeman and Carroll also investigated direct and indirect outcomes of the interventions. Their findings showed that curriculum interventions, which generally involve a smaller allotment of resources and effort and were aimed at changing attitudes to bullying, were seldom effective in impacting the level of bullying. They argued that attempting to change attitudes and behaviors at the classroom level is unlikely to have an effect since bullying is a systemic group process. As they pointed out: "If bullying is a systemic group process involving bullies, victims, peers, adults, parents, school environments, and home environments, an intervention on only one level is unlikely to have a significant consistent impact" (p. 86). According to these researchers, crucial to effective anti-bullying programs are interventions that are well-planned, involve multiple disciplines and a whole-school community, and are championed by committed staff.

In 2011, Ttofi and Farrington undertook another systematic and meta-analytic review of anti-bullying programs. They examined the effectiveness of 44 school-based programs to reduce bullying. The programs they examined were quite varied, diverse, and were across different age groups and countries. For example, they examined the Finish KiVa program (Kärnä et al., 2011), which is a well-structured program that seeks to change attitudes to bullying using visual learning envirionments, such as computer games and role-playing. The KiVa program has been widely disseminated and subject to a wide range of evaluations. In the Australian context a widely used and evaluated anti-bullying program is Friendly Schools (Cross et al. (2015). The systematic analysis by Ttofi and Farrington (2011) found that overall, school-based anti-bullying programs effectively reduced bullying (i.e. bullying of others) on average by 20%–23% and victimization (i.e. being bullied by others) by 17%–20%, and that intensive programs were the most effective. Common elements of effective programs included meetings with parents, firm disciplinary measures, the use of videos and cooperative group work, and improved supervision of young people's play area. Noteworthy is that work with peers, such as peer mediation, peer mentoring, and encouraging bystander intervention to prevent bullying, generally increased victimization. Citing other research that supported their findings (Dishion, McCord, & Poulin, 1999; Dodge, Lansford, & Dishion, 2006), Ttofi and Farrington recommended that work with peers should not be used as an anti-bullying intervention.

An important feature of interventions influencing the effectiveness of anti-bullying programs is the "dosage" or intensity of the program (Slee, 2017). Dosage refers to the degree of exposure to the program. Ttofi and Farrington's (2011) findings showed that intensive and long-lasting programs with large amounts of program exposure were more likely to be effective in reducing involvement in bullying. This suggests that anti-bullying programs that continue to be implemented in schools year after year are beneficial as anti-bullying sentiment would build an appropriate (long-term) school ethos. Overall meta-analytic and meta-ethnographic research studies, such as those mentioned above, suggest that whole-school approaches may be quite effective in reducing involvement in bullying. However, it could still be the case that other types of interventions have yet to be tried and tested. It would certainly be advantageous to find an intervention program that was effective yet was not as time- and resource-intensive as one which required the involvement of all school community members.

The P.E.A.C.E. Pack

In the following sections we describe the "Coping With Bullying" (CWB) program designed by the authors to reduce bullying victimization, enhance the coping skills of students, and promote well-being. The program was developed from an anti-bullying intervention developed by the authors and called the P.E.A.C.E. pack: A program for reducing bullying in our schools (Slee, 2001).

The P.E.A.C.E. pack is a successful intervention framework dealing with bullying in schools (Slee, 1996; Slee & Mohyla, 2007). The framework was developed in consultation with teachers, students, principals, and parents, and school administrators from daycare centers, kindergartens, and primary and secondary schools have all contributed to the development of the P.E.A.C.E. pack. Particularly valuable contributions to the package were made by the representatives of various secondary and primary schools who met in focus groups over the course of two years to develop, implement, and evaluate intervention programs for reducing school bullying.

The acronym P.E.A.C.E. has been used to help organize the material presented in this package under the following headings:

P   Preparation and consideration of the nature of the problem
E   Education and understanding of the issues by those concerned
A   Action taken and strategies developed to reduce bullying
C   Coping strategies which are implemented for staff, students, and parents
E   Evaluation and review of the program in place at school

Theoretically the framework draws on essential systemic principles (Shute & Slee, 2015) whereby the issue of school bullying is nested within relationships and understood in terms of social constructivist thought. Systemic thinking is sharply at odds with more conventional western scientific thinking with its emphasis on remediation, deficits and weaknesses in the individual (Shute & Slee, 2015). In contrast to this "deficit" approach, systemic thinking emphasizes the active role of the individual in socially constructing meaning and has a strong focus on competency, success, and individual strengths. It embraces the idea of the "social", whereby meaning is constructed within the social setting of relationships, interactions and communication.

Evidence-based Support

It is widely used in Australia and has been translated and evaluated in countries such as Japan, Malta, and Greece, adapted for culture. In Australia year-long P. E.A.C.E. pack intervention programs in five primary schools involving 806 students were successful in significantly:

Reducing the amount of bullying
Increasing students' knowledge about how to stop bullying
Increasing students' awareness of who to talk to about bullying

In Japan the P.E.A.C.E. pack has been translated into Japanese and implemented in two Japanese junior high schools. Consistent with the Australian research, the program was effective in reducing the level of school bullying. (Slee, 1997). In Malta the P.E.A.C.E. pack was adapted in the 2014 Ministry for Education and Employment documents "Respect for All" and "Addressing Bullying Behavior in School" and subsequently implemented as the Malta school-based intervention program "Flourishing at School and at Home" across nine schools involving pre and post evaluations with almost 3,000 12-year-old students. Following the delivery of the six-lesson "Flourishing at School and at Home" intervention, which was expressly designed for Maltese schools, there was a significant reduction in the level of self-reported bullying amongst seriously bullied students, a significant reduction in the amount of verbal bullying for seriously bullied students, and reductions in other forms of bullying, but there was a small increase in self-reported cyberbullying and being ignored. In addition, seriously bullied students were less likely post-intervention to engage in nonproductive coping strategies, but they were also less likely post-intervention than other students to use productive coping strategies. The intervention was associated with positive changes in seriously bullied students' positive feelings about school. In Greece the outcomes of an anti-bullying intervention program based on the P.E.A.C.E. pack placed emphasis on the training of students in coping strategies for handling bullying. The program consists of eight lessons of two hours and was conducted during the years 2012–2014 and involved 932 students along with their teachers from 14 secondary schools in Thessaly, central Greece (two schools participated in the control group). The results from the intervention group showed that under repeated assessments, those partici-pants who were identified as seriously bullied reported decreased victimi-zation experiences and increased sense of safety in school. Regarding coping with bullying, it was found that the strategies of: a) reduced optimism, b) improving the relationship with the bully, c) wishful thinking, and d) pretending that it is not happening, significantly distinguish the seriously bullied group of students from their peers in the moderate bullied and safe (from bullying) categories. The coping strategies that were found to have predictive value for serious victimization are wishful thinking and pretending it is not happening. At the end of the program, there was a significant decrease in the use of wishful thinking and of pretending it was not happening

Multicultural Counseling Considerations

Research by the author on coping with school bullying has been conducted in Japan and other Pacific rim countries and is ongoing in Greece, Malta, and Italy (Slee, 2017). At the broadest level this cross cultural research has identified significant differences in how school bullying is defined, its fre-quency and effects, the priority attached to addressing it by schools and government agencies, and the intervention and counseling approaches adopted. A range of resources for addressing and counseling this issue may be found at www.caper.com.au

In particular, research (e.g. Slee, 2017) has identified that children on the autism-spectrum disorder are up to four times more likely to be seriously bullied than are their counterparts. Counseling resources in the form of DVDs to assist teachers and parents have been developed and are available on the website www.caper.com.au. It is also clear from the latest research regarding cyberbullying that very particular resources to assist teachers, parents, and students are needed, given the legal ramifications of such bullying (Slee, 2017).

Procedure

Implementing the P.E.A.C.E. Pack in your School

The P.E.A.C.E. pack is an intervention program dealing with bullying in schools and presents school-based strategies that have been shown to reduce school bullying. The framework will be described identifying the steps that can be taken to implement the intervention in your school (Figure 10.1).

"P" Preparation

The P.E.A.C.E. pack is generally implemented by an individual such as the school counselor, well-being coordinator, or senior teacher. The first step in

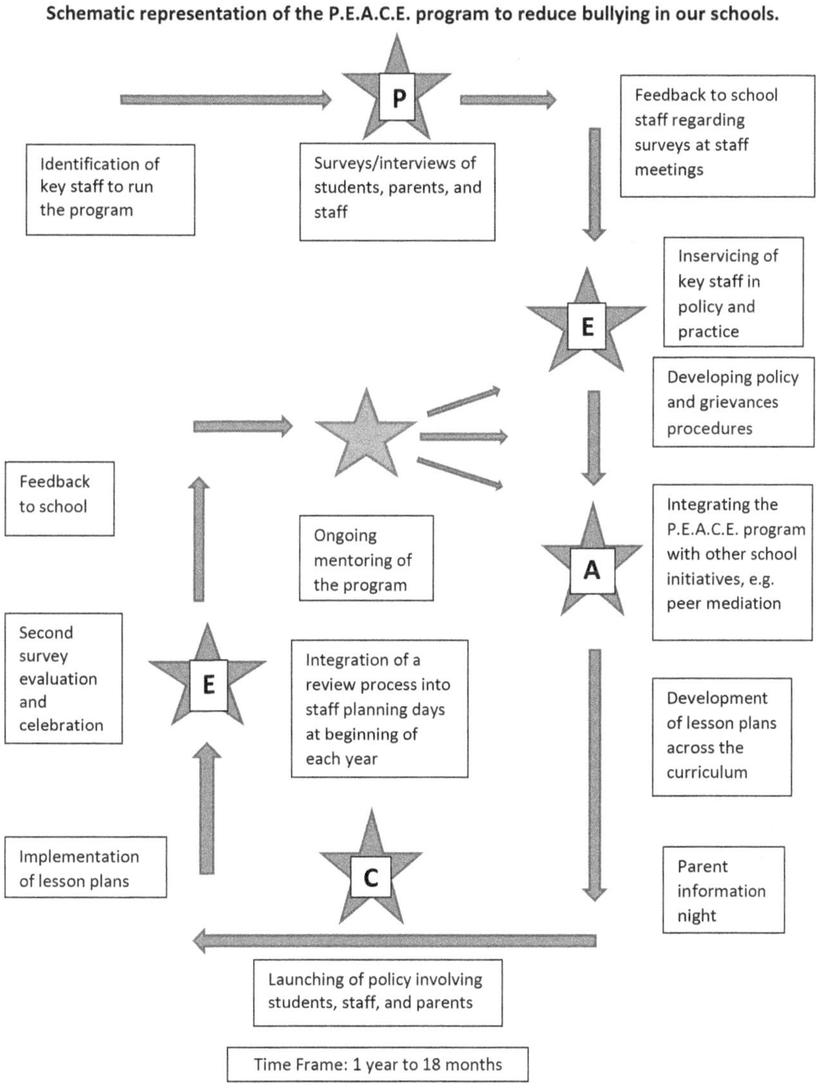

Schematic representation of the P.E.A.C.E. program to reduce bullying in our schools.

Identification of key staff to run the program	Surveys/interviews of students, parents, and staff

Feedback to school staff regarding surveys at staff meetings

Inservicing of key staff in policy and practice

Developing policy and grievances procedures

Feedback to school

Ongoing mentoring of the program

Integrating the P.E.A.C.E. program with other school initiatives, e.g. peer mediation

Second survey evaluation and celebration

Integration of a review process into staff planning days at beginning of each year

Development of lesson plans across the curriculum

Implementation of lesson plans

Parent information night

Launching of policy involving students, staff, and parents

Time Frame: 1 year to 18 months

Figure 10.1 The P.E.A.C.E. Process

preparing a school intervention program involves collecting information regarding the nature of the bullying experience, as a basis for policy development, program development, and parent and student involvement. As such the counselor would familiarize her/himself with contemporary information regarding the definition of bullying, its manifestation, the types of bullying that could occur including cyberbullying, the impact of bullying on the well-being of those involved, the importance of school safety and classroom climate, and the evidence base for interventions.

Critical Questions

"What do I know about the issue of bullying?"
"What do I need to learn more about in relation to the issue?"
"Where can I find the information?"

"E" Education

Having prepared oneself with some basic information about the topic of bullying, the next step involves educating others about the issue and collecting information upon which to base an intervention program. Education may occur through:

A review of school policies and procedures for addressing bullying
Direct observations
Interviews
Anonymous surveys

The review of current school practice regarding bullying should provide an understanding of school policy and the nature of the action needed to address the issue of bullying. Slee (2017) has described a variety of methods that could be used to collect information, e.g. direct observation, questionnaires, school records, together with the strengths and weaknesses of the various methods. The importance of this step in the framework is that it provides an evidence base for the intervention and importantly a baseline to examine the effectiveness of the intervention.

Critical Questions

"What has my review about the issue of bullying indicated?"
"What needs to be done in my school?"
"Who can assist me?"

"A" Action

The third step in the P.E.A.C.E. process involves identifying the ACTION that can be taken by staff, students, and parents to address bullying at school. From a systems perspective, action should engage the various subsystems of the school environment including students, parents, and teachers. Broadly, interventions can involve "first-order" change where individuals caught up in the bully-victim cycle may need some assistance and strategies to deal with bullying. The school system remains the same with the bully viewed as the "bad" student in need of control and change, and the victim viewed as an individual needing help and protection. If the view of the situation is accurate and constructive, and if in fact the students do simply need to acquire some new skills, then "first-order" interventions have a place in an intervention program.

"Second-order change" will occur when the system itself changes. For example the school may gain some insight through a review of policy and practice as to how current procedures maintain and even amplify or encourage bullying. The school, in modifying attitudes, perceptions, and beliefs, may approach a student's bullying behavior from a very different perspective. In shifting the focus and thinking in more systemic terms, change will resonate throughout the school system. Instead of focusing on changing the "bad" behavior of the bully and on "helping" the victim, consideration might be given to roles, relationships, and interactions and communication within the system which encourage or discourage bullying. When the system itself begins to change or realign, "second-order" change has occurred.

Shute and Slee (2015) note that the idea of "student voice" has gained increased emphasis in research. This reflects a move away from viewing young people as passive and vulnerable individuals to an outlook that values them as active agents in the research process. For a long time, however, children and young people have not had a voice in either the research process or the outcomes of research. Rather, they participated at the behest of adults, whose views have long been privileged over those of children. Children's and young people's role in research consisted solely of responding to adult instructions or demands, e.g. filling out questionnaires or responding to interview questions: as passive recipients or objects at the center of adult enquiry. Schools genuinely seeking reform and change in relation to school bullying should actively seek out children's and young people's ideas and views regarding interventions.

Critical Questions

"Who needs to be involved in addressing the issue of bullying?"
"What are the barriers and facilitators to change regarding this issue?"
"Who can best help me address the issue?"

"C" Coping

Coping relates to how one deals with stress, where stress refers to environmental elements that impact on physical or psychological functioning in a disruptive manner. In reviewing the coping strategies literature, Skrzypiec, Slee, Murray-Harvey, and Pereira (2011) note that it is possible to categorize strategies as involving "approach" or "avoidance" (Causey & Dubow, 1992; Lazarus and Folkman, 1984). "Approach" types include positive strategies that may decrease the likelihood of continued victimization (e.g. help seeking to stop the victimization). "Avoidance" approaches (e.g. denial and refusal to think about an incident) are generally regarded as less effective. Overall, though, much remains to be done to understand the dynamics underpinning a successful intervention program.

In the P.E.A.C.E. pack "COPING" is considered in terms of:

Attitudes (ethos) of the school
Behaviors to develop
Curriculum to implement

Critical Questions

"How can the intervention be implemented across the curriculum?"
"What do I know about the coping literature?"
"Where can I find the information?"

"E" Evaluation

The final step in the P.E.A.C.E. pack involves evaluating the effects of any school-based program for reducing bullying. This may be accomplished using:

Surveys

If a survey has been conducted then it may be appropriate to conduct a brief follow-up survey to understand the impact of any intervention.

Interviews

Interviews with students, staff, and parents following an intervention are another way of evaluating the usefulness of a program.

Observations

Examination of records of reported incidents of bullying or direct observations in the playground may be useful in evaluating an intervention.

Celebration

It is important that opportunity be found to celebrate the accomplishments of the whole school intervention program. Avenues that schools have used to achieve this end include:

- Announcements of progress at school assemblies
- Class letters circulated amongst classes detailing ideas and accomplishments
- School newsletters that are sent home to parents

- Parent information nights
- Open days at the school which might incorporate a display of the outcomes of the program e.g. class rules, school policy, etc.

Critical Questions

"What is the best way to collect information about the intervention?"
"Who can help me collect this information?"
"How will this information be disseminated to the school community?"
"How do we celebrate our achievements?"

Implementing the P.E.A.C.E. Pack Framework: A Step-by-step Guide for Schools

Coping with Bullying

The Coping with Bullying (CWB) program has been substantially developed by the authors from the "Coping" component of the P.E.A.C.E. pack. The CWB program brings together related, but until recently separate, areas of research interest: bullying, coping, and social and emotional well-being. Individually these areas are connected to research that has focused on improving well-being and academic outcomes for children and young people. The CWB program is based at the individual classroom level, but it involves a whole-year level approach as complete cohorts of students are participants in the intervention.

The way in which young people respond to bullying is important in terms of re-victimization. It is not clear why some young people become the victims of bullies or why they generally find it difficult to defend themselves. While victims are not to be blamed for being bullied, research suggests that vulnerable children who appear to be socially withdrawn, anxious, or submissive, or who respond in counter-productive ways to bullying (e.g. with angry and emotionally charged responses), may actually reinforce victimization. The way in which victims cope with bullying and the strategies they employ may also influence the likelihood of persistent victimization.

Clearly identified in the research literature are effective and ineffective ways for coping with problems in general. Effective coping strategies may be referred to as "approach" or "productive" strategies. Ineffective coping strategies may be referred to as "avoidance" or non-productive' strategies. (The terms approach/avoidance and productive/non-productive strategies will be used synonymously in this chapter.)

With regard to bullying, approach strategies are actions that are likely to decrease the likelihood of continued victimization. These approach strategies include seeking help or support from others to stop the victimization. On the other hand, avoidance strategies are ineffective approaches. Ineffective strategies include such actions as denial and refusal to think about an incident after it has happened. However, whether a strategy is effective in all instances may be dependent on the context. For example, talking back may sometimes be seen by some as an effective strategy for a victim defending him/herself while at other times it could be ineffective, particularly if the victim is overpowered by the bully.

Several studies have shown that victims manage bullying less effectively by using coping strategies which are non-productive, such as responding passively, walking away, or fighting back (see review in Slee, 2017). Such non-productive responses to bullying may increase the likelihood of continued victimization. Murray-Harvey and Slee as reported in Slee (2017) revealed that ineffective or unproductive coping was strongly correlated with adolescent students' reports of being victimized and with negative effects on their psychological health (e.g. apathy, depression, aggression, somatic symptoms).

However, research conducted by Frydenberg (2004) has provided some direction for assisting victims develop better coping strategies and hence reduce the likelihood of further victimization. In their research Frydenberg et al. (2004) showed that through explicit teaching, young people can be taught how to cope with stressful life situations, such as bullying. As a response to stress, Frydenberg et al. (2004) argued that young people can develop resilience by mastering more effective strategies and reducing ineffective coping strategies. In three settings involving over 400 youths aged 11–17 in Australia and Italy, Frydenberg et al. (2004) demonstrated that it was possible for trained teachers to increase students' self-efficacy and to engender their use of new and more effective coping strategies. These findings informed the development of the CWB intervention and the development of the CWB questionnaire. The CWB questionnaire was adapted from Frydenberg and Lewis's (1993) Adolescent Coping Scale, and it was used to assess students' coping with bullying before and after the CWB intervention.

"Coping with Bullying Intervention" Package

The P.E.A.C.E. pack includes an important element associated with assisting students to cope with bullying. An important element of the program is "C", i.e. enhancing the coping skills and strategies of staff, students, and parents. All too frequently the focus of anti-bullying programs is on helping students cope, but in an important systemic sense any intervention should also address how important other individuals (e.g. parents) cope with bullying.

The teacher package includes the *Coping with Bullying* DVD (including four bullying scenarios, namely physical, verbal, relational, and cyber bullying), outlines for eight lessons, supporting information and class activity materials and resources, and pre and post questionnaires. The package also includes a short 5-minute PowerPoint presentation for the teachers involved.

Delivery of the Program

Teachers typically deliver the program as eight lessons as part of pastoral care or home-group curriculum (35–45 minutes). The teachers participating in the training receive a half-day training session which includes student workbooks, teacher feedback sheets, pre and post questionnaires, and recommendations for bullying/harassment policy.

In related research in the schools, data was collected regarding the multiple ways in which students reported they were bullied, and the relationship to coping. Data was also collected regarding the coping strategies that "seriously" bullied students use compared with what school counselors would advise. The framework is theoretically based on a systems perspective emphasizing that we must identify key aspects of school systems that influence students' abilities to achieve well-being and promote their learning. The five generally agreed-upon core socio-emotional learning (SEL) competencies include:

Self-awareness
Self-management
Social awareness
Relationship skills
Responsible decision making

These SEL competencies form the foundation for the lessons whereby awareness is raised of the issue of bullying (e.g. nature, types, and effects) and strategies for coping, and the lessons have particular activities to allow students to practice and enhance their coping skills and well-being with attention given to activities in the lessons associated with the five core SEL competencies.

The Child and Adolescent Psychological and Educational Resources (CAPER) Website

This site has been active since 2001 and, over time, has built up a large information base, accessed internationally by students, teachers, researchers, and other professionals interested in research and practical resources relating to children, adolescents, and families. Particular focus is given to issues relating to peer relationships, including bullying, as well as stress and well-being. The site hosts the P.E.A.C.E. pack and the CWB program described in this chapter, and can be accessed at

Challenges and Solutions

> I have been impressed with the urgency of doing. Knowing is not enough; we must apply. Being willing is not enough; we must do.
>
> (Leonardo da Vinci)

Box 10.1 An Exercise for Disputing Misconceptions about Bullying

Raising the Issue of Bullying: Disputing Misconceptions – a Staff Exercise

Raising the issue of bullying may elicit a range of BELIEFS, ATTITUDES and OPINIONS amongst staff. The following exercise provides a framework for disputing common misconceptions about bullying. These misconceptions may be presented, discussed, and disputed as a means for lowering staff resistance towards any school program for reducing bullying (e.g. at a staff meeting or workshop).

MISCONCEPTION	DISPUTING THE MISCONCEPTION
There is no bullying at school	-view literature, statistics (see resources) -present the results of a school survey -interview students and present the findings
There may be bullying but it is not harmful	-review the literature (see resources) -talk to students about the harmful effects -talk to adults who have been bullied
Bullying may be harmful but adult students will get over it depression	-bullies are more prone to juvenile and offending -victims are prone to ill health and -see resources
There may be bullying but it is not harmful	-review the literature (see resources) -talk to students about the harmful effects -talk to adults who have been bullied
The school does not have the bullying expertise to deal with bullying of	-the most effective programs to reduce are school-based and utilize the expertise students, staff, and parents
Let the school deal with the staff problem of bullying and do not involve me the student	-stopping bullying begins with individual and students taking responsibility -action against bullying involves action at the classroom level and individual staff, and parent level
I can't do something to help stop bullying	-identify the ACTION individuals can take

In this chapter we take to heart da Vinci's general admonishment and, in relation to the topic of school bullying following decades of research, argue that there is an urgent need to act on what we best know and understand. That said, the challenges facing researchers and teachers in implementing evidence-based programs to address bullying are quite evident. It is frequently the case that when a teacher or counselor attempts to introduce an anti-bullying program into a school they are met with the response, "We don't need that program here; we don't have a problem with bullying". This is surprising given the focus on the issue. The following activity is useful for disputing such a claim. Box 10.1 provides a simple exercise for helping dispute such claims.

Further challenges include the evaluations of programs in the 'messy' real world of schools and classroom, the issues faced with implementing programs with integrity, and promoting evidence-based programs in a world where increasingly 'quick fixes' are demanded by legislators and politicians.

Resources

Child and Adolescent Psychological and Educational Resources (CAPER) www.caper.com.au

The Flinders Centre for Student Well-being & Prevention of Violence (SWAPv) www.flinders.edu.au/ehl/swapv/

Bibliography

Baumrind, D. (1966). Effects of authoritative parental control on child behavior. *Child Development, 37*(4), 887–907.

Campbell, M. & Bauman, S. (2017). *Reducing cyberbullying in schools*. Amsterdam, The Netherlands: Elsevier.

Campbell, M.A. & Bauman, S. (Eds.) (2018). *Reducing cyberbullying in schools : International evidence-based best practices*. London: Elsevier.

Causey, D.L. & Dubow, E.F. (1992). Development of a self-report coping measure for elementary school children. *Journal of Clinical Child Psychology, 21*(1), 47–59. http://dx.doi.org/10.1207/s15374424jccp2101_8

Craig, W., Harel-Fisch, Y., Fogel-Grinvald, H., Dostaler, S., Hetland, J., Simons-Morton, B., et al. (2009 Sep). A cross-national profile of bullying and victimization among adolescents in 40 countries. *International Journal of Public Health, 54*(Suppl 2), 216-224. doi: 10.1007/s00038-009-5413-9.

Cross, D., Shaw, T., Hadwen, K., Cardoso, P., Slee, P., Roberts, C., et al. (2015). Longitudinal impact of the cyber friendly schools program on adolescents' cyberbullying behavior. *Aggressive Behavior, 42*, 166–180.

Dishion, T.J., McCord, J., Poulin, F. (1999). When interventions harm: Peer groups and problem behavior. *American Psychologist, 54*(9), 755–764.

Dodge, K.A., Dishion, T.J., & Lansford, J.E. (Eds.) (2006). *Deviant peer influences in programs for youth: Problems and solutions*. New York: Guilford.

Frydenberg, E. (2004). Coping competencies: What to teach and when. *Theory into Practice, 43*(1), 14–22.

Frydenberg, E. & Lewis, R. (1993). Boys play sport and girls turn to others: Age, gender and ethnicity as determinants of coping. *Journal of Adolescence, 16*(3), 253–266.

Frydenberg, E., Lewis, R., Bugalski, K., Cotta, A., McCarthy, C., Luscombe-Smith, N., & Poole, C. (2004). Prevention is better than cure: Coping skills training for adolescents at school. *Educational Psychology in Practice, 20*(2), 117–134, doi: 10.1080/02667360410001691053.

Goodman, R. (1997). The strengths and difficulties questionnaire: A research note. *Journal of Child Psychology and Psychiatry, 38*, 581–586. https://doi.org/10.1111/j.1469-7610.1997.tb01545.x

Mrazek, P.J. & Haggerty, R.J. (Eds.) (1994). *Reducing Risks for Mental Disorders: Frontiers for Preventive Intervention.* Washington DC: National Academies Press.

Kärnä, A., Voeten, M., Little, T.D., Poskiparta, E., Kaljonen, A., Salmivalli, C. (2011). A large-scale evaluation of the KiVa antibullying program: grades 4–6. *Child Development, 82*(2), 311–330. doi: 10.1111/j.1467-8624.2010.01557.x.

Lazarus, R. & Folkman, S. (1984). *Stress, Appraisal, and Coping.* New York: Springer.

Monks, C.P., Smith, P.K., & Swettenham, J. (2005). Psychological correlates of peer victimisation in preschool: Social cognitive skills, executive function and attachment profiles. *Aggressive Behavior, 31*(6), 1–18.

Olweus, D. (1993). *Bullying at school: What we know and what we can do.* Malden, MA: Blackwell.

Shute, R. & Slee, P.T. (2015). *Child development: Theories and critical perspectives.* London, UK: Routledge.

Shute, R. & Slee, P.T. (2016). *Mental health and well-being through schools: The way forward.* Routledge.

Skrzypiec, G., Slee, P., Askell-Williams, H., & Lawson, M. (2012). Associations between types of involvement in bullying, friendships and mental health status. *Emotional and Behavioral Difficulties, 17*(3–4), 259–272.

Skrzypiec, G., Slee, P.T., Murray-Harvey, R., & Pereira, B. (2011). School bullying by one or more ways: Does it matter and how do students cope? *School Psychology International, 32*, 288–312.

Skrzypiec, G.K., Slee, P.T., & Askell-Williams, H. (2017). Collaboration with parents/carers in KidsMatter schools. In C. Cefai & P. Cooper (Eds.) *Mental health promotion in schools: Cross cultural narratives and perspectives* (pp. 181–196). Rotterdam, Netherlands: Sense Publications.

Slee, P.T. (1996). The P.E.A.C.E. Pack: A program for reducing bullying in our schools. *Australian Journal of Guidance and Counselling, 6*, 63–69.

Slee, P.T. (1997). *The P.E.A.C.E. Pack: A programme for reducing bullying in our schools.* Tokyo: JiJi-tsushin.

Slee, P.T. (2001). *The PEACE Pack: A program for reducing school bullying* (1st Ed.). Adelaide: Flinders University.

Slee, P.T. (2017). *School bullying: Teachers helping students cope.* London: Routledge.

Slee, P.T., Campbell, M., & Spears, B. (2012). *Child, adolescent and family development* (2nd ed.). Melbourne: Cambridge University Press.

Slee, P.T., Cross, D., Campbell, M.A., & Spears, B. (2012). Bullying-Cyberbullying: Translating theory into practice to assist with coping in school settings. *CSE Occasional Paper 118.* Melbourne: CSE.

Slee, P.T., Ma, L., Hee-Og, S., Taki, M., & Sullivan, K. (2003). *School bullying in five countries in the Asia-Pacific region.* In *The handbook on educational research in the Asia Pacific region.* J. Keeves & R. Watanabe (Eds.) Alphen aan den Rijn, Netherlands: Kluwer Academic Publishers, 425–439.

Slee, P.T. & Mohyla, J. (2007). The PEACE Pack: An evaluation of a school-based intervention to reduce bullying in four Australian primary schools. *Educational Research, 49*(2), 103–115.

Slee, P.T. & Skrzypiec, G. (2016). *Well-being, positive peer relations and bullying in school settings*. Basel, Switzerland: Springer.

Smith, P.K., Kwak, K., & Toda, Y. (2016). *School bullying in different cultures: Eastern and western perspectives*. Cambridge: Cambridge University Press.

Smith, P.K., Morita, J., Junger-Tas, J., Catalorio, R., & Slee, P.T. (Eds.) (1999). *The nature of school bullying*. London: Routledge.

Spears, B., Costabile, A., Brighi, A., Del Rey, R., Porhola, M., Sanchez, V., et al. (2013). Positive uses of new technologies in relationships in educational settings, In P. Smith & G. Steffgen (Eds.), *Cyberbullying through the new media: Findings from an international network*. (pp. 178–200). London: Psychology Press.

Spears, B. A., Taddeo, C. M., Daly, A. L., Stretton, A. J., & Karklins, L. T. (2015). Cyberbullying, help-seeking and mental health in young Australians: implications for public health. *International Journal of Public Health, 60*(2), 219–226.

Troy, M. & Sroufe, L. A. (1987). Victimization among preschoolers: Role of attachment relationship history. *Journal of the American Academy of Child & Adolescent Psychiatry, 26*(2), 166–172. http://dx.doi.org/10.1097/00004583-198703000-00007.

Ttofi, M.M. & Farrington, D.P. (2011). Effectiveness of school-based programs to reduce bullying: A systematic and meta-analytic review. *Journal of Experimental Criminology, 7*, 27–56.

Vreeman, R.C. & Carroll, A.E. (2007). A systematic review of school-based interventions to prevent bullying. *Archives of Pediatrics and Adolescent Medicine, 161*(1), 78–88.

Ybarra, M.L. & Mitchell, K.J. (2008). How risky are social networking sites? A comparison of places online where youth sexual solicitation and harassment occurs. *Pediatrics 121*(2), e350–357. doi: 10.1542/peds.2007-0693.

11 How to Develop Community Resources

Michael S. Kelly

Overview:

The Curious Case of (the lack of) Community Involvement in SBFC

This chapter will explore a present and persistent challenge for any SBFC practitioner, namely how to meaningfully involve community resources and stakeholders in the provision of SBFC. I lead with characterizing this as a challenge because, as we will see, everyone agrees that the work of helping at-risk youth is enhanced (and, in many cases, is only effective) when a variety of community stakeholders are able to work together to serve that young person and their (gender neutral) family. Despite the widespread agreement that this is what is needed, there are enormous gaps between what we know works and what is actually happening in day-to-day mental health provision for young people and their families. This is a pronounced challenge in most school and community settings around the world, but is an acute problem here in the largely resource-rich United States, where a crazy quilt of local, state and federal programs create particular challenges for SBFC practitioners even when there are community and school resources that could be mobilized. In this chapter, I will share what we know about creating effective community resources to further the important work of SBFC practitioners, with a particular emphasis on deploying needs assessment strategies like resource mapping and wraparound supports to bring the key community resources to bear in assisting SBFC clients and their families. Because the skills involved in developing community resources are both a macro-level issue that requires policy-practice skills as well as a problem that can be rooted in just one family and their child, attention will be paid throughout the chapter on how the skills of developing community resources requires SBFC practitioners to operate at multiple levels of intervention within the client system. Starting at Tiers 1 and 2 (typically characterized as the "primary prevention" tiers in the Multi-Tiered System of Supports (MTSS) public health framework), I will start by showing how needs assessment and resource mapping at those tiers can directly impact SBFC practitioners' practice with specific school clients as well as enhancing the overall school environment. After showing how these skills can work for SBFC practitioners at Tiers 1 and 2, I will move to showing how the same skills can be adapted through more intensive clinical work at Tier 3, through a wraparound framework. Finally, I will describe how these practices look like in actual practice, drawing on some case studies from my recent consulting work with agencies and practitioners providing SBFC.

Background

In Chapter 2 of this volume, Gerrard (Gerrard & Soriano, 2018) writes that a key part of conceptualizing a case for SBFC practitioners is determining the answer to this question: "Does the school have the resources to address this problem?" Assuming the answer is no, the SBFC practitioner is encouraged to "Develop Community Resources" and deliver a "Community Intervention." (Chapter 2, Box 2.13. This seemingly straightforward process is actually fraught with complications, based on the research literature on SBFC practice, multi-tiered systems of supports (MTSS), and school resource needs assessments (Franklin, Harris, & Allen-Meares, 2012; Massat, Kelly, & Constable, 2016). Just as SBFC practitioners' clients often have a host of complicating details and presenting problems, schools and their surrounding communities present their own sets of challenges as SBFC practitioners seek to answer the seemingly simple question, "Does the school have the resources to address this problem?"

Before getting more fully into this chapter, here are a few definitions of terms, to help us differentiate between the different practices and levels of intervention as we discern how best to identify and develop community resources in SBFC: Multi-tiered Systems of Supports (MTSS), sometimes also referred to as Positive Behavior Interventions and Supports (PBIS), School-Wide Positive Behavior Interventions and Supports (SWPBIS), Response to Intervention (RTI), and the Inter-Connected Systems Framework (ISF), form a well-developed public health prevention framework that is evidence-informed and data-driven, and has been widely adopted in American K-12 schools (Franklin, Harris, & Allen-Meares, 2012). Though all of the above abbreviations differ somewhat in terms of whether they emphasize academic, mental health, or behavioral interventions, all of them rely on a three-tier model with levels of universal prevention/intervention (Tier 1), selective prevention/intervention (Tier 2) and Indicated prevention/interventions (Tier 3). School-Based Needs Assessment refers to a systematic process of gathering information about a significant problem in a school setting that is impacting social/academic/behavioral outcomes. Resource Mapping (often a key component of a larger needs assessment) refers to the process of looking at what formal and informal supports exist within the school and surrounding community (including community agencies, government, non-profits, churches) to address the needs of the school population. Evidence-informed practice refers to the application of the best available empirical evidence (combined with SBFC practitioners' expertise and client values) to address presenting problems, and can be used across all. Wraparound refers to "an intensive, holistic method of engaging with individuals with complex needs (most typically children, youth, and their families) so that they can live in their homes and communities and realize their hopes and dreams." (National Wraparound Initiative, 2017).

Answering the Question: "does the school have the resources to address the SBFC client's presenting problem?"

The key word I want to unpack from the above question is "resources," and then I shall go on to provide some strategies for how SBFC practitioners can efficiently utilize needs assessment and resource-mapping tools to help their clients. At its root, dictionary.com defines a resource as "a source of supply, support, or aid, especially one that can be drawn upon when needed." Schools, not being simply static, inanimate objects, but rather buildings that contain people, systems of care, practices, and policies (Ball in Massat, Kelly, & Constable, 2016), offer a range of possible supports for SBFC practitioners' clients. These can be staff members who are willing to give more of their time to the SBFC practitioner's client, possibly by mentoring them 1:1; school policies that promote parental involvement and welcoming practices for parents going through difficult times; or schools that intentionally create culturally responsive after-school programs for immigrant youth. All of these examples indicate that a school may have the "resources" at that specific time for the specific SBFC practitioner's client and their family. (And as we'll see, SBFC practitioners are often masterful at linking families to the resources the school is offering.) Likewise, schools may present very differently to specific SBFC clients and their families: schools may have staff or school policies that treat the student unfairly, or define the student's problems in overly pathological ways that actually impede the student's progress and the family's willingness to work with the school (Kim, Kelly, & Franklin, 2017). These examples rely largely on the specific school context and key school-level variables like principal leadership, staff readiness, and overall school-level knowledge about mental health and family-related issues (Barrett, Eber, & Weist, 2013; Dadaczynski & Paulus, 2015; Owens et al., 2014).

But there are other ways in which the school/resources question can be answered, ones that may not be as immediate to the specific SBFC case but that can have long-range impacts on the school's ability to address the SBFC practitioner going forward. Resources can be viewed in terms of funds, budgets, and time commitments that schools and districts are able to make to address the kinds of problems that SBFC practitioners typically encounter (Anderson-Butcher et al., 2017; Owens et al., 2014). Resources can also be reflected in state and federal-level funding priorities (Barrett, Eber, & Weist, 2013; Massat, Kelly, & Constable, 2016). Finally, school resources are often contingent on the very communities they are located in and the families they serve, making some SBFC practitioner clients more likely to have good school and/or community resources based on where they live and how many resources the community has (Anderson-Butcher et al., 2017; Oakes, Maier, & Daniel, 2017).

Developing Community Resources in the Absence of School Resources: No Resources? Not So Fast!

As we will see later in this chapter, SBFC practitioners have a wealth of evidence-informed strategies to identify resource gaps and to foster stronger school-community partnerships. For now, I want to focus on what a SBFC practitioner might do if they reach the conclusion that the school does not have the resources needed to address the specific SBFC practitioner concern. And from the outset, I want to challenge the way in which many SBFC practitioners reach that conclusion. We often assume the lack of resources without engaging in formal needs assessment planning (detailed a little further into this chapter) and/or without engaging a team around the SBFC client to produce a resource map. We know from survey research I and other scholars have conducted on school mental health practice that few SBFC practitioners who are employed by schools are consistently engaging in the kinds of policy-practice, needs assessment, and resource development work as part of their usual practice repertoire (Dupper et al., 2014; Kelly et al., 2016; Kelly & Lueck, 2011). Many SBFC practitioners report that caseload demands impact their ability to do this work (Kelly et al., 2015); but there are other issues embedded in our data that indicate that lack of comfort with using and applying data systematically also plays a role in many SBFC practitioners choosing to refrain from this work (Phillippo et al., 2017).

Needs Assessment and Resource Mapping: Two Crucial and Related Intervention Strategies for SBFC

These two strategies, needs assessment and resource mapping, are crucial for any SBFC practitioner who wishes to extend and deepen their work with their school-based clients, and also to build school and community capacity. The process of conducting a needs assessment can be as intensive or brief as is needed, and can involve a formal resource mapping process when it's deemed to be necessary to understand what kinds of services and interventions are already available in the school and community to help SBFC clients. Fortunately, many SBFC practitioners can also build their needs assessments into an extant public health prevention model that is firmly embedded in many schools today. There has been wide adoption in the United States of Multi-Tiered Systems of Supports (MTSS), an approach rooted in a three-tier public health prevention framework. This approach has been adapted to address academic, behavioral, and mental health issues in schools (called everything from RTI, PBIS, to now the Interconnected Systems Framework or ISF), and is now the most widely implemented, evidence-based public health strategy in American K-12 schools (Barrett, Eber, & Weist, 2013). A well-functioning MTSS allows for SBFC practitioners to identify the resource gaps within a school and community and tailor their interventions to developing those resources further. As shown in Figure 11.1, a three-tier model can be adapted well to the SBFC Meta-Model (see Figure 11.2). But to best target the resources of a school and community to

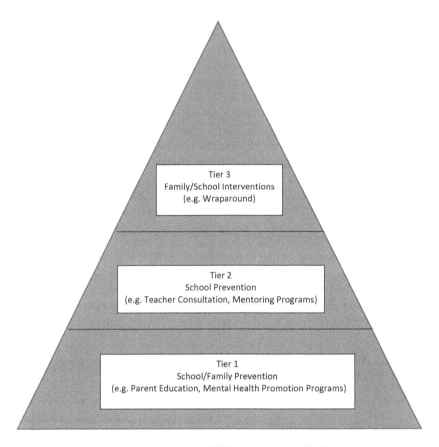

Figure 11.1 Connecting the Three-Tier MTSS Model to the SBFC Meta-Model

address the typical concerns faced by SBFC clients, SBFC practitioners have to become involved in performing needs assessments (usually including resource mapping) to make the most of the school and community resources that exist, and to identify where the resource gaps are.

Key Components of Needs Assessments and Resource Mapping

Bleyer and Joiner (2016) describe the skills involved in conducting and completing needs assessments as

> crucial … a needs assessment provides a broader context for the problems that students are experiencing … it provides school social workers (SSW) with a powerful, data-based means of customizing their roles to fit the needs of a particular school or district.
>
> (Bleyer & Joiner in Massat, Kelly, & Constable (2016), pp. 315–16).

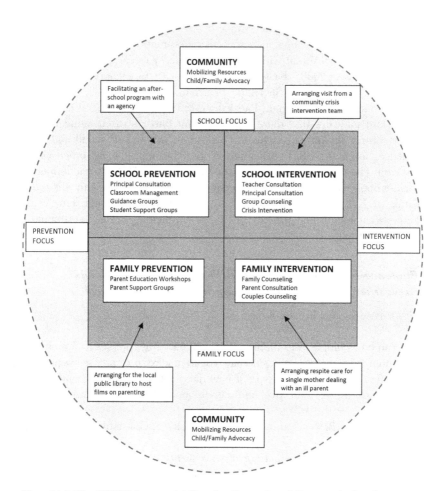

Figure 11.2 The SBFC Meta-model Showing Examples of Community Involvement
Source: Gerrard, B. & Soriano, M. (2018). The role of community intervention in school-based family counseling. *International Journal for School-Based Family Counseling*

Adelman and Taylor (2012) emphasize that having a clear map of school and community resources is essential in developing a range of learning supports that current and future SBFC clients can benefit from. At all three tiers, having data on what the school's overall social/emotional/behavioral needs are provides the SBFC practitioner with a means to tailor their services to what schools need and to measure the impact of those services. Because the quality and quantity of SBFC practitioner referrals are related to a school's overall climate and functioning, needs assessments and resource maps are also essential tools for SBFC practitioners to expand their unique contributions to schools.

However, a recent study of Ontario SSW (School of Social Work) survey data revealed that 83% of the sample (n=377, 90% response rate) reported "seldom" or "never" engaging in needs assessment activities (Kelly, under review). This is consistent with other recent survey research for school social workers (Kelly, 2008; Kelly et al., 2010, 2016), school psychologists (Newman et al., 2017; Shernoff, Bearman, & Kratochwill, 2017), and school counselors (Ockerman, Patrikakou, & Hollenbeck, 2015; Olsen et al., 2017) and indicates that there are significant barriers to engaging in these more community-based practices. To be sure, this is a new skill and set of practices for many SBFC practitioners, but the impact these practices can have on schools and on enhancing the unique role of SBFC practitioners as socio-emotional learning and prevention leaders seems worth the effort (Brake & Kelly, 2017; Kelly & Lueck, 2011). I now will detail some of the best evidence-informed practice (EIP) for conducting needs assessments in a school setting.

Evidence-Informed Practices (EIP) for Conducting Needs Assessments and Resource Mapping in School Settings

Needs Assessments in schools

> can be as simple as examining existing data, or as complex as a multiyear, multiphase study … it is generally wise to first explore and use existing data before considering any type of new data collection … analyzing existing data can be very effective, and schools generally have a wealth of data on hand.
> (Bleyer & Joiner in Massat, Kelly, & Constable (2016), p. 317).

Typically, an SBFC practitioner who wants to create a comprehensive Tier 1-level needs assessment will want to look at some tools that help to assess school functioning and climate. Additionally, the SBFC practitioner can supplement those tools with focus groups, in-depth interviews, and analyzing school-level data (often called BAG, for "Behavior, Attendance, Grades") (Barrett, Eber, & Weist, 2013). Because the process of doing needs assessment can be highly time-consuming, it's important that SBFC practitioners try to join with other interested partners in and outside the school to engage in these processes, often using a framework drawing on the principles of asset-based community development, wherein communities are invited to view their challenges through the lens of community assets and capacities, rather than deficits (Boyd et al., 2008). Those partners can assist the SBFC practitioner from the beginning in identifying the scope and depth of the needs assessment. As part of the needs assessment process, a resource map of all school and community-based resources that fit within the typical range of problems experienced by SBFC clients provides a potential treasure trove of information that the SBFC practitioner can return to again and again as they serve SBFC clients in that school or district (Adelman & Taylor, 2012). Table 11.3 shows the key components of resource mapping, using it to map out potential resources for an SBFC practitioner to help a school and community create mentoring programs for at-risk youth.

Table 11.1 shares some of the tools and strategies that SBFC practitioners can use to collect needs assessment data, and then in Table 11.2 I share some of the best practices on how to present these findings to engage the school community, as well as some of the best EIP strategies for sharing needs assessment data with schools.

Table 11.1 Needs Assessment Tools for SBFC practitioners

Tools For SSW	Type	Age Range	Social Feasibility rating (SF)	Link
Consortium on Chicago Public Schools Research Survey (5 Essentials) (Completed by all stakeholders)	A	K-12	High	https://safesupportive learning.ed.gov /survey/consortium-chicago-school-research-survey-chicago-public-schools
The Organizational Climate Description For Schools (OCDQ) for Elementary, Middle, and High Schools	A	K-12	High	www.waynekhoy. com/ocdq-re.html
REACH Survey for Schools	A	12+	Low/$$	www.search-institute.org/surveys/ REACH
School Success Profile (a suite of needs assessment tools for all grade levels and for assessing schools as a learning organization)	A	K-12	Low/$$ + Time	www.schoolsuccesson line.com/
School Survey on Crime and Safety (completed by principals)	A	K-12	High	https://nces.ed.gov/ surveys/ssocs/ques tionnaire.asp
Strengths and Difficulties Questionnaire (SDQ)	S, A	4–18	High	http://www.sdqinfo. com/

Notes: A=Assessment Tool; S=Screening Tool.
SF (Social Feasibility Rating): High (free, brief, easy-to-use, minimal training); Medium (low cost >$100, some training needed); Low (cost<$100, training needed, concerns about complexity of the tool or intervention for regular practice)

Table 11.2 Needs Assessment Steps

EIP Strategy	Sample Links to Strategy
Step 1: Identifying and Engaging the Appropriate Stakeholders	www.ideapartnership.org/usingtools/learning-together/collections.html?id=1598:sisp-tools
Step 2: Identifying Relevant Data Sources (Ideally From Multiple Perspectives and Stakeholders, Including Students, Educators, and Families)	https://tea.texas.gov/index2.aspx?id=25769811842 http://sitool.ascd.org/Default.aspx?ReturnUrl=/ www.nd.gov/dpi/uploads/1228/SpecEd PlanningGuide.pdf
Step 3: Resource Mapping	http://smhp.psych.ucla.edu/pdfdocs/resourcemapping/resourcemappingandmanagement.pdf
Step 4: Preparing Your Needs Assessment Team's Findings	Both steps have many examples of assessing needs and implementing needs assessments here at www.midwestpbis.org/interconnected-systems-framework/tools
Step 5: Implementing Your Team's Recommendations	

Sources: "Assessing school-level and district-level needs" Bleyer & Joiner in Massat, Kelly, and Constable, (2016).

Table 11.3 identifies the key components of resource mapping, going from a step-by-step process identified by Adelman and Taylor (2012) at the UCLA Center for Mental Health in Schools (2015) and using the example of the mentoring program to frame how the resource mapping can identify both assets and gaps for SBFC practitioners to address in their planning.

As can be seen from the range of tools and strategies described here, the process of needs assessment and resource mapping is one that should be carried out by the SBFC practitioner in a team, with some overarching goals established up front, including a deadline for completion. Ideally, a good needs assessment will help build the capacity of the school and community that participates in it, and also allow the SBFC practitioner to refer back to it for future clients (Bleyer & Joiner in Massat, Kelly, and Constable, 2016; Kelly, 2008). This can also form the basis of helping a school develop a community school framework, where many of the services that are identified in this process can be co-located in the school itself (Anderson-Butcher et al., 2017; Oakes, Maier, & Daniel, 2017). This needs assessment process, as valuable as it can be, is obviously also no substitute for the many informal ways in which SBFC

Table 11.3 Resource Mapping Examples

Resource Mapping Step: Building a Youth Mentoring and Family Support Program to Engage Economically Disadvantaged Families	Example
Step 1: Identify the "Who's Who" in the school and community, focusing on those who provide services related to SBFC clients and their families	Defining all the school-based mental health professionals, community providers, and lead teachers who are involved in mentoring youth (creating that circle of care)
Step 2: List the extant programs, activities, and services already available in the school and community to address SBFC client and family needs	Generating a list of the mentoring programs offered in the school and community, to build connections and minimize redundant services
Step 3: Map the financial and in-kind resources that are available to provide services within the school and community for SBFC clients and families	Learning through the mapping process that the school board has made a budget line item for mentoring program to decrease the achievement gap through mentoring programs, and that the local community Big Brothers Big Sisters of America is looking for more sites for its mentoring program.
Step 4: Coordinate and align the policies of the school and community context to the needs Identified in the initial needs assessment data	Identifying the key stakeholders (principal, superintendent, BBBS program director) who will create policies to fund and support the mentoring program; coordinating the referral and screening process with the SBFC practitioner coaching the school-based mental health professionals; creating a framework where the SBFC practitioner will provide ongoing clinical consultation for the mentors and BBBS program managers.

practitioners already access community resources for their clients, whether it's finding them temporary housing, getting them into low-cost community health services, or helping them complete paperwork for government assistance. The point of the needs assessment/resource mapping processes outlined here is to create a "resource bank" of tools, strategies, and referral sources that the SBFC practitioner can continue to rely on and develop further, and to possibly limit the need for SBFC practitioners to continually "reinvent the wheel" in finding community resources for their clients. I will now share a brief case example of how an SBFC practitioner used resource mapping and needs assessment tools to build community resources for their clients.

Community Mental Health Services Made Accessible or How to "DO Something"

Ms. Jones, the school social worker for Forest Glen Middle School, was frustrated. Her school had recently experienced a few suicide attempts by two students and the staff were spooked. While it was fortunate that neither student had completed their suicide attempt, both had taken Ms. Jones and the school community by surprise. It had shaken everyone up, leading more than one school administrator to tell her that we have to "DO something" about "these kids." Ms. Jones found herself thinking, "what can I do, what can the school do, when we don't have the resources in the community to address these kids' mental health needs?" She felt the weight of these two young people's situation, and was worried about how she might move forward to try to build better supports into the school mental health service delivery process.

In conversation with her team (the school counselor, school psychologist, and school nurse), they all agreed that the current mental health crisis protocol for their school wasn't consistent and relied too much on an individual parent's willingness to seek mental health services for their child, and their ability to pay for those services. Being in a working-class/working-poor community, the Forest Glen team had seen again and again that parents couldn't or wouldn't seek mental health services, even when kids had had a mental health emergency like these two kids had. They decided to engage in a needs assessment process, which included looking at developing a resource map for the community. They started with identifying the key stakeholders in this process (lead teachers, administration, and members of the parent-teacher organization, as well as some youth they had on their caseload who had experienced depression and anxiety) and inviting them to share their perspective on how to improve mental health referrals in the school community. These contacts revealed that most school stakeholders didn't know how to refer students who were showing signs of depression, and weren't sure what would happen after SBFC practitioners got involved. The parent teacher organization focus group indicated that there was a lot of fear and stigma still around mental health issues, but also some real concern about how families could access and pay for mental health services. The next step, identifying relevant data sources, involved applying a brief screening tool (the SDQ) for all students in the school, revealing that roughly 10% of the middle school had clinically significant scores on the SDQ which could indicate a possible risk for a mental health crisis. And looking further at nurses' visits, there was a high number of students with somatic complaints that hadn't been referred for mental health support.

Looking at those two data points (and the high caseloads of the SBFC practitioners), the group decided to next map what resources existed in the community to help the SBFC practitioners make more successful community referrals. This part of the process was illuminating, as there were a number of community agencies that had been hoping to increase their collaborations with the schools in the district. One agency had a consulting psychiatrist who told the team that she would be willing to work with the school to do additional mental health screening in the event that a student was suicidal or showing other significant mental health distress. Another agency had just received a mental health grant to provide family therapy in after-school settings and was looking for a middle school as a place to provide its low-cost SBFC. The team was energized by these contacts, and took this information to their student services director who, in collaboration with the central administration, was able to create a mental health exclusion policy whereby any family who had a youth in crisis could be referred for a psychiatric screening and referral for services that the district would pay for, and where the other community agency would provide follow-up family counseling. Ms. Jones was thrilled. In just a few months, Forest Glen had moved from being a school that was fearful and reactive to one that was willing to build meaningful and affordable community resource connections. They had truly "done something."

As this case example shows, the process of doing a needs assessment and developing a resource map doesn't require a lot of money, just time and a team to carry it out. The combination of stakeholder buy-in, good data sources, and community resources helped create a plan fairly quickly that can be easily adapted and utilized for many future SBFC clients to increase those families' ability to access and use community resources. This approach, which aligns well with Tier 1 and 2, could also be built into a Tier 3 approach of Wraparound, a teaming approach where SBFC practitioners work closely with educators, community partners, youth, and parents to build the capacity of everyone to help address a youth's struggles. I will discuss the basics of Wraparound in the next section.

Tier 3 Community Resource Development for iNtensive Client Issues: The Example of Wraparound

The Wraparound model is nothing new, having been around in some form since the 1980s (National Wraparound Initiative, 2017). Given the focus of this SBFC book, it could be argued that family-based clinicians have long been deploying some of the ideas inherent in Wraparound since family therapy first began (e.g. noting family strengths, identifying natural supports for troubled youth, creating a supportive network around a family in crisis to build their resilience). Wraparound has the crucial distinction here of being an approach that has wide empirical support (Midwest PBIS, 2017; Suter & Bruns, 2009) for helping schools and community providers help the hardest-to-reach families and youth, the very clients that many SBFC practitioners specialize in (Suter & Bruns, 2009). I detail some of the key features of the Wraparound approach here, paying specific attention to how the tools of needs assessment and resource mapping can be vital in helping a specific

SBFC practitioner client and their family. For example, a typical Wrap-around process would involve identifying key stakeholders for the SBFC client, mapping the relevant community resources, and agreeing on a plan to link those resources and providers together to better assist the young person and their family. A student who has a history of depression and anger problems could be receiving psychiatric care in the community, participating in an after-school mentoring program focused on learning social skills and practicing mindfulness, and engaging in a service learning project at their church, all in conjunction with the services provided by the SBFC practitioner.

Box 11.1 shares the best practices identified by Wraparound experts at Midwest PBIS for how a Wraparound facilitator (often referred to as a "Wrap Facilitator") can best use their skills to bring school and community resources to help school clients. Even a cursory look at this role description makes it clear how much the skills SBFC practitioners have overlap with this role. As previously noted, Wraparound is first and foremost a teaming process (Midwest PBIS, 2017) that brings together the SBFC practitioner, school staff, and other community providers in close collaboration with the family and their child to address their complex needs. It is not only case management (though good case management is part of the role of a Wrap facilitator, as I note in Box 11.1), and is not simply about putting services in place. Rather, it strives to make "family voice and choice" central to the entire planning and service delivery process. Appendix A shares a sample set of forms for how a Wrap process can be completed, starting with the initial Wrap meeting with the youth and their family. By engaging in a more personal version of a needs assessment and mapping the family, personal, school, and community resources, Wraparound helps SBFC practitioners develop community resources and work with the natural strengths of the family to create conditions for lasting change.

Box 11.1 Selecting Facilitators for Individualized Wraparound Interventions

Recommended Qualities, Attributes & Role

1) **Position in school/district allows**:
   a. Time to facilitate individualized meetings and do all preparation
   b. Flexibility to meet at unusual times (when needed) and to meet outside school (when needed)
   c. Collaboration and meetings with community agencies/resources

2) **Professional beliefs:**

   a. Families and youth need to be supported
   b. Family and youth outcomes can improve with the right support
   c. Families and youth need voice, choice and access to make improvements in quality of life
   d. When families' lives improve, their children do better in school

3) **Professional is skilled at:**

   a. Interacting positively with school staff, community service providers, students and families
   b. Effective team facilitation
   c. Time management
   d. Staying solution-focused
   e. Supporting all members to give input
   f. Maintaining a "safe" environment (no blaming, no shaming)
   g. Self-initiating activities (and is highly motivated)
   h. Knowing community agencies/resources

4) **Role description:**

   a. Assist Systems Planning Team in identifying youth in need of support
   b. Begin conversations with families and youth
   c. Assist in building individualized teams and have conversations with team members about the individualized process
   d. Begin gathering baseline data
   e. Schedule first team meetings
   f. Keep all team meetings focused on strengths, needs, and action planning
   g. Input and track data regularly (before/after each individualized meeting)
   h. Assure that team meetings continue to happen at least every two weeks in the beginning, phasing to monthly as improvements are noted
   i. Use data to progress-monitor students weekly to assess response to intervention/support

Multicultural Counseling Considerations

It likely goes without saying that no good needs assessment, whether it's of a school and surrounding community, or an individual family, can be failsafe. The challenge with thinking about multicultural counseling here is that there are so many different directions in which to look that I choose to frame it around a more broad idea of anti-oppressive practice (AOP) in human services, particularly given that so many SBFC clients are themselves subject to a variety of oppressive systems in their day-to-day travels. I excerpt a lengthy but potent quote here to help clarify what AOP is and what it might mean to SBFC practitioners and their developing community resources:

> The theoretical rationale for an anti-oppressive transformation of social services may include developing non-hierarchical work relations between clients and social workers, promoting social rights, adopting structural and contextualised views of clients' social problems and developing client representation. In addition, the rationale includes responding to social, class, gender and ethnic diversity, acknowledging unequal power relations with clients, creating a non-bureaucratic organisational culture, developing alliances with clients and critical consciousness among clients and workers, as well as promoting reflexivity between workers and clients.
>
> (Strier & Binyamin, 2013, p. 3)

As with all the interventions and tools summarized here in this chapter, there is a high level of EIP on offer, but these EIP tools are neither an exhaustive list of EIPs nor a completely sufficient one. Part of the reason for this is related to the quote above about AOP: AOP is far from being realized in our schools and communities, and within the framework of mental health treatment itself more broadly. The nature of engaging in EIP calls us to carefully examine all the interventions and tools we choose to use for how they do (or don't) fit within the "social, class, gender, and ethnic diversity" of our SBFC clients and their families. To be sure, none of the EIP noted in this chapter has been shown to be harmful to any specific population that SBFC practitioners serve; but saying that alone is no guarantee that these strategies are going to be acceptable to the specific client sitting in front of us. The hard work of doing AOP in applying EIP is ahead of all of us in assessing the needs of our schools, communities, and families. For example, the very real issue of stigma and mental illness is not one that can be simply waved away by having a great referral process; SBFC practitioners need to have the skills to engage diverse families around their beliefs about mental illness and to identify culturally responsive ways to encourage families to understand mental health problems and to seek help for them. In many ways, the location of many SBFC practitioners (in schools) is itself a strength of developing a meaningful approach to AOP: families are more likely to identify known adults in their child's lives, i.e. educators, as ones that they will trust with their family secrets and struggles, and SBFC practitioners can build on their location in the schools to foster a sense of trust that allows families to access the services they need.

Conclusion: Challenges and Solutions

I hope I've made clear in this chapter how vital the process of developing community resources through careful, systematic processes can be in enhancing your SBFC practitioner practice. Threaded throughout this chapter though, is the very real and serious issue I referred to at the start: namely, how few SBFC practitioners are doing this work, as described here. A recent secondary data analysis of 2013 SSW survey data my team did showed that roughly 17% of a national sample of SSW (n=3,769) were practicing in the community-based, prevention-oriented ways that we've discussed in this chapter (Thompson, Frey, & Kelly, under review). Many others in our sample (and in other surveys of other SBFC practitioners) do some of this work some of the time, if they can find the time. This issue of time can't be overstated; without a clear focus on making the time at the start of a school year with a school-level needs assessment team (or at an initial intake session with a family), this kind of community resource work simply won't happen in a consistent and replicable way. Doing good needs assessment work takes time and planning; having a real Wraparound process takes time, will, and money from the school and related stakeholders. Without those commitments up front, many of the great EIP strategies delineated here won't become reality for most SBFC practitioners. Still, the rewards for approaching our work in schools in this way are significant, and having found an SBFC practitioner team to do this work remains one of my most valuable experiences as a practitioner.

Resources

Needs Assessment Resources

Midwest PBIS
The leading three-tier PBIS/MTSS training group in the U.S., with a site containing a wide range of free EIP tools for use for Tier 2, student social and emotional regulation skill development, needs assessment, and professional development work; they are also vital members of our PLC Project's Advisory Board! www.midwestpbis.org/home

School Climate Survey Compendia
A great reference guide to school climate surveys in the U.S. https://safesupportive learning.ed.gov/topic-research/school-climate-measurement/school-climate-survey-compendium

SMH ASSIST
The site where a lot of good resources for our toolkits has originated, including ideas for how to assess the needs of your schools and deliver EI) https://smh-assist.ca/

UCLA Center for School Mental Health in Schools
A detailed guide to using resource mapping to create a working needs assessment to address a variety of social/emotional/behavioral needs in schools http://smhp.psych.ucla.edu/pdfdocs/resourcemapping/resourcemappingandmanagement.pdf

EIP Resources Consulted (Books and Monographs)

Barrett, S., Eber, L., & Weist, M. (2013). Advancing education effectiveness: Interconnecting school mental health and school-wide positive behavior support. Center for School Mental Health. Retrieved from www.pbis.org/school/school-mental-health/interconnected-systemsLots of good templates and strategies to use across all the Core SSW Services.Corcoran, K., & Fischer, J. (2013). *Measures for Clinical Practice and Research, Volume 1: Couples, Families, and Children.* Oxford, UK: Oxford University Press.A range of free and/or low-cost rapid assessment instruments to use to screen and assess students.Franklin, C., Harris, M. B., & Allen-Meares, P. (Eds.). (2012). *The School Services Sourcebook: A Guide for School-Based Professionals.* Oxford, UK: Oxford University Press. *Seventy-three chapters on EIP-related SSW topics, written by leading SMH scholars.*Harrison, J. R., Schultz, B. K., & Evans, S. W. (Eds.). (2017). *School Mental Health Services for Adolescents.* Oxford, UK: Oxford University Press. *A strong focus on EIP for adolescent school mental health issues.*Kelly, M. S., Raines, J. C., Stone, S., & Frey, A. (2010). *School Social Work: An Evidence-Informed Framework for Practice.* Oxford, UK: Oxford University Press. *Provides a critical review of the best available EIP for some key domains of SSW practice identified in the authors' 2008 National SSW Survey, many of which are relevant to the current Ontario PLC Project.*Kelly, M. S. (2008). *The Domains and Demands of School Social Work Practice: A Guide to Working Effectively with Students, Families and Schools.* Oxford, UK: Oxford University Press. Offers some step-by-step ideas about how to "do" EIP in a real-world school setting, with lots of practice examples from the author's time as a SSW in the Chicago area.Massat, C. R., Kelly, M., & Constable, R. T. (2016). *School Social Work: Practice, Policy, & Research* (8th Ed.). Oxford University Press. *The foundational guide for SSW for 40+ years; the 36 chapters and appendices provide a range of EIP for all 12 of the Key Domains and Core SSW Services identified by the Ontario SSW PLC Project.*

EIP Resources Consulted (Websites)

Blueprints for Healthy Youth Development
A well-curated EBP site that provides specific information and ratings on programs to address youth risk and resilience factors in school and community settings. www.blueprintsprograms.com/search

California Evidence-Based Clearinghouse for Child Welfare
While focused on child welfare, there are a number of programs and interventions for which this site provides detailed appraisal and which relate to SSW practice. www.cebc4cw.org/home/

Campbell Collaboration
An international repository of systematic reviews on mental health and social work topics, including several that are pertinent to the Key Domains/Core Services of SSW Practice. www.campbellcollaboration.org/

Bibliography

Adelman, H., & Taylor, L. (2012). Mapping a school's resources to improve their use in preventing and ameliorating problems. In C. Franklin, M. B. Harris, & P. Allen-Meares (Eds.). *The School Services Sourcebook*. New York, NY: Oxford University Press, pp. 977–990.

Anderson-Butcher, D., Paluta, L., Sterling, K., & Anderson, C. (2017). Ensuring healthy youth development through community schools: A case study. *Children & Schools*, 40(1), 7–16.

Barrett, S., Eber, L., & Weist, M. (2013). Advancing education effectiveness: Inter-connecting school mental health and school-wide positive behavior support. Center for School Mental Health. Retrieved from www.pbis.org/school/school-mental-health/interconnected-systems

Bleyer, L.R., & Joiner, K. (2016). Needs assessment: A tool of policy-practice in school social work. In C. R. Massat, M. Kelly, & R. T. Constable (Eds.). *School Social Work: Practice, Policy, & Research* (8th Ed.). Oxford, UK: Oxford University Press, pp. 320–345

Boyd, C. P., Hayes, L., Wilson, R. L., & Bearsley-Smith, C. (2008). Harnessing the social capital of rural communities for youth mental health: Asset-based community development framework. *Australian Journal of Rural Health*, 16(4), 189–193.

Brake, A., & Kelly, M.S. (2017). New directions in leadership? Early lessons from Chicago's school social work professional learning community project (Project Monograph, Northeastern Illinois University).

Dadaczynski, K., & Paulus, P. (2015). Healthy principals—healthy schools? A neglected perspective to school health promotion. In V. Simovska and P. McNamara (Eds.) *Schools for Health and Sustainability* (pp. 253–273). New York, NY: Springer Netherlands.

Dupper, D. R., Rocha, C., Jackson, R. F., & Lodato, G. A. (2014). Broadly trained but narrowly used? Factors that predict the performance of environmental versus individual tasks by school social workers. *Children & Schools*, 36(2), 71–77.

Franklin, C., Harris, M. B., & Allen-Meares, P. (Eds.). (2012). *The School Services Sourcebook: A Guide for School-Based Professionals*. Oxford, UK: Oxford University Press

Gerrard, B. & Soriano, M. (2018). The role of community intervention in school-based family counselling. *International Journal for School-Based Family Counseling*, 10, 1–11.

Green, G. P., & Haines, A. (2015). *Asset Building & Community Development*. Thousand Oaks, CA: Sage publications.

Huebner, A. J., Mancini, J. A., Bowen, G. L., & Orthner, D. K. (2009). Shadowed by war: Building community capacity to support military families. *Family Relations*, 58(2), 216–228.

Kelly, M. S. (2008). *The Domains and Demands of School Social Work Practice: A Guide to Working Effectively with Students, Families and Schools*. New York, NY: Oxford University Press.

Kelly, M. S. School social work in Canada: Results from a province-wide survey. Manuscript under review.

Kelly, M. S., Berzin, S. C., Frey, A., Alvarez, M., Shaffer, G., & O'Brien, K. (2010). The state of school social work: Findings from the National School Social Work Survey. *School Mental Health*, 2(3), 132–141.

Kelly, M. S., Frey, A., Thompson, A., Klemp, H., Alvarez, M., & Berzin, S. C. (2016). Assessing the National School Social Work practice model: Findings from the second National School Social Work Survey. *Social Work*, 61(1), 17.

Kelly, M. S., & Lueck, C. (2011). Adopting a data-driven public health framework in schools: Results from a multi-disciplinary survey on school-based mental health practice. *Advances in School Mental Health Promotion*, 4(4), 5–12.

Kelly, M. S., Thompson, A. M., Frey, A., Klemp, H., Alvarez, M., & Berzin, S. C. (2015). The state of school social work: Revisited. *School Mental Health*, 7(3), 174–183.

Kim, J. S., Kelly, M. S., & Franklin, C. (2017). *Solution-Focused Brief Therapy in Schools: A 360-Degree View of Research and Practice* (2nd Ed.) New York, NY: Oxford University Press.

Massat, C. R., Kelly, M., & Constable, R. T. (2016). *School Social Work: Practice, Policy, & Research* (8th Ed.). New York, NY: Oxford University Press.

MIdwest PBIS. (2017). Training materials for wrap-around person-centered planning. Retrieved from http://www.midwestpbis.org/materials/wraparound

National Wraparound Initiative. (2017). Wraparound basics. Retrieved from https://nwi.pdx.edu/wraparound-basics/

Newman, D. S., Hazel, C. E., Barrett, C. A., Chaudhuri, S. D., & Fetterman, H. (2017). Early-career school psychologists' perceptions of consultative service delivery: The more things change, the more they stay the same. *Journal of Educational and Psychological Consultation*, 28(2), 105–136.

Oakes, J., Maier, A., & Daniel, J. (2017, June 5th). Community schools: An evidence-based strategy for equitable school improvement. Retrieved from https://learningpolicyinstitute.org/product/community-schools-equitable-improvement-brief

Ockerman, M. S., Patrikakou, E., & Hollenbeck, A. F. (2015). Preparation of school counselors and response to intervention: A profession at the crossroads. *Journal of Counselor Preparation and Supervision*, 7(3), 105–136.

Olsen, J., Parikh-Foxx, S., Flowers, C., & Algozzine, B. (2017). An examination of factors that relate to school counselors' knowledge and skills in multi-tiered systems of support (Featured Research). *Professional School Counseling*, 20(1), 159–171.

Owens, J. S., Lyon, A. R., Brandt, N. E., Warner, C. M., Nadeem, E., Spiel, C., & Wagner, M. (2014). Implementation science in school mental health: Key constructs in a developing research agenda. *School Mental Health*, 6(2), 99–111.

Phillippo, K. L., Kelly, M. S., Shayman, E., & Frey, A. (2017). School social worker practice decisions: The impact of professional models, training, and school context. *Families in Society: The Journal of Contemporary Social Services*, 98(4), 275–283.

Shernoff, E. S., Bearman, S. K., & Kratochwill, T. R. (2017). Training the next generation of school psychologists to deliver evidence-based mental health practices: current challenges and future directions. *School Psychology Review*, 46(2), 219–232.

Strier, R., & Binyamin, S. (2013). Introducing anti-oppressive social work practices in public services: Rhetoric to practice. *The British Journal of Social Work*, 44(8), 2095–2112.

Suter, J.C., & Bruns, E.J. (2009). Effects of Wraparound from a meta-analysis of controlled studies. *Clinical Child and Family Psychology Review*, 12, 336–351.

Thompson, A., Frey, A., & Kelly, M. S. A latent profile analysis of school social work ecological practice. *School Mental Health*, 11(1), 129–140.

Appendix A

Sample Wraparound Forms, including the Wraparound Action Plan Form (Shared with permission from Midwest PBIS)

INITIAL MEETING WITH CHILD AND FAMILY

Pre-Meeting Preparation
Meeting goals for Wrap Facilitator: BUILD TRUST - GATHER INFORMA-TION - EDUCATE - PREPARE

1. Are my talking points in order?

    *   Can I clearly define my role as a school employee and Wraparound Facilitator (WF)?
    *   Can I clearly describe PBIS and how wraparound fits in the continuum?
    *   Can I clearly explain that wraparound is a process defined by 10 principles and implemented in 4 phases?
    *   Do I have literature on wraparound, blank copy of SNP, Student Disposition Tool, Education Information Tool, and Home School Community Tool?

2. Meeting should be approximately 60–90 minutes.

    *   It may take two meetings to gather information to address action steps.
    *   Don't rush the meeting. If family appears preoccupied or over-whelmed, it is OK to stop and arrange to meet again.
    *   If family is in crisis, offer assistance/support/direction. Do not leave without addressing child safety concerns.

3. Explain that wrap is different than any school meeting they have been a part of in the past.

    *   Wraparound is NOT a continuation of their child's IEP.
    *   Be prepared to give specific examples of how wraparound is different.

4. The conversation should feel like a "coffee chat," rather than a psycho-social, check-the-box assessment.

    *   While talking with the family, listen for what is said around their strengths, needs and culture.
    *   If needed, utilize the "Coffee Chat Questions" document to help guide conversation.

5. Explain that participation in wraparound is voluntary. If family decides to not participate or drops out during the process, there will be no repercussions (a family deciding to not participate in wraparound does not mean we stop engaging).
6. Have available copies of required consent or confidentiality forms for family signature.
7. Explain that wraparound is a "transparent" process.

   - Family will be able to review and approve all notes, documents and forms.
   - Family will have final voice on action plan items and interventions.
   - Decisions about the student and family will not be made outside the meetings.
   - You will never offend a family by asking for their opinion, approval or permission.

NOT ABOUT ME – WITHOUT ME

8. Make sure to schedule a follow-up meeting with the family, within 3–5 days.

"Helping Students & Families Learn the Skills to Manage their Needs"
Wraparound Observation Form

INITIAL MEETING WITH CHILD & FAMILY

Wraparound Facilitator: _____ Date: _____

Reviewer: _____

ACTION STEP	*In place/ Not in Place*	*COMMENT*
1. Wraparound Facilitator (WF) introduces self, defines their role as a school employee, provides a brief overview of PBIS and introduces wraparound.		
2. WF describes how wraparound could be used to help the family address challenges they may be experiencing.		
3. WF engages the family in a "coffee chat" type conversation, answering questions the family may have about wraparound, the role of a WF and the wrap team.		
4. WF explains that participation in wraparound is voluntary and helps the youth and family decide if wraparound is a good fit for them.		

ACTION STEP	In place/ Not in Place	COMMENT
5. WF explains confidentiality (gets release of information signed if needed) and their role as a mandated reporter.		
6. WF asks child and family about any urgent situations that need to be addressed. If yes, discuss short-term solutions.		
7. WF ensures that the family has the ability and resources needed to address current crisis.		
8. WF answers all final questions the child and family may have and schedules a follow up meeting within 3–5 days.		

Adapted with permission from John VanDenBerg

INITIAL MEETING WITH CHILD AND FAMILY
Post-Meeting Tasks

1. Immediately after the meeting, revise list of:

   - Strengths identified during coffee chat with child & family
   - Needs identified with child & family
   - Potential team members, current service providers and natural supports
   - Culture aspects unique to child and family

2. Review and organize notes, identify domains that need to be discussed in follow-up meeting(s) with family. Begin preparation for next meeting.
3. SIMEO* documents to complete afterwards & after each additional coffee chat

   - Begin *draft* SD-T. Review w/family at next meeting. Enter in SIMEO when competed
   - Begin *draft* HSC. Review w/family at next meeting. Enter in SIMEO when completed
   - With teacher(s) assistance, begin Education tool. Enter in SIMEO after reviewed w/family
   - Develop a *draft* Strengths Needs Profile

4. Complete all tasks you may have agreed to do in the meeting, i.e. send family additional information about wraparound, contact current service provider.

- The easiest way to "lose" a family is to not complete a task you agreed to do

At least 1–3 follow-up coffee chats with the child and family during the engagement phase will occur. Remember the goals of each coffee chat: build a trusting relationship, continue gathering information in each of the life domains, educate family (and in time the team) about the wraparound process, and begin preparing the family for their first Team meeting.

"Helping Students & Families Learn the Skills to Manage their Needs"

****

* Note: the tools referred to in this appendix are part of a suite of assessment and benchmarking tools Systematic Information Management for Educational Outcomes (SIMEO) to help with the Wraparound assessment and service delivery process. Specific tools referred to here include: SD-T (student disposition tool, collecting demographic information), HSC (home/school/community tool), and Education tool (collecting student performance data on academics and behavior). For more information on these assessments and the whole suite of SIMEO tools, please go to www.pbis.org/evaluation/evaluation-tools

12 How to Overcome Barriers to SBFC

Danielle C. Swick, Joelle D. Powers, and Caroline Doyle

__Overview__: In order to support students' socio-emotional, behavioral, and academic needs, School-Based Family Counseling (SBFC) practitioners need to consider and address the effect that the family can have on children's functioning (Gerrard, 2008; Negreiros & Miller, 2014; Valdez, Carlson, & Zanger, 2005). The SBFC framework is an integrated approach to mental health intervention that focuses on involving both the school and family in order to help children overcome personal challenges and be successful in school (Evans & Carter, 1997; Gerrard, 2008; Gerrard & Soriano, 2013). However, there are often challenges with implementing SBFC. In this chapter, we identify common school-level, family-level, and inter-professional barriers to successfully implementing SBFC, and offer several strategies and practical advice for how to overcome these barriers.

School-level Barriers to SBFC

There are a number of school-level barriers that may prevent the successful implementation of the SBFC model. First, there is a shortage of qualified professionals in the school system, resulting in heavy caseloads. For example, the National Association of School Psychologists (2010) recommends a ratio of one school psychologist for every 1,000 students and when school psychologists are providing comprehensive and preventive services (as in the SBFC model), NASP recommends that the ratio not exceed 500 to 700 students for every school psychologist. However, the current student-school psychologist ratio in the United States far exceeds this number at 1,381 students per one school psychologist (NASP, 2017). The American School Counselor Association recommends a ratio of one school counselor for every 250 students (ASCA, 2018). However, as with the national shortage of school psychologists, the actual national average student-to-school staff ratio is almost doubled at 1 school counselor per 482 students (ASCA, 2014).

Second, even when there are qualified professionals present in the school district, they are not necessarily trained in the SBFC model. Mental health professionals practicing from an SBFC framework must have a specific setup of specialized skills. As a foundation, they should be trained in family systems approaches (Ehrhardt-Padgett, Hatzichristou, Kitson, & Meyers, 2004; Star, 2010). While the American School Counselor Code of Ethics (2016) suggests a family systems training paradigm for counselor education programs, data show that over half (51.9%) of all school counselors are not required to take a course in family counseling or systems theory (Perusse, Goodnough, & Noel, 2001). Professionals implementing SBFC should also have a solid understanding of the structure and organization of schools (Ehrhardt-Padgett, Hatzichristou, Kitson, & Meyers, 2004; Star, 2010). Additionally, they need to be competent in interacting with families and partnering with them to keep them actively engaged. Unfortunately, research indicates that less than half of counselors (49% of high school and 39% of middle school counselors) report knowing how to implement interventions in ways that keep students' parents and families actively involved (College Board Advocacy & Policy Center National Office for School Counselor Advocacy, 2012). Further, professionals should be trained in delivering services from an evidence-based practice approach and in a culturally competent manner (Ehrhardt-Padgett, Hatzichristou, Kitson, & Meyers, 2004; Gerrard, 2008).

Third, many school staff lack mental health awareness (Froese-Germain & Riel, 2012). Classroom teachers play an important role in promotion of mental health for youth because they are on the front line to detect problems early and make referrals that connect students with SBFC services (Jorm, Kitchener, Sawyer, Scales, & Cvetkovski, 2010; Loades & Mastroyannopou-lou, 2010; Rothi, Leavey, & Best, 2008). However, without adequate education and training, teachers are less likely to have the capacity to detect early warning signs or recognize symptoms of mental illness in students. Teacher pre-service education programs currently provide little to no preparation for adequately instructing and meeting the unique needs of vulnerable students with mental health problems (Koller & Bertel, 2006; Rones & Hoagwood, 2000). Therefore, it is not surprising that many teachers perceive themselves as inadequately prepared to support students with these challenges (Rothi, Leavey, & Best, 2008). A survey of teacher attitudes toward mental health services in schools found that a large majority of teachers recognized the need for mental health services and felt that it should be the school's role to offer such services, but only 4% strongly agreed with the statement that they had the knowledge and skills to meet their students' mental health needs (Reinke, Stormont, Herman, Puri, & Goel, 2011). In another study, school counselors were asked how they would define mental health awareness at their school and 20 of them responded that it was average while only one thought it was excellent and six thought it was poor (Bain, Rueda, Mata-Villarreal, & Mundy, 2011). Teachers and administrators have identified their own lack of information and training as one of the most significant obstacles preventing students from receiving appropriate mental health services in schools (Short, Weist, Manion, & Evans, 2012; Walter et al., 2011; Walter, Gouze, & Lim, 2006). Educators not only recognize their lack of training, but also have expressed an explicit desire to become more informed about child mental health. When asked to identify topics on which they desired further training, the second most common answer among teachers in one study was recognizing and understanding mental health needs in students (Reinke, Stormont, Herman, Puri, & Goel, 2011).

A final barrier to implementing SBFC is potential resistance from school administrators. The roles and functions of mental health professionals at schools may vary widely, depending on the expectations of the school administrators (Negreiros & Miller, 2014). Unfortunately, there are often competing priorities in schools, such as the increased pressure to focus on academics to meet accountability demands of legislation (Short, Weist, Manion, & Evans, 2012). Therefore, school district administrators may not place value on school professionals implementing SBFC if the school prioritizes testing over addressing students' mental health needs and implementing prevention and intervention services.

Strategies for Overcoming School-level Barriers to SBFC

Below are several suggestions, based on the literature, for SBFC practitioners on how to overcome school-level barriers to SBFC.

1 Seek Out Outside Training Opportunities

Qualified professionals who would like to engage in SBFC, but do not feel adequately prepared to do so, should seek out outside training opportunities to become well-versed in the SBFC model. This could include taking additional counseling courses (e.g., on family counseling or family systems theory) through universities' mental health departments (e.g., school counseling, counseling psychology, counseling and educational development, and social work) and attending annual and summer conferences (NASP, 2011). SBFC practitioners should ask their principals to financially support these efforts since these learning opportunities are part of their professional development.

2 Have Staff Development / On-site school Trainings

Schools should have staff development/on-site school trainings related to mental health, behavior management, and partnering with parents. There are several examples in the literature on how this can be done. One example is when a school brought in university experts to deliver a two-hour professional development workshop to school staff (Powers, Wegmann, Blackman, & Swick, 2014). The training was designed to provide information on seven of the most common mental health disorders among children, including prevalence, symptoms, and diagnostic criteria to counter misconceptions about the disorders, increase factual knowledge, and give school staff the basic knowledge necessary to facilitate referrals to school-based mental health services. The short- and long-term consequences of untreated mental health disorders in children were discussed, as was information about common barriers that can prevent families from accessing consistent, quality mental health care. Ultimately, the training was effective in increasing school staff members' knowledge of the signs and symptoms of common childhood mental health disorders.

Another example of training is when SBFC personnel (e.g., counselor or psychologist) provided a training to teachers in both behavior management and in how to effectively partner with parents (Carter & Evans, 2008). The first session provided teachers with positive strategies for managing challenging behaviors in the classroom. The second session focused on how to develop more effective partnerships with parents in order to improve student learning. Trainings similar to this one and the one discussed above could be feasibly implemented on-site at schools at minimum cost.

3 Advocate for the Importance of SBFC

SBFC practitioners should advocate at multiple levels for the importance and effectiveness of SBFC. At the school level, school staff should continuously discuss in staff meetings the importance and positive impacts of family-school partnerships (Negreiros & Miller, 2014). School administrators and other school staff may be unaware of what SBFC is and its value – SBFC practitioners must educate individuals on what SBFC entails and how it can be effective. School mental health professionals should also advocate to expand their roles by assisting in coordinating parent-teacher organizations, provide workshops to school staff on home-school partnerships and to families on parenting skills or home interventions that address behavior and academic issues (Negreiros & Miller, 2014).

SBFC practitioners should also advocate to the school board and their county commissioners for the importance of SBFC. Again, these individuals may never have heard the term SBFC before. Therefore, it is important that SBFC practitioners educate these individuals about the components of SBFC and how it can be of value to schools, families, and communities. Advocacy can take the form of a simple letter to a county commissioner or asking to speak at a school board meeting.

4 Utilize Undergraduate and Graduate Interns

SBFC practitioners may already spend a large portion of their time on testing students during the assessment process. If there are colleges or universities near the school that have counseling programs, one alternative might be to utilize undergraduate and graduate interns to assist with this process (Negreiros & Miller, 2014). In one study, when school counselors were asked whether they thought that having a graduate counseling intern could be beneficial in helping the school provide mental health services to students, 96% of the counselors who responded agreed (Bain, Rueda, Mata-Villarreal, & Mundy, 2011). If undergraduate and graduate students are receiving training in their programs on administering tests (without interpreting the results), they could assist SBFC practitioners with the assessment process, so that SBFC practitioners could focus more of their time on intervention and partnering with families and the larger community (Negreiros & Miller, 2014).

5 Demand Adequate Space

SBFC is an intensive process that involves meeting with students, teachers, and families on an ongoing basis. These meetings often involve discussions around sensitive and confidential matters. Additionally, it is important that families feel welcomed and comfortable in the space where these discussions take place. Given these considerations, it is important that SBFC practitioners demand from their school administrators that they are provided with a family-friendly and private space to meet with students, teachers, and families (Negreiros & Miller, 2014). The space does not need to be big, but it does need to be enclosed so that families can openly share their thoughts without worrying that someone will overhear them. Additionally, SBFC practitioners should think about putting bright and inviting pictures on the walls and/or having a few toys in the room for younger siblings to play with if families need to bring their other children along to the meetings.

6 Seek Grant Funding from Private Foundations or Collaborate with Local Universities for Funding Opportunities

If a school does not have the necessary resources to effectively implement the SBFC model, the SBFC practitioner should think about seeking grant funding to bring in additional resources to the school. There may be local, state, or national private foundations that may be interested in funding initiatives around education and/or mental health. An SBFC practitioner could also collaborate with a local university to pursue a funding opportunity. In this instance, the university members could use their expertise in grant-writing to help write the grant and get funds for the school. A great example of this is a partnership that developed between an urban school district in the southeastern United States and a university (Powers & Swick, 2017; Powers, Swick, Sneed, & Wegmann, 2016; Swick & Powers, 2016; Swick, Powers, Wegmann, & Watkins, 2015; Wegmann, Powers, Swick, & Watkins, 2017). This partnership began when a university member and school district wrote a grant together to obtain $75,000 to pilot-test an SBFC program in one school. At the time, the university was funding innovative university-community partnerships. After the first year, the school district decided not only to assume the majority of the funding for the partnership, but also to expand the program to six additional schools.

Family-level Barriers to SBFC

Since children spend more of their waking hours at school than they do at home, the school setting offers an ideal place for prevention, intervention, positive development, and communication between the school and family (Nealis, 2016). The SBFC approach seeks to fulfill this need for communication and collaboration between the family and the school, focusing on the strengths of both and eliciting the need for the parent's input in developing ways for their child to succeed academically. The task of the SBFC practitioner is to cultivate an atmosphere of mutual understanding and support between teacher and parent to collaboratively find new strategies for dealing with their child's behavioral and/or emotional problems. In order to effectively carry out this task it is critically imperative to know the barriers that keep families from accessing SBFC and school-based mental health in general. Once we know what may be keeping families from seeking services, then we can design an approach to help mitigate or breakdown those barriers.

One barrier to obtaining family involvement in SBFC is that families often do not understand the link between what's happening at home and how that impacts their child's academic and social success at school. This connection is often not clearly explained to parents by school personnel (e.g., teachers and school mental health professionals). The less that is explained to them about how important their involvement is and how family factors influence their child's performance at school, the more hesitant parents will be to access SBFC services and school-based mental health services in general (Evans & Carter, 1997). Other barriers to parents accessing school-based mental health services include fear of stigma, lack of awareness, lack of school resources, affordability, accessibility, language barriers, conflicts with time and work, lack of childcare, perceptions of school psychology as ineffective, concerns about confidentiality, mistrust in providers, and child's unwillingness to go.

Ohan, Seward, Stallman, Bayliss, and Sanders' (2015) identified the types of barriers parents of elementary school children perceive when seeking help from a school psychologist and the frequency with which they were reported over a 10-month period. Barriers most frequently reported by both groups were concerns of stigma, belief the school or school psychologist lacked the resources to deal with their child's problem, beliefs the school psychologist was ineffective or unhelpful, and concerns over confidentiality within the school setting. In regard to stigma, the themes that emerged from both groups were the fears of being blamed, labelled, and treated differently. Of specific concern to parents was teachers' stigma directed towards the child and fear their child would be diagnostically labelled or put in a "box." Lastly, a small number of the parents held the belief that no outside help was needed for their child and viewed their child's problem as a developmental stage or that their own efforts would remedy the problem. This belief was reported more by the group of parents who had concerns about their child's behavioral/emotional issues than those who did not have concerns. Also notable was that the parents who reported they would readily seek the school psychologist also expressed having a good relationship with school staff and felt confident in approaching them (Ohan, Seward, Stallman, Bayliss, & Sanders, 2015).

In addition to stigma, lack of knowledge about and awareness of services is another family-level barrier. The Foundation for People with Learning Disabilities (2002) found there were two kinds of knowledge barriers keeping families from accessing mental health services in general. These were: (1) parents were unsure about how to seek mental health services and (2) parents who lacked knowledge of exactly what services were available to them. More specifically, families did not know what their treatment options were and the referral routes needed to access those services (Foundation for People with Learning Disabilities, 2002). These barriers were notably significant for certain minority and ethnic groups, particularly for those whose primary language was not English (Sin, Francis, & Cook, 2010).

Language, cultural barriers, and lack of diversity within schools also keep parents from connecting with services. According to an article titled, *Engaging Youth and Families in Mental Health Services,*

> both nationally and locally, Asian American youth continue to be most under-represented in the children's mental health system and to have unmet mental health needs. Parents of Asian descent are less likely to identify their children as having a mental health concern.
>
> (Ferris, Hane, & Wagoner, 2014, p. 2)

Some ethnic groups think of mental health in terms that are more somatic, describing their symptoms as physical, such as a stomachache or headache, which makes mental illness difficult to identify. Refugee children, who have faced the horrors of war, poverty, culture shock, discrimination, and other challenges are especially at risk of being overlooked. Because of this, teachers and parents may not know the child has a mental health concern. In many cultures such as the American Indian culture and in new immigrant or refugee communities, the parents will seek advice from elders or traditional healers before seeking mental health services. Southeast Asian families support the clan, and traditional healing methods are sought before or along with Western mental health services. Additionally, many Asian cultures believe it is not appropriate to share mental health issues with outsiders (Ferris, Hane, & Wagoner, 2014).

There has been some research that has specifically looked at what students see as barriers to accessing services. One study compared high schoolers' perceptions of stigma as a barrier to seeking school-based mental health services with service providers' perceptions of stigma as a barrier (Bowers, Manion, Papadopoulos, & Gauvreau, 2013). A larger number of young people versus providers reported stigma as the biggest barrier to accessing services. The second most common barrier reported by young people with a mental health concern was not knowing where to go for help. Those without mental health concerns ranked peer pressure and not knowing one has a problem as the second most common barrier. What needs to be stressed here is that both of these barriers, *not knowing where to go* and *not knowing one has a problem*, stem from a lack of mental health literacy not just within the schools but within the community as well (Bowers, Manion, Papadopoulos, & Gauvreau, 2013).

Health literacy in general is a real issue in our society and this is true within the mental health arena as well. In fact, knowledge about mental health helps to dispel other barriers such as stigma and discrimination and gives a person more control over their mental disorder. Possessing mental health literacy builds resilience, encourages positive lifestyle change, empowers individuals (families and children) to effectively manage their condition, reduces the burden on the mental health and social care services and reduces mental health inequalities (Mental Health Literacy: Mental Health Foundation, n.d.). A lack of mental health literacy amongst health and social care staff, as well as teachers and educators, can lead to misunderstandings and discrimination towards those suffering with mental health problems and act as a barrier keeping families from seeking services for their children, whether they be school-based mental health services or mental health services in general.

Strategies for Overcoming Family-level Barriers to SBFC

Below is a list of suggestions for breaking down some of the barriers mentioned above and possible strategies for implementing them. Some of these strategies, specifically literacy, overlap and serve to dispel or lessen more than one barrier.

1 Train Teachers (not just school mental health professionals) in Family Systems Theory and Mental Health as Part of Early Childhood Education

Carter and Evans (2008) discuss how they train teachers to develop more effective partnerships with parents. To build these partnerships, teachers were trained to focus on what might be going on at home with a family in order to understand the situation versus engaging in the "parent-bashing" that often occurs when teachers are frustrated (Carter & Evans, 2008). Since teachers are usually the first ones to recognize behavioral and/or emotional problems with a child in the classroom, it becomes even more important to know how to approach the family regarding these matters. Because family systems theory is a complex and extensive training it needs to begin with university curricula. Although the SBFC model can and does implement this approach, starting at the university level would provide more extensive training for teachers and provide schools with teachers already trained in this theory. Seeing the bigger picture of what causes mental illnesses and how families are impacted by them would be beneficial to both the teacher and the family. Having a knowledge base about family systems would also give them the "language" tools needed to effectively discuss issues with parents involving their child's behavioral and emotional problems (Christian, 2006). This would greatly enhance mental health resources within the school system as a whole and possibly make parents more receptive to accessing school-based mental health services for their child.

2 Integrate Mental Health Literacy as Part of the Curriculum Within the School System

Implement mental health literacy into the curriculum that is culturally competent and caters to the needs of all students. Making it part of the learning process in every classroom early on would help dispel stigma, and provide information about mental disorders and services available within the school and community. It would be important to word the curriculum in such a way that reduces pathology and emphasizes treatment and framing it to be culturally competent in order to reach those populations who are more ethnically diverse. Talking about stigma and what that is on a level elementary students can understand would be a powerful strategy to dispel stigma. Part of this would include hiring interpreters to assist teachers and to be a part of the planning process in order to reach diverse populations within the school system.

3 Implement a Community-based Effort to Bring Schools and Families Together

Students and even teachers or other community leaders with and without mental disorders interacting with each other, to educate other students and families, could dispel some of the misperceptions surrounding mental health disorders. An advocacy event or meeting where people within the community (even students and teachers) who have mental health concerns come together with the purpose of speaking out about their challenges would serve as a way to lessen stigma and discrimination about mental health. This event would be one where parents and other community leaders would be encouraged to attend. The event would serve to increase parents' awareness of the efficacy of school-based mental health in reducing mental health problems. This event could be a fair where food, games, and prizes are given in order to engage students and parents. It could serve as a support system for parents who have children with mental health concerns to come together and find ways to access services within the school setting.

A similar way to engage parents would be to advertise and hold a support group at the school for parents who have children with mental health concerns. On the school and community level, SBFC practitioners could facilitate group discussions with school personnel to discuss ways to engage at-risk families. SBFC practitioners could also collaborate with social service agencies outside the schools, local health clinics, law enforcement agencies, and faith institutions to refer at-risk families to access SBFC services (Carter & Evans, 2008). It would be good to design and place flyers within schools and other social service agencies (in different languages) advertising SBFC services and to pass these flyers out at school functions such as PTA meetings.

4 Actively Involve Students in Mental Health Advocacy, Outreach, Support and Literacy Efforts

Having high school students in particular (and middle school students) form support groups within the school, even online support groups surrounding mental health literacy, could help build knowledge about mental health and ways to access services within the schools. Actively involving students in the design, promotion and implementation of mental health and substance abuse programs within their schools and local community would offer support regarding their own mental health concerns and help to dispel stigma and discrimination surrounding mental health. It would also provide them the knowledge to access services and directly influence their perceptions of the availability of services and strengthen the efficacy of school-based mental health in general.

In regard to stigma, it is important to note that eliminating it altogether would be difficult, but talking about stigma in regard to mental health stresses the need for literacy. Dispelling stigma involves dispelling ignorance. Mental illness is stigmatized because people lack knowledge about it. Once mental health becomes a more universal subject in schools and within communities, then we will begin to see a reduction in stigma surrounding mental disorders (Bowers, Manion, Papadopoulos, & Gauvreau, 2013).

Outreach and advocacy could consist of putting help-seeking services in the pathway of adolescents with mental health or substance use issues. Bringing the knowledge to them could be an alternative approach because most teenagers tend to try to deal with their personal and emotional issues alone. A way to do this would be to recognize that while young people are reluctant to seek help for themselves, they are much more likely to advocate for and/or seek help for a friend or partner. Instead of focusing on encouraging them to seek help for themselves, more emphasis could be placed on them seeking help for their friends. Teaching young people how to effectively seek help for their friends could reach those reluctant to seek help and at the same time encourage their own help-seeking behavior (Rickwood, Deane, Wilson, & Ciarrochi, 2005).

5 Set Clear-cut Confidentiality and Informed Consent Guidelines

In order to reduce fears parents may have of their child being "labelled" or stigmatized by teachers, the SBFC practitioner can set clear-cut boundaries early on with teachers and other school personnel by being clear about informed consent and confidentiality. One step towards eliminating this barrier would be meeting with school personnel about this issue and discussing with them the guidelines regarding confidentiality of students and what can or cannot be shared with them regarding a students' mental health status and progress. A vital first step would be to talk up front with parents about their confidentiality concerns and take measures to assure parents and adolescents that their information will not be disclosed without their consent (Ohan, Seward, Stallman, Bayliss, & Sanders, 2015).

Mental Health Inter-professional Barriers to SBFC

There is an increasing need for inter-professional collaboration in order to meet the complex needs of school-age youth (Sosa & McGrath, 2013; Villarreal & Castro-Villarreal, 2016). Unfortunately, a long history of barriers exists between mental health providers, which impedes effective collaboration (Carter, Garner, Geiger, Gerrard, & Soriano, 2017). Conflict between the disciplines can result in an array of negative outcomes such as reduced and less coordinated care for vulnerable students and their families. These obstacles actively detract from the goals and intentions of SBFC. It is therefore critical for us to understand the existing inter-professional barriers in order to better identify strategies for overcoming them.

Sosa and McGrath define inter-professional collaboration as "two or more professionals from different disciplines or agencies working together to meet the needs of the child and family" (2013, p. 36). In a truly collaborative approach, each practitioner is considered an expert but also recognizes that there is a great deal to be learned by working with other disciplines. Sharing knowledge and skills across disciplines allows for creative solutions to the complex problems our clients face (Hall, 2005), and partnerships within the school and community offer a better opportunity to meet the needs of children and families (Rose, 2011). Unfortunately, effective teamwork across multiple disciplines can be challenging (Sosa & McGrath, 2013). Many factors can contribute to a lack of effective collaboration between mental health practitioners (Widmark, Sandahl, Piuva, & Bergman, 2011). These barriers include but are not limited to: professional identity and lack of understanding of other disciplines, poor communication, and power and territory. Each of these barriers is described in more detail below.

Professional identity and poor understanding of other disciplines can contribute to a lessened capacity for collaboration with other mental health practitioners (Barnes, Carpenter, & Dickinson, 2000; Glasby & Lester, 2004). People are socialized and indoctrinated into their chosen disciplines early in their education and training. Professional identity develops and can deepen over time spent practicing throughout a career. Soon practitioners may find themselves immersed in a specialist perspective with a narrowed scope or approach (Hall, 2005; Rose, 2011). This professional culture can reinforce common values, approaches, and even the jargon of their own discipline (Hall, 2005). This is not necessarily a negative quality, but it can impede capacity to broaden our scope of practice or fully collaborate with those from other professions. This is especially true if there is not a good understanding of what other disciples do and what they contribute. A lack of knowledge of other professionals' areas of expertise can hinder the success of a multidisciplinary team (Ambrose-Miller & Ashcroft, 2016), and result in a lack of appreciation and loss of inter-professional partnership opportunities.

Poor communication is another barrier to collaborative practice amongst professionals (Wood, Ohlsen & Ricketts, 2017). Diverse training and unique philosophical orientations can add to difficulty with effective communication (Villarreal & Castro-Villarreal, 2016). Practitioners may use different jargon, assessments, and approaches to assist a family. Without ongoing and effective dialogue and listening, care delivery could be disjointed and confusing for clients. Coordinated treatment plans will require regular meetings and conversation to ensure that critical information is shared in a way that is most beneficial.

Issues of power and territory can also promote barriers between disciplines. Power is related to status and is described as an imbalance in influence or discrepancy in decision-making authority. When one professional is perceived as having more or less say in an important decision, it can cause tension and fracture opportunities for partnership. Power, whether overt or covert, can also be tied to discrepancies in compensation across professionals (Ambrose-Miller & Ashcroft, 2016). Territory is the understanding of roles and boundaries, both personal and those of others (Rose, 2011). Confusion around boundaries can lead to practitioners feeling either over- or under-utilized and can increase conflict with a team (Hall, 2005). Ultimately, poorly managed issues of power and territory serve as obstacles that can lead to increased mistrust between practitioners (Widmark, Sandahl, Piuva, & Bergman, 2011).

It is necessary for diverse practitioners to collaborate when working with children and families in order for us to provide comprehensive treatment (Widmark, Sandahl, Piuva, & Bergman, 2011). While the list of barriers described here is certainly not comprehensive, these barriers warrant attention as they impede SBFC practitioners from working effectively together and with other mental health professionals. Therefore, it is imperative that we learn to identify and address such obstacles.

Strategies for Overcoming Inter-professional Barriers

This section will highlight four practical strategies for overcoming inter-professional barriers and increasing effective collaboration.

1 Improve Communication

Actively working on improving communication with SBFC practitioners from diverse disciplines is a good first step toward collaboration (Wood, Ohlsen, & Ricketts, 2017). Ongoing and meaningful communication is critical when dealing with complex client issues, as multiple professionals are often working with the same clients. In order to prevent duplication of services while also providing comprehensive care we need to be aligned. This is only possible with consistent communication. Establishing set times to communicate on a regular basis may make it more likely to become a part of the culture of the SBFC practice.

A key aspect of successful communication is listening to our colleagues, just as we would our clients. By actively listening to each other we also increase the opportunity to recognize when there may be tension stemming from issues of power or territory amongst diverse practitioners. Establishing good communication early on may better position us to be able to effectively address issues that could detract from our ability to collaborate.

2 Focus on Shared Purpose

Though we may view our clients' treatment through a different philosophical lens, the primary goal of improving the wellbeing of youth and families remains the same across all SBFC practitioners. By focusing on this shared aim rather than our professional differences we can begin to work together in more productive ways (Rose, 2011; Widmark, Sandahl, Piuva, & Bergman, 2011). The shared purpose can serve as a tie that binds us regardless of our unique disciplines.

3 Focus on SBFC as a Process

It can be easy to get caught up in a narrow focus or specialized approach when treating clients. Sometimes different ways of assessing or working with clients can feel threatening to our own professional identity. However, framing SBFC as a process that can be used by any mental health professional may be a more comfortable approach (Carter, Garner, Geiger, Gerrard, & Soriano, 2017). Similarly, using discipline-inclusive language such as "practitioner" rather than counselor or social worker may make this approach more encompassing and even welcoming to diverse professionals.

4 Be Familiar with Other Disciplines

An easy way to get out of our discipline-specific silos is to proactively learn more about our colleagues' professional lenses. Looking up websites for the accrediting or licensing body of our other colleagues is a simple way to learn more about the theories, philosophies, and approaches they might use. Another simple and straightforward approach is to find a time to meet with a colleague and ask them to teach you more about their methods of working with clients. Taking the opportunity to learn more about other SBFC practitioners' professional orientations will likely lead toward a greater appreciation for what they offer clients and may open the door for increased collaboration (Carter, Garner, Geiger, Gerrard, & Soriano, 2017).

There is increased recognition for the importance of effective interprofessional collaboration (Hall, 2005), and it is considered to be more beneficial to the client (Glasby & Lester, 2004). The primary and shared goal of all mental health professionals is to provide the highest quality of care to those we have the privilege of treating. Therefore, it makes good sense that we would strive to work more effectively with each other through partnership and collaboration.

Bibliography

Ambrose-Miller, W., & Ashcroft, R. (2016). Challenges faced by social workers as members of inter-professional collaborative health care teams. *Health & Social Work, 41*(2), 101–109.

American School Counselor Association (ASCA). (2014). *Student-to-school-counselor ratio 2013–2014*. Retrieved from www.schoolcounselor.org/asca/media/asca/home/Ratios13-14.pdf

American School Counselor Association (ASCA). (2016). *ASCA ethical standards for school counsellors*. Retrieved from www.schoolcounselor.org/asca/media/asca/Ethics/EthicalStandards2016.pdf

American School Counselor Association (ASCA). (2018). *School counselors: Careers/roles*. Retrieved from www.schoolcounselor.org/school-counselors-members/careers-roles

Bain, S. F., Rueda, B., Mata-Villarreal, J., & Mundy, M. A. (2011). Assessing mental health needs of rural schools in South Texas: Counselor's perspectives. *Research in Higher Education Journal, 14*, 1–11.

Barnes, D., Carpenter, J., & Dickinson, C. (2000). Inter-professional education for community mental health: Attitudes to community care and professional stereotypes. *Social Work Education, 19*(6), 565–583.

Bowers, H., Manion, I., Papadopoulos, D., & Gauvreau, E. (2013). Stigma in school-based mental health: Perceptions of young people and service providers. *Child and Adolescent Mental Health, 18*, 165–170.

Carter, M., Garner, W., Geiger, P., Gerrard, B., & Soriano, M. (2017). Reducing inter-professional barriers affecting school-based family counseling. *International Journal for School-Based Family Counseling, 9*(2), 1–18.

Carter, M. J., & Evans, W. P. (August 2008). Implementing school-based family counseling: Strategies, activities, and process considerations. *International Journal for School-Based Family Counseling, 1*(1), 1–21.

Christian, L. G. (2006). Understanding families: Applying family systems theory to early childhood practice. *Young Children, 61*(1), 12–20.

College Board Advocacy & Policy Center National Office for School Counselor Advocacy. (2012). *2012 National survey of school counselors*. Retrieved from www.civicenterprises.net/MediaLibrary/Docs/2012_NOSCA_Report.pdf

Ehrhardt-Padgett, G. N., Hatzichristou, C., Kitson, J., & Meyers, J. (2004). Awakening to a new dawn: Perspectives of the future of school psychology. *School Psychology Review, 33*, 105–114.

Evans, W. P., & Carter, M. J. (1997). Urban school-based family counseling: Role definition, practice applications, and training implications. *Journal of Counseling and Development: JCD, 75*(5), 366–374.

Ferris, M., Hane, A., & Wagoner, B. (2014). Engaging youth and families in mental health services: Lessons learned for creating a culturally-responsive system of care in Ramsey County. *Amherst H. Wilder Foundation: Wilder Research* 651-280-2660.

Froese-Germain, B., & Riel, R. (2012). *Understanding teachers' perspectives on student mental health: Findings from a national survey*. Ottawa, ON: Canadian Teachers' Federation.

Gerrard, B. (2008). School-based family counseling: An overview, trends and recommendations for future research. *International Journal of School-Based Family Counseling, 1*, 6–24.

Gerrard, B., & Soriano, M. (Eds.). (2013). *School-based family counseling: Transforming family school relationships*. Phoenix, AZ: Createspace.

Glasby, J., & Lester, H. (2004). Cases for change in mental health: Partnership working in mental health services. *Journal of Interprofessional Care*, *18*(1), 7–16.

Hall, P. (2005). Inter-professional teamwork: Professional cultures as barriers, *Journal of Interprofessional Care*, (Supplement 1), 188–196.

Jorm, A. F., Kitchener, B. A., Sawyer, M. G., Scales, H., & Cvetkovski, S. (2010). Mental health first aid training for high school teachers: A cluster randomized trial. *Biomedcentral Psychiatry*, *10*(51), 1–12.

Koller, J. R., & Bertel, J. M. (2006). Responding to today's mental health needs of children, families, and schools: Revisiting the preservice training and preparation of school-based personnel. *Education and Treatment of Children*, *29*, 197–201. Retrieved from www.educationandtreatmentofchildren.net/

Loades, M. E., & Mastroyannopoulou, K. (2010). Teacher recognition of children's mental health problems. *Child and Adolescent Mental Health*, *15*, 150–156.

Mental health literacy. (n.d.). *Mental health foundation*. Retrieved from www.mental health.org.uk/a-to-z/m/mental-health-literacy

National Association of School Psychologists (NASP). (2010). *Model for comprehensive and integrated school psychological services*. Retrieved from www.nasponline.org/standards-and-certification/nasp-practice-model

National Association of School Psychologists (NASP). (2011). *What is a school psychologist?* Retrieved from www.nasponline.org/about_sp/whatis.aspx

National Association of School Psychologists (NASP). (2017). *Shortages in school psychology: Challenges to meeting the growing needs of U.S. students and schools*. Retrieved from www.nasponline.org/research-and-policy/nasp-research-center/research-summaries

Nealis, L. (2016). The importance of school-based mental health services. *NEA Healthy Futures, National Education Association*. Retrieved from http://healthyfutures.nea.org/importance-school-based-mental-health-services/

Negreiros, J., & Miller, L. D. (2014). Integrating school-based family counseling into school psychology practice. *British Journal of Education, Society & Behavioural Science*, *4*, 883–896.

Ohan, J. L., Seward, R. J., Stallman, H. M., Bayliss, D. M., & Sanders, M. R. (2015). Parents' barriers to using school psychology services for their child's mental health problems. *School Mental Health*, *7*(4), 287–297. doi:10.1007/s12310-015-9152-1.

Perusse, R., Goodnough, G., & Noel, C. (2001). A national survey of school counselor preparation programs: Screening methods, faculty experiences, curricular content, and fieldwork requirements. *Counselor Education and Supervision*, *40*, 252–262.

Powers, J. D., & Swick, D. C. (2017). Establishing and maintaining successful university-school partnerships in school-based research. *International Journal for School-Based Family Counseling*, *9*, 1–7.

Powers, J. D., Swick, D. C., Sneed, C., & Wegmann, K. (2016). Supporting prosocial development through school-based mental health services: A multi-site evaluation of social and behavioral outcomes across one academic year. *Social Work and Mental Health*, *14*, 22–41.

Powers, J. D., Wegmann, K. M., Blackman, K. F., & Swick, D. (2014). Increasing awareness of common child mental health issues among elementary school staff. *Families in Society*, *95*, 43–50.

Reinke, W. M., Stormont, M., Herman, K. C., Puri, R., & Goel, N. (2011). Supporting children's mental health in schools: Teacher perceptions of needs, roles, and barriers. *School Psychology Quarterly*, *26*(1), 1–13.

Rickwood, D., Deane, F. P., Wilson, C. J., & Ciarrochi, J. (2005). Young people's help-seeking for mental health problems. *Advances in Mental Health*, *4*, 218–251.

Rones, M., & Hoagwood, K. (2000). School-based mental health services: A research review. *Clinical Child and Family Psychology Review, 3*, 223–241. Retrieved from www.springerlink.com/content/104849/

Rose, J. (2011). Dilemmas of inter-professional collaboration: Can they be resolved? *Children & Society, 25*(2), 151–163.

Rothi, D. M., Leavey, G., & Best, R. (2008). On the front-line: Teachers as active observers of pupils' mental health. *Teaching and Teaching Education, 24*, 1217–1231.

Short, K. H., Weist, M. D., Manion, I. G., & Evans, S. W. (2012). Tying together research and practice: Using ROPE for successful partnerships in school mental health. *Administrative Policy in Mental Health, 39*, 238–247.

Sin, C., Francis, R., & Cook, C. (2010). Access to and experience of child and adolescent mental health services: Barriers to children and young people with learning disabilities and their families. *Mental Health Review Journal, 15*(1), 20–28.

Sosa, L. V., & McGrath, B. (2013). Collaboration from the ground up: Creating effective teams. *School Social Work Journal, 38*(1), 34–48.

Star, M. (2010). Teachers' perceptions of students' needs for family counseling and attitudes toward school-based family counseling (PhD dissertation, Capella University). Retrieved from Pro Quest Information and Learning database.

Swick, D. C., & Powers, J. D. (2016). School-based mental health programming: Summary of results and recommendations for future evaluations. *International Journal for School-Based Family Counseling, 7*, 1–15.

Swick, D. C., Powers, J. D., Wegmann, K. M., & Watkins, C. S. (2015). Promoting academic achievement through school-based mental health programming: Evaluation of math outcomes across one academic year. *Journal of Behavioral and Social Sciences, 2*(2), 113–123.

The Foundation for People with Learning Disabilities. (2002). *Count us in: The report of the committee of inquiry into meeting the mental health needs of young people with learning disabilities.* London: The Mental Health Foundation.

Valdez, C. R., Carlson, C., & Zanger, D. (2005). Evidence-based parent training and family interventions for school behavior change. *School Psychology Quarterly, 20*, 403–433.

Villarreal, V., & Castro-Villarreal, F. (2016). Collaboration with community mental health service providers: A necessity in contemporary schools. *Intervention in School and Clinic, 52*(2), 108–114.

Walter, H. J., Gouze, K., Cicchetti, C., Arend, R., Mehta, T., Schmidt, J., & Skvarla, M. (2011). A pilot demonstration of comprehensive mental health services in inner-city public schools. *Journal of School Health, 81*(4), 185–193.

Walter, H. J., Gouze, K., & Lim, K. G. (2006). Teachers' beliefs about mental health needs in inner-city elementary schools. *Journal of the American Academy of Child and Adolescent Psychiatry, 45*, 61–68.

Wegmann, K. M., Powers, J. D., Swick, D. C., & Watkins, C. (2017). Supporting academic achievement through school-based mental health services: A multi-site evaluation of reading outcomes across one academic year. *School Social Work Journal, 41*(2), 1–22.

Widmark, C., Sandahl, C., Piuva, K., & Bergman, D. (2011). Barriers to collaboration between health care, social services and schools. *International Journal of Integrated Care, 11*, 1–9.

Wood, E., Ohlsen, S., & Ricketts, T. (2017). What are the barriers and facilitators to implementing collaborative care for depression? A systematic review. *Journal of Affective Disorders, 214*, 26–43.

13 Effective Referral Processes in School Mental Health

Multicultural Considerations in a Eurocentric System

Michael J. Carter and Emily J. Hernandez

Overview: *A prevalent problem in school settings is the lack of follow-through by families on mental health referrals provided by school personnel. This chapter provides an overview of the background and challenges involved in mental health referrals to mental health agencies outside the school environment, particularly by families with multicultural backgrounds. An example is provided of an effective referral process in school mental health with a focus on multicultural considerations within a predominantly Eurocentric system. Two case studies are provided, one reflecting the challenges of a referral to a traditional Eurocentric mental health agency, and the other involving a referral to an agency that utilized a more multiculturally appropriate conjoint family therapy intervention. Promising trends in multicultural mental health are also described.*

Background

Providing mental health referrals is a key aspect, and obligation, of the mental health profession. Historically, and in the present, schools identify students who demonstrate emotional and behavioral difficulties (EBDs) that indicate the need for referral to a mental health professional. Often, these referrals are made by a school counselor, school social worker, or school psychologist, but in the many schools that do not have these personnel on campus, administrators or even office staff will provide this referral. Several research studies indicate, however, that many school referrals to mental health services are not successfully followed through by families.

When children are referred to a mental health provider, evidence suggests that family compliance with mental health referrals is quite low, with one study finding that fewer than half of children referred for specialty mental health services ever obtained care (Glied & Cuellar, 2003). Research also shows that a significant number of school professionals (48%) report feeling "frustration" with parents not following through on referrals/recommendations they make (Ritchie & Partin, 1994). Disparities also exist in mental health care utilization for African American and Hispanic children and the disparity for these children is independent of socio-demographics and child mental health needs. Researchers indicate that efforts to reduce this disparity may benefit from addressing not only access and diagnosis issues, but also parents' help-seeking preferences for mental health care for their children (Coker et al., 2009).

These challenges to utilizing mental health services are also seen with elementary school-aged children. According to one study (Simon et al., 2015), in 2010–2012, 23.1% of children ages 6 to 11 years old in the United States were identified as having EBDs. Of these children, 5.8% had serious EBDs and 17.3% had minor EBDs. Among all children with EBDs, 17.8% were receiving both medication and psychosocial services, 28.8% psychosocial services only, 6.8% medication only, and 46.6% neither type of service. In 2011–2012, nearly two-thirds of children identified as having EBDs (64.2%) received no school-based psychosocial services and 71.2% of children with EBDs did not receive non–school-based psychosocial services. These findings illustrate the current lack of effectiveness in school referrals for mental health services outside the school, and the lack of intervention for many children who need emotional and behavioral support in order to be successful academically.

Other studies indicate that the relationship with the referring party is a critical factor in the follow-through of referrals to mental health agencies. For example, using the relationship between primary care providers and their patients to integrate mental health providers was found to be an effective strategy for enhancing the provision of child development and mental health services to children and adolescents (Tynan, Woods, & Carpenter, 2015). Additional studies indicate that there is a positive impact on referrals related to the location and availability of behavioral health services for children (Wildman & Langkamp, 2012). Close location and flexible schedules of availability enhance the follow-through of these referrals.

These findings and other professional anecdotal experiences of providing mental health services to students and families in both school and clinic settings provide some insights into the possible causes of the lack of follow-through with school referrals for mental health services. There appear to be several obstacles involved in this lack of follow-through, most notably multi-cultural factors in families' viewpoints, beliefs, attitudes, and stigmas of mental health and the value of mental health services for their children.

One important obstacle is that the American mental health system has historically viewed the individual as the primary focus of pathology and treatment. This is reflected in the prevalent use of the *Diagnostic and Statistical Manual of Mental Disorders* (DSM) to assess the symptoms of an individual as a means of making a diagnosis, which then leads to treatment of the individual. These treatments do not typically involve consistent conjoint therapy with the individual and family members, although family members may sometimes be interviewed regarding the history of the individual and their symptoms in the initial assessment. This individualistic approach to the provision of mental health services may result in a lack of alignment in the value and utility of these services for families from collectivist cultures. This has been referred to as a "Eurocentric" approach to mental health treatment because it focuses on European culture or history to the exclusion of a wider view of the world, implicitly regarding European culture as pre-eminent. This approach focuses primarily on individual factors versus social, ecological and systemic factors such as environment, family, culture, and history (Eurocentrism, 2018).

Many families from multicultural backgrounds have great value for family and the interactions between family members, but may not specifically value mental health services that do not actively address their views and concerns. These families may have different viewpoints about the nature of the problem and the indicators of successful treatment than a Eurocentric-oriented mental health system and may want to be more actively involved in the ongoing treatment of family members. In addition, there is a wealth of knowledge and resources that family members can contribute to the therapeutic processes of evaluation and treatment. For example, one study (Kouyoumdjian, Zamboanga, & Hansen, 2003) states that, "When therapists are well educated about the Latino culture, they can also better understand the supportive role of family members (Acosta, 1984; Rogler, Malgady, & Rodriguez, 1989) and the potential benefits for Latino clients of incorporating the extended family in treatment plans (Keefe & Casas, 1980; Padilla & Salgado de Snyder, 1985)." Another study reported that low income African American caregivers described schools as being rigid, unwelcoming, and uncaring which directly impacts follow-through on referrals due to trust, fear, and safety issues (Tucker, 2009). Frequently, caregivers didn't understand the school system process or the roles of school professionals with a limited understanding about the reason for the referral (Tucker, 2009). While school counseling preparation programs and textbooks offer instruction on consultation for making referrals outside the school, most do not include any guidance for referring families from diverse cultural, racial, or social class backgrounds to mental health services (Tucker, 2009).

Over the past 30 years, there has been a movement to address school mental health issues through School-Based Family Counseling (SBFC). SBFC is an approach to helping children succeed in school and overcome personal, interpersonal, and family problems. It integrates a broad-based systems meta-model that is used to conceptualize the child's problems in the context of all interpersonal networks: family, peer group, classroom, school, family, and community (Soriano & Gerrard, 2013). The main areas of strengths in the SBFC model include maintaining a systems focus, being strength-based, having partnerships with parents, being multiculturally sensitive, being advocates for children and families, and actively promoting the transformation of schools (Soriano & Gerrard, 2013).

SBFC can typically involve a one- to five-session treatment approach that focuses on actively involving the parents and family in their child's education (see Chapter 3, Family Intervention: How to Build Collaboration Between the Family and School using Conjoint Family Counseling). A major component of this collaborative process is to help the parents understand the importance of their involvement with the school in maximizing student success. This also includes helping families to follow through with referrals to receive counseling from local mental health agencies. However, before the referrals are made, parents need to truly understand how their child's emotional and mental health status affects academic achievement. It is also important that parents understand how they affect these factors and how they can participate in addressing these factors to maximize the academic success of their children.

One of the most important factors to enhance this collaboration is to understand what the parents' ultimate goals are for their child. When asked a question regarding this, most parents will indicate that they want their child to get a good education in order to maximize their opportunities to live a good life. For most parents, their value for education is manifested in their hopes that their child will someday find a job that will provide them the means to live a full life with less stress than the parents themselves have experienced. Accordingly, it is important for school personnel to work collaboratively with parents to help them understand how they can participate in the successful completion of their child's education, which can lead to their child actualizing this hope for improved employment.

In order to accomplish this, it is often helpful to use a chart produced by the US Department of the Interior that indicates the weekly salary and percentage of unemployment associated with an individual's educational achievement (see Chapter 3). Once this chart is presented to the parents and student, it is often kept in full view for continued reference throughout the session. An important part of this presentation is a discussion of the average expenses incurred per person for that local community area. These expenses include housing, food, transportation, clothing, television and other technological devices and subscriptions, and what would comprise the rest of a typical household budget. There is then an exploration of the nature of specific barriers to children's learning, especially emotional and behavioral factors. The concept of how "available a child is for learning" is discussed, including the role of anxiety in reducing this availability for learning.

Parents also are assisted in understanding how their own emotional state is affected when they are anxious, especially if they are experiencing any conflicts between people they love. The parents then explore the possible sources of anxiety in their child's lives. A major source of anxiety for children is any difficulties in the relationships between other family members, most notably their parents. The main point is to help parents understand how what is happening at home can affect their child's functioning in school: academically, behaviorally, and socially. This approach is multicultural in nature because it focuses on the family's worldview and actively facilitates the family's identification and expression of their own values and priorities for their children.

Following are two actual case studies that exemplify the discussion above and include a multiculturally focused school intervention and referral process to two community mental health agencies with drastically different outcomes. Any identifying information has been removed or modified to protect client confidentiality.

The Case of "Eddie"

"Eddie" is a fifth-grade boy of Mexican heritage attending an urban public school in South Los Angeles. Although Eddie has been assessed with above-average intelligence, his grades have been inconsistent since second grade, when he received mostly "A" grades. Since then, Eddie has had many behavioral referrals for lack of attention, incompletion of tasks, and disruptions in the classroom and on the playground. In October of last year, Eddie's behavior deteriorated significantly to the point where he was suspended from school for inappropriate touching of a student and aggressive behavior towards a teacher. This occurred three weeks after Eddie's father was released from state prison after serving two and a half years of a three-year sentence for drug trafficking.

The counselor at Eddie's school had a Pupil Personnel Services credential in school counseling and was also a licensed mental health professional, who had been specifically trained in the SBFC approach. She contacted Eddie's parents to ensure that they would both attend the post-suspension meeting with school administrators. Eddie's mother stated that his father would be unable to attend because a condition of his release was his restriction to his residence and transportation to and from work. The SBFC practitioner then contacted the parole officer to obtain permission for father to travel to and from his home to attend the post-suspension meeting.

During the posst-suspension meeting, school personnel asked Eddie's parents to comment on Eddie's current situation and their hopes for his future. They talked about him getting a good job, having friends who were loyal, and avoiding prison. These were summarized consistent with the three outcomes of young adulthood (i.e., be self-maintaining, have at least one good friend, and stay out of jail). Eddie's parents were also asked what they did *not* want in Eddie's future. They spoke of wanting Eddie to avoid the things that they had gone through as adolescents: substance abuse, teen pregnancy, and gang involvement. These were summarized consistent with the three high-risk behaviors of adolescents (i.e., substance and alcohol abuse, issues related to romantic relationships, including early pregnancy and STDs, and negative influence from peers). There was then discussion of what helps kids avoid these behaviors or the primary protective factors against these high-risk behaviors (i.e., being really good at something, having constructive and supportive friends, having an open and trusting relationship with a significant adult).

Eddie's parents were then shown a US Labor Department chart regarding "earnings and unemployment rates according to educational attainment." There was then a discussion about how to increase Eddie's future happiness through increased earning power (increased access to resources), less unemployment (reduced anxiety resulting in less substance abuse), and receiving education about many different aspects of life with different people (the benefits of general education in community college).

The SBFC practitioner then obtained a commitment from Eddie's parents to attend from three to five subsequent weekly sessions with her to focus on beginning the process of addressing Eddie's current situation and maximizing his prospects for the future. This work focused on learning about the family factors that may have contributed to Eddie's problem behaviors, such as the father's absence and re-entry into the family, providing psycho-education about issues of development and positive discipline, specific practice of active listening and conflict resolution skills, and the need for Eddie's parents to co-parent with a focus on school-related behaviors including following directions and playground skills (i.e., discipline & emotional/social-peer skills). This led to the parents' understanding of the need for more focused work outside school in order to go deeper with treatment and intervention to heal the "wounds" of the family and to build their capacity to increase learning during future developmental stages to keep Eddie's education progressing into increased earning power (i.e., referral to a community clinic).

It appeared that Eddie's family was all set with a referral to a community clinic with: (1) the name of a specific counselor to contact; (2) specific instructions to tell the counselor why they were coming to counseling; (3) a request to sign a release of information so that the community clinic mental health practitioner could contact the SBFC practitioner for information about the family and the previous work that had been done. Eddie's family attended the clinic together and informed the SBFC practitioner of this. They said that the mental health practitioner had spent time with Eddie and then the parents alone. The SBFC practitioner reminded them of the need to also give consent for the clinic mental health practitioner to contact the SBFC practitioner for information and to collaborate regarding school services in order to support Eddie while not duplicating services.

Two weeks went by without the SBFC practitioner receiving any calls from the clinic or family. The SBFC practitioner contacted the clinic and waited for a response. After three more weeks, Eddie's behavior in school began to deteriorate and the SBFC practitioner called his mother in for a meeting. Unfortunately, his father refused to attend. The SBFC practitioner asked Eddie's mother about the therapy and she stated that it did not go well and that Eddie refused to go after four sessions. Further questioning revealed that Eddie's parents were only asked to attend the first session to answer questions regarding Eddie's background and history. Since then, Eddie had only been seen individually, had become angry at his parents, and started refusing to go saying, "Why am I the only one who has to go? It's not all my fault." The father then refused to attend any more sessions at the school, despite several attempts by the SBFC practitioner to help him understand the importance of his participation. The mother reported that the father told her, "I was willing to go to counseling, but I'm through with that now."

What happened to Eddie appears to be a result of a Eurocentric approach where the individual exhibiting symptoms was the primary focus of evaluation, and treatment excluded the family as an active participant on a consistent and conjoint basis. While Eddie and his family were willing to attend all of the sessions with the SBFC practitioner at the school site,

Eddie's and his family's frustration at the narrow focus of the clinic's individualistic approach resulted in their giving up on counseling as a means of addressing Eddie's difficulties in the future.

The Case of "Joseph"

This is in direct contrast to the case study of "Joseph," a fourth grader with similar symptoms and background who went through a similar multiculturally focused intervention with the same SBFC practitioner. In Joseph's case, however, the SBFC practitioner was able to refer the family to a community clinic with an SBFC focus where the entire family was required to participate in each phase of counseling, including evaluation and treatment. The evaluation included interviews of all family members, school personnel, and relevant community members and treatment focused on assisting the family to address the presenting problem *together*, while also improving family functioning. This included frequent conjoint sessions that included dyad work to improve all the relationships in the family, especially between the parents.

Throughout the process, there was a consistent emphasis on participation in conjoint family counseling with an educational focus to increase financial power and to realize happier outcomes for the parents and all of their children. Joseph's family missed only one of the 20 scheduled sessions (for his sister's quinceañera), and reports from the school indicated continued improvement by Joseph in his behavior, academic achievement, and social interactions throughout the rest of fourth grade until his culmination at the end of fifth grade.

The major difference between these two cases is the use of a multiculturally relevant approach that incorporated the worldview of the family versus that of a traditional mental health approach. This multicultural approach also actively involved the whole family in each step of evaluation and treatment, including the specific goals of therapy, which allowed each member of the family to improve their mental health and wellness. This constitutes a preventative approach to mental health that results in a positive view of mental health services that can be activated later in the development of the family.

Multicultural Considerations in Traditional Mental Health Services

The above discussion is not intended to imply that individual treatment and group participation are not necessary. They are, in fact, important aspects of any effective mental health service delivery system. If parents are unavailable or unwilling, then individual and group counseling can be critical to the child's progress. Groups are also vital to secondary school students (ages 11–18) as part of a multimodal approach to treatment. An effective multicultural approach, however, must always include family and community in these interventions whenever possible. This may not mean that the family or community participate in the counseling, but they must be informed at each step of the process as to how it may affect their children and the rest of the family. For example, many high school suicide prevention programs focus on increasing awareness and expression of the students' feelings, including negative emotions. This can often lead to more conflict in the student's home if the parents are not made aware of the specific nature and possible consequences of the group interventions. This often results in parents' resenting the high school's intervention and withdrawal of consent for their child to participate in the program.

It's also important to emphasize a broader view of what constitutes a "family" in mental health services, one that includes extended family members and functional family members who may not be biologically related, but who provide the same critical functions as more traditional families (e.g., foster families).

Promising Trends in Multicultural Mental Health

While most community agency mental health approaches continue to be more Eurocentric in nature, there are several recent trends in mental health services that are promising. In many urban areas, the concept of "wrap-around services" is being implemented. These typically involve sending mental health professionals to the home where they provide mental health and social services, including family counseling, to all family members. In addition, there has been a recent focus of many public mental health agencies on creating "systems of care" for the chronically mentally ill that actively include family members and the community in the evaluation, treatment, and follow-up of services for the identified patient. In the DSM-5 (the most recent edition of the *Diagnostic and Statistical Manual of Mental Disorders*), there is inclusion of environmental factors and family influence on the diagnosis of mentally ill persons. In the past few years, many insurance companies have included payment for a therapist's communication with extended family members and other community members such as employers, schools, and law enforcement agencies.

Finally, the movement towards a more multiculturally relevant mental health service delivery system is a promising trend in many ways. The idea is to bring more energy, resources, and support to children and families experiencing mental health issues by *using* multicultural factors rather than *avoiding* them. And this must always come from a wellness and strengths-based approach that respects all members of the family and their viewpoints, and builds healthy structures and growth, with as much fun as possible (e.g., family fun nights). Utilizing and developing more effective collaborative communication and relationships with families is an important foundational step in shifting the existing paradigms and moving forward. While this may be an abstract concept, simple concrete steps can be taken: inviting parents/

caregivers in the problem-solving process at the first signs of any issues, asking for solutions they have implemented at home, assessing how they may be receiving school staff members' suggestions by attending to their nonverbal communication and body language, asking open-ended questions, and asking how they feel about what is happening and what is being said (Tucker, 2009). It seems clear that we need the inclusion of the above-mentioned multicultural considerations in the initial intervention and referral process to be successful in getting the family to follow through with mental health referrals to community clinics. Despite this success, however, if community mental health agencies continue to use a Eurocentric approach to evaluation and treatment, many families will probably not continue with their attendance, and school services professionals will continue to feel frustration with the lack of follow-through on referrals and recommendations. Box 13.1 shows some recommendations for making culturally responsive referrals.

Box 13.1 Recommendations for Making Culturally Responsive Referrals (Tucker, 2009)

- Be aware of cultural stigmas and fears, as well as practical concerns parents/caregivers may be facing.
- Be aware of any negative past personal experiences related to counseling and mental health services before making a referral, and address these concerns with the family by asking them what their past experiences have been, validating their experiences, providing psycho-education, demystifying and normalizing the process.
- Explore existing concerns (paying for services, finding time, practical concerns, fears) with parents/caregivers prior to making referrals in order to improve the changes that families will access the services.
- Create warm, egalitarian relationships with caregivers prior to the development of a problem. This can assist in preventing negative outcomes and increase chance family will access the referral services.
- SBFC practitioners could lead other members of school faculty in creating a welcoming and collaborative climate at the school.
- Create collaborative communication and relationships with families.
- Make sure that parents/caregivers understand precisely what the referral entails.
- Take time to make sure parents/caregivers understand what is being said in the referral meeting, and make time for answering all questions that may come up after the meeting.
- Referral meetings should begin by introducing all members present to parents/caregivers with an explanation of their role and reason for being in the meeting.

Bibliography

Acosta, F. X. (1984). Psychotherapy with Mexican Americans: Clinical and Empirical Gains. In J. L. Martinez, Jr., & R. H. Mendoza (Eds.), *Chicano Psychology* (pp. 163–189). Orlando, FL: Academic Press.

American Psychiatric Association. (2013). *Diagnostic and Statistical Manual of Mental Disorders* (5th ed.). Washington, DC: American Psychiatric Association.

Coker, T. R., Elliott, M. N., Kataoka, S., Schwebel, D. C., Mrug, S., Grunbaum, J. A., Cuccaro, P., & Peskin, M. F. (2009). Racial/Ethnic Disparities in the Mental Health Care Utilization of Fifth Grade Children. *Academic Pediatrics, 9*(2), 89–96.

Eurocentrism. retrieved 2018 July 19 from https://en.wikipedia.org/wiki/Eurocentrism

Fantuzzo, J., Stoltzfus, J., Lutz, M. N., Hamlet, H., Balraj, V., Turner, C., & Mosca, S. (1999). An Evaluation of the Special Needs Referral Process for Low-Income Preschool Children with Emotional and Behavioral Problems. *Early Childhood Research Quarterly, 14*(4), 465–482.

Glied, S., & Cuellar, A. E. (2003). Trends and Issues in Child and Adolescent Mental Health. *Health Affairs, 22*(5), 39–50.

Keefe, S. E., & Casas, J. M. (1980). Mexican Americans and Mental Health: A Selected Review and Recommendations for Mental Health Service Delivery. *American Journal of Community Psychology, 8*(3), 303–326.

Kouyoumdjian, H., Zamboanga, B., & Hansen, D. (2003). Barriers to Community Mental Health Services for Latinos: Treatment Considerations. *Clinical Psychology: Science and Practice, 10*(4), 394–422.

Padilla, A. M., & Salgado de Snyder, N. (1985). Counseling Hispanics: Strategies for Effective Intervention. In P. Pedersen (Ed.), *Handbook of Cross-Cultural Counseling and Therapy* (pp. 157–164). Westport, CT: Greenwood Press.

Ritchie, M., & Partin, R. (1994). Referral Practices of School Counselors. *School Counselor, 41*(4), 263–272.

Rogler, L. H., Malgady, R. G., & Rodriguez, O. (1989). *Hispanics and Mental Health: A Framework for Research.* Malabar, FL: Krieger.

Simon, A. E., Pastor, P. N., Reuben, C. A., Huang, L. N., & Goldstrom, I. D. (2015). Use of Mental Health Services by Children Ages Six to 11 with Emotional or Behavioral Difficulties. *Psychiatry Services, 66*(9), 930–937.

Soriano, M., & Gerrard, B. (2013). *School-Based Family Counseling: Transforming Family-School Relationships.* Phoenix, AZ: Createspace.

Tucker, C. (2009). Low-Income African-American Caregivers' Experiences of Being Referred to Mental Health Services by the School Counselor: Implications for Best Practices. *Professional School Counseling, 12*(3), 240–252.

Tynan, W. D., Woods, K., & Carpenter, J. (2015). *Integrating Child Psychology Services in Primary Care.* Washington, DC: American Psychological Association. Retrieved from www.apa.org/pi/families/resources/primary-care/integrating-services.aspx

Wildman, B. G., & Langkamp, D. L. (2012). Impact of Location and Availability of Behavioral Health Services for Children. *Journal of Clinical Psychology in Medical Settings, 19*(4), 393–400.

14 Case Study

A Family in Distress

Gertina J. Van Schalkwyk

Overview: *In this chapter the focus is on exploring the various relationships impacting the intervention planning for a youth struggling at school and in life. The Collage Life-story Elicitation Technique (CLET) was employed with the family unit and analysed to assess the underlying challenges, after which intervention planning proceeded based on the SBFC meta-model. Further techniques stimulated by solution-focused and narrative family counseling with groups and individuals were employed to generate change in relationship patterns and resolve the initial referral problem for a school student and his family.*

Referral and Assessment

A secondary school student, Xander (aged 17) was referred to the SBFC practitioner, Ms. Yoli, for consultation after continuous failure to meet expectations set by his classroom teachers. (Note: All clients and the SBFC practitioner are referred to by pseudonyms to protect confidentiality.) Apart from his non-compliance, Xander was also causing problems in the classroom, disrespecting the authority of the teacher and performing poorly in his schoolwork, failing most subjects in the past semester. He had already once failed a year prior to being transferred to his current school where he had to repeat the year. Xander carried with him the label of being a "bad" student, and the school administrators were now considering suspending him and he would again have to transfer to another school in the next semester.

During the first interview with Ms. Yoli, the SBFC practitioner, Xander appeared sullen and uninterested, and reluctant to talk about what bothered him. He commented that "school was a drag and boring" and that he preferred the extra-curricular sport activities more than having to sit in class listening to "boring" teachers. He would often pick up additional basketball games with friends from his previous school and stayed out late rather than going home. He also confessed having had to meet with the disciplinary teacher at school because of cheating or forgetting to submit homework. He further claimed that even if he did study hard, he still got poor grades, and felt that it was useless even to try.

Ms. Yoli made an initial assessment of Xander's problems considering a broader systems model—the School-Based Family Counseling (SBFC) meta-model—as framework. It seemed that Xander's problems at school, his low achievement orientation, and reluctance to go home were related to his family, and she suggested to Xander that she would like to speak with his parents and younger brother (family consultation) before moving forward with a treatment plan. Because Xander apparently did not like his current school, Ms. Yoli also suggested that she would want to consult further with the teachers and administrators on his behalf, but Xander was adamant that he did not want her to speak with the school staff as he was afraid that he would be further stereotyped as unwelcome and would not be able to complete his schooling. Even though he did not like school, he did not want to embarrass his parents by failing to complete his final two years of secondary school education at the current school, a school favoured by his parents and extended family. Finally, and given that Xander apparently still favoured interactions with peers from his former school, Ms. Yoli suggested that she would also like to speak with some of his classmates in his current school and that Xander could propose who should be included in a group consultation session. Xander agreed that his family could be involved and also proposed the names of a few classmates with whom he was most friendly.

Following his agreement, Ms. Yoli set up a consultation session with the family in order to further assess the directions of possible intervention and frame the problem within the broader system of Xander's interpersonal relationships. Ms. Z (Xander's mother) immediately agreed to meet with her, but it took some convincing getting Mr. Z to agree to a meeting time as he was apparently exceedingly busy at work and did not have time to deal with matters concerning the children's education. After much deliberation, Ms. Yoli managed to get both parents and Xander's younger brother to attend a joint meeting at their home.

Family Consultation

The Zhang family (not their real names) and Ms. Yoli gathered at their house on a weekday evening after Mr. Z returned from a business meeting. Since it was not easy to conduct extended family therapy with multiple sessions, Ms. Yoli decided to use the Collage Life-story Elicitation Technique (CLET) with the family to further explore the underlying problems and direct further interventions with Xander (Van Schalkwyk, 2010b, 2013a). The CLET is known for its transformative nature and for assisting family members to uncover issues still below the level of awareness. Ms. Yoli had limited access to other forms of assessment and she had to develop her case conceptualisation based on the information she could gain from a brief history taking and the CLET, as well as other observations in the natural setting.

Box 14.1 Steps in the Collage Life-story Elicitation Technique (CLET)

Step 1: Collage making

The first step in the CLET entails making a collage, selecting images and/or cuttings from magazines and print media provided. Instructions to the family: Create your family's life story collage representing important and memorable experiences and using at least 10–12 pictures, images, cuttings and text.

Step 2: Storytelling

In Step 2 the family engages actively in constructing micro-narratives stimulated by the images on the collage in a semi-structured interview setting. The counsellor asks the participant:

a) To tell a (short) story about the image/picture/drawing on the collage
b) Why he/she chose this image, picture or drawing
c) How the image, picture or drawing relates to something important or memorable event in the family life

Other prompts are also used to encourage each family member to tell a rich and vivid story (micro-narrative) about the images on the collage.

Step 3: Self-positioning and missing image

The third step continues the autobiographical remembering and reminiscing, asking each family member to comment on two issues:

a) A place on the collage where she or he would like to position the self (a picture of him/herself)
b) An image he or she could not find but would have liked to add to the collage

Step 4: Juxtaposition (comparing similarities and differences)

In this step, each family member reflects upon the dynamic conflict portrayed in the similarities and differences of images on the collage. After selecting three images, the individual is asked to describe the similarities and differences and to give reasons.

Step 5: Reflection and Closure

For the final step in the CLET interview, the participating family has the opportunity to reflect upon the process of making the collage and telling their stories, and to add further information any person thinks is relevant to the narrating of memorable life events. This step also provides some form of debriefing, and allows individuals to ask questions about things that created confusion during the collage making and storytelling.

See also Van Schalkwyk (2013a) for further elaboration regarding each step in the CLET as assessment tool for SBFC.

After briefly explaining the procedures of the CLET to the Zhang family, all members agreed to participate voluntarily, and completed basic demographic background information (see genogram in Figure 14.1). Ms. Yoli carefully followed each of the five steps of the CLET (see Box 14.1) in sequence and allowed family members sufficient time to respond to the question prompts. Ms. Yoli, with the full consent of all family members, audio-recorded the interview for further exploration and case conceptualisation. The completion of the CLET with the Zhang family took about two hours and Ms. Yoli thanked them for their constructive collaboration. Ms. Yoli also asked for a second meeting with the family during which she would discuss the outcomes emerging from her initial narrative analysis of the CLET. This would give all family members a chance to reflect on their own performance on the CLET and she would be able to conduct member checking. The family agreed to the follow-up meeting, which was set for the following week at the same time.

Zhang Family Structure and Functioning

Following the solution-focused and narrative approaches, Ms. Yoli evaluated the Zhang family members' interactional patterns, compiling a genogram and exploring the nuclear and extended family relationships (Van Schalkwyk, 2010a). The genogram and demographic information provided an initial understanding of the Zhang family structure and functioning.

Mr. Z is 44 years of age and a manager in a financial setting where he was recently promoted. He has two older siblings who are both married but who do not live close by and they only meet once a year for the annual Chinese New Year celebrations. His older brother has two children. His mother is

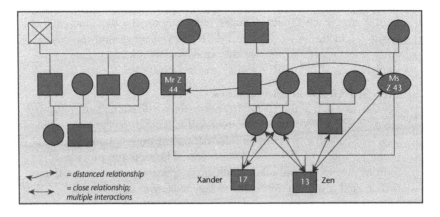

Figure 14.1 Zhang Family Structure/Genogram

alive and living close by, and they meet occasionally when Mr. Z has time to visit.Ms. Z is 43 years of age and a trained nurse working night shifts with only three evenings per week at home with her sons. Her husband, Mr. Z, is rarely home early on these evenings and Ms. Z has to act as both carer and disciplinarian. She has two siblings who are both married and have children (boys and girls) of similar ages to Xander and Zen.Xander (17, Grade 11) is the older of the two siblings.Zen (13, Grade 7) started the school year as a junior secondary student at the same school Xander is attending.

Ms. Yoli also learned, from the history taking, how the family functioned in interaction with the extended family members. Although not much different from how families function in the collectivist context, Ms. Yoli was concerned about the extent of pressure placed on Xander and Zen to meet expectations.

> Mr. and Ms. Z are both well educated and the family could be considered as upper middle class and of high socio-economic status. The two boys attend the same school as their maternal cousins, and apart from meeting at school, the families meet once a month with all the children and grandchildren for Sunday lunch. At these family gatherings, the parents discuss and compare their children's academic performances. Xander and Zen are expected to make their parents proud, perform well academically and not disgrace both the nuclear and the extended family systems (Van Schalkwyk, 2011, 2017). However, Xander feels that his parents and family members exert a lot of pressure on him to meet expectations—specifically academic expectations—and as an adolescent, he does not like attending these (extended) family gatherings.

Case Conceptualisation using the CLET

The CLET analysis proceeded after Ms. Yoli transcribed the audio-recorded stories and prepared the CLET protocol. The protocol comprised the (i) collage and (ii) micro-narratives (CLET Step 2), as well as (iii) the family members expressed self-positioning and missing images (CLET Step 3). Figure 14.2 represents the collage (CLET Step 1) that the Zhang family completed during the first consultation with the images numbered in the order in which the family members told the stories (CLET Step 2; numbers 1–16). All four family members collaborated in selecting images and pasting these on the collage. They also independently and without guidance told stories about the images and the micro-narratives. Micro-narratives refer to the stories told for each image by each of the family members and are briefly summarised below to explicate the core content. In the summaries, Ms. Yoli extracted the underlying meanings and emotional intensity (Haefner, 2014) relevant to the challenges that could have

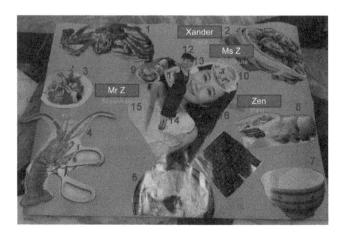

Figure 14.2 The CLET Performances of the Zhang Family

contributed to Xander's distress at school, while also acknowledging that alternative meanings could be interpreted under different circumstances. The family members also expressed their self-positioning (CLET Step 3a)— marked with their names on the collage (Figure 14.2). The self-positioning was done in private during the first interview so that family members did not, at the time, know where each had positioned herself or himself on the collage. Each family member identified an image she or he could not find, but would have liked to add (CLET Step 3b), indicated below each person's name on the collage (Figure 14.2). Ms. Yoli interpreted the missing images as representing suppressed memories and unspoken feelings, as well as family members' sources of strength and hopes for solutions to the underlying problems the family was experiencing at the time.

Ms. Yoli analysed and interpreted the CLET protocol, first the collage separately and then in conjunction with the micro-narratives. She also checked her interpretations with the Zhang family during the second meeting in order to confirm or change her inferences as necessary. From the conjoint analysis, the following case was conceptualised. During the second consultation with the family, Ms. Yoli also engaged with all family members to propose an intervention that would strengthen family coherence and communication, these been considered the most pressing issues at the time.

CLET Analysis and Interpretation

The initial prompt for making the collage was to elicit each family member's perceptions regarding their family life and everyday functioning as a unit more generally (Lijadi & Van Schalkwyk, 2014). Giving a more generic prompt was considered helpful as Ms. Yoli suspected difficulties and socio-emotional distress within the family as a possible reason for Xander's school problems. A brief analysis of the collage and a summary of the micro-narratives suffice to explicate the presenting concerns and each family member's response. Although not specifically asked during the CLET interview to comment on this, all family members expressed their interpretations of Xander's pending suspension from his current school in one way or another.

Except for a few images, family members pasted pictures of expensive food and travelling to exotic places on the collage (Figure 14.2). Only three of the 16 images represented people, and these were single faces of women with expensive clothing and jewellery. Food obviously seemed an important issue for all family members. Most of the images, however, were of individual food portions rather than of a family gathering. To some extent, this confirmed Ms. Yoli's observation that Xander was discontent with the monthly family gatherings as mentioned above and that his parents were perhaps also distressed or embarrassed about having to relate his poor performance during these gatherings. From her reading of the collage, Ms. Yoli concluded two further assumptions regarding the relationship patterns within the family:

1. Expensive items could relate to skewed family values for material things rather than quality relationships.
2. Much of the family members' current distress evolved around unmet needs regarding family meetings around the dinner table, both in the nuclear family and in the extended family circle.

These assumptions were further tested in Ms. Yoli's reading and analysis of the micro-narratives. Below is a brief summary of each person's narratives regarding the images pasted on the collage.

Mr. Z's stories: Mr. Z related stories about his heavy workload and how he often had to work overtime as a way to improve his career opportunities. He did not spend much time at home and often worked till late at night meeting with clients and business partners, and rarely getting home while the boys were still awake. His hard work had secured him a promotion a month before the consultation with Ms. Yoli, which benefited the whole family as he could now take them travelling, and his sons each received a brand new electronic device following a raise in his salary. Although Mr. Z was concerned about Xander's poor academic results, he felt helpless not knowing how to motivate Xander to achieve better.

Ms. Z's stories: Unrelated to the images on the collage, Ms. Z only expressed her consistent worry about Xander's poor academic results and added that she was frequently summoned to the school which complained about his disruptive behaviour in class and on the school grounds. She maintained that Xander was seemingly the troublemaker also in the family, although she had tried her best to set him straight. As a traditional wife and mother, Ms. Z had always been responsible for the boys' academic performance and other family-related issues, while Mr. Z was responsible for financial support and major decision-making. Because Mr. Z was often unavailable, Ms. Z, for the most part, raised her sons by herself, setting the rules, and disciplining them when necessary.

Xander's stories: Xander narrated stories about how he loved Japanese food, and cooking with his younger brother, but felt it was useless because his father would not be at home to share in the meals they prepared. Despite being good at sports and having received many awards for his performance in basketball and football, Xander felt that he was still considered worthless in the family context. He talked about how his parents, specifically his father, compared his academic performance to that of his brother and cousins while not acknowledging his sport achievements. He also wished for time with his father watching football on TV. Overall Xander related stories about feeling extreme pressure because of charges from his father that he was a disgrace to the family pending the possible suspension from school and again having to transfer to a new school.

Zen's stories: On a somewhat similar note, Zen claimed that his parents only cared about Xander and no matter what he (Zen) did or wanted, his father disregarded him, viewing him still as the "baby" in the family. His academic results were much better than those of his older brother, yet he felt that nobody really cared about him because they only attended to matters concerning Xander's performance. He liked cooking and often made food for himself and his brother when they were home alone in the evenings with mother working and father staying late at the office. Although he saw himself as easy-going, he felt rejected by his parents and by his brother who ignored and made fun of him at school.

From reading the micro-narratives, Ms. Yoli partially confirmed her two assumptions made in terms of the collage:

1. Mr. Z was particularly concerned about his ability to provide financially for the family, valuing wealth accruement and giving his children material things he could afford after his promotion at work. He also complained that Xander was unthankful for these and was causing the family to lose face because of his (Xander's) failure to meet expectations.
2. Both Xander and Zen commented on the lack of time spent with their father and feeling disregarded for their academic or sport achievements.

Interactional Patterns and Potential Conflict Escalation

Interpreting the family members' respective self-positioning, missing images and juxtaposing on the collage (CLET Steps 3 and 4), Ms. Yoli inferred furthermore that there were concerns regarding the interactional patterns and relationship boundaries with and between family members.

Couple relationship: Positioning himself (CLET Step 3a) on one side across from mother and sons, labelled on the collage with each person's name (Figure 14.2), Mr. Z expressed anxious/avoidant attachment almost as though he wanted to disengage himself from the problem by staying emotionally and physically at a distance from his wife and sons. Also, being more traditional, it seemed that Mr. Z expected his wife and sons to serve him, seeing himself solely as the provider (breadwinner) of material goods to secure their good behaviour and seeking unconditional compliance to his demands, particularly from his oldest son Xander. Ms. Z, in her self-positioning, appeared anxious even though she had her sons positioned at either side of her. To some extent, Mr. and Ms. Z had a distant relationship, perhaps due to their busy work schedules and limited time to talk about and/or attend to family matters together. On the other hand, Ms. Z seemed rather enmeshed in her relationship with both her sons, continuously worrying about how to handle Xander's misbehaviour at home and at school and relying on Zen to provide emotional closeness and support when she felt tested by the older boy's troubles and her husband's absence.

Sibling relationship: The boys' attachment patterns to their parents seemed somewhat secure and enmeshed for Zen and avoidant/distant for Xander. Throughout the CLET consultation, Zen sat close to his mother, often leaning into her and cuddling despite the presence of the father and SBFC practitioner, while Xander seemed distant and on edge, almost as though he was looking in on the family from a distance. Xander's distancing of himself could be interpreted as typical behaviour of a youth in late adolescence striving for autonomy, and resulting in arguments, quarrels and fights with his younger brother and even with his parents. Zen's need for attention and recognition for being the "good boy"—as opposed to Xander being the "bad" student—could on the other hand explain his cuddling up to his mother, almost as though he wanted to protect her from further hurt.

Regarding conflict escalation, neither Mr. nor Ms. Z knew how to control Xander's behaviour as he was apparently getting more rebellious over time. Ms. Z was particularly worried that he would get involved with gangs if he had to transfer to a new school known for accommodating youths with conduct problems. Apparently, seeking support from Mr. Z was not possible as he was too busy at work and also did not know how to deal with his son's problems. When Ms. Z reproached Xander for his poor academic performance and behaviour at school, he argued back, and she was at a loss as to how to handle the boy. Her over-involvement with Xander's difficulties at school also limited the time she had available to attend to the needs of her younger son, Zen, leading to him feeling rejected and unwanted. Despite these feelings, Zen was still the only one who could soothe his mother and brother after their arguments.

Critical Evaluation of Using the CLET with a Chinese Family

Several issues should be taken into consideration when using the CLET with a Chinese family. Chinese mothers tend to respond to factual questions and tell low-elaborative and interdependent conversational style stories when talking about their children (Wang, Leichtman, & Davies, 2000). Conversing about highly emotional and elaborative content while their children are present seems to be difficult, and Ms. Yoli had to proceed with caution. Furthermore, in the Chinese culture, harmony is a very important concept emphasising stability and peace in the system, and family members avoid relating negative socio-emotional content in their narratives (Dias, Chan, Ungvarsky, Oraker, & Cleare-Hoffman, 2011; Keeling & Piercy, 2007). In particular, they tend to hide negative events and feelings from others as a way of saving face (Van Schalkwyk, 2011). This resulted in the family focusing on positive content for the images pasted on the collage and for the storytelling about their family life. For the most part, the Zhang family omitted talking about problems or difficulties—except for Ms. Z's worries about Xander—and tended to maintain a harmonious front for the SBFC practitioner.

Nonetheless, the CLET provided a workable solution to the initial phase of treatment, allowing Ms. Yoli to develop a working therapeutic relationship with the family. In lieu of further assessments, which Ms. Yoli was not licensed to perform, she had to depend on using the CLET for screening and treatment planning. Completing the relatively non-threatening task such as picture selection, cutting and pasting, Ms. Yoli and the family members were given the opportunity to develop a collaborative relationship, and she was able to inspire hope and optimism, adopting a "beginner's mind" listening for strengths and opportunities. The collage making also aims to elicit content that is still hidden from awareness and Ms. Yoli was able to discern this hidden content with careful analysis of the metaphors and denotations embedded in the collage, assessing the individual, systemic and broader cultural dynamics evident in the problem description.

Intervention Planning

During the second consultation with the Zhang family, Ms. Yoli discussed her initial interpretations of the CLET protocol and problem description with the family members and they were also given an opportunity to share their reflections and interpretations. Ms. Yoli empathised with Mr. Z's busy work schedule, with Ms. Z's distress and heavy workload as a nurse and taking care of her two sons, and with the boys' need for more connectedness with their father. Although both boys valued their independence, they also had a great desire to spend more time with their father and for him to share in their hopes and dreams for the future. Ms. Yoli discussed her proposed treatment plan and intentions to assist the family with solutions to their expressed concerns, particularly the parents' concerns about Xander's pending suspension from yet another school. In this regard, Ms. Yoli proposed two treatment plans: (i) for

Box 14.2 Treatment Goals and Implementation for the Zhang Family

1. Increase time for family members eating together at dinner time.

- Mr. Z agreed to come home for dinner early at least four times per week to share dinner with the boys when Ms. Z was at work (she is a nurse working night shifts) and to spend time with the boys before bedtime.

2. Increase Mr. Z's overall involvement with his sons and decrease Ms. Z's triangulation of the children.

- Mr. Z agreed to accompany Xander when the latter played sport over the weekends for the period of one month to express his appreciation for Xander's achievements in sport. Ms. Z agreed to allow Mr. Z more involvement with family activities and to reduce her triangulation with the children, particularly with Zen from whom she sought emotional support in times of distress.

3. Increase sleep time for Xander and Zen.

- Having an early dinner, Xander and Zen agreed to sleep earlier and track their schedules regularly to ensure they had sufficient sleep time. Because they sometimes had to wait up late for Mr. Z to return home after work just to see him for a brief period, Xander and Zen did not get good quality sleep and they often felt sleepy in class affecting their concentration and academic performance.

the family (Box 14.2), and (ii) for Xander (Box 14.3), focusing on solution-focused and systemic approaches for family and individual counseling.

Because Ms. Yoli could not continue with family counseling, she trained the family to use two solution-focused strategies to keep track of their progress and self-evaluate their success with the agreed treatment goals:

Desired Situation activity: Once per week and during a shared dinner, each family member (i.e. parents and children) had to describe how he or she would like the family relationship and functioning to change. During this activity, and practising turn-taking, each family member was encouraged to vividly describe the desired situation in terms of concrete and behaviourally defined solutions. Listening actively, other family members (i.e. the listeners) would give positive feedback in terms of how he or she would be able to notice that things had become better. The main objective was for everyone in the family to develop a supportive, non-confrontational and appreciative manner in which to build positive relationships amongst all members of the family.

Progress evaluation: Using the "what's better" question each family member also had to evaluate his or her progress in achieving the treatment goals. For example, both Xander and Zen would evaluate the degree in which Mr. Z increased his involvement in family activities and Ms. Z reduced her triangulation of the children. Mr. Z and Ms. Z had to focus on evaluating whether they improved on giving positive feedback to the boys for their respective achievements (at school). The objective of this activity was to help the family focus on the progress that had been made in the past week and on what had worked well. It had a motivating effect leading to more awareness of achieving their goals even though they could not attend family counseling.

Box 14.3 Treatment Goals and Implementation for Individual Family Counseling with Xander

1. Increase Xander's communication skills and mechanisms for voicing his frustration in the family.

- During their weekly meetings, Ms. Yoli taught Xander how to actively listen and to voice his thoughts and needs in a non-aggressive manner. Xander had to practise his newly acquired communication skills at home and report back the next week. Ms. Yoli used scaling questions about the desired situation, earlier successes, current position, and already achieved goals to help Xander improve on his communication skills with his parents and brother.

2. Utilise Xander's strengths in sport to develop positive relationship with peers and enhance his sense of belongingness to the school community.

- Xander had to decrease the time spent playing sports with peers from his former school and increase the time spent playing sports with peers from his current school.

3. Help ease the tensions between Xander and his teachers in an effort to increase his academic performance

- Using the exception-seeking question, Ms. Yoli explored with Xander the times when he was not bored with his classes and did not engage in disruptive behaviour in class. Ms. Yoli helped

---

Xander to identify times when things were different in class and how he could make this happen more frequently.
- Xander's disruptive behaviour in class also decreased notably after he started attending the student group consultation set up by Ms. Yoli to help the Grade 11 (see more below), and with acquiring new learning skills.

Continuing her weekly individual consultations with Xander for a period of 10 weeks, Ms. Yoli was able to evaluate his progress and the family's success implementing the proposed treatment goals. During the closing phase of treatment, Ms. Yoli obtained the following feedback from Xander: although Mr. Z was still busy at work getting more assignments after his recent promotion, he had made a concerted effort to spend more time with his sons and be more involved in family activities. Mr. Z wanted to do this for his sons as he was keen to understand them better and build a solid foundation for their future relationships.

Furthermore, Ms. Yoli discussed the following tasks with Xander for completing the family counseling with individuals and to develop an after-care plan to maintain the gains:

1. The first task was to increase Xander's sense of emotional closeness to reduce his helplessness and conflict both at school and at home. Xander was encouraged to implement the strategies he had learned in his weekly consultations with Ms. Yoli by setting new goals for himself and evaluating his progress. For example, he could use the past successes and exception seeking to concretely identify alternative behavioural descriptions for satisfying his relationship with his father, his mother, and his brother respectively. Xander could also use the scaling exercise (i.e. rating success on a scale from 1 to 10) to continuously evaluate his own goal achievement, both relationally and academically, and build on his newly acquired communication skills and learning strategies.
2. The second task was to increase Xander's sense of belongingness at his current school using his strengths in sport. When he was busy with his sport practices, Xander had less conflict with peers and teachers. Xander also agreed to help a teacher with coaching the junior basketball team at his school which included his younger brother Zen. This could enhance his communication with his brother outside the home environment and improve the bond between the brothers.

School Consultation

Although Xander initially did not want Ms. Yoli to discuss his difficulties at school with the referring teacher, she convinced him during a follow-up meeting that she was trustworthy and would not cause further problems for him or his family. Thus, he consented to her consulting with the senior adviser of the Grade 11 group and the principal. During their meeting following an open consultation agenda, Ms. Yoli identified a need at the school to develop two group interventions: one for the teachers and one for the students.

Teacher Group Consultation

Ms. Yoli prepared a brief psycho-education workshop for the teachers in which she focused on the developmental challenges that adolescents face and how teachers could assist the youth in the challenging time of identity development. In the workshop, Ms. Yoli encouraged teachers to avoid negative labelling (e.g. "bad" student) as this demotivated the youth and could lead students to distance themselves further from authority figures. Ms. Yoli also offered stress management techniques for the teachers, which they could incorporate in the classroom management strategies in order to help students alleviate the pressure from home to perform well and enhance their attention/concentration in class.

Student Group Consultation

Given her knowledge of local customs of parents pressuring students for academic achievement beyond their abilities, Ms. Yoli established group consultation sessions for students who experienced excessive stress. A group of Grade 11 female and male students (including Xander) met weekly throughout the semester to talk about the stressors that limited their motivation at school. Although the students were initially reluctant to participate in the group and had to be commanded by the principal to attend the weekly meetings, they soon realised the benefits of sharing and gaining support for dealing with the challenges they faced. Because the group consultation also included mentoring the students regarding different study habits and mechanisms to enhance their achievement through mindfulness training, they decided collectively to form learning communities to support and tutor one another. This was particularly beneficial to Xander who no longer felt isolated from his classmates, both during school hours and after school, and he became eager to improve his grades. The success of the student group consultation sessions (they met for 10 consecutive weeks) quickly spread across the school, and Ms. Yoli subsequently set up several group counseling sessions with different groups as well as met with distressed students individually.

Conclusion

The interventions presented in this case and the application of the CLET for assessment of the family dynamics were configured within the SBFC meta-model showing the linkages to various communities influencing the youth's performance in school and in life. After the first meeting with Xander, Ms. Yoli evaluated his situation as being influenced both by the family dynamics and by the school (i.e. teachers and peers). In lieu of inviting both parents to join a parent education workshop—Mr. Z was too busy at work to attend any meetings at the school—Ms. Yoli opted to implement the CLET to assess the family dynamics in a home-school visit. This was done with a focus on family intervention providing family counseling through participatory brief solution-focused counseling (Hanton, 2011; Macdonald, 2007; Nichols & Schwartz, 2008; Winbolt, 2011) and narrative collaborative counseling (Chang & Nylund, 2013).

The CLET is a powerful intervention tool to make conscious perceptions lurking below the surface of awareness and to transform these perceptions and change the family dynamics (Van Schalkwyk, 2013a). Focusing her attentions on the family and using the CLET, Ms. Yoli conducted family counseling using characteristics of participatory and brief solution-focused therapy to counsel the family. For example, Mr. Z, a rational and intelligent, but concerned parent, quickly realised—while collaborating with Ms. Yoli to analyse the embedded meanings in the collage and narratives—what role his overly involved business endeavours was playing in his son's distress and pending suspension. Mr. Z adopted new behaviour patterns that changed the relationship between father and son and resolved the underlying distress Xander was experiencing that his father rejected him as bad for the family reputation. Other family members also gained insight into their respective roles, allowing everyone to adopt new patterns of interacting and satisfying their relationship needs.

Regarding the school focus in the SBFC meta-model, Ms. Yoli focused on school prevention. Engaging the teachers in a psycho-education program to review their approaches to classroom management with adolescents, Ms. Yoli changed how teachers interacted with the students in a more positive manner. In her consultation with the staff at the school, Ms. Yoli focused on an important phase of adolescent development, and engaged the teachers as positive role models guiding the students towards their identity achievement. Ms. Yoli also engaged with the students, setting up student group counseling that provided the students with new insights into the challenges they faced. As mentioned above, peer group counseling became a regular feature at the school and in general the school climate is changing to provide all students with an optimal context in which to flourish.

A challenge that still remains unresolved is mobilising resources at the community level and in particular advocating for changes at the local education department. Schooling in the local community is still characterised as having a "limited responsiveness to consumers and inadequate information to parents; and few quality assurance systems" (De Robertis & Morrison, 2009, p. 153). Although education has received more attention since the transition of Macao—the context of this case study—to the People's Republic of China (PRC) in 1999, there are still concerns about its quality, particularly for students such as Xander and others with special needs. For example, schools are ranked in terms of their academic performances and some schools are rather elitist and highly selective of students based, for the most part, on family background and academic performance. Academic performance is highly regarded and if students continue to fail (i.e. after failing the second time in a grade) they are usually expelled (De Robertis & Morrison, 2009). Non-compliant students, poor academic performance and conduct problems are all used as an excuse to stereotype the students as "bad", and they carry this label with them to the next school when transferred. Other schools seem to accept all students, but with low standards and often receiving a reputation amongst the local population because of their willingness to accept the stereotyped "bad" students. Amidst these differences in the ranking of schools in Macao, there is also a gap with regard to providing adequate psychological services, and school-based family counseling is almost non-existent in the territory (Van Schalkwyk, 2013b).

In Ms. Yoli's approach of integrating both a family and a school focus in her interventions, she was one of only a few school mental health professionals adopting the principles embedded in the SBFC meta-model. Based on the psychological and educational needs of Xander and his family, the SBFC meta-model provided a way to enhance family functioning, empower Mr. Z and Ms. Z in their parenting of Xander and Zen, and to help the family cope with the challenges they experienced in their parent-child and extended family relations. The SBFC meta-model also enabled Ms. Yoli to provide preventive interventions at the school where these were most needed. Working within this model, Ms. Yoli was able to access and engage all members of Xander's interpersonal network (i.e. parents, teachers and peers) to develop psychological openness and generate positive attitudes towards help-seeking behaviour that were to the advantage of all. Given the importance that Chinese parents attach to their children's education, the home-school partnership in accordance with the SBFC meta-model should be encouraged to strengthen the relationships amongst all parties who influence the youth's success in school and in life.

Bibliography

Chang, J., & Nylund, D. (2013). Narrative and solution-focused therapies: A twenty-year retrospective. *Journal of Systemic Therapies, 32*(2), 72–88. doi: 10.1521/jsyt.2013.32.2.72

De Robertis, C., & Morrison, K. (2009). Catholic schooling, identity and social justice in Macau. *International Studies in Catholic Education, 1*(2), 152–169. doi: 10.1080/19422530903138044

Dias, J., Chan, A., Ungvarsky, J., Oraker, J., & Cleare-Hoffman, H. P. (2011). Reflections on marriage and family therapy emergent from international dialogues in China. *The Humanistic Psychologist, 39*(3), 268–275. doi: 10.1080/08873267.2011.592434

Haefner, J. (2014). An application of Bowen family systems theory. *Issues in Mental Health Nursing, 35*, 835–841. doi: 10.3109/01612840.2014.921257

Hanton, P. (2011). *Skills in solution focused brief counseling & psychotherapy*. London: SAGE.

Keeling, M. L., & Piercy, F. P. (2007). A careful balance: Multinational perspectives on culture, gender, and power in marriage and family therapy practice. *Journal of Marital and Family Therapy, 33*(4), 443–463. doi: 10.1111/j.1752-0606.2007.00044.x

Lijadi, A. A., & Van Schalkwyk, G. J. (2014). Narratives of third culture kids: Commitment and reticence in social relationships. *The Qualitative Report, 19*(49), 1–18. Retrieved from www.nova.edu/ssss/QR/QR19/lijadi49.pdf

Macdonald, A. J. (2007). *Solution-focused therapy: Theory, research & practice*. Los Angeles, CA: SAGE.

Nichols, M. P., & Schwartz, R. C. (2008). *Family therapy: Concepts and methods* (8th). Boston, MA: Allyn & Bacon.

Van Schalkwyk, G. J. (2010a). Mapping Chinese family systems and parental involvement in educational settings in Macao. *International Journal of School-Based Family Counseling, 2*(5), 1–20.

Van Schalkwyk, G. J. (2010b). Collage Life-story Elicitation Technique: A representational technique for scaffolding autobiographical memories. *The Qualitative Report, 15*(3), 675–695. Retrieved from www.nova.edu/ssss/QR/QR15-3/vanschalkwyk.pdf [ISSN 1052-0147].

Van Schalkwyk, G. J. (2011). Face and hierarchical positioning of parents in the family-school relationship in Macao. *International Journal of School-Based Family Counseling, III*, 1–12. [ISSN 2159-4589].

Van Schalkwyk, G. J. (2013a). Assessing individual or family dynamics through the Collage Life-story Elicitation Technique (CLET). In B. Gerrard, & M. Soriano (Eds.), *School-based family counseling: Transforming family-school relationships* (Chapter 24, pp. 419–439). Phoenix, AZ: Createspace.

Van Schalkwyk, G. J. (2013b). School-based counseling and psychological services in Macao. *International Journal of School & Educational Psychology, 1*(3), 207–216. doi: 10.1080/21683603.2013.8228-40

Van Schalkwyk, G. J. (2014). Perceptions of school-based child and family counseling in Macao (SAR). *Journal of Asia Pacific Counseling, 4*(2), 147–158.

Van Schalkwyk, G. J. (2017). Socio-cultural barriers to entry for school-based family counseling. *International Journal for School-Based Family Counseling, Special Topic Issue, 9*(4), 1–10.

Wang, Q., Leichtman, M. D., & Davies, K. I. (2000). Sharing memories and telling stories: American and Chinese mothers and their 3-year-olds. *Memory, 8*(3), 159–177. doi: 10.1080/096582100387588

Winbolt, B. (2011). *Solution focused therapy for the helping professions*. London: Jessica Kingsley Publishers.

15 The Case of Collaboration

A Closer Look at a University/ K-12/nonprofit Partnership

Deborah Ribera

Overview

This chapter explores the implementation of SBFC-based intervention programs from the perspective of the three collaborative partners: a university, a K-12 school, and a nonprofit. The purpose of this alternative descriptive case study is threefold. First, it is meant to provide an example of how a school can expand SBFC programming through collaboration. Second, it provides insight into how one can develop SBFC programming through the structure of a nonprofit organization. Third, it details how university training programs can partner with local schools to deliver SBFC services.

Throughout this book, you have seen that School-Based Family Counseling can be practiced in multiple different modes and settings. This case study features yet another way to practice SBFC, focusing on the benefits of collaboration. The case describes the relationship between a middle school (called Bayside Middle School or Bayside MS here), a nonprofit organization, and a university, as opposed to describing an individual or a family. The purpose of this alternative descriptive case study is threefold. First, it is meant to provide an example of how a school can expand SBFC programming through collaboration. Second, it provides insight into how one can develop SBFC programming through the structure of a nonprofit organization. Third, it details how university training programs can partner with local schools to deliver SBFC services. The overall goal of this chapter, however, is to demonstrate the dynamic, interdisciplinary nature of SBFC. As SBFC practitioners, it is important to understand the ways in which we can effect change not only on an individual level, but also on a systemic level. When community-based collaborative partners come together with school-site practitioners to create SBFC programming, a shift in culture can occur.

The efforts depicted in this case study mainly address the SBFC meta-model quadrants of school intervention (group counseling), school prevention (global awareness/dropout prevention program), and family prevention (parent education/support groups). Understood as a whole, the partnerships here represent community intervention, as the school partnered with both a nonprofit organization and a local university in order to bring much-needed services to both students and their parents. Figure 15.1 uses the SBFC meta-model diagram to identify the specific interventions made.

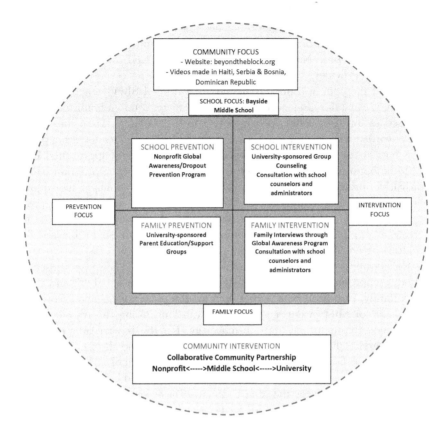

Figure 15.1 The SBFC Meta-model with University/K-12/Nonprofit Partnership Interventions

This chapter will be written largely in the first person because I (the author) both founded the nonprofit that worked with Bayside MS and teach at the university that partners with Bayside for group counseling services. My only connection to Bayside MS is that I attended the same SBFC training program as their assistant principal. My experiences began in 2010 and continue today (2018).

The School

Many school-based readers may find that they are the only professional at their school who has an SBFC perspective. Implementing any SBFC programming beyond your own practice might seem challenging, if not impossible. If you are an administrator, as opposed to a counselor, the challenge of incorporating SBFC may seem even more daunting. This section of the case description is meant to demonstrate that in order to deliver SBFC services at your site, service providers do not necessarily need to be at your school. Finding outside partnerships and creating collaborative relationships with nonprofits and universities is a creative way to expand the SBFC offerings your school provides.

One of the administrators at Bayside is a trained SBFC practitioner. As a former counselor and current assistant principal, this administrator has focused on bringing SBFC programming to his students. When the school was awarded a significant grant, he contracted with an educational nonprofit that had an SBFC foundation. When the local university approached him with the opportunity to work together on a group counseling program based on SBFC principles, he immediately approached his principal to explore how they could accommodate the group. Being in an administrative position, this SBFC practitioner knew that he would not have enough time to create and implement SBFC programming on his own, so he focused on prioritizing collaborative community partnerships.

Collaborative relationships are similar to marriages. They take conscious effort, compromise, listening, understanding, patience, negotiation, and most importantly, trust from both parties. Sharing the philosophical and theoretical shorthand of SBFC went a long way towards nurturing the trust between the school, the nonprofit, and the university. For the Bayside administrator, finding service providers who understood the school and the issues that the families there faced was essential. Bayside Middle School is located in an urban area, has a student population of almost 2,000, and is 99% Latino. The current dropout rate for the area is about 26% according to the California Department of Education. Bayside feeds into a high school that has historically had one of the city's highest dropout rates, averaging around 40%. Based on grades, test scores, and behavioral patterns, administrators at the school estimate that 30%–40% of the students currently enrolled at Bayside are at high risk for school dropout. The collaborators that the administrator chose then needed to understand how to provide culturally relevant services to a Latino population, how to address the various aspects of school dropout, and how to create content that addressed not only the individual aspect of a child's life, but also the systemic aspects of family, community, and culture. The administrator felt that he could trust fellow SBFC providers because they are trained at doing all those things.

When collaborating with outside providers, it is crucial to discuss evaluation methods from the beginning. A school will undoubtedly have expectations for the level of service they would like to see from collaborators. How will the school assess the effectiveness of the services being provided by partners? What is the partner's capacity to collect data and provide the school with interpretation of that data? Who are the stakeholders that the school answers to (e.g., parents, the district, the state educational board, grant funders)? Who are the stakeholders the partners answer to (e.g., grant funders, peer-review boards for tenure and publishing, donors)? How can you make a data plan that is mutually beneficial? Will you need permissions from a human subjects review board to collect data?

As a school-site SBFC practitioner and a community-based collaborative partner, evaluation methods should be established well before interventions begin in order to ensure the best data collection. Partners should communicate with each other about this process in order to ensure that the data being collected fits their needs. The field of SBFC is still growing in terms of how we feature our services through data. Qualitative data was gathered for both the nonprofit and group counseling interventions at Bayside from surveys and pre- and post-tests that students and parents completed. Quantitative data such as grades or attendance was not gathered. Such quantitative data would likely only have correlational effects as opposed to causation effects; however, efforts to create such studies would still be helpful in moving the field forward and in positioning SBFC practitioners for partnerships.

The Nonprofit

While working as a dropout prevention counselor for a K-12 school district, I began teaching a personal development course for middle school students (ages 12–14) at risk of school dropout. I taught these classes at three middle schools throughout the district, Bayside Middle School being one of them. While teaching at Bayside I noticed that my students, who were in my class because they were disengaging from learning, always responded well when my co-teacher and I showed documentary videos. There was one video in particular that had a significant impact on my students; it profiled students who were the first in their family to go to college. Those in the video represented diverse life experiences and my students related to their stories and felt connected to the students profiled. I began to use film regularly in my personal development classes—both fictional and documentary—with much success.

Concurrently, I was beginning to internalize a message I often heard when meeting with my students' parents who were from Mexico and Central America: "If only my son/daughter could see where I was from, they would understand how lucky they are to be able to attend school here." These parents were experiencing severe intercultural estrangement from their children. Many of them had not been able to attend school past the elementary level in their home country because they could not afford to pay the school fees or forgo earning wages at a job. These parents felt that their children did not understand the conditions their families faced growing up in developing countries, a poverty unlike that of the United States, with unstable governments, civil wars, and an overall lack of access to basic resources such as running water, electricity, and social services. Complicating this estrangement, many of the children I worked with would never have the opportunity to travel to their parents' homeland even if they wanted to, because they were undocumented or lacked the financial means to travel. Their geographical isolation extended from national borders to neighborhood boundaries, as many could barely travel beyond the block their homes were located on due to the risk of crossing into rival gang territory. Some students seemed to internalize this imposed isolation, professing they had no desire to leave their neighborhoods because all they cared about lay within a few square blocks.

Enough parents related the same message to me that I took note of this intercultural issue. I realized that issues of identity and culture were not being addressed in the classroom. Based on my observation that film was a useful and effective pedagogical tool for my population, I developed the idea to make documentaries about places like the ones my students' parents came from. I was not attempting to be a documentary filmmaker; rather, I was attempting to use video as a teaching tool in order to address a need that had been voiced to me by my students' parents. I started out thinking that this would be an excellent idea to incorporate into a comprehensive dropout prevention program at the school I was working at, but I saw how the creative freedom of the dropout prevention unit I was working in was becoming increasingly stymied with the drive to standardize and regulate interventions. I felt that starting my own nonprofit organization would protect the program from district politics, educational policy, and institutionalization. From this space, Beyond the Block developed.

Beyond the Block is an educational nonprofit organization designed to provide culturally relevant global awareness education to students of color who have an identified risk of school dropout (i.e., failing grades, low attendance, disciplinary problems), students who attend majority-minority schools, and students who attend under-resourced schools in urban areas. The purpose of our global awareness curriculum is to help students become more globally aware by improving their understanding of others and themselves (family focus), developing their critical thinking skills (school and community focus), and increasing their future-thinking habits (school and community focus). Global awareness (also known as global competence or global citizenship) is a key 21st-century learning skill that broadens students' knowledge about various issues and cultures outside the United States. We seek to create emotional and intellectual connections across borders. By providing students with a way to locate themselves globally, we open up new local pathways through which they can interpret who they are, who they could be, and who they want to be locally.

Beyond the Block's family, school, and community focus is an example of a prevention-oriented SBFC approach. Carter and Perluss (2008) describe prevention programs as macro efforts that address systemic, ecological issues such as school culture, institutional racism, transitions, risk factors, and developmental issues. Prevention programs can be delivered in the form of psycho-educational groups, assemblies, classroom guidance sessions, campaigns, or professional development. At Bayside, Beyond the Block was delivered through assemblies that included anywhere from 50–200 students as well as classroom sessions that included 30–40 students. The frequency of our sessions was determined by the grant; however, the basic program consists of four units, with each unit consisting of five lessons. These lessons are designed for class periods of at least 55 minutes for a total of 1,100 minutes of instruction (or about 18 hours) over one year. When working with a school, you must accommodate various types of schedules including block scheduling. Many schools, including some teachers at Bayside, were only interested in having one presentation for their students. Though this is not ideal service delivery (and affects data collection), it is important to be flexible and understanding. My first presentation at Bayside was a one-off presentation. One lesson, then, might turn into a longer partnership down the road, as it did with Beyond the Block and Bayside.

The cornerstone of Beyond the Block's global awareness curriculum is the educational travel video. These videos, also known as ethnographic documentary videos, are 35-minute explorations into the lives of children and adults around the world. *Beyond the Block: The Dominican Republic* examines the everyday lives, education, cultural values, and dreams and goals of students living in a small rural village in the Dominican Republic. *Beyond the Block: Serbia and Bosnia* is a travel narrative that reflects on the history of the Balkan war and the effects it has had on the region. *Beyond the Block: Haiti* profiles the lives, experiences, and dreams of several children who live in an orphanage in post-earthquake Port-au-Prince, Haiti. Beyond the Block's website (www.beyondtheblock.org) provides more photo and video representations of these videos that will give you a better idea of the feeling behind them.

There are a few stylistic aspects of the videos, such as music and editing, that draw the students in. But the greatest draw by far are the people who are at the heart of the video, particularly the children. When I interview the video participants, I explain the type of work I do in the United States (dropout prevention counseling) and the type of student that will be watching this video (one that is disengaged from or at risk of becoming disengaged from education). As a result, the students in the US feel as if those in the video are speaking directly to them—because they are! Making this video for a very specific audience, then, was key to using it as a teaching tool. This intentionality is part of a larger commitment, rooted in the foundation of SBFC, to using culturally relevant interventions with my students.

Student responses to Beyond the Block's programming were heartfelt and encouraging. In a qualitative study that explored the affective impact the video *Beyond the Block: Haiti* had on the students, I found that students who viewed the video were able to enter into a change-space of relation, position themselves in the world, and recognize their own contextualized privilege (Ribera, 2018). Student responses were gathered after every presentation. Select comments representing the identified themes are in Box 15.1. Teacher responses were also encouraging. Teacher and student responses are also featured in an informational video on Beyond the Block's website.

Box 15.1 Bayside Middle School Student Feedback to Beyond the Block Global Awareness Program

Student 1: I think that this video changed how I feel about wars. It was life-changing … I feel more aware now.

Student 2: This presentation changed the way I think about my education. I feel that we take things for granted here in the US. Our school system is free and we take it for granted. An ordinary kid in Haiti dreams to be a politician, teacher, doctor, or the president so they can help the people and kids. We can at least take advantage of our school system and grow up and be successful.

Student 3: I learned that no matter what struggles I face, I can either run away from it or face it with my head held high. While watching this video I did shed tears, and it made me think, what can I do to change the world? I'm still trying to discover it.

Student 4: I've learned today, even though Haitians have a difficult life, they help each other out. Not like Americans. Sometimes I have food that I don't like and I don't eat it. I'm going to start being more grateful.

Student 5: Getting an education will help yourself and others because it has an effect worldwide, not only with the people around you.

Student 6: I have learned to never drop out of school.

The Family Connection

In terms of directly reaching parents and caregivers at Bayside Middle School, Beyond the Block was not able to gain access to that population due to time constraints and the parameters of the grant. However, much of the curriculum focused on the students' relationship with their families. For instance, in one follow-up activity with a class, the students received a lesson on values. They were asked to reflect on the values they grew up with in their family. These values, and the impact family has on our belief system, were discussed in the class and compared and contrasted to the way family influenced the lives of those children featured in the educational travel documentaries. So although I was not reaching caregivers directly, this activity encouraged students to explore issues of family influence and my SBFC training allowed me to facilitate discussion from a family systems perspective.

Another lesson taught students interview skills. Using the information they had learned about cultural identity development, they interviewed a member of their class. Their homework was to interview a member of their family in the same way. Again, though I was not able to include the caregivers in the classroom activity, I was able to encourage students to generalize the skill they were practicing in the classroom with their family. For various reasons in our various roles, we may have access only to parents or may have access only to children. Even if you don't have direct access to the whole family, you can still incorporate an SBFC perspective into the work you do.

The University

At our university, students can receive a Master's degree in Counseling through our SBFC program. This program prepares students to be school counselors and marriage and family therapists. University counseling training programs typically require that certain classes contain a practicum component. Our SBFC program decided to incorporate part of this component into our group counseling class, a course that takes place in the second semester of the first year of our graduate program. Our program is specifically an SBFC program, so partnering with a school for our group counseling practicum was a natural fit. Programs that do not have a stated SBFC focus can still incorporate SBFC training into their curriculum, however. Seeking out school partnerships for practicum opportunities is a great way to do this.

During the first nine weeks of the class our students worked on developing group counseling proposals. During the last six weeks our students implemented those group proposals directly at the Bayside school site, providing these services for free to students and parents. I approached Bayside to be the site because they are in our feeder area; that is, many of the students who attend Bayside who go on to college end up attending our university. Serving our immediate community is key to our university's mission, so this partnership made sense for us. Whether or not your university receives students from your immediate area, partnering with local schools is an excellent way to build community relations and resource networks. Conversely, if you work at a school site, reaching out to counseling, social work, education, and psychology programs at your local university to initiate a partnership can prove to be a fruitful and productive connection.

Logistically, I specified upfront that the groups would take place once a week and begin at 4:45 pm. This was key to mention because although our university classes begin at 4:30 pm, the Bayside school day ends far earlier. We would need an administrator to stay with us until about 7 pm. Though we were offering these services for free, we knew this would be a huge inconvenience for staff. Keeping in mind the importance of negotiation when collaborating, we let the school know that we would need their assistance in recruiting, but that we could have our counseling interns who were placed at the school take on the majority of the responsibility for that. The administrator and counselor immediately agreed to a meeting to explore this option. When entering the meeting, it was important for me to be prepared, but to also be flexible. In this meeting we discussed logistics as well as possible group topics. Box 15.2 contains all of the information we discussed in our initial meeting in regards to logistics.

Box 15.2 Group Counseling Partnership Logistical Information

WHAT: Nine (9) total Psychoeducational and Counseling Groups made up of 6–10 students or parents per group, with each group led by two (2) university counseling students. (On-site Licensed Marriage and Family Therapist/PPS credentialed counselor will be supervising.)

WHO: For Bayside MS students AND parents.

WHEN: Each group will meet for 5 sessions, all meetings on Mondays from 4:45–5:45.

WHERE: Bayside Middle School (can each group have their own classroom?)

- Assistant Principal, Counselor, Psychiatric Social Worker, and counseling interns from university will work with counselors, students, parents, and any other relevant staff to determine what nine (9) groups will be offered.
- Each group will consist of two co-leaders from university and 6–10 students or parents from Bayside.
- University will work with Assistant Principal, Counselor, Psychiatric Social Worker, counseling interns, and any other relevant staff to recruit and orient students and parents to the groups.
- University will provide a referral form that Bayside staff can fill out so that co-leading counselors can learn about their students and parents before first session.
- University will provide an Informed Consent form that Bayside staff can ideally have students and parents sign for collection before the first session.
- University will provide food and drink at the group sessions for all participants.
- University will provide certificates of completion for all participants.
- Bayside will offer incentives for their students to participate, including:

  - Detention hours served
  - Consideration towards culmination behavioral requirements

As the university coordinator of this collaboration, I volunteered to speak with the Bayside parent group and to advertise the groups in multiple classrooms over a period of four weeks. This was time- and labor-intensive; however, it gave me enough face time with students, teachers, and counselors that they began to recognize me. The school even provided me with my own mailbox where students could place their parent consent forms. This relationship-building is essential to successful partnerships between school and community. Though I outreached to many, I was able to form an especially strong relationship with one counselor and two teachers. The counselor referred a number of her students and parents to the group and reminded the students to bring in their consent forms. The teachers did the same.

The university students suggested groups they would be interested in leading; however, it was ultimately Bayside that chose which groups they wanted. Our students chose the group they wanted to research and design from that selection. This was a key step in teaching our students the critical nature of culturally responsive counseling. We could not impose upon Bayside our own ideas of what they needed. We had to listen to them first, then design our interventions in response to their needs.

The university provided eight student counseling groups with 5–10 students in each group, and two parenting counseling groups. The Spanish language parenting group had an unexpected 15 parents in it. Though we were only expecting 10, we did not want to turn away the additional parents. There were four parents in the English-language parent group and all of those parents were bilingual. What we learned was to have two Spanish language parenting groups. Unfortunately, we did not have enough Spanish-speaking student therapists to accommodate for this. Attendance was good and the free pizza after the groups was a large draw for both students and parents.

Both the Bayside students and the university students responded positively to this collaboration. Based on feedback gathered at the last group session, Bayside students reported that they learned new things, understood themselves better, and were able to express themselves in the group because they felt the group leaders listened to them. Based on class feedback, the university students felt it was invaluable to have a chance to work in a school setting with students and parents within the first year of their graduate studies. Though they found it challenging to have only five sessions, they also were able to get a taste of how rewarding group counseling interventions can be. The parents of the Bayside students, however, were the most vocal in their feedback. The vast majority of them were dissatisfied with the length of each session and the length of the group counseling program in general ... because they wanted it to last longer! As of the writing of this article (almost one year after the sessions took place), the SBFC practitioner at Bayside reports that parents have been asking whether or not the program is going to return because they want to enroll themselves and their children in the university group counseling program. Thankfully, we will be returning to meet this need! And in response to the feedback from the SBFC practitioner, we will be expanding the parent groups. Box 15.3 contains reflections on the group counseling experience from the university counseling graduate students who led the groups at Bayside.

Box 15.3 University Counseling Students' Reflections on Bayside MS Group Counseling Collaboration

Student 1: Ultimately, this experience reaffirmed for me that I enjoy, and am good at, working with adolescents. Their humor and deep feelings are assets to the therapeutic process, and I have an appreciation for these traits. I was also initially intimidated by leading group therapy; there are so many personalities to reach and help. However, this group showed me that I am able to successfully lead a group and when reflecting on their evaluations, I am proud that they felt helped and better prepared to handle the high school transition—the overall goal.

Student 2: One of my greatest fears in life is that I am afraid to fail. I am scared of doing bad on tasks that I am assigned to do especially in school and work. I am afraid to feel incompetent and unintelligent. In the past I have said no to job positions because I did not think I could do it. It is not until I force myself to try that I prove myself wrong. I know I will not be perfect and I will make mistakes but everything in life is a learning experience. Just as in this group I learned more about parents and what they need, I also learned about myself and how I feel about my Spanish. I learned about working with a co-leader, and benefits as well as the disadvantages of working with a partner. There are ups and downs in all we do just like in our Spanish parenting group but I would not change this experience for the world.

Student 3: Group counseling was quite the experience at [Bayside] Middle School. I have not worked in a school setting in 15 years, and I have not worked with middle school students. My experience comes from my volunteer work at my church where I was in charge of small groups with high school students. I was able to use this experience in planning the activities and organizing the proposal for this boys' group. I was not sure my leadership style would translate well with middle school students … I have learned to be flexible with the plans we have for the sessions in order to have unconditional positive regard for the boys. Following through with the plans only satisfies my agenda, and not what the boys are feelings at that moment. I learned that my own childhood experiences couldn't always translate into the experiences of today's youth. Each of the boys brings in their individuality and I should not expect them to have same experiences as one another. Being open to change and having the flexibility in the group sessions has helped me be more present with the boys in the group.

Student 4: I felt very appreciative to be able to co-facilitate this counseling group since topics such as cultural identity are barely covered during middle school. For the students in the group, this was their first exposure to this type of content … The students in our group were engaged, curious to learn, and asked many questions about the content.

Reflections

Personally, the opportunity to collaborate with Bayside Middle School has been one of the most rewarding growth-experiences of my career. By entering into partnerships with the SBFC-trained administrator, we were able to provide creative interventions to students that addressed the needs of the school. In general, the students at Bayside love the enrichment programming they have received through Beyond the Block and our university. Of course there are those who get bored during a video or who just want to talk to their friends in group counseling. However, I and my university students are routinely surprised at just how engaged the students are. In regard to Beyond the Block, students who see the videos for the first time inevitably want to make their own video so that they can speak to the children featured in them. In regard to group counseling, it is wonderful to see students hesitantly show up for the first group and slowly head upstairs. By the end of the sessions they are running to their room to make it on time and asking us, as their parents do, why the groups cannot last longer.

The administrators have been extremely supportive of all of our collaboration and have routinely stated to us how much the students and parents need the services we are providing to them. Teachers with whom I work directly say the same thing. Teachers are overworked and underpaid, yet still so many of them wish they had the time to do more. The main feeling that they convey to me about the services we offer to students is relief—relief that someone is offering the extra services that they cannot. In my conversations with the school administrators, counselors, and teachers at Bayside, it is clear that if the various partnerships have taught them anything, it is how underserved their students and families are, not just by the school, but within the community. Free counseling groups, for instance, are incredibly difficult for their families to access, especially if they are undocumented.

As SBFC practitioners, we are professional gap-finders. We work with a family and we assess how they are interacting with the system of a school. We work with a school and we assess how it is interacting with the system of a family. We try to strengthen those interactions in order to form stronger bonds and connections between these two interdependent systems and then take it a step further by assessing how each system fits into the larger community. This is challenging work, but doing our best to comprehensively and competently address the needs of our students and their families is essential and gratifying. Working in a collaborative team with like-minded individuals makes our job easier and our service provision more effective.

Conclusion

This case study looked at two programs that were brought into Bayside Middle School in order to increase their SBFC service provision. The first was a global awareness and dropout prevention program implemented by an educational nonprofit organization, Beyond the Block. The second was a group counseling program implemented by a partner university, California State University, Los Angeles. The efforts depicted in this case study address the SBFC meta-model quadrants of school intervention (group counseling), school prevention (global awareness/dropout prevention program), and family prevention (parent education/support groups). From this case, we can learn the following:

1. Prioritizing community partnerships allowed one SBFC practitioner at a school to extend SBFC programming to many students and parents.
2. Using an interdisciplinary approach allowed an educational nonprofit to develop an innovative prevention program based on SBFC principles.
3. Using a collaborative approach allowed a university counselor training program to establish a mutually beneficial partnership with a K-12 school site and bring much-needed counseling resources to the school.

As SBFC practitioners, we are ultimately tasked with developing and implementing interventions and processes that encourage opportunities for connection and growth among the student, school, and family. Through community partnerships and taking an interdisciplinary, collaborative approach, we can do just that.

Resources

Please visit Beyond the Block's website to watch an informational video with student and teacher responses to the global awareness lessons. You can also link to the educational travel video trailers from there. www.beyondtheblock.org

Bibliography

Carter, M. and Perluss, E. (2008). Developments in training school-based family counselors: The school-based family counseling (SBFC) graduate program at California State University, Los Angeles. *International Journal for School-Based Family Counseling*, 1(1), 1–12.

Ribera, D. (2018). (Re)presenting the subject: A critical reflection on the use of ethnographic documentary video with students of colour in K-12 urban school settings. *Ethnography and Education*, 1–16. doi: 10.1080/17457823.2018.1452041.

Index